DATE DUE

OCT 1 8 1994	JAN 2 3 2002
NOV - 5 1994	MAR 1 4 2002
DEC 2 0 1994	APR 0 3 2002
JUL 0 8 1995	APR 2 6 2002
	MAY 2 2 2002
JUN 0 6 1996	OCT 2 9 2002
	NOV 1 2 2003
JUN 1 4 1997	MAR 2 5 2004
	AUG 2 7 2004
AUG 2 1 1997	
SEP 1 8 1997	FEB 1 6 2006
JUN 2 9 1998	APR 0 8 2006
AUG 0 3 1999	
OCT 2 8 1999	
MAR 0 6 2000	
SEP 1 8 2001	

GAYLORD   PRINTED IN U.S.A.

JUN 86 C1

739.27   Cartlidge, Barbara, 1922-
C   Twentieth-century jewelry / Barbara
          Cartlidge. -- New York : H.N. Abrams,
          1985.
             238 p. : col. ill. ; 28 cm.

             Bibliography: p. 231.
             Includes index.
             ISBN 0-8109-1685-1 : $60.00

          1. Jewelry--History--20th century.
       I. Title.
SAN RAF   860513   860512
E000009   /NBG   86-B10299
                              85-6028

TWENTIETH-CENTURY JEWELRY

Barbara Cartlidge

TWENTIETH-CENTURY JEWELRY

Harry N. Abrams, Inc., Publishers, New York

For DERRICK, with all my love

Library of Congress Cataloging in Publication Data

Cartlidge, Barbara 1922–
    Twentieth-century jewelry.

    Bibliography: p.
    Includes index.
    1. Jewelry–History–20th century. I. Title.
NK7310.C37 1985   739.27'09'04   85–6028
ISBN 0–8109–1685–1

Copyright © 1985 by Office du Livre, Fribourg, Switzerland

Printed and bound in Switzerland

C 1

Contents

Introduction

The history of jewellery in the twentieth century is as manifold as the century's events and their consequences. This fact is perhaps not as surprising as it seems at first, considering that jewellery is a quite extraordinary artifact: it is not essential for survival like food, shelter or clothing; yet it has existed since time immemorial and is found, in one form or another, in every civilization from the most primitive to the highly sophisticated.

Jewellery and jewels have aroused unequalled passions as emblems of deities to be worshipped or as tokens of love, magic and power. This concept is still with us, albeit in a somewhat muted form: the basic need for reassurance and the desire to convey certain aspects of our personality that go beyond mere ornamentation or pure material considerations. Within almost all of us is a primal urge to possess a small, tactile object with very personal associations; and no matter what the material value of this object may be, its fundamental purpose lies in its spiritual and emotional content. The eventual importance and intensity is awakened by the creator of the jewellery in much the same way as a painter or sculptor seeks to find a rapport with his public.

For many people, the word 'jewellery' is synonymous with 'luxury', 'glamour' and 'precious object'. Some do not consider jewellery made from intrinsically worthless materials worthy of the name. This view is often justified by the argument that cheap and common materials do not last. Time has taught us otherwise—for much ancient jewellery was made of iron, bronze or copper; and with paste, glass or ceramics in conjunction with gold and silver. Certainly precious metals have a greater chance of survival because of their durability, but there is no evidence to suggest that jewellery made of base metals or other materials was less important to its owners.

Luckily for us, since it is so recent, much of the twentieth century's jewellery has survived in all its varied forms. Obviously there are some periods for which evidence is less abundant than others: the periods of the two World Wars with their appalling consequences for so many people. Wanton destruction and plunder have never been the friends of the historian. Yet such circumstances may serve to high-light another aspect of jewellery: the light it throws on our changing patterns and styles of life; the way it mirrors the public and private events in our lives as almost no other artifact does. Personal landmarks like birthdays, confirmation, engagement, marriage; special occasions like coronations or investitures and religious ceremonies are often marked by gifts of jewellery. Customs, traditions and social structure can all be expressed in terms of jewellery, and in addition it can offer a host of information that tells us not only a great deal about people's lives in past centuries but also a lot about our own lives.

Whether we admit it or not, all of us try to present a certain image of ourselves to the outside world. Styles and customs change to fit in with life styles and varying needs, but the basic methods we use remain the same: with our bodies, our clothes and our jewellery, we convey certain messages that vary with the occasion and inform the onlooker. Consciously and subconsciously, we allow other people to conclude in a glance what kind of a person we are—or aim to be—with which social group we want to identify. By the cut of our hair, the shape of our clothes and the sort of jewellery we wear, we transmit both the desire to conform and the need to differentiate ourselves from the crowd—to stand out as individuals. A wedding ring is universally agreed to be a band of metal (mostly of precious metal), decorated or plain, but without a stone. We wear it to conform, but it is engraved inside to make it specific, individual and our own. We might wear more jewellery for an evening out because it is the custom in our social group, but nothing pleases as much as a special piece, something unique and 'different'. This constitutes a decided need, at every level of society, regardless of whether it is done with immense expenditure or indeed by the very opposite, the total lack of such means of self-expression.

Almost every walk of life is identifiable through some form of jewellery. We expect the monarch or the president and their families to appear all-aglitter on state occasions; we enjoy the glamour and flamboyance of theatre and film stars. A nun, however, dresses in stark simplicity, in sombre black with just a touch of white or totally in white, thus demonstrating her negation of worldly and materialistic values. She is a figure apart from the world, uniform only with those who share her devotion—but she wears jewellery to emphasize that devotion: a rosary, a cross and a plain wedding ring to symbolize her union with God. For centuries in fact, the Church has accepted many gifts in the form of jewellery that embellishes the statues and paintings of saints or stays in the treasure chambers of various cathedrals. Such a gift is seen as a sacrifice, and thus meritorious. This is in itself proof of the importance of jewellery in people's lives. Most churches and other religious bodies make use of jewellery to denote the status of the wearer within the hierarchy.

Uniforms too, with their buttons, badges and medals, are another important area that demonstrates very clearly how jewellery indicates belonging to a group as well as the rank within that group. This jewellery may be purely functional, but without it, we could not tell a colonel from a private, an admiral from a captain, the commander-in-chief from a constable, or the hero from the rest of us. Civic regalia and sheriff's badges, the insignia of clubs and sporting medals are other examples of 'public' jewellery that is still very much with us in the twentieth century.

The criteria of taste and fashion affect jewellery only in limited ways for several reasons: partly because the pendulum swings back and forth too quickly, particularly in this century, for most jewellery trends to have a lasting character; partly because it has always been acceptable to wear heirlooms from any previous era, so much so, that historical styles have been reproduced time and again in large quantities. At different times, various revivals of 'Egyptian' or 'Graeco-Roman' designs have occurred (the fashion sparked off by new excavations) or simple repetitions of eighteenth- and nineteenth-century jewellery for its undeniable classic and conventional appeal. Moreover, at any given time our 'fashion/taste' tends to oscillate between a reappreciation of whatever happened about forty of fifty years ago and something very modern, or even futuristic, completely new to the present. In the 1940s and 1950s, there was a distinct harking back to late nineteenth-century Victorian fashions that was coupled with the emergence of Dior's and Chanel's classic look, which owed nothing to that tradition. Today we have moved on to a reappraisal of the 1930s and 1940s, yet we also enjoy objects that project us into the Space Age.

All this has a strictly limited effect on the basic meaning and function of jewellery, however, because jewellery has such personal connotations for the owner. People become deeply attached to it and wear it long after its 'fashionable' appeal has worn off; and its small format allows it to be stored until it finds favour again with other generations. Curiously enough, the more precious the materials used in the jewellery, the more at risk it is of being broken up and refashioned. Even pieces by great masters, renowned in their lifetime, have suffered this fate for one reason or another and were in this manner lost to posterity. Sometimes this happened because the stones in the jewellery were cut in an 'old-fashioned' way and new faceting techniques could improve their brilliance and quality, thereby increasing their commercial value; other reasons were often that the owners wished to have their jewels remodelled so they would be more modern without the additional expense of new materials. With jewellery as with most other things, there is a time when it is new, exciting and very much in demand; then it falls into a period of neglect because it is 'old-fashioned', and its price drops; this is the time for the discerning bargain hunter. Finally, if its quality and craftsmanship as well as its design are classic and typical of its day, it becomes valuable once more and a desired commodity.

These last three points—design, quality and craftsmanship—and not always in that order, are the criteria underlying this book. Perhaps a fourth—basic—concept should be added for, as previously mentioned, much repetition of earlier designs and historical revivalism took place at the same time as new, unique and original ideas were conceived. The focus of this book is on those new concepts that typify our day and age. It concerns itself, with particular emphasis during the last twenty years, with 'unconventional' jewellery because that is the area where the most exciting developments can be seen. In this context it is well to remember that much of the jewellery of the earlier part of the century was considered 'unconventional' in its time.

It is of real importance for both jewellery-makers and wearers to understand the fundamental meaning and function of all forms of jewellery, which is as powerful and essential to the individual today as it ever was—jewellery is very much a part of our modern culture and a vital component of our spiritual and emotional well-being.

I   1900–1920

One of the most fascinating aspects of jewellery in the twentieth century is that attitudes and designs have changed so drastically, that it is possible to recognize the styles of different decades, or even of specific years. During earlier periods of history, the same kind of jewellery often remained in use over prolonged spans of time, making it difficult for historians to date jewels by appearance or techniques of construction. The pace quickened during the eighteenth and nineteenth centuries when improved production methods increased output and more documentation became available. But the last hundred years have seen such enormous changes in social structure, in technological and ethical fields, not to mention world-shattering events like wars, revolutions and the exploration of space, that it was inevitable that they would be reflected in jewellery.

The turn of the century—1900—had a magic ring to it, and in many ways people saw it in much the same way as we regard the year 2000, as a turning point, although events do tend not to consider the calendar. The year 1900 marked the end of a century characterized by many historical events of worldwide importance, with far-reaching impact. The early rumblings of revolution and uprisings were felt; the Industrial Revolution and colonial expansion took place, and radical movements in art came to the fore. Yet life was much slower paced; the worldwide communications network was in its infancy, and intercontinental travel, by boat and train, was reserved for the privileged.

The social structure remained much the same after the turn of the century, and changes that did occur in it, took much longer to affect the majority of people everywhere than they would nowadays. In that first decade of this century, the royal houses of Europe still retained a certain amount of political power, and they were certainly considered the apex of society.

Fabergé, who reigned supreme in the world of jewellery, was still creating his astounding masterpieces, which brought him fame far beyond his native Russia. In 1842, Gustav Fabergé established his first workshop in St Petersburg. His eldest son, Peter Carl (1846–1920) took over the control of the firm in 1870, and it was the son's achievements that won the house its first gold medal at the Pan-Russian Exhibition in Moscow in 1882. In 1884, Tsarina Marie Feodorovna was given the first of the many legendary Imperial Easter Eggs. The firm enjoyed international acclaim for its exquisite products, each one executed with such finesse and ingenuity that it became a by-word for virtuosity in terms of craftsmanship and expertise, and the reputation lasted well into the early twentieth century. Perhaps Fabergé was the last and greatest Court Jeweller of all time; he had royal clients all over Europe and later in the Far East; he allowed his fantasy and imagination free reign unlimited by costs for labour or materials. Fabergé supplied royalty with jewels and bejewelled objets d'art that defy present-day notions of 'good taste' by their sheer magnificence and extravagance. For example, it took two entire years to complete the Trans-Siberian Railway Egg that Nicholas II presented to Alexandra Feodorovna (probably in 1901) to commemorate the ceremonial opening of that railroad. Ten and three-quarter inches high, it was made of gold, enamelled translucent green and set with blue and orange enamel mounts. Surmounted by a gold eagle bearing the Imperial Crown, the egg was supported by three Romanoff griffins on a white onyx base. Concealed within was a complete replica in miniature of the train, consisting of engine, tender and five coaches, all made of gold and platinum. The locomotive was driven by a clockwork motor. The egg can still be admired in the Armoury Museum, housed within the Kremlin in Moscow.

The firm of Fabergé had its headquarters and workshops in St Petersburg; in the late 1890s it established branches at Odessa and Kiev; later, in 1906, it opened a London branch, which finally closed when the firm went out of business just after the outbreak of World War I. In Russia Fabergé continued sales until 1918, when the premises and stock were seized by the Bolsheviks and Peter Carl Fabergé fled, via Latvia and Germany, to Switzerland; he died in Lausanne in 1920.

Two other famous names, whose work still dominated the jewellery scene in that first decade of the twentieth century, were Castellani and Giuliano.

The Castellani brothers, Alessandro (1824–1883) and Auguste (1829–1914) were the sons of a Roman goldsmith and jeweller, Fortunato Pio Castellani (1793–1865). In the wake of the archaeological discoveries in the nineteenth century, which aroused tremendous public interest and enthusiasm, Etruscan-style jewellery became very popular. The Castellanis studied the archaeological treasures in great detail and became masters in reproducing gold jewellery in Neo-Classical styles imitating ancient Greek and Roman jewellery, including the use of a type of granulation, although the rediscovery of the truly ancient technique of granulation would have to wait until 1920.

Carlo Giuliano (1831–1895) had worked some time for Castellani in Naples, then moved to London, where he also specialized in fine reproductions of historical jewels, though he worked in the 'archaic' style rather than making actual copies. His two sons, Carlo and Arthur, carried on the family business in London until 1914.

Art Nouveau and the Arts and Crafts Movement

So while the famous International Exhibition of 1900 in Paris celebrated the turn of the century, nothing changed drastically for just over another decade or so, until the outbreak of World War I—at least not on the surface. Where change could be observed dramatically, however, was in the art world, as demonstrated by the Pre-Raphaelites and the Impressionists who were breaking new ground in the visual arts during the 1880s and 1890s with their radical changes of artist techniques and concepts. This was followed by the birth of both Art Nouveau and the Arts and Crafts Movement. The declared aim of the latter was to bring art to the masses.

In the wake of the Industrial Revolution, when mass production became the pride and joy of the nineteenth-century entrepreneur, people revelled and glorified in the luxury of consumer goods, including jewellery, now available at economic prices to a fast growing middle class. Larger sections of the population, enjoying greater prosperity, wanted to consolidate and demonstrate their affluence—a development that provided a powerful stimulus to the jewellery industry in both Europe and the United States.

In this avalanche of mass production, many artists, craftsmen and craftswomen felt that the human touch, respect for materials and the satisfaction of a fine finish were being lost. Jewellery, like other articles, was becoming impersonal, carelessly constructed, unimaginatively designed. Labelled romantic and idealistic, the followers of John Ruskin and William Morris sought to produce individually conceived and executed pieces in workshop situations similar to those of the mediaeval guilds. They wanted to produce hand-made jewellery from less expensive materials for the general public, yet with the same care and commitment a court jeweller might apply to work for his wealthy and aristocratic clientele. In the past there had always been craftsmen in towns and villages, working for ordinary people on a one-to-one basis; the adherents of the Arts and Crafts Movement felt there was an urgency to return to this special relationship. It was considered particularly important that artists be involved in the design and making of artifacts, which would result in the production of a more meaningful object, whether it be pottery, furniture or, especially, jewellery.

The Art Nouveau style (also known as *stile Liberty* in Italy, *Jugendstil* in Germany, *le style moderne* in France and *Secessionstil* in Austria) with its liberating concepts, fired enthusiasm and inspired artist/craftsmen all over Europe, across the Atlantic and back again. Its flowing lines and graceful forms, drawing on nature in its perfection and portraying idealized images, pervaded all areas of design from fabrics, furniture and cutlery to painting and sculpture. Perhaps it was in jewellery that Art Nouveau reached its highest pinnacle. Born out of a direct reaction and opposition to both Historicism and unbridled mass production, its declared aim was to bring aesthetic values within the reach of ordinary people and into functional areas. Away from the cluttered over-ornamentation of the past, it also hoped to reintroduce respect for hand-made articles in place of the admired machine-made products, by employing new and more natural forms, executed in fluid and elegant lines.

The ideals of the Arts and Crafts Movement were in complete sympathy and agreement with the concepts of Art Nouveau and implemented them in practical ways by forming small groups, guilds and workshops in Britain, Germany and Austria. Charles Robert Ashbee (1863–1942) founded the School and Guild of Handicrafts in London in 1887 with two retail shops in Brook Street and Bond Street, W. 1, and workshops in Chipping Camden, Gloucestershire. Members of the Guild were almost all amateurs who were taught their craft in the workshops that executed, predominantly, Ashbee's own designs. Although the enterprise lasted merely ten years (it went into voluntary liquidation in 1908), its very existence and Ashbee himself had made a decisive impact on the movement as a whole.

In Scotland, Charles Rennie Mackintosh (1868–1929), his wife Margaret Macdonald (1865–1933), her sister, Frances (1874–1921), and Frances's husband, Herbert MacNair (1868–1955) were becoming known as the 'Glasgow Four'. Although perhaps most famous for his architecture and furniture design, Mackintosh collaborated with the other three in designing and making jewellery, though sadly none of it seems to have survived. As a group, the 'Glasgow Four' were much admired by their contemporaries, and they influenced many of the well-known artists and craftsmen on the Continent, where they took part in several international exhibitions.

In Austria, Josef Hoffmann (1870–1956) founded the 'Wiener Werkstätte' in Vienna in 1903, together with Koloman Moser (1868–1918) and Fritz Waerndorfer, a banker. A great admirer of C. R. Ashbee, Hoffmann organized his workshops on lines similar to that of Ashbee's Guild of Handicrafts, except that he insisted on employing only fully qualified craftsmen. Hoffmann, like Mackintosh, was an architect by profession, but practised jewellery design as well.

In 1901, Grand Duke Ernst Ludwig of Hessen invited the well-known Austrian architect Joseph Olbrich to build an artists' colony on the Mathildenhöhe in Darmstadt. Here too, workshops were part of the scheme, involving a number of extremely talented and well-known artists in making jewellery, among them Peter Behrens, Rudolf Bosselts, Patriz Huber and Olbrich himself. Many of their designs were mass-produced for very inexpensive jewellery by Theodor Fahrner (1868–1919), a jewellery manufacturer in Pforzheim, Germany, whose wares were marketed all over Europe and even exported to America.

It was around that same time, in 1904, that Georg Jensen (1866–1935) opened his workshop in Copenhagen, Denmark. Trained in the traditional manner as a gold- and silversmith, Jensen had also studied sculpture at the Danish Royal Academy. He had worked together with Mogens Ballin, a Danish artist, making experimental jewellery in silver and pewter. Then he turned to making silver jewellery with semi-precious stones, the first models of the long-lasting and highly influential designs that made his enterprise flourish to this day and made Scandinavian jewellery a household word. Jensen's early years were, however, a continuous struggle for survival. Trying to appeal to the more progressively minded in the middle class, he tended to under-price his jewellery, and although he exhibited frequently at the Danske Kunstindustrimuseum, which also purchased some of his work, he did not achieve any measure of commercial success until 1909, when Carl Dyhr opened a shop in Berlin exclusively devoted to Jensen's jewellery.

The Arts and Crafts Movement, despite its unaggressive and 'uncommercial' approach to business, produced far-reaching repercussions long after the movement itself had died an early death. Its international associations, its ideals of artists' involvement with the crafts, of artist/craftsmen's integrity and social awareness were to inspire whole generations to come.

It was ironic that, eventually, it was the rich and cultured who appreciated and valued the exquisite work, the exciting designs, the unusual and ingenious use of materials characteristic of the Arts and Crafts Movement and of the exponents of Art Nouveau. What had begun as a deliberate attempt to bring art to the masses, turned into an elitist exercise for the affluent. It was the rich, with their education, culture and money, who had the courage and the means to be avant-garde. It was easy for them to accept that artists should involve themselves in creating functional objects. The past had provided many precedents: Dürer designed medals and coins; Cellini, Ghirlandaio and Leonardo da Vinci were all outstanding artists who practised the art of the goldsmith.

But in spite of all the artists' efforts and the support they did receive, the Arts and Crafts Movement could not survive its lack of wider commercial appeal. The exception was Georg Jensen (though Carl Dyhr's shop in Berlin closed down with the outbreak of World War I), who scored an enormous success at the Baltic Exhibition in Malmö, Sweden in 1914: a Swedish art dealer, Niels Wendel, bought all his exhibits and later became his partner. In 1915, at the Panama-Pacific International Exhibition in San Francisco, the newspaper magnate William Randolph Hearst purchased the major part of Jensen's exhibited works. But perhaps the true secret of Jensen's success story is the combination of two principles in his enterprise: he never compromised about producing jewellery of high artistic merit and design in affordable price ranges, and he always gave full credit to the many artists with whom he collaborated. Moreover, he had the good fortune (or judgment) to be associated with people like his brother-in-law Thorolf Møller, P.A. Pedersen and Frederick Lunning among others, whose business acumen was responsible for the financial success of the firm, yet who never demanded that Jensen lower his standards or depart from his original ideals.

At the other end of the scale, during the Edwardian era in England and its equivalent elsewhere, established 'jewellery houses' like Cartier and Fouquet along with comparative newcomers such as Bulgari and Tiffany enjoyed enormous success. The world was, in fact, in a sort of economic crisis even in the early days of the twentieth century, but this had rather more to with a shifting of wealth from one section of society to another than the later recessions of the 1920s and 1970s. Those who had acquired wealth more recently, vied with each other to spend it, modelling themselves very much on those who had always enjoyed the privilege of wealth and emulating the aristocratic taste for large and resplendent jewellery. Apart from royal and aristocratic clients in Europe, enough jewels of outsize proportions were commissioned or purchased by American millionaires and Eastern princes to turn the fortunes of these 'houses' into legends. Their jewellery turned into legends too—made to stun, dazzle and impress, it had to be large so it could be seen from afar; it had to contain important and valuable stones, so that their reflective sparkle would evoke awe and wonder. The shape and precious quality of this jewellery was designed deliberately to touch archaic responses within the onlookers, to remind them of the ancient magic and power attributed to precious stones and metals. It is hardly surprising that

artists and craftsmen alike responded to such an opportunity—to work under such conditions, unlimited by price or size, is indeed the dream of any creative mind. Consequently, the art of the jeweller flourished at that time, and these 'houses' continued to do very well into the 1920s and 1930s.

France

In the world of jewellery, France reigned supreme in those days, and Paris became the mecca for all those in search of the spectacular, the exquisite and the expensive, as well as for those capable of producing it with superlative skills and imagination.

The name that springs perhaps most readily to mind in this context is that of the House of Cartier. For over a hundred years, starting in 1847, Cartier was owned and managed by the direct descendants of its founder, Louis-François Cartier (1819–1904). Even he could trace his talent for making and dealing in jewellery back to a grandfather who had worked as a metallurgist at the Louvre in Paris and to his own father who had taught him as a boy to carve wood and ivory, and the technique of alloying metals.

The chronicle of the House of Cartier and the individual contributions to its rise in fame made by each successive member of the family is a fascinating story of nineteenth-century standards and attitudes constantly being adapted and, finally, giving way to new situations.

Court Jewellers *par excellence*, Cartier boasted some thirteen Royal Warrants by the early 1920s, when Louis Cartier (1875–1942) managed the firm together with his brothers Pierre and Jacques. In 1898, Cartier moved into 13 Rue de la Paix in Paris, employing thirteen designers; and the firm still occupies the same impressive premises today. Little wonder that Louis always considered thirteen his lucky number. In 1902, Cartier's London branch opened in Bond Street under the patronage of King Edward VII, and in 1908 they established themselves in New York. Throughout their existence as a family business (Cartier-New York was sold in 1962, and by 1970 all the other branches had passed into public ownership), the Cartiers were close bystanders and witnesses to the many amazing events that beset their illustrious clients. They were advisers and confidantes of royalty in power and in exile; with all their knowledge of the intrigues and *affaires de cœur* of the famous they exercised impeccable discretion, handled crown jewels and priceless trinkets for sultans from the Orient and sovereigns from Europe.

In Paris, *le style moderne* reached perhaps greater heights than anywhere else. It was here that artists like Bonnard, Vuillard, Van de Velde, Mucha, Beardsley, Gaillard and Gallé (to name but a few) worked, designing and making all kinds of furnishings, household utensils and personal items like jewellery. Their work was often shown at important international exhibitions such as the one organized in Paris in 1900 and, in successive years, in Vienna, Berlin, London and Chicago. These artists were also greatly encouraged by Samuel Bing, who opened a shop in Paris in the early 1890s called 'La Maison de l'Art Nouveau', with an exterior designed by the English artist Frank Brangwyn. Bing commissioned, stocked and displayed decorative art from all over the world, including the famous Tiffany glass and mosaics, which he saw for the first time at the World's Columbian Exhibition in Chicago in 1893, immediately recognizing their enormous potential.

Among the most outstanding artist/jewellers of the period, René Jules Lalique (1860–1945) indisputably stands out. For over twenty-five years, from the late 1880s to about 1910, he created spectacular jewellery of highly original design and superb quality, including a fantastic collection of stage jewellery for the legendary actress Sarah Bernhardt and a magnificent group of 145 pieces, made between 1895 and 1912, for the collection of Calouste Gulbenkian, which is now housed and displayed in the Fundação Calouste Gulbenkian in Lisbon, Portugal.

From the age of sixteen, Lalique had served a formal apprenticeship with the Parisian jeweller Louis Aucoc. At the end of his training, Lalique continued with further studies at the Ecole des Arts Décoratifs in Paris; and after spending a couple of years in London, he opened his own workshop in Paris in 1884. A man of great talent and imagination, Lalique perfected the finest techniques in casting and *plique-à-jour* enamel to execute designs of extravagant beauty. In glowing colours, obtained by using iridescent enamels, superbly large baroque pearls and a gamut of semi-precious stones set in gold, he created exquisite images of classic quality. Dreamy and tranquil, his soft reliefs, with female faces and bodies surrounded by voluptuous, free-flowing hair merging into clouds and echoed by long-stemmed flowers, symbolize the very spirit of that era. In his long working life, Lalique achieved crowning success in two quite separate media: jewellery, and glass—the material to which he devoted the second part of his career as an artist with phenomenal results.

Georges Fouquet is another great name, whose jewellery expressed superbly the idyllic view of nature so typical of Art Nouveau. His forms, even when they are partly abstract, are none the less deeply rooted in exotic flora and fauna and display an ingenious sense of composition.

Georges's father, Alphonse Fouquet, founder of the House of Fouquet, had risen to fame through forty years of steady work, to be counted finally among the top ten jewellery creators at the turn of the century; however, Alphonse's preoccupation with, and commitment to, commercial considerations had prevented him from reaching that position sooner. He was unwilling and unable to detach himself from his regular workshop production in order to create the kind of jewellery that would command attention at prestigious exhibitions.

In 1895, the year in which the Salon des Artistes français included exhibits of jewellery for the first time, Georges Fouquet took over the direction of the House of Fouquet. Georges showed his jewellery there from 1897 onwards, and at the Exhibition of 1900 especially, he gained widespread recognition and acclaim for his work in collaboration with the well-known artist Alphonse Mucha (1860–1939). Inspired and stimulated by the renowned Lalique, Georges Fouquet was sensitive to the importance of artistic content in his own work and often enlisted the aid of other fine artists from different disciplines such as painting, sculpture or even architecture. He had an enviable talent for successfully combining the skills of various craftsmen, each an expert in his own field, giving form and perfection to an artistic concept conceived by someone else.

Then as now, the dilemma and argument over the validity of jewellery as an art form was ever present: can and should the artistic content take precedence over craftsmanship; is 'artistic' jewellery wearable, and does it fulfil the 'proper' function of jewellery?

At the Salon des Artistes français and other important exhibitions, the jewellery exhibits drew wide attention and admiration, but there were also critics like Henri Vever, who wrote in 1898, "some of the pieces are too heavy for wear, clumsily executed and the overall outlines appear to be more the work of a bronze-caster than that of a goldsmith'. Others deplored the large format of the jewellery that made it quite unsuitable for wear by any but the most daring.

The master jewellers whose names now stand like hallmarks for the very best that their era produced also continued making ranges of less ambitious, more commercially viable jewellery, of high standard and quality, accessible to a wider public. Their concern with, and understanding of, art expressed in terms of jewellery directly influenced and improved the designs used for their more commercial output; they exploited their own ingenuity and innovative skills without any apparent loss of artistic integrity—a feat that is rarely attempted or achieved nowadays.

The commercial potential and spread of Art Nouveau was greatly furthered by its connection with certain enterprises whose names have also become synonymous with the movement as a whole: Bing's 'La Maison de l'Art Nouveau' (which actually gave its name to the style, at least as far as England was concerned), Liberty's and Tiffany, the other two businesses that completed a Paris–London–New York triangle.

The United States

During the earlier part of the nineteenth century, comparatively little jewellery was actually produced in the United States. Society ladies preferred to buy their sparkling ornaments in Europe, predominantly in France, or from Tiffany, which imported the best European jewellery in large quantities. By the end of the last century, however, the main jewellery centres in the United States —Newark, New Jersey, and Providence, Rhode Island—had grown to rival their European counterparts, spurred on by the discovery of their own gold resources in the West.

Louis Comfort Tiffany (1848–1933), who had taken over the firm from his father, Charles Lewis Tiffany (1812–1902), studied painting in Paris and Spain. He became keenly aware of the new trends in art and jewellery and devoted himself first to glass, which he registered with the 'Favrile' trademark in 1894 and supplied to Bing's shop. In 1900, metalwork in the form of lamps and ornaments, and jewellery began to be produced in Tiffany's workshops, the management of which Louis took over after his father's death in 1902. His highly skilled craftsmen certainly equalled those in Europe, and they developed a subtle yet quite distinct American version of Art Nouveau.

Liberty's of London

In London, Arthur Lasenby Liberty (1843–1917) founded his famous store in 1875, originally to specialize in the sale of oriental arts and crafts, which had become very popular in the wake of Queen Victoria's proclamation as Empress of India and the newly established trade links between Japan and the Western world.

Arthur Liberty's lifelong interest in oriental art has been perpetuated to the present day: Liberty's retain a specialist department that offers art and craft work of all kinds from all over the Far East. This interest brought Arthur Liberty into contact with artists like Burne-Jones, Rosetti and Whistler, who shared his enthusiasm and were in turn dominant in the development of Art Nouveau.

Some of the best examples of Art Nouveau jewellery were specially made for Liberty's in Birmingham, by W. H. Haseler amongst others, who employed many artists including Oliver Baker, Archibald Knox and Arthur Gaskin. Under the tradename of 'Cymric' they produced an enormously popular range of silver jewellery, much of it with semi-precious stones, mother-of-pearl and enamel.

Japan

The opening of trade links with Japan not only awakened widespread interest in Japanese art and culture in the United States and Europe, but Western influence also brought Japan firmly into the twentieth century. Isolated from the outside world since the seventeenth century to prevent the spread of Christianity, it preserved its own strong traditions and customs that did not include jewellery as we know it, which arrived in Japan after the 1860s. The techniques and skills were present but were used only on items like hair ornaments, netsuke, objets d'art and ceremonial weaponry. By late in the nineteenth century and early in the twentieth, Japan was already briskly producing jewellery, mostly of European design, but with astounding workmanship and quality. More than that, certain Japanese techniques were brought into play like the ancient art of *mokume gane* (*mokume* = 'wood grain', *gane* = 'metal'), a method of laminating different non-ferrous metals, including precious ones, by heat, then reducing the laminate to a workable thickness of metal sheet. Depending on the different methods used to achieve the reduction, the final sheet will contain a permanent pattern of varied metal colours. Another technique, *shakudo* (an alloy of 75 to 95 per cent copper with pure gold), produced a metal with a patina ranging from reddish brown to a velvety black.

Lalique, Gaillard and other contemporaries were great admirers of Japanese expertise with metal, wood and horn, to the extent that they even employed Japanese craftsmen in their workshops in Paris. In London, the Royal College of Art invited two Japanese professors, Unno Bisei and T. Kobayashi, to lecture to their students on these techniques as early as 1905.

The Mikimoto Company, which introduced cultured pearls in 1920, was already flourishing at that time, dealing in pearls all over the world, as well as in made-up jewellery from their own workshops in the current style (with pearls and diamonds) but with a distinctive touch that made the products unmistakably Japanese.

Etiquette

It is important to remember that during the entire pre-World War I period the social structure was still essentially nineteenth-century with clearly defined rules and etiquette that were observed, or at least aspired to, by a majority of people in all classes. There were specific forms of jewellery like tiaras for appearances at the royal court, their size carefully graduated according to rank and age; matching sets of earrings, necklace and bracelet were considered proper for gala occasions, and smaller sets of jewellery were appropriate for day wear. Modest jewellery was designated for the lower-income groups in keeping with their station. It would have been unthinkable for a person of low social standing to appear wearing jewellery of quality without arousing the gravest suspicions about their honesty or morals. There were strict rules, too, as to what kind of jewellery was suitable for a girl, a young lady, a young married woman or a matron. Obviously, these rules applied equally to dress and to manner in general, but it is quite hard these days to imagine that they were strong and powerful enough to cause scandals if contravened. Books were written on etiquette, upper-class girls everywhere were sent to finishing schools to learn its disciplines, and the lower orders knew their place.

To illustrate the point, there is an amusing anecdote quoted by Gilberte Gautier in her marvellous book entitled *13 Rue de la Paix*, the history of the House of Cartier. The story comes from *Vingt Ans Maître d'Hôtel chez Maxim*, the memoirs of Hugo, head-waiter for two decades at Maxim's, the famous Parisian cafe-restaurant frequented by the great beauties of the day—actresses and courtesans like La Belle Otéro, Liane de Pougy and Gaby Deslys. Madame Otéro was dining at Maxim's, covered with sparkling jewellery from head to foot. Madame Liane de Pougy's table was empty; finally Madame Liane swept in, dressed in a simple robe of black velvet, totally unadorned, and followed by her personal maid. After a moment, astonishment changed to stupor as Madame Liane removed the hat and cloak from her servant's shoulders—to reveal the girl wearing all her priceless jewels. Madame Liane, accompanied by Count de T., took her seat amidst applause. Madame Otéro got up in a rage and left, swearing violently in Spanish, as she passed Liane's table.

In the present social climate, such a scene is unimaginable anywhere. In those days, however, people of all social levels tried their best to conform, the only exception being a few intellectuals and artists, and perhaps some eccentrics. It was easy to shock others, since it required only a subtle, small, personal gesture to invite punitive results that could range from social ostracism to loss of employment, which at that time (when unemployment benefits and social security were unknown) could spell abject poverty. The nearest comparison one could make, though without such dire consequences, is with today's punks who certainly wear their jewellery of pins and razor blades to shock the Establishment.

World War I

The outbreak of World War I and the Russian Revolution put jewellery, like everything else, into an altogether different perspective. Glittering galas and receptions vanished overnight; valuables were put into safes and bank vaults by those who could afford to keep them, while others bartered their priceless possessions, for their lives sometimes, as in the case of the Russian aristocracy. Stories abound of countesses exchanging emerald, ruby and diamond necklaces for the peasants' milk and bread; or of others who fled to Germany, France, England and the United States, taking their splendid heirlooms with them to sell there and so finance a new start in life.

Everywhere jewellers and artists were called up to join the armed forces of their own countries; those remaining in the workshops often had to use their fine mechanical skills to produce what the arms industry required. Precious metals became scarce; many people in countries like Germany donated their gold jewellery to the government to help its war effort.

For general wear, patriotic jewellery became the order of the day; it was made of less valuable materials like silver, copper, aluminium and even iron. The meaning of personal jewellery intensified with the common experience of separation from loved ones and the tragic losses suffered by so many on both sides of the conflict. Yet even during the dark and gruesome periods of prolonged trench warfare, soldiers in dug-outs fashioned rings from bits of wire lying around or made other forms of jewellery from metal fragments, shell-cases, bullet cartridges, etc.

The nineteenth century had come to an end, more truly than at the actual turn of the century. The physical, emotional and economic shock suffered by everyone—particularly in Europe, but the repercussions were felt everywhere—is mirrored in jewellery only too clearly.

1 Brooch/Pendant. 18-carat gold and enamel with a baroque pearl drop. French, by René Jules Lalique (1860–1945). Ca. 1898/1900. H. 8.5 cm, W. 8.5 cm. Schmuckmuseum, Pforzheim (SCH 1736).

Throughout his long working life as an artist, jeweller and later sculptor, renowned glass-maker and designer, Lalique's work epitomized the spirit of his times. This brooch/ pendant was made when he had already won wide-spread recognition for his exquisite and stunning jewellery. Two idealized female heads in profile amidst swirling gold swallows en-amelled blue, completed by the iridescent whiteness of a baroque pearl drop, make this piece a classic example of its period. The free-flowing forms on a background of *plique-à-jour* enamel and the irregular shape of the ba-roque pearl embody all the essential features of the Art Nouveau concept of design. A slight abstraction and idealization of nature and the soft, fluid overall outlines that give this brooch a dreamy, romantic look were the hallmarks of Art Nouveau during the entire era.

2 Waist Clasp. Sterling silver, set with an opal. British, probably designed by Oliver Baker (1856–1939), made by W. H. Haseler & Co, Birmingham. Ca. 1899/1900. L. 10 cm, W. 6 cm. Victoria and Albert Museum, London (M. 306–1975).

Wide belts with ornamental buckles and clasps were very much in fashion at the turn of the century. This waist clasp is a fine example of design, typical of the jewellery of the Arts and Crafts Movement for which Liberty's became so well-known in England and abroad at that time. This piece was made for Mrs John Lle-wellyn, wife of the director of Liberty & Co, who was in charge of 'Cymric' jewellery, which was specifically designed and made for Lib-erty's by W. H. Haseler & Co. of Birmingham.

Liberty's owned a large part of the shares in Haseler & Co. which, in turn, produced the greater part of Liberty's jewellery and silver ware. Many well-known artist/jewellers who belonged to the Arts and Crafts Movement were responsible for Haseler's designs: among them, Oliver Baker, Arthur Gaskin and Archi-bald Knox.

3 Pendant. 18-carat gold with enamel and rubies. French, by Emile Froment-Meurice (1837–1912). 1900. L. 4.5 cm, W. 6 cm. Vic-toria and Albert Museum, London (M. 347–1940).

Cast in gold and finely enamelled, this pendant represents a woman's body to the waist; in a typical Art Nouveau pose, against a background of irises, she is holding her flowing tresses in her hands. The pendant originally had a pearl drop as well; however, it was lost before the donor (Captain Walter Dasent, R.N.) bequeathed it to the museum.

For most of his working life, Emile Froment-Meurice, a jeweller like his father and grand-father before him, produced jewellery in the Neo-Classical styles of the Renaissance; but, towards the end of the nineteenth century, he was inspired, albeit in a somewhat restrained manner, by Art Nouveau.

4 Brooch. Gold with diamonds and Missis-sippi pearls. U.S.A., by Tiffany & Co, New York. Ca. 1900. L. 10.5 cm, W. 5.8 cm. Private Collection.

Unusually large for the period, this brooch is made to resemble a chrysanthemum with pearl petals and pavé-set diamonds on the stem and leaves. These uncommonly large, irregularly shaped pearls are named after the valley of the river in which they are found. They are fresh-water pearls and grow inside the Niggerhead mussel, a species of pearl mussel with a shell that can attain a diameter of up to 10 centi-metres.

Tiffany's, founded in the late 1830s by Charles Lewis Tiffany, is a name which, to this day, is synonymous with fabulous jewellery. By the end of the nineteenth century, Tiffany's had its own workshops and the founder's son, Louis Comfort Tiffany, had joined the firm. Louis took over the direction of the business in 1902 on his father's death.

5 Necklace. Gold with black-and-white enamel, rose diamonds and a single baroque pearl drop. British, by Carlo and Arthur (1864–1914) Giuliano. Ca. 1900. Top circum. 38 cm, L. (drop) 7 cm. Private Collection.

The Giuliano family became well-known for their particular style of jewellery design, inspired by that of the Renaissance, which was very popular in the second half of the nine-teenth century and continued to be produced well into the early decades of the twentieth.

This necklace opens out from the single chain of links into three strands fastened to two diamond-set rosettes, one on either side. Each link is finely enamelled and joined by a small diamond to the next one; finally, the three cen-tre sections are connected and culminate in a baroque pearl drop. The design is light and perfect for wearing with the low-cut dresses of the period that leave the neck and shoulders bare.

6 Brooch. Silver, gold and enamel, set with opals. British, by Murrle, Bennett & Co, Lon-don, made for Theodor Fahrner & Co. Ca. 1910. Diam. 4 cm. John Jesse/Irina Lasky Gal-lery, London.

The design of this brooch and the use of silver together with gold and enamel demonstrate the gentle transition from the florid exuberance of Art Nouveau styles towards the bolder, simpler forms of the much later Art Deco.

This is a typical example of a range of jewel-lery produced in great quantities at that time for the German market, where Art Nouveau was known as *Jugendstil*. The London firm of Murrle, Bennett & Co manufactured such jewellery for Theodor Fahrner & Co of Pforz-heim. The back of this brooch bears the marks of both firms.

7 Two Rings. (*left*) 18-carat gold with am-ethyst. L. 3 cm; (*right*) 18-carat gold set with turquoise. W. 2 cm. French, (*left ring*) by A. Bricteux; (*right ring*) anon. Ca. 1900. John Jesse/Irina Lasky Gallery, London.

Finely wrought in gold, both rings are good examples of the high standard of French crafts-manship, coupled with an unmistakably Art Nouveau design.

The unusual shape of the amethysts on the left ring suggests that they were probably cut specially for this piece with its stylized floral motif.

The ring on the right is set with a large cab-ochon turquoise matrix. Turquoise matrix had become very popular at that time for its beauti-ful bright colour, accentuated by fine dark-brown veins. The bezel of this ring is joined to the shank on either side by an exquis-itely modelled dragon-fly, spreading its wings around the collet.

8 Buckle. Silver with green-dyed agates. Ger-man, designed by Patriz Huber (1878–1902) in Darmstadt. Ca. 1900/1901. W. 8.7 cm. Schmuckmuseum, Pforzheim (SCH 1768).

Inspired by ancient Indian and Chinese decor-ative motifs, Patriz Huber was much attracted by symmetrical forms, which he adapted to his own aesthetic principles. This piece with the spiral motif formalized into triangular shape, with lines radiating from the centre and topped by triangular cabochon stones, is characteristic of his design, as is the overall sobriety of the piece.

In 1899, Huber was one of a number of young creative talents from all over Europe invited by Grand Duke Ernst Ludwig of Hes-sen to live and work in a specially constructed artists' colony at Darmstadt, which produced significant and interesting work but lasted only a few years.

9 Pendant. Gold, diamonds, enamel and pearl drop. German, by Max Friedrich Koch (1859–1930). Ca. 1900/1903. L. (incl. pearl drop) 7.5 cm. Schmuckmuseum, Pforzheim (1966/14).

Finely modelled in relief, this gold pendant expresses the favourite Art Nouveau concept of idealized womanhood: a female profile is surrounded by flowing hair in gentle curls; the woman's dreamy gaze is fixed on two playful dragonflies with spread wings gliding over the water's edge. The scrolled sides of the pendant are topped with diamonds and edged with a graceful arrangement of iris and foliage. The top loop glitters with pavé-set diamonds, and a large pearl is suspended from the lowest point of the triangular shape.

Max Friedrich Koch belonged to the very small group of German artist/jewellers (see Pl. 44) who were undoubtedly inspired and influenced by the great French exponents of Art Nouveau but who created their own original versions of the style.

10 Pendant. Gold, enamel, Australian opal, diamond sparks and three tourmaline beads. British, by Charles Robert Ashbee (1863–1942). Ca. 1903. H. 7.6 cm, W. 2.3 cm. Victoria and Albert Museum, London (M. 4.–1964).
Making ingenious use of the unusual, irregular shape of the beautiful opal, the stone in this piece is mounted like a sail on a golden boat. Known as the Ship Pendant (the 'Craft of the Guild'), it was designed by Charles Robert Ashbee, a prolific English designer, a great idealist and an important figure in the Arts and Crafts Movement, who founded the School and Guild of Handicrafts. By 1902, the Guild had become a limited company and its workshops had been moved from London to Chipping Campden in Gloucestershire, where this pendant was made.

11 Brooch. Gold, silver, aquamarine and diamonds. Russian, by Carl Fabergé (1846–1920). Ca. 1900. L. 4.2 cm, W. 6.7 cm. Private Collection.
This is a rather severe, geometric design, which echoes beautifully the cut of the unusually large aquamarine and sets off the sparkle of the pavé-set rose diamonds against the blue of the stone. The brooch is mounted in gold but the diamonds are set in silver, a method quite commonly practised because silver is deemed to enhance better the colour of diamonds. It is also a softer metal than gold and, therefore, easier to use for setting small stones.

This brooch bears the mark of August Wilhelm Holmström, a workmaster for Carl Fabergé at his St Petersburg workshop: it comes from the collection of Irene, Princess Heinrich of Prussia, a sister of Tsarina Alexandra Feodorovna.

12 Brooch. Gold with *plique-à-jour* and translucent enamel. French, by Georges Fouquet (1862–1957) and Charles Desrosiers. 1901. H. 6.1 cm, W. 12.9 cm. Victoria and Albert Museum, London (957–1901).
The Hornet Brooch, as this piece is known, was acquired by the Victoria and Albert Museum at the Paris Salon in 1901. The brooch is a bold piece of large dimensions, even by present-day standards, the generous sweeping curves of the floral stem superbly enamelled in translucent green over the etched texture. The hornet (slightly smaller than life-size), with stripes of dark-brown enamel on gold and spread-out wings, rests on the edge of the flower's delicate petals that are supported by a crescent shape with stylized floral motifs. Petals and wings are filled with *plique-à-jour* enamel in subtle shades of pink and green.

This is one of the many classic pieces of Art Nouveau jewellery made by Georges Fouquet in collaboration with artists, in this case with Charles Desrosiers.

13 Two Brooches. Gold, enamel and diamonds. Russian, by Carl Fabergé (1846–1920). Ca. 1900/1910. (*top*) L. 3.9 cm, W. 4.2 cm; (*bottom*) L. 2.1 cm, W. 5.2 cm. Private Collection.
The incredible versatility and virtuosity of Carl Fabergé's design and craftsmanship is well demonstrated by these two comparatively small brooches and by the one illustrated in Pl. 11. In great contrast to the stark simplicity of the previous design, these two brooches are ornate and complex in structure, features more often associated with Fabergé. The top brooch is made of gold in the form of a bow, the 'ribbon', delicately etched to resemble moiré silk, covered with bright pink, translucent enamel and edged with rose diamonds pavé-set in silver.

The second brooch, in the shape of a lozenge, is also of gold, enamelled in pink over an etched, textured surface and surmounted by a gold leaf at either end. In the centre, there is a tiny diamond-encrusted crown over Queen Marie of Rumania's cypher, also composed of tiny pavé-set diamonds.

Unfettered by costs, since his customers were the Russian and other European courts, Carl Fabergé created jewellery and bejewelled objects of such magnificence that, even today, visitors to exhibitions, or to the collection in the Kremlin in Moscow, are astounded by their sheer extravagance and unequalled perfection.

14 Pendant. Silver, with moonstones and opals. British, by Charles Robert Ashbee (1863–1942). Ca. 1904/1905. Diam. 5 cm. John Jesse/Irina Lasky Gallery, London.
Wrought in silver and using the opals and moonstones so much in favour at the time, this pendant by Charles Robert Ashbee is more influenced by Art Nouveau than is usual in the more modest styling of the Arts and Crafts Movement.

The peacock is well defined and finely modelled, its fully spread feathers accentuated by moonstones and bordered by a silver wire, which frames the edge with small silver grains soldered to the end of each pointed feather. The drops consist of three irregularly shaped opals, held in mounts of twisted wire.

15 Hair Ornament. Gold, horn and diamonds. French, by Lucien Gaillard. (1861–unknown). Ca. 1903. W. 11 cm. Schmuckmuseum, Pforzheim (1963/201).
This hair ornament by the third-generation jeweller Lucien Gaillard is sensitively carved in horn to represent cowslip flowers; each small part of the flower cluster is set with a tiny diamond.

Gaillard, who was encouraged by his friend and contemporary René Lalique (see Pls 1, 23) to turn from silversmithing to jewellery-making, won much acclaim for his 'oriental'-style jewellery, including the First Prize for Jewellery at the Paris Salon in 1904; Gaillard is known to have employed Japanese craftsmen in his workshop in Paris.

16 Pendant. Silver and opals. Austrian, by Koloman Moser (1868–1918). 1904. L. 15 cm, (chain) 39 cm. Österreichisches Museum für angewandte Kunst, Vienna (Bi. 1495).
In addition to his undoubted capacity as an artist, Koloman Moser, co-founder of the Wiener Werkstätte, was a man of vision and commitment, a fervent supporter of the ideals of Ruskin and Morris, untiring in his efforts to put his strong beliefs and principles into practice. Moser made jewellery in the Arts and Crafts style.

A weasel-like animal, made of silver, curls itself around the opal, holding the stone with its feet; its long tail ends in a spiral at the base of the oval outer frame. Squares of silver, irregular in size and placement, connect the frame with the centre and are also attached to the chain that dangles at the bottom of the oval.

1 Brooch/Pendant. 18-carat gold and enamel ▷ with a baroque pearl drop. French, by René Jules Lalique (1860–1945). Ca. 1898/1900. H. 8.5 cm, W. 8.5 cm. Schmuckmuseum, Pforzheim (SCH 1736).

2 Waist Clasp. Sterling silver, set with an opal. British, probably designed by Oliver Baker (1856–1939), made by W.H. Haseler & Co, Birmingham. Ca. 1899/1900. L. 10 cm, W. 6 cm. Victoria and Albert Museum, London (M. 306–1975).

3 Pendant. 18-carat gold with enamel and rubies. French, by Emile Froment-Meurice (1837–1912). 1900. L. 4.5 cm, W. 6 cm. Victoria and Albert Museum, London (M. 347–1940).

4 Brooch. Gold with diamonds and Mississippi pearls. U.S.A., by Tiffany & Co, New York. Ca. 1900. L. 10.5 cm, W. 5.8 cm. Private Collection.

5 Necklace. Gold with black-and-white ▷ enamel, rose diamonds and a single baroque pearl drop. British, by Carlo and Arthur (1864–1914) Giuliano. Ca. 1900. Top circum. 38 cm, L. (drop) 7 cm. Private Collection.

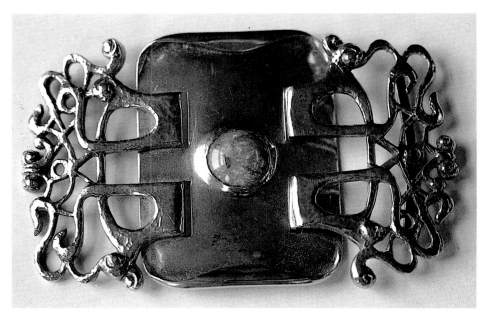

6 Brooch. Silver, gold and enamel, set with opals. British, by Murrle, Bennett & Co, London, made for Theodor Fahrner & Co. Ca. 1910. Diam. 4 cm. John Jesse/Irina Lasky Gallery, London.

7 Two Rings. (*left*) 18-carat gold with amethyst. L. 3 cm; (*right*) 18-carat gold set with turquoise. W. 2 cm. French, (*left ring*) by A. Bricteux; (*right ring*) anon. Ca. 1900. John Jesse/Irina Lasky Gallery, London.

8 Buckle. Silver with green-dyed agates. German, designed by Patriz Huber (1878–1902) in Darmstadt. Ca. 1900/1901. W. 8.7 cm. Schmuckmuseum, Pforzheim (SCH 1768).

9 Pendant. Gold, diamonds, enamel and pearl drop. German, by Max Friedrich Koch (1859–1930). Ca. 1900/1903. L. (incl. pearl drop) 7.5 cm. Schmuckmuseum, Pforzheim (1966/14).

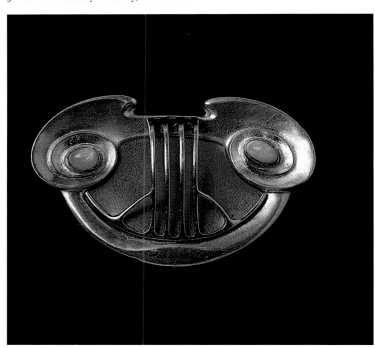

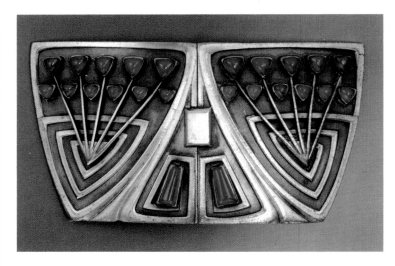

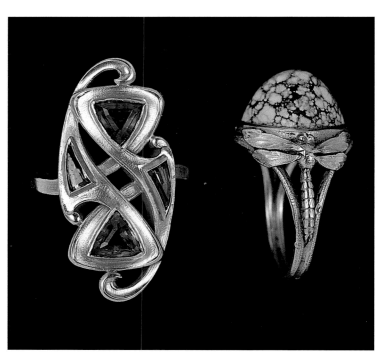

10 Pendant. Gold, enamel, Australian opal, diamond sparks and three tourmaline bead drops. British, by Charles Robert Ashbee (1863–1942). Ca. 1903. H. 7.6 cm, W. 2.3 cm. Victoria and Albert Museum, London (M. 4.–1964).

11 Brooch. Gold, silver, aquamarine and diamonds. Russian, by Carl Fabergé (1846–1920). Ca. 1900. L. 4.2 cm, W. 6.7 cm. Private Collection.

12 Brooch. Gold with *plique-à-jour* and translucent enamel. French, by Georges Fouquet (1862–1957) and Charles Desrosiers. 1901. H. 6.1 cm, W. 12.9 cm. Victoria and Albert Museum, London (957–1901).

13 Two Brooches. Gold, enamel and diamonds. Russian, by Carl Fabergé (1846–1920). Ca. 1900/1910. (*top*) L. 3.9 cm, W. 4.2 cm; (*bottom*) L. 2.1 cm, W. 5.2 cm. Private Collection.

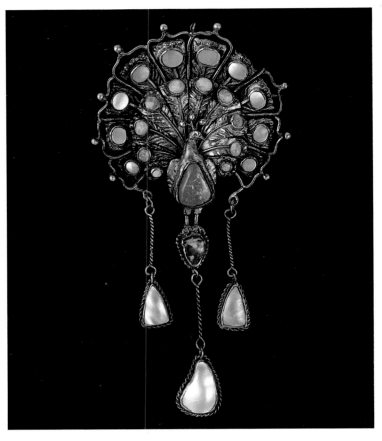

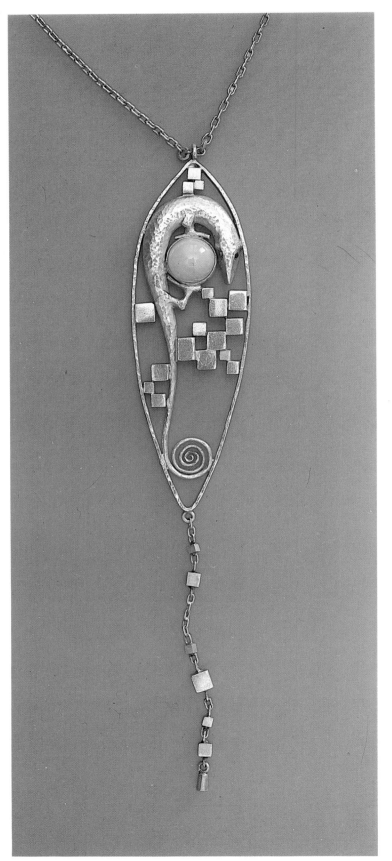

◁◁ **14 Pendant.** Silver, with moonstones and opals. British, by Charles Robert Ashbee. (1863–1942). Ca. 1904/1905. Diam. 5 cm. John Jesse/Irina Lasky Gallery, London.

◁◁ **15 Hair Ornament.** Gold, horn and diamonds. French, by Lucien Gaillard. (1861–unknown). Ca. 1903. W. 11 cm. Schmuckmuseum, Pforzheim (1963/201).

◁ **16 Pendant.** Silver and opals. Austrian, by Koloman Moser (1868–1918). 1904. L. 15 cm, (chain) 39 cm. Österreichisches Museum für angewandte Kunst, Vienna (Bi. 1495).

17 Three Brooches, Two Combs, a Buckle and a Bracelet. Silver, amber, green agates and garnets. Danish, by Georg Jensen (1866–1935). 1904/1910. (*From left to right*) top: W. 6 cm, 12.5 cm, 4 cm; *2nd row*: W. 11 cm, 12 cm, 10 cm; *bottom*: L. 19 cm. Georg Jensen Sølvsmedie A/S, Copenhagen.

Georg Jensen's success story is extraordinary; his business still flourishes world-wide today. Designs by Georg Jensen himself, from the first decade of the twentieth century, as well as many others by fine artists added over the years are in the firm's current stock.

Although the examples of Jensen's early designs illustrated here, with their floral and insect motifs, are not dissimilar to those produced elsewhere by the exponents of the Arts and Crafts Movement, they are still (or perhaps again) popular. Later Jensen designs by other artists became more abstract, sober and streamlined: this was the famous 'Scandinavian look', which made Jensen's name a hallmark in 'modern jewellery' during the 1930s, 1940s and 1950s.

18 Pin. Gold, set with a milky opal, pearls and topazes. British, probably designed and made by May Morris (1862–1938). Ca. 1903. L. 7.6 cm, W. 2.3 cm. Victoria and Albert Museum, London (M. 21–1939).

This is a very pretty piece in the style of the Arts and Crafts Movement's jewellery, probably by the daughter of the movement's founder, William Morris. The opal is surmounted by a tiny gold flower with a pearl in its centre and a pearl on either side. Two topazes are suspended from the lower edge on links of gold intertwined with pearls and beads of twisted gold wire.

The pin once belonged to May's mother; other examples of May Morris's delicate jewellery can be seen in the National Museum of Wales, Cardiff.

19 Necklace. Gold, enamel, sapphires, emeralds and diamonds. U.S.A., by Tiffany & Co, New York. 1905. L. (pendant) 6.5 cm, (chain) 61 cm. Private Collection.

A few years before this necklace was made, Louis Comfort Tiffany had taken over the running of the company from his father. The necklace is in the revived Renaissance style popular then and made in gold with elaborate floral motifs. The main feature of this design, attributed to Louis himself, is the large oval-cut sapphire in the centre of the pendant (weighing ca. 37.49 cts), surrounded by enamelled floral ornamentation set with circular emeralds, sapphires and fancy-coloured diamonds. The pendant is suspended from a chain composed of gold and enamelled links of foliage, alternating with clusters of round sapphires, round and baguette-cut emeralds and square, round and marquise-cut multicoloured diamonds. The necklace, signed 'Tiffany & Co', was last offered for sale at auction on 25 October 1983, at Christie's in New York.

20 Brooch. White gold, diamonds, pearl and jade. Japanese, by the Mikimoto Company, Tokyo. Ca. 1905. L. 7.4 cm. Mikimoto Company, Tokyo.

Jewellery, as we know it, was not included in Japan's cultural and artistic heritage, which did however contain many jewel-like objects and artifacts. In the mid-nineteenth century, with the opening of Japan, Western customs and artifacts – including jewellery – were introduced, while the newly discovered Japanese art exerted a strong influence on the arts and crafts of Europe and the United States.

This brooch, entirely in the European style of the turn of the century, was made in the workshops of the Mikimoto Company, which was established in 1893. A tribute to the rich materials and skilful master artist/craftsmen of the country, it features a magnificent pearl surrounded by jade and pavé-set diamonds.

21 Brooch. Gold with turquoise. Dutch, by Frans Zwollo Sr. (1872–1945). Ca. 1906. L. 6.9 cm, W. 1.8 cm. Private Collection.

Although the small group of artist/jewellers that existed in Holland did not become the leaders of major movements, their work of this period was both original and competent.

Deeply influenced as an artist by his belief in theosophy, Zwollo lectured on 'The Symbolic of the Jewellers' Art' and spoke of the powerful symbolism of silver, a metal representative of mankind and central, for him, between the heavenly spirit (gold) and the material earth (copper). Symbolic shapes (*yin* and *yang* motifs within circles, for example) were often part of his designs for brooches. This brooch is shaped like a pair of spread-out wings; the large turquoise in the centre is encircled by two snakes.

22 Two Pendants. (*Left*) gold, enamel and glass; (*right*) gold and enamel. British, by Phoebe Anna Traquair (1852–1936). (*Left*) H. 6.2 cm, W. 3.5 cm; 1902; (*right*) H. 6.1 cm, W. 3 cm; 1906. Victoria and Albert Museum, London (M. 193–1976, Circ. 210–1953).

These two pendants, splendid examples of the jewellery of the Arts and Crafts Movement, were designed and made in Edinburgh, Scotland, by Phoebe Traquair.

The pendant on the left depicts Cupid (the Earth-Upholder), flanked on either side by pierced gold curves that form a point at the bottom, from which dangles an imitation stone made of coloured glass backed with foil. The pendant on the right represents the Virgin and Child and is enamelled on both sides; the figures are set against a background cross, and the pendant is signed on the reverse with the artist's initials and the date.

23 Brooch. Gold and citrines. French, by René Jules Lalique (1860–1945). Ca. 1904/1910. W. 4.1 cm. Land Baden-Württemberg, on loan to the Schmuckmuseum, Pforzheim (LBW 1/1978).

Although this brooch is dated to the first decade of the twentieth century, it is undoubtedly an early forerunner of Art Deco design. The square shape, echoed by the five square-cut citrines on either side and emphasized by the three centre panels, is very much in advance of its time. The graceful figures decorating the centre section are superbly carved into the paler citrines from below and demonstrate Lalique's great ability as a sculptor. The outline and composition are also characteristic of much of his later work, particularly in glass and in larger format.

17 Three Brooches, Two Combs, a Buckle and a Bracelet. Silver, amber, green agates and garnets. Danish, by Georg Jensen (1866–1935). 1904/1910. (*From left to right*) top: W. 6 cm, 12.5 cm, 4 cm; *2nd row*: W. 11 cm, 12 cm, 10 cm; *bottom*: L. 19 cm. Georg Jensen Sølvsmedie A/S, Copenhagen.

18 Pin. Gold, set with a milky opal, pearls and topazes. British, probably designed and made by May Morris (1862–1938). Ca. 1903. L. 7.6 cm, W. 2.3 cm. Victoria and Albert Museum, London (M. 21–1939).

19 Necklace. Gold, enamel, sapphires, ▷ emeralds and diamonds. U.S.A., by Tiffany & Co, New York. 1905. L. (pendant) 6.5 cm, (chain) 61 cm. Private Collection.

20 Brooch. White gold, diamonds, pearl and jade. Japanese, by the Mikimoto Company, Tokyo. Ca. 1905. L. 7.4 cm. Mikimoto Company, Tokyo.

21 Brooch. Gold with turquoise. Dutch, by Frans Zwollo Sr. (1872–1945). Ca. 1906. L. 6.9 cm, W. 1.8 cm. Private Collection.

22 Two Pendants. (*Left*) gold, enamel and glass; (*right*) gold and enamel. British, by Phoebe Anna Traquair (1852–1936). (*Left*) H. 6.2 cm, W. 3.5 cm; 1902; (*right*) H. 6.1 cm, W. 3 cm; 1906. Victoria and Albert Museum, London (M. 193–1976, Circ. 210–1953).

23 Brooch. Gold and citrines. French, by René Jules Lalique (1860–1945). Ca. 1904/1910. W. 4.1 cm. Land Baden-Württemberg, on loan to the Schmuckmuseum, Pforzheim (LBW 1/1978).

24 Pendant. Gold, silver, rubies, chrysoprases, sapphires, aquamarines and opals. British, by John Paul Cooper (1869–1933). 1906. H. 13.2 cm, W. 7.2 cm. Victoria and Albert Museum, London (M. 30–1972).
Like so many other artist/jewellers in his day (and quite a few in the present), John Paul Cooper's background was architecture. The Gothic influence was strong in his design and shared by several of his contemporaries, for Wagner's operas were all the rage.
This pendant in the form of an open ring, on which are mounted tiny gold stars that alternate with stars set with rubies, consists of a Madonna and Child set in a niche surrounded by chrysoprases, sapphires, aquamarines and opals. Above the ring, suspended from the loop, is a dove—the symbol of the Holy Spirit—under an opal, and below the ring is a second round pendant set with an opal and a chrysoprase drop.

25 Pendant on Chain. Gold, enamel, moonstones and ruby. British, by John Paul Cooper (1869–1933). Ca. 1900. Diam. 5 cm. John Jesse/Irina Lasky Gallery, London.
Another charming example of John Paul Cooper's design, again strongly influenced by his interest in the popular Gothic style, this pendant has a mediaeval castle in the centre, complete with three turrets and portcullis. There is foliage on either side of the castle, which is surrounded by an openwork ring set with gold stars on the upper half. Above, in a smaller ring, a dove is suspended in flight; it carries three gold links and a tiny ruby in its beak. The chain is fed through a wide gold loop adorned with bands of twisted gold wire.

26 Brooch. Platinum and diamonds. French, by Cartier. 1907. H. 5.7 cm, W. 8.8 cm. Private Collection.
Ribbons and bows were a popular theme for brooches around the turn of the century (see Pl. 13). In this example by the famous French jewellers Cartier, the 'ribbon' is quite narrow, and the entire piece is covered with diamonds pavé-set in platinum, a metal that was coming more and more into use around the turn of the century. The loops are held by a pierced centrepiece, set with a larger diamond. Three pendants are suspended at the centre, each bearing five graduated diamonds within an outer frame.

27 Two Brooches. Bronzed copper with red and white enamel and a blue stone. Dutch, by Jan Eisenloeffel (1876–1957). (*Left*) 1904, (*right*) ca. 1908. Diam. (*left*) 5 cm; (*right*) 3.5 cm. Private Collection.
Jan Eisenloeffel's designs are governed by a strict sense of symmetry and by patterns carefully worked out to balance within the given shape. The round brooch has lines radiating outwards from the stone set in its centre; they connect it to an enamelled circle with zigzag lines. The brooch is bordered by a granulated edge. The smaller brooch has a large blue stone in the centre, which is surrounded by four semicircular shapes, studded with enamel dots.
Frequently, Eisenloeffel was known to make up different versions of his basic designs in varying materials: for example, the round brooch illustrated has the same motif as the centre of a plate and the top of a teapot and sugar-bowl. The smaller brooch also exists in a different version: ivory enamel on the outer half-circles and a large round lapis lazuli in the centre, surrounded by an edge decorated with small black-enamel dots.

28 Buckle. Silver, opals, malachite and coral. Austrian, by Josef Hoffmann (1870–1956). 1908. L. 5.8 cm, W. 2.5 cm. Österreichisches Museum für angewandte Kunst, Vienna (Bi 1302).
A gifted and prolific artist, designer and craftsman as well as co-founder of the famous Wiener Werkstätte, Hoffmann became an early rebel artist and an active founding member of the Secession Movement, where he came into contact with many leading figures in the arts and crafts.
The design of this silver buckle, with its straight lines and symmetric arrangement of stone settings, is geometric and slightly architectural in approach—a feature quite characteristic of much of Hoffmann's work.

29 Tiara. Gold, enamel, crystal, pearls and semi-precious stones. British, by Henry Wilson (1864–1934). 1909. H. 9 cm, L. 19.5 cm (from centre to either end). Worshipful Company of Goldsmiths, London.
Henry Wilson was a regular exhibitor from 1889 with the Arts and Crafts Exhibition Society and became their president in 1915 and Master of the Art Workers' Guild in 1917.

This tiara is made of solid gold and weighs 195.4 grams. The nude figure of Orpheus is leaning against an open ring banded with blue enamel; he is set above a golden rose with green enamel leaves and a blue stone in the centre. Two lions on either side of the ring sit obediently with heads turned towards Orpheus. On both sides of the tiara are differently coloured semi-precious stones, mounted on the round base with green enamel foliage, and towards the back, a gold angel's wing spreads out. The back of the tiara is also fitted with a detachable golden roundel, designed to hold three ostrich feathers, the customarily required head-dress for the presentation of young ladies at court. For such an occasion, for the sake of modesty, a removable gold loin-cloth was also originally included and could be clipped in place on the nude figure.
The tiara was first lent to the Worshipful Company of Goldsmiths by Lady Llewellyn Smith for the 1961 International Contemporary Jewellery Exhibition; some years later the company bought it.

30 Necklace. Silver, enamel, pearls and turquoise. British, by Georgina Cave Gaskin (1868–1934). Ca. 1910. L. 46 cm; H. (pendant) 8.2 cm, W. 3.1 cm. Victoria and Albert Museum, London (Circ. 359–1958).
Subtitled 'Love-in-the-Mist', this delightful necklace is very typical of both the period and the delicate but sure touch of Georgina Gaskin's work. It was designed for Mrs Emmeline H. Cadbury, who presented it to the museum in her later years. Each link is elaborately wrought from silver, with chased leafage and little flowers; the centre one contains a pearl, the smaller ones are set with tiny turquoise and silver grains. The same motifs surround the larger oval pearl in the centre of the pendant and the smaller shape with a drop suspended from it. A fine, separate silver chain is attached to the top of the pendant, an additional feature quite commonly used at the time: when worn, it falls into two large loops, one on each side of the necklace, giving the whole piece extra width.
This necklace was made at Georgina and Arthur Gaskin's own workshop in Olton, Warwickshire.

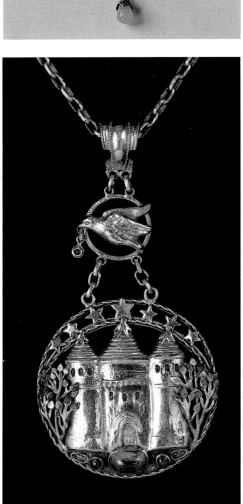

24 Pendant. Gold, silver, rubies, chrysoprases, sapphires, aquamarines and opals. British, by John Paul Cooper (1869–1933). 1906. H. 13.2 cm, W. 7.2 cm. Victoria and Albert Museum, London (M. 30–1972).

25 Pendant on Chain. Gold, enamel, moonstones and ruby. British, by John Paul Cooper (1869–1933). Ca. 1900. Diam. 5 cm. John Jesse/ Irina Lasky Gallery, London.

26 Brooch. Platinum and diamonds. French, by Cartier. 1907. H. 5.7 cm, W. 8.8 cm. Private Collection.

27 Two Brooches. Bronzed copper with red and white enamel and a blue stone. Dutch, by Jan Eisenloeffel (1876–1957). (*Left*) 1904, (*right*) ca. 1908. Diam. (*left*) 5 cm; (*right*) 3.5 cm. Private Collection.

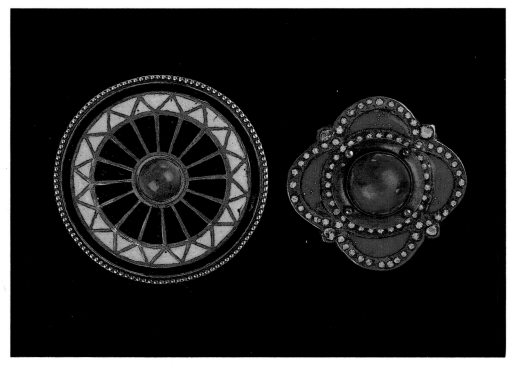

28 Buckle. Silver, opals, malachite and coral. Austrian, by Josef Hoffmann (1870–1956). 1908. L. 5.8 cm, W. 2.5 cm. Österreichisches Museum für angewandte Kunst, Vienna (Bi 1302).

29 Tiara. Gold, enamel, crystal, pearls and semi-precious stones. British, by Henry Wilson (1864–1934). 1909. H. 9 cm, L. 19.5 cm (from centre to either end). Worshipful Company of Goldsmiths, London.

30 Necklace. Silver, enamel, pearls and turquoise. British, by Georgina Cave Gaskin (1868–1934). Ca. 1910. L. 46 cm; H. (pendant) 8.2 cm, W. 3.1 cm. Victoria and Albert Museum, London (Circ. 359–1958).

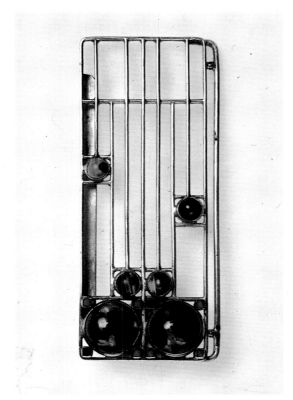

31 Four Brooches, Pendant on Chain, Ring and Cufflinks. Gold, enamel, peridot, cornelian, topaz, coral, pearls, sapphire and rubies. Dutch, by Lambert Nienhuis (1873–1960). 1905–1911. L. (pendant) 3 cm; Diam. (ring) 1.8 cm; (cufflinks) 1.4 cm; (brooches: *left top*) 2.5 cm; (*left below*) 2.5 cm; (*right top*) W. 2.5 cm, L. 3.6 cm; (*right below*) W. 2.2 cm, L. 3.6 cm. From several private collections.

Although Nienhuis's first engagement in the Arts and Crafts Movement was in the field of ceramics, when he became teacher of general subjects at the Kunstnijverheidschool in Haarlem in 1905, he began to design gold (and silver) jewellery, typical examples of which are illustrated here. These pieces were designed by Nienhuis for the firm W. Hoeker of Amsterdam and made in their workshops by L. W. van Kooten.

The ring is set with a cornelian; the brooch below it has an openwork border accentuated with black enamel and a topaz in the centre. The lower brooch on the left is round with a border of white enamel and has a red coral centre. The pendant is decorated with green enamel and small rubies, and the cufflinks have pale blue enamel around the small sapphires. The brooch below them is oval with a scalloped border, enhanced with white enamel and small pearls, and there is a large oval topaz in the middle. The last brooch on the right contains a large faceted peridot surrounded by mauve enamel.

Nienhuis's design is distinctive and recognizable; he favoured the use of enamel to emphasize the ornamental, symmetric lines and scrolls that surround his settings for semi-precious stones.

32 Buckle. Silver and enamel. British, by Edith and Nelson Dawson (1859–1942). Ca. 1900. W. 8 cm. John Jesse/Irina Lasky Gallery, London.

A classic example of Arts and Crafts jewellery of the period, this buckle was designed and made by Nelson Dawson; it is chased in silver with leaves pierced on either side. The enamelled painting of a pansy inside the frame is by Nelson's wife, Edith.

The couple met during the time Nelson spent working in an art shop in Scarborough, Yorkshire. Edith Robinson was then an accomplished watercolour artist. In 1893 they married in London, where Nelson became interested in metalworking and enamelling, which he subsequently taught to Edith, who practiced the art with distinctive style and skill.

33 Diadem. Gold, enamel, aquamarines and diamonds. French, by Georges Fouquet (1862–1957). Ca. 1910. H. 2.45 cm, L. 20 cm. Private Collection.

The diadem was a form of jewellery much in demand in the upper social circles, fashionable at this time and very effective worn over the era's elaborate hair-styles.

This piece with its large rectangular aquamarines, set with claws on a band patterned with green enamelled leaves against a background of pavé-set diamonds, is unusual for its time because of the simplicity of its design. The combination of blue with green was a favourite with many Art Nouveau artists and recurs in much of the jewellery, fabric designs and ceramics of the period.

34 Pendant on Chain. Platinum and diamonds. French, by Cartier. 1910. Diam. 5 cm, L. (chain) 63 cm. Private Collection.

This classic piece of Cartier's superb craftsmanship and design is a round pendant in 'Arab' style—a regular pattern of symmetrical openwork lines, enriched with pavé-set diamonds. One large diamond is mounted in the middle, and two smaller ones are set into the pattern, one on each side. The pendant is attached to a chain consisting entirely of small links set with diamonds.

This entire piece is made in platinum, a metal that Cartier were among the first to use (see also Pl. 26). Since it is harder than gold, platinum is eminently suitable for fine and complex constructions like this pendant.

35 Two Brooches, Two Pendants, One Brooch/Pendant. Gold, enamel, diamonds, rubies, synthetic rubies, sapphires and pearls. Spanish, by Luis Masriera (1872–1958). Ca. 1900–1910. Brooch/pendant (*top left*): W. 5.2 cm, L. 6.4 cm; pendants (*top right, centre*): W. 4.4 cm, L. 7.8 cm; W. 4.5 cm, L. 5.9 cm; brooches (*bottom left and right*): W. 4.6 cm, L. 7.8 cm; W. 5.7 cm, L. 7.7 cm. Private Collection.

This group of jewellery by Luis Masriera was part of a collection of thirty-six pieces offered for auction by Christie's of Geneva on 15 May 1980. The occasion afforded a rare chance to see a wider range of work by this creative and talented artist/jeweller. Although not a leader of Art Nouveau, but influenced by several of its prime exponents, Masriera created exquisite designs, sensitively executed, which show a distinctive and original interpretation. His work is much sought after by collectors, but many of his designs were remade by his firm in later years with a noticeably lower standard of finish, and some have been copied by others since.

Masriera, like some of his contemporaries, was inspired by the popularity of Wagner's operas. The brooch/pendant represents Isolde; she is carved in ivory, wearing a rose-cut diamond crown with an eagle crest. Her hair is set against a *plique-à-jour* enamel stained window. The piece, set with square sapphires and diamonds, has a golden eagle at the base, holding a diamond and pearl drop in its claws.

The shield-shaped pendant (centre) depicts three Breton girls inside a circle wearing brocade caps, watching a seascape with a sailing boat in *plique-à-jour* enamel. The wing-shaped top is enamelled in two shades of blue and decorated with pavé-set diamonds; two diamond-set leaves form the base, with a pearl at the centre and a pearl drop. The other pendant represents Arachne, seated within a circular mount before clouds and a cobweb; she is holding a cultured pearl. The mount is set around the edge with square-cut synthetic rubies.

The two brooches are shaped like figures of nymphs, with spread wings made of *plique-à-jour* enamel; they hold pearls against a background of pavé-set diamonds that is bordered with rubies. The edges of their robes are superbly ornamented and set with diamonds.

31 Four Brooches, Pendant on Chain, Ring and Cufflinks. Gold, enamel, peridot, cornelian, topaz, coral, pearls, sapphire and rubies. Dutch, by Lambert Nienhuis (1873–1960). 1905–1911. L. (pendant) 3 cm; Diam. (ring) 1.8 cm; (cufflinks) 1.4 cm; (brooches: *left top*) 2.5 cm; (*left below*) 2.5 cm; (*right top*) W. 2.5 cm, L. 3.6 cm; (*right below*) W. 2.2 cm, L. 3.6 cm. From several private collections.

32 Buckle. Silver and enamel. British, by Edith and Nelson Dawson (1859–1942). Ca. 1900. W. 8 cm. John Jesse/Irina Lasky Gallery, London.

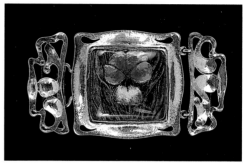

33 Diadem. Gold, enamel, aquamarine and diamonds. French, by Georges Fouquet (1862–1957). Ca. 1910. H. 2.45 cm, L. 20 cm. Private Collection.

34 Pendant on Chain. Platinum and diamonds. French, by Cartier. 1910. Diam. 5 cm, L. (chain) 63 cm. Private Collection.

35 Two Brooches, Two Pendants, One ▷ Brooch/Pendant. Gold, enamel, diamonds, rubies, synthetic rubies, sapphires and pearls. Spanish, by Luis Masriera (1872–1958). Ca. 1900–1910. Brooch/pendant (*top left*): W. 5.2 cm, L. 6.4 cm; pendants (*top right, centre*): W. 4.4 cm, L. 7.8 cm; W. 4.5 cm, L. 5.9 cm; brooches (*bottom left and right*): W. 4.6 cm, L. 7.8 cm; W. 5.7 cm, L. 7.7 cm. Private Collection.

36 Pendant. Silver and enamel. British, by Omar Ramsden (1873–1939). Ca. 1900. W. 4cm (when closed). John Jesse/Irina Lasky Gallery, London.

This pendant in the popular Neo-Gothic style of the period is made in the form of a triptych. The enamelled picture in the centre represents England's patron saint, St. George, in full armour, carrying shield and sword. Omar Ramsden set up his own workshop and business in London, in partnership with Alwyn Carr, a former fellow-student at art school, and made his name and reputation by his business acumen rather than through the exercise of his creative talents; his workshop, however, produced much jewellery of distinctive quality.

37 Pendant. Silver, *plique-à-jour* enamel and amethyst. British, by May Hart Partridge (?–1917). Ca. 1912. H. (pendant) 2.9cm, W. 2.2cm; L. (chain) 17cm. Victoria and Albert Museum, London (M. 32–1968).

Designed and made by May Hart Partridge, this pendant is in a colour scheme much favoured at this period—green and blue. The *plique-à-jour* enamel on the foliage sets off the large cabochon amethyst in the silver frame.

May Hart Partridge made up her own jewellery designs as well as doing the enamelling on some of C.R. Ashbee's jewellery and silverwork.

38 Necklace. Gold and opals. Austrian, by Carl Otto Czeschka (1878–1960). 1912. L. 28cm, W. 12cm. Österreichisches Museum für angewandte Kunst, Vienna (WI 1061).

Four oval pendants suspended by fine gold chains make up this delicately wrought gold necklace. Each pendant consists of chased gold leaves connected by wire stems and tendrils curled at the ends, interspaced with varying sizes of opals in hues of blue and green. In addition, in the largest pendant in the centre, there are two gold birds sitting in the foliage. The three opal drops at the bottom of the necklace are held by curled gold wire. Ingenious use is made of the extra loops of the fine gold chain to ensure correct spacing between the pendants and to give the entire piece greater width (cf. Pl. 30).

Carl Otto Czeschka was another important member of the Wiener Werkstätte, multitalented and prolific, capable of creative activities in almost every field of the arts.

39 Comb. Horn and pearls. Japanese, by the Mikimoto Company, Tokyo. 1914. L. 11cm, W. 6.2cm. Mikimoto Company, Tokyo.

Carved in the Art Nouveau style, with openwork foliage, this comb is set with a cluster of pearls in the centre, above which are larger pearls. Inevitably, the early jewellery produced in Japan followed closely the styles then current and favoured abroad. It is difficult to establish the origin of the designs the Mikimoto jewellers worked from, or indeed the names of the designers, who were surely Japanese, for many of Mikimoto's pieces, in spite of their apparently European style, also have distinctly Japanese elements incorporated into the design and execution. This haircomb provides an obvious example, but there are other pieces, of which, alas, only workshop drawings remain, that are even more typical of Japanese concepts.

40 Ring. Gold and chrysoprase. Austrian, by Dagobert Peche (1886–1923). 1914. L. 2.4cm, W. 2cm. Österreichisches Museum für angewandte Kunst, Vienna (WI 1236).

In this example of Arts and Crafts jewellery, a very beautiful, large chrysoprase has been set with a wide collet on the graduated shank of the ring. The collet is ornamented with square panels alternating with panels of pierced leaves and banded by rows of gold grains. The bezel is supported by two V-shapes joined to the shank, one on either side.

Dagobert Peche, who joined the Wiener Werkstätte in 1915 and later managed their Zurich branch (from 1917 to 1918) was a versatile artist/craftsman (see also Pl. 43): he designed wall-paper, textiles, carpets, china, ceramics, glass, furniture and posters in addition to jewellery.

41 Locket. White metal, gilt and enamel. German, by unknown maker. 1915. Diam. 1.7cm. Private Collection.

An example of patriotic jewellery, this locket is made from a German 1-*pfenning* piece, domed and hinged, with a snap fastening at the top loop.

The front of the locket is gilded, and on it the head of Kaiser Wilhelm II seems to be bursting through the centre. The Kaiser is depicted wearing his familiar helmet and moustache. The German eagle ornaments the reverse of the locket (original as on the coin), which has a circle in the centre enamelled in the German national colours: stripes of black, white and red.

A second version exists, made with the same technique and design but with the head of Field Marshal von Hindenburg, one of the chief commanders of the German army in World War I, breaking through the centre.

42 Bracelet. Aluminium and brass. British, by unknown maker. 1917/1918. Diam. 5.7cm, H. 3cm. Private Collection.

This is a touching example of war-time jewellery, made under conditions of great hardship. The size of the bracelet is small; it was probably made for a very young girl by a loving father or brother, to pass the time in the trenches. The bracelet, made from a section of an aluminium shell case, has been skilfully carved and filed into a shield shape in the front and inlaid with brass; it is quite professionally engraved with floral motifs, ornamental scrolls and the word YPRES in large letters across the shield. Ypres, in southern Belgium, was one of the battlefields where the opposing armies in World War I fought bitterly over a period of several months.

43 Brooch. Gold and pearls. Austrian, by Dagobert Peche (1886–1923). 1917/1918. L. 5.8cm, W. 2cm. Österreichisches Museum für angewandte Kunst (BI 1461).

Although still inspired by floral forms—leaves, buds and tendrils—the design of this gold brooch with pearls begins to show some abstraction, a progression from the more ornate handling of the same theme in the Art Nouveau or the Arts and Crafts styles (see Pl. 40).

This brooch was made when Dagobert Peche was manager of the Zurich branch of the Wiener Werkstätte, a post he relinquished in 1918, although he continued to work for them until he died.

44 Necklace with Pendant. Gold, diamonds, emeralds, rubies and pearls. German, by Wilhelm Lucas von Cranach (1861–1928). 1917/1918. L. (pendant) 4 cm. Schmuckmuseum, Pforzheim (1964/40).

Cranach was one of the few outstanding German designers of Art Nouveau jewellery (see also Pl. 9) with a distinctive style, flamboyant and full of fantasy tinged with symbolism.

The heavy gold chain of this necklace is fastened on to the tails of two snakes whose heads are connected to the loops that hold the pendant. The large snake that forms the pendant is curled around a 'clutch of eggs', represented by three pearls still attached to the shell of the pearl mussel. The snakes are encrusted with pavé-set diamonds and emeralds; there are cabochon rubies on their heads. This necklace was made in the jewellery workshop of Louis Werner in Berlin.

45 Necklace. Silver, gold, opals, tourmalines and emerald pastes. British, by Georgina Cave Gaskin (1868–1934). Ca. 1920. (Pendant): L. 6.3cm, W. 3.9cm. Victoria and Albert Museum, London (Circ. 223–1921).

Links of silver wire wrought into openwork floral motifs alternate with little birds set on circles in this necklace. The circular pendant with its heart-shaped opal at the centre includes two rosettes on the foliage, one on either side, and is completed with an opal drop.

This necklace was one of five purchased in 1921 by the museum directly from the Gaskins, who had moved their workshop to Edgbaston near Birmingham by then (see also Pl. 30).

36 Pendant. Silver and enamel. British, by Omar Ramsden (1873–1939). Ca. 1900. W. 4 cm (when closed). John Jesse/Irina Lasky Gallery, London.

37 Pendant. Silver, *plique-à-jour* enamel and amethyst. British, by May Hart Partridge (?– 1917). Ca. 1912. H. (pendant) 2.9 cm, W. 2.2 cm; L. (chain) 17 cm. Victoria and Albert Museum, London (M. 32–1968).

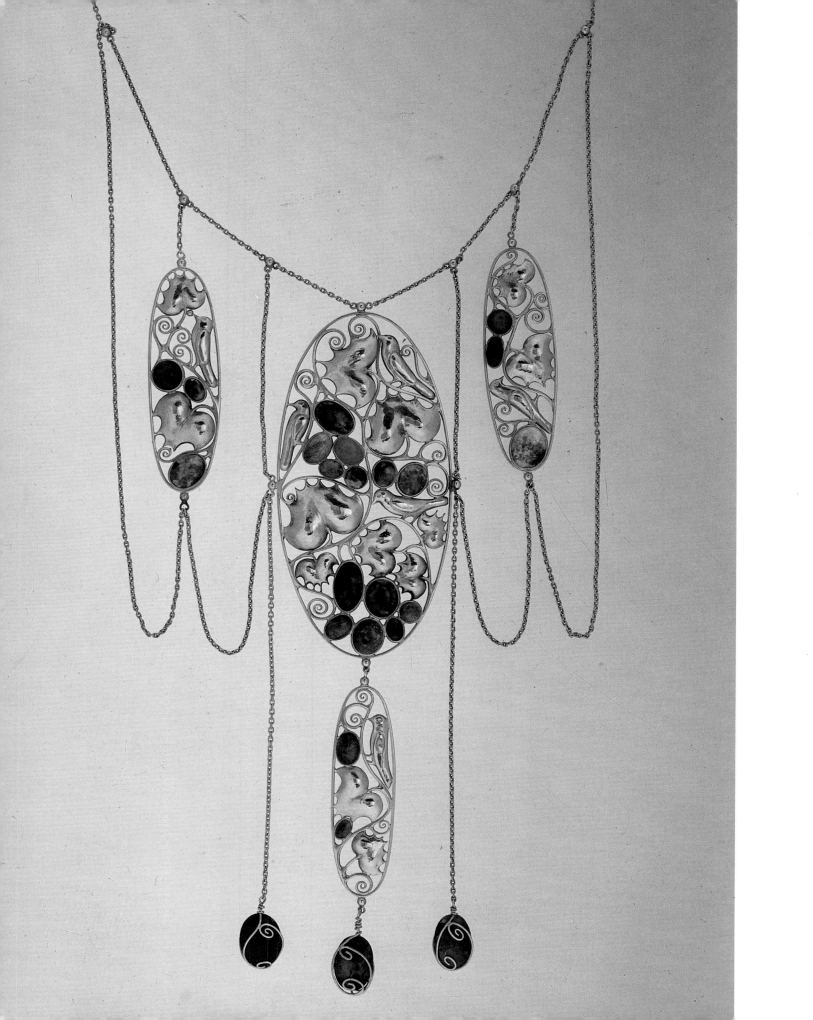

38 Necklace. Gold and opals. Austrian, by Carl Otto Czeschka (1878–1960). 1912. L. 28 cm, W. 12 cm. Österreichisches Museum für angewandte Kunst, Vienna (WI 1061).

39 Comb. Horn and pearls. Japanese, by the Mikimoto Company, Tokyo. 1914. L. 11 cm, W. 6.2 cm. Mikimoto Company, Tokyo.

40 Ring. Gold and chrysoprase. Austrian, by Dagobert Peche (1886–1923). 1914. L. 2.4 cm, W. 2 cm. Österreichisches Museum für angewandte Kunst, Vienna (WI 1236).

41 Locket. White metal, gilt and enamel. German, by unknown maker. 1915. Diam. 1.7 cm. Private Collection.

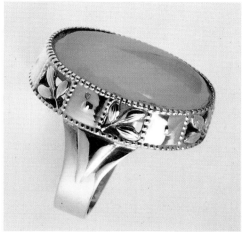

42 Bracelet. Aluminium and brass. British, by unknown maker. 1917/1918. Diam. 5.7 cm, H. 3 cm. Private Collection.

43 Brooch. Gold and pearls. Austrian, by Dagobert Peche (1886–1923). 1917/1918. L. 5.8 cm, W. 2 cm. Österreichisches Museum für angewandte Kunst (BI 1461).

44 Necklace with Pendant. Gold, diamonds, emeralds, rubies and pearls. German, by Wilhelm Lucas von Cranach (1861–1928). 1917/1918. L. (pendant) 4 cm. Schmuckmuseum, Pforzheim (1964/40).

45 Necklace. Silver, gold, opals, tourmalines ▷ and emerald pastes. British, by Georgina Cave Gaskin (1868–1934). Ca. 1920. (Pendant): L. 6.3 cm, W. 3.9 cm. Victoria and Albert Museum, London (Circ. 223–1921).

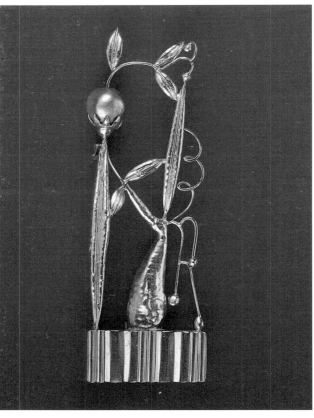

II 1920–1950

Four years of bitter fighting on the battlefields of Europe and the shock waves of the Russian Revolution left victors and vanquished alike counting the cost and trying to rebuild a new and better life. For Germany, the defeat was followed by an economic crisis that reached its climax with an inflation that devalued everything to such an extent that by 1922, a loaf of bread cost several million marks. With paper money and coinage losing value from day to day, small items like jewellery became useful currency for barter. People were crying out everywhere for social reforms and better working conditions. Enlightened sections of the middle class were adopting a decidedly restrained attitude towards flamboyance in clothes and jewellery.

Everywhere the social structure changed dramatically: women were taking a greater part in public life, speaking out for equality, fighting for the right to vote and engaging in careers, however modest by present-day standards. They were no longer content either to be placed on pedestals or to remain drudges immersed in their own households. Women needed an entirely different kind of jewellery to wear on bodies that moved freely and contained active minds, voices that could be heard and personalities that longed for expression.

Of course, these developments did not occur overnight; yet within a few years after the war, designs in jewellery already reflected very strongly the basic changes in concept that could also be observed in other forms of art. The shock and pain of the war years, followed by the harsh realities of the immediate post-war period, had had their sobering effect. The romantic, idealistic and sometimes slushy sentimentality of Art Nouveau, with its perfectly formed nymphs surrounded by all that spelt grace and beauty in flora and fauna, gave way to a stylization based on simpler variations of natural forms, which finally became complete abstraction, and with the emergence of the new style known as Art Deco, a geometric element was added.

Art Deco

The Exposition des Arts Décoratifs held in Paris in 1925, was the show-case of the new style and gave it its name. There, demonstrated visibly for all to see, was a radical change in design for architecture, furniture, fabrics and, of course, jewellery. The use of bold colours and basic shapes—squares, circles and triangles —frequently overlapping or linked by lines is the principle underlying Art Deco design. The outer contours of Art Deco buildings and furniture are streamlined, stripped of fussy and over-ornamented facades and surfaces: instead they present generous, sweeping curves and bold straight lines. Any decorative element follows the outer edges, emphasizing them with echoed reliefs that harmonize with the overall concept.

In Germany, the Hochschule für Bau und Gestaltung, a state school known as the 'Bauhaus', was founded in Weimar in 1919 by Walter Gropius; later (from 1925–1932), under Mies van der Rohe, it was moved to Dessau and finally to Berlin, until it was closed in 1933. The leading principle of the Bauhaus was to return art and the crafts to basic formal concepts; it developed its own style of combining aesthetics with the functional, placing extreme emphasis on non-ornamentation. Teachers, who included Moholy-Nagy, Klee, Kandinsky and Schlemmer, exerted a strong influence on the development of contemporary design, which was to last to the present day and perhaps beyond, and to spread over many continents.

But it was in Paris in the mid-twenties that Art Deco reached one of its highest points. It was there that painters and sculptors employed the skills of expert craftsmen to produce superb examples of fabrics, furniture, ceramics and jewellery so typical of the period, using an enormous variety of different materials with no regard to cost.

This was an extraordinary era in many ways, full of radical change in many fields: social outlooks were broadening, science and technology were making great strides. Often referred to as 'fast times' or the 'roaring twenties', it saw the first mass-produced motorcars, the start of air travel, radio and the 'movies'—all this after just having survived what was thought to be the war to end all wars.

The same period also produced great changes in the economic fabric of many countries; fortunes were made as entrepreneurs seized the opportunities offered by a growing demand for consumer goods, while the employees had to fight harder to gain certain rights and better working conditions, which had been promised to them when they returned from the battlefields.

Georges Fouquet was elected Chairman of the Selection Committee for the 1925 Exposition des Arts Décoratifs, a position in which he played an important part in drafting the guide lines for the presentation of that show. It was decided that only works of 'new direction and true originality' would be considered. The declared intention of the exhibition's organizers was not to introduce designers to manufacturers but to exhibit jewellery made by artists alone or by artists in co-operation with manufacturers and craftsmen. The pieces for display were anonymous when chosen, and only afterwards exhibited with their respective name plates. Amongst some thirty exhibitors who qualified were Louis Aucoc, Boucheron, Chaumet, Lacloche, Mauboussin and Van Cleef & Arpels.

In the world of *haute joaillerie*, big names like Cartier, Boucheron, Mellerio, and so forth were careful to adapt themselves to the new demands of a changing clientele. As the royal courts of Europe began to disappear, and with them many of the wealthy aristocrats, a new elite stepped into their place. The descendants of those who had amassed their fortunes in the second half of the nineteenth century during the Industrial Revolution, now often became the 'playboys' of the Western world and spent their inherited riches on opulent jewels.

The urge to wipe out the miseries of war, revolution and economic catastrophies was felt by all. It drove the grand houses of fashion and jewellery, as well as society hostesses, into a frenzy of organizing gala events, often in aid of charities, which once more provided glamour and glitter. Even those who could not afford to take part in these events revelled in the detailed newspaper accounts of such occasions or of the morganatic marriages between impoverished aristocrats and industrial princesses. The rags-to-riches story became a favourite theme for innumerable films that alternated with the now legendary spectaculars lavishly churned out by Hollywood. Diamonds, big ones especially, were 'a girl's best friend' as the famous song proclaims. Frankly, for the majority that meant imitation diamonds, but nearly everyone emulated fashions that often copied designs first shown in films and cut their hair and hemlines to demonstrate their new freedom.

Fouquet's shop in the Rue Royale, designed by Alphonse Mucha at the turn of the century, was remodelled in keeping with the times: a much simpler facade of marble was designed by the architect Ernest Bertrand, who was also responsible for the new interior wall panelling of light oak. Semi-precious stones like amethyst, lapis lazuli, coral, turquoise, onyx and jade became popular sources of the colours so necessary to the new Art Deco design concepts; sometimes they were used in conjunction with diamonds. In order to compete with rising young artist/jewellers like Raymond Templier, Gérard Sandoz and others, Georges Fouquet now collaborated with artists like the architect Eric Bagge (1890–1978), the poster-designer Adolphe Mouron (known as Cassandre) (1901–1968) and the painter André Léveillé (1880–1961). Together they created jewellery of astounding quality and beauty, much of it still in existence in various public collections in museums the world over. A large part of the work was shown at an exhibition in Paris and Zurich in 1984, the 'House of Fouquet, 1860–1960', though it was sad to note on that occasion how many important pieces had been lost in the course of time, leaving only a black-and-white photograph or a workshop drawing as a record.

It was also at the famous 1925 Paris exhibition that Jean Fouquet, Georges's son, born in 1899, showed his talent for design for the first time. From then on, until 1939, Jean continued to participate in all the jewellery exhibitions at which the 'Maison Fouquet' was present. There is no doubt that Jean Fouquet's contribution to the overall reputation and standing of the 'Maison Fouquet' was equal to that of his father and grandfather, the founder of the firm. Although less concerned with the technical aspects of jewellery, Jean was a most original and innovative artist, deeply concerned with aesthetics, the perfection of, and harmony between, design and technique.

Apart from his own creative activities in the field of jewellery design, Jean Fouquet was a man deeply interested in all aspects of the arts, intellectually active and politically involved. In 1931 he published an illustrated folder under the title 'Bijoux et Orfèvrerie' ('Jewellery and Goldsmiths' Work'), containing his personal view of jewellery and his definition of creative design: 'Jewellery and any other work by a goldsmith must fulfil the criteria of a work of art and at the same time conform to the functional demands of a product'. Recalling the end of the 1920s in an article written in 1946 on Jean Puiforçat (1897–1945), a superb and famous silversmith of the time, Jean Fouquet wrote: 'What criticisms were levelled against those of us who were in favour of sobriety, just as we were in the process of forming the Union des Artistes Modernes? We were told we were too simplistic; we were neglecting beautiful craftsmanship, the essential French characteristic, amongst others.... Does this beautiful French craftsmanship mean a florid, baroque design covering up poor technique and inadequate material and form with over-ornamentation, or rather ought it not to be employed to bring out the inherent beauty of the material?'

Jean Fouquet counted the poets Paul Eluard and Louis Aragon among his personal friends, attended the meetings of the Association des Ecrivains et Artistes Revolutionaires and in 1940 became the Chief Curator of the Musée National d'Art Moderne in Paris. He tended to keep his various interests quite separate from each other; so it was not until 1950 that one day, as he and Louis Aragon passed the shop-window of an antique dealer where the famous snake-bracelet designed by Alphonse Mucha and made for Sarah Bernhardt by Georges Fouquet was displayed, that Aragon noticed the name and was surprised to learn that Georges Fouquet was Jean's father, and that Jean was also a noted jeweller.

Cartier, as always, demonstrated its astuteness and was sensitive to the current trends. It stayed on top by moving with the times and was helped in this by Louis Cartier's new girlfriend, Jeanne Toussaint, who began to take an active interest in the business, particularly in matters concerning design. She stayed on well after her affair with Louis was over, and only retired because of age in the late 1950s. Nicknamed 'the Panther' by Louis Cartier, Jeanne Toussaint was responsible for the range of jewellery with that name, which was first produced in 1925 but is still available from Cartier today.

Cartier continued to count among its clients the famous and the wealthy, among them the Duke and Duchess of Windsor, Princess Bibesco, Paul Claudel, Coco Chanel, Prince Youssoupoff, and, of course, the remaining members of the royal courts of Europe. Many of these people became their personal friends. Together with Prince Youssoupoff, the three Cartier brothers were involved in the gradual disposal of the Romanoff jewels that had been brought out of Russia packed in the coffin of an American seaman, James Jones, who had died in the Black Sea and whose coffin was shipped home. From this collection of treasure, Pierre Cartier acquired the Imperial Crown and a 120-carat emerald that had belonged to Catherine the Great. For the sake of discretion, the remaining jewels were sold off piecemeal over a period of some nine years, during which time the Cartier brothers bought several more items.

In the United States at this time, Harry Winston was at the start of his career, in the course of which he was to become known as the 'King of Diamonds', his name synonymous with legendary and priceless jewels. Born in New York in 1896, Harry Winston began working at the age of fifteen in his father's modest jewellery shop in California. An astute judge of quality gems from the start, Harry was obsessed with the 'drama, romance and excitement' of real and expensive stones. He was also a skilful and adventurous dealer, unafraid of handling millions of dollars worth of gems, even in the early stages of his career, when he had no personal capital to finance his transactions. In the United States, Harry Winston became renowned as a purchaser relentless in his pursuit of fabulous jewellery collections from the estates of multimillionaires whose names he obtained from *Who's Who*, the *Social Register* or as tip-offs from the legal circles that dealt with the probate. In 1926, after a great deal of persuasion, Winston's bank financed him so he could acquire a fantastic collection of superb diamonds and pearls that had belonged to the late Arabella Huntington (widow of Collis P. Huntington, the American railroad builder, and later the wife of his nephew, Henry Huntington). The collection cost Winston $1,200,000.–, a fraction of its original cost, and included a necklace of 160 perfectly matched, natural pearls, 5 feet long, which had cost Mrs Huntington over one million dollars to assemble. Most of the pieces in the Huntington Collection were considered 'outdated' in form and, in any case, were much too large and opulent for current taste. Winston proceeded to break them up, remodelling them into smaller units which were more economical and, therefore, more profitable to sell. He was fond of saying that the Huntington pearls now graced the necks of at least two dozen women in various parts of the world.

Harry Winston was very much a man of his time; his flair as an entrepreneur enabled him to seize the opportunities provided by the depression and the Wall Street crash on a grand scale. For him and his clients, design and artistic concept were at all times secondary to the material value of the stones.

The great artist/jewellers of the 1920s—Raymond Templier, Jean Després, Jean Fouquet, Jean Dunand and Gérard Sandoz—saw jewellery in a totally different light. They used the materials, precious or otherwise, not for their intrinsic value but solely for their suitability and effectiveness in expressing the design concepts that were typical of their work and epoch. These artists were aware of cultural and social changes, of new movements in art and architecture; they were sensitive to people's needs for jewellery that was more than mere ornamentation or a symbol of status and wealth. At the same time, there is no doubt that these men counted the wealthy amongst their customers too, especially the cultured and sophisticated rich.

Arts and Crafts

The Arts and Crafts Movement had died by the outbreak of World War I. Its spirit, however, continued to live on—in a somewhat changed form—and found its way into the educational systems of many countries during the 1920s and 1930s. *Kunstgewerbe*, *l'art décoratif* or 'arts and crafts' gained wider appeal and became a subject taught at lower levels in progressive kindergartens and schools, and at more advanced levels in art colleges and adult-education classes.

Margaret Craver was an American artist/teacher whose contribution to the craft revival in the United States in the late 1940s and 1950s was crucial to the later flowering of the art.

Originally a silversmith predominantly interested in hollow-ware, Craver was trained in the 1930s in metalsmithing at an art school and studied in Sweden in the studio of Baron Erik Fleming. After returning to America in 1938, she became part-time curator, part-time teacher at the Wichita Art Museum, Kansas, for a few years. At the end of World War II, at her suggestion, the firm of Hardy & Harman, a metal refinery, commissioned her to draw up a rehabilitation programme in metalwork for returning war veterans, a course that was eventually incorporated into the hospitals of the thirteen army commands in the United States as well as into others in that country, Canada and Great Britain.

More regulated working hours and working days shorter than before the war for the employed, led to the development of the concept of 'leisure-time activities', which could be spent in the pursuit of outside interests—the 'hobby' was born. Enthusiasts and amateurs enrolled in evening classes to learn crafts such as pottery, weaving and, in some places, even jewellery-making. There was a growing interest in hand-made things and a few craftshops opened, providing outlets for some craftsmen and craftswomen that enabled them to earn a modest living.

Australia

Here it is particularly interesting to look at the historical background of a faraway newcomer to the world of contemporary jewellery: Australia; it illustrates vividly the various factors that have made modern jewellery so interesting and exciting.

Colonized by Great Britain in 1788, Australia's population at the beginning of the nineteenth century consisted mainly of several thousand convicts who were serving out their sentences under the watchful eyes of a small military force and a few government officials. However, soon after the establishment of the penal settlement, Australia began to attract growing numbers of immigrants from Britain and Europe, particularly in the latter half of the last century, by which time the population had quadrupled, to nearly 100,000. They were drawn there by the usual hopes for better opportunities and cheap land for agricultural development; and some of them were lured by the discovery of gold in New South Wales and Victoria in 1851, and silver in the late 1880s. Today, with a population of some thirteen million, Australia still represents a microcosm of many different European cultures (the Aborigines form only about 1 per cent), and yet a certain element of Australian identity has been achieved in this short span of time.

During the nineteenth century, jewellery production in Australia was minimal, most items available in retail shops were imported from Europe and Britain. But with the discovery of precious metals and the fine quality of Australian opals, a small number of highly skilled and creative jewellers began to work on unique pieces of jewellery with a distinctly Australian flavour. Today some very fine examples of their work are in the collections of the Art Gallery of South Australia, the Museum of Applied Arts in Sydney and the National Gallery of Victoria. Mostly in the form of brooches (but also some bracelets, pendants and pins), they are made from Australian gold with designs inspired by the indigenous flora and fauna. Other designs feature figurative motifs of specifically local interest—trains, or the shovels and pans used by gold-miners, often with the addition of a piece of gold quartz or a tiny nugget.

Made mostly for private commissions, for instance to commemorate a lucky find or for the completion of a railway line, such pieces are more meaningful and valuable than the run-of-the-mill, gem-set variety. Their emotive appeal, closely followed by their exquisite craftsmanship will survive further centuries, reflecting the essence and spirit of their time and place.

In the early twentieth century, with Sydney, Melbourne and Adelaide rapidly expanding and becoming more prosperous, the growing demand for jewellery was mostly satisfied by mass-produced, conventional jewellery imported from abroad. A very small group of artist/jewellers became followers of the Arts and Crafts Movement in the early 1920s. Rhoda Wager in Sydney, James Fawcett and David Grieve in Melbourne, and James Linton in Perth are perhaps the best known. Like some of the European pioneers of the Arts and Crafts Movement, James Fawcett was an architect, chief of the Victoria Railway Department. David Grieve (born in 1886 in Melbourne) trained at the Detroit Craft Center in the United States during the 1920s but returned to Australia in 1938. Rhoda Wager was perhaps the most prolific artist/jeweller of the group, producing literally thousands of pieces of jewellery over a period of some twenty-five years from the early 1920s to the middle 1940s. Her designs were distinctly Australian, making use of semi-precious stones found locally, baroque pearls and settings that incorporated gum leaves, berries and other Australian plants.

Jewellery Industry

The jewellery industry in general lagged behind the new ideas by the usual fifteen to twenty years. The reason was twofold, then as now. Manufacturing jewellers were, as always, reluctant to risk putting into production innovative designs; they favoured making repetitions of earlier and conventional models, which could be produced without going to the expense of employing artists or designers, on the grounds that it satisfied the market. This is certainly to some degree a justifiable argument—the general public's attitude towards jewellery is more conservative than it tends to be in other areas like fashion, but it should not serve as an excuse for never venturing and striking out to produce something new. It is very much part and parcel of people's psychological pattern that they oscillate between an inner drive to revolutionize and improve things, while, at the same time, hanging on to prescribed, traditional values and ways of thinking. Jewellery with all its implications, emotional and material, tends to last a long time. Unlike the fashion industry, which produces brand new ideas at affordable prices every season, jewellery is often too expensive an acquisition for people to experiment or be adventurous.

This is not so in the field of costume jewellery however, where new materials like bakelite and German silver (an alloy of copper, nickel and zinc), as well as older ones like marcasite, pewter and rhinestones were becoming popular. It had become socially acceptable to wear 'imitation' jewellery, so low in price that one could afford to take risks and be bold with shapes and colours. Quite a lot of such jewellery from the 1920s and 1930s has survived and is currently highly sought after by collectors of Art Deco and people with a penchant for the period. Some enterprising manufacturers are even reproducing and copying the designs now.

The late 1920s and 1930s also saw the birth of the 'badge', 'button' or 'sticker' in great profusion. Mass-production machinery swung into action to supply emerging political organizations with the enormous amount of badges and other insignia they required. Members of political parties, from the extreme left to the extreme right, took to wearing the emblem of their convictions, if not an actual para-military uniform, which needed all kinds of distinguishing buttons and pips to denote rank and station.

World War II

The outbreak of World War II brought the jewellery industry, like many others, to a standstill for the second time this century. This time not only was production as such disrupted in Europe, the military operations destroyed the very premises and means of production as well. The industrial centres of Britain, Germany and France were the targets of wholesale bombing, which laid waste entire regions of factory-occupied land. Small workshops closed as their craftsmen were called up to fight or to work in munition factories, where their skills were much in demand for the precision-engineering work more than ever needed for producing modern weaponry. Precious metals became scarce or unobtainable again; less precious materials were also in short supply, and second-hand jewellery was much in demand. A certain amount of patriotic jewellery made its appearance, as wives and sweethearts of men serving in the armed forces proudly wore the emblems of their loved ones' regiment or unit in the form of a brooch.

Among Europe's millions of refugees, the luckier ones often had nothing but their jewellery, portable wealth, to help them on their road to freedom. People lost their valuables in a thousand different ways, through pilferage and looting, corruption and persecution, betrayal and fear. In the last uncertain days at the end of the war in Europe, jewellery was sometimes a better currency than money; at least it was tangible and had an international, negotiable value. Just like at the end of World War I, no one had faith in bank notes.

In Britain and the United States, the situation was obviously less desperate. In spite of the extensive bombing, no enemy set foot on British soil, and the United States was far away from the main theatres of war. None the less, while people's confidence remained intact, it took considerable time for social life to return to normality—in Britain, for example, it was ten years before austerity gave way to the brighter side of life.

46 Brooch/Earrings. Platinum, diamonds, sapphires and fine pearls. French, by Cartier. 1921. L. (together) 13.5 cm, W. 11.3 cm. Private Collection.

The beautiful design of this brooch demonstrates again the close relationship that often exists between concept and execution: in this case, the perfect symmetry and precision of the supporting platinum frame are crucial to the realization of the design concept.

Although still somewhat ornate, the style heralds the starker, bolder outlines of Art Deco design with its pavé-set diamonds, graduated in size to emphasize the pattern, surrounded by a narrow band of small stones tipped at the points with larger ones. The centre drop is composed of two diamonds and has a pearl suspended from it. The two longer drops on either side each consist of one long and one short link, again with pavé-set diamonds; a sapphire is set in the centre of the bottom link. These drops can be detached and worn separately as earrings, a novel and most practical feature.

47 Bracelet/Brooch. Platinum and diamonds. French, by Cartier. 1921. L. 15.7 cm, W. 4.2 cm. Private Collection.

A superb example of innovative design, with matching craftsmanship, this bracelet is made of over a hundred carefully graduated links in the form of fish-scales, each link encrusted with pavé-set diamonds. The floral motif in the centre features a square-cut diamond surrounded by eight round ones. The centre of this bracelet can be detached and worn separately as a brooch. The entire bracelet is set in platinum, which heightens the brilliance of the stones and gives strength to is flexible construction.

48 Bracelet. Platinum, coral and diamonds. French, by Cartier. 1922. L. 17.2 cm. Private Collection.

In a sober yet colourful Art Deco design, the rectangular platinum links forming this bracelet glitter with pavé-set diamonds that alternate with square links cut from coral.

Cartier always had a keen eye for coming trends and quickly adapted to new ideas, knowing that its clients were not likely to be inhibited by modesty and restraint, particularly in the days when most of them belonged to the set whose actions defined the period as the 'Roaring Twenties'.

49 Pendant. Silver, enamel, emerald and diamonds. Dutch, by Johannes Steltman (1891–1961). Ca. 1923. H. 5.2 cm. Private Collection.

Johannes Steltman was an important figure in Dutch jewellery design of the 1920s and 1930s. He was keenly aware of the importance of the artistic concept in jewellery.

This pendant is a fine example of his ability to express the spirit of his time: the winged form of black enamel finely edged with silver, resembles a body in flight. The centre is set with graduated diamonds in a vertical line ending with a large emerald drop.

50 Pendant/Brooch. Carved jade, platinum, diamonds, black lacquer. French, by Georges Fouquet (1862–1957). 1924. L. 12.5 cm. Private Collection.

The wave of orientalism, which was first felt in the second half of the nineteenth century and later exerted strong influence on Art Nouveau design, now made its impact on the stricter forms of Art Deco.

The large piece of jade is finely carved in relief with floral motifs, studded with two diamonds and suspended from a jade ring by links of black lacquer that contrast with the alternate platinum links of pavé-set diamonds. The stone is held by two black lacquer bands with scrolled ends, surmounted, for extra support, by platinum and diamonds.

51 Brooch/Pendant. Sketch on paper for design, in poster paint. French, by Cassandre [Adolphe Mouron] (1901–1968) for Georges Fouquet. 1925. H. 9.2 cm, W. 10.5 cm. Fouquet Archives.

It had always been Georges Fouquet's policy to involve talented artists in working with him and his superb craftsmen to create unusual and meaningful jewellery. In order to participate in the Exposition des Arts Décoratifs in Paris, in 1925 Fouquet sought to produce original, new ideas with the help of, among others, Cassandre, a pseudonym for Adolphe Mouron, who was a poster designer and graphic artist.

The sketch represents a typical Art Deco design for a brooch/pendant, intended to be made in crystal, onyx, lapis lazuli, coral and topaz. It bears the rubber stamp used by Cassandre for all drawings he submitted to the selection committee for the 1925 exhibition. The strong geometric element in this design is very characteristic of many of the classic pieces of jewellery produced by Fouquet from Cassandre's sketches.

52 Brooch. Gold, coral, onyx and diamonds. French, by Boucheron, Paris. Ca. 1925. L. 6 cm, W. 2 cm. John Jesse/Irina Lasky Gallery, London.

A classic and simple design of the Art Deco period, this brooch is very effective, particularly in its strong colour contrasts of red and black, illuminated by the pavé-set diamonds on the centre bands and at each end.

Boucheron was founded in Paris in 1858 by Frédéric Boucheron (1830–1902) and is still a family firm and a leading name for high-quality, gem-set jewellery.

53 Brooch. Platinum, rock crystal, coral, onyx and diamonds. French, by unknown maker. Ca. 1925. L. 6.3 cm, W. 6.3 cm. John Jesse/Irina Lasky Gallery, London.

Matt rock crystal acts here as the perfect foil for the panel of onyx in the centre and the three triangular corals set against the lower edge. Double bands of platinum with pavé-set diamonds serve as claws to hold the stones in place.

The brooch is a typical Art Deco design in its choice of colours (white/red/black) and in the way the outer edges of the rock crystal echo the contours of the onyx.

54 Brooch. Platinum, diamonds, rock crystal and enamel. French, by Cartier. 1925. 6.3 cm × 3.5 cm. Private Collection.

Rock crystal was a popular semi-precious stone, used in much Art Deco because it is large and cheap enough to be cut into any desired shape. Moreover, it is very effective, as the brooch illustrated proves, giving emphasis and width to the centre section consisting of a large diamond mounted on a black enamel backing and surrounded by pavé-set diamonds in an openwork pattern constructed in platinum.

55 Pendant. Platinum, diamonds, rock crystal and amethysts. French, by unknown maker. Ca. 1925. L. 6.3 cm. John Jesse/Irina Lasky Gallery, London.

This is a charming period pendant, featuring a large cabochon amethyst held against matt rock crystal by pavé-set diamonds. A tiny superstructure above the stone, also set with diamonds, contains the attachment for the fine platinum chain. Such pendants were usually worn on long chains, and looked very good with the low-waisted dresses and short hemlines fashionable during the 1920s.

46 Brooch/Earrings. Platinum, diamonds, ▷ sapphires and fine pearls. French, by Cartier. 1921. L. (together) 13.5 cm, W. 11.3 cm. Private Collection.

47 Bracelet/Brooch. Platinum and diamonds. French, by Cartier. 1921. L. 15.7 cm, W. 4.2 cm. Private Collection.

48 Bracelet. Platinum, coral and diamonds. French, by Cartier. 1922. L. 17.2 cm. Private Collection.

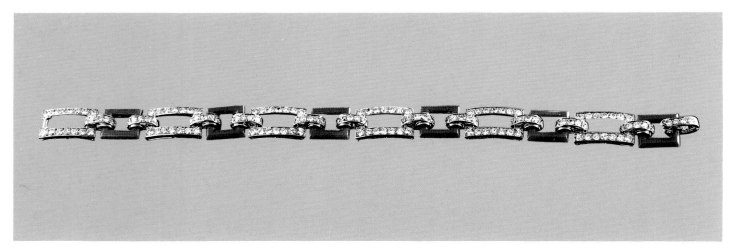

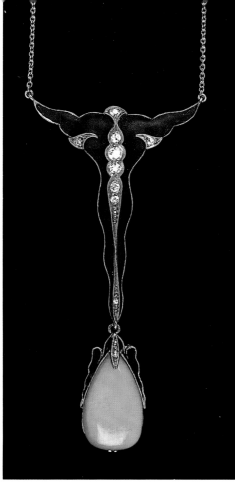

49 Pendant. Silver, enamel, emerald and diamonds. Dutch, by Johannes Steltman (1891–1961). Ca. 1923. H. 5.2 cm. Private Collection.

50 Pendant/Brooch. Carved jade, platinum, diamonds, black lacquer. French, by Georges Fouquet (1862–1957). 1924. L. 12.5 cm. Private Collection.

51 Brooch/Pendant. Sketch on paper for design, in poster paint. French, by Cassandre [Adolphe Mouron] (1901–1968) for Georges Fouquet. 1925. H. 9.2 cm, W. 10.5 cm. Fouquet Archives.

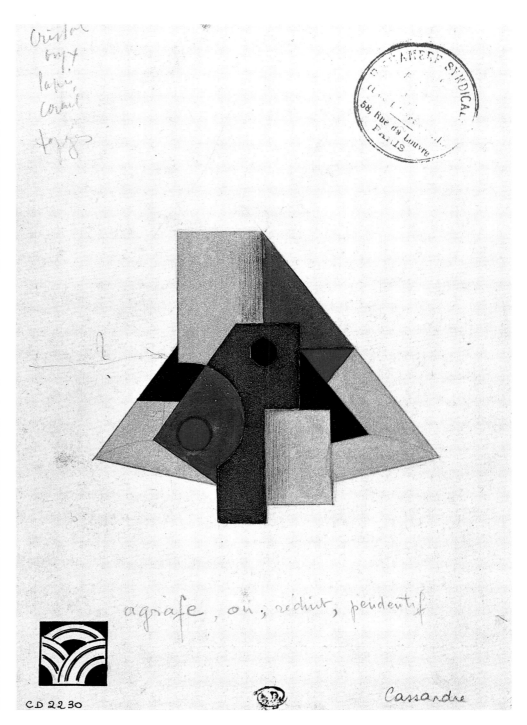

52 Brooch. Gold, coral, onyx and diamonds. French, by Boucheron, Paris. Ca. 1925. L. 6 cm, W. 2 cm. John Jesse/Irina Lasky Gallery, London.

53 Brooch. Platinum, rock crystal, coral, onyx and diamonds. French, by unknown maker. Ca. 1925. L. 6.3 cm, W. 6.3 cm. John Jesse/Irina Lasky Gallery, London.

54 Brooch. Platinum, diamonds, rock crystal and enamel. French, by Cartier. 1925. 6.3 cm × 3.5 cm. Private Collection.

55 Pendant. Platinum, diamonds, rock crystal and amethysts. French, by unknown maker. Ca. 1925. L. 6.3 cm. John Jesse/Irina Lasky Gallery, London.

56 Necklace. Gold and cornelian. Italian, by ▷ Alfredo Castellani (1853–1930). 1925. L. 38 cm. Private Collection.

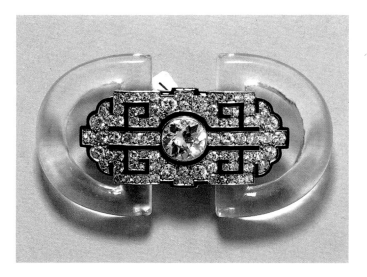

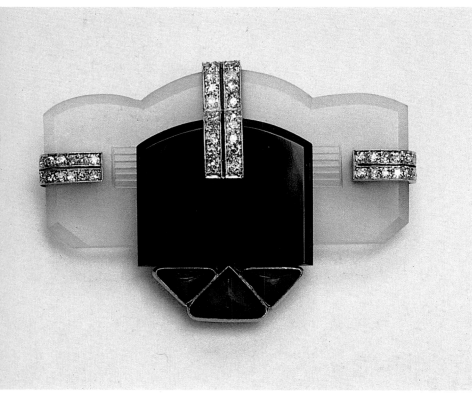

56 Necklace. Gold and cornelian. Italian, by Alfredo Castellani (1853–1930). 1925. L. 38 cm. Private Collection.

A late example of historical revivalism, this necklace continues a tradition, popular throughout the nineteenth century, of jewellery made in the Greek/Roman/Etruscan styles by the famous family firm of Castellani. Successive generations of this firm made pain-staking research into the techniques and designs of archaeological jewellery, particularly the art of granulation, though they did not discover the genuine method (see Pl. 63). Castellani's reigned supreme in the field for their imaginative adaptations and excellence of craftsmanship.

This necklace, made to lie close to the base of the neck, is composed of round gold beads, textured all over with granulation, alternating with plain gold links edged with granules and set with cornelian scarabs held by granulated collets. Some of the scarabs are genuine antiques; others are modern and cut to match.

57 Sheet of Designs. Pencil, crayon and gouache. French, by Raymond Templier (1891–1968). Ca. 1925. 64 × 49.5 cm. Private Collection.

This sheet of designs by one of the most important artist/jewellers of the time illustrates many of the classic features of jewellery typical of the period. They are designs for ear-clips and brooches, a range within which Templier explores the endless possibilities and variations of inter-related surfaces, either by repeating the basic form in graduated steps on different levels or by opposing circular movements and stark colour contrasts. To heighten the effect, much use is made of doming and of reflections on highly polished surfaces.

58 Pendant/Pin. Diamonds, sapphires, black chalcedony, jade, platinum and gold, ribbon. French maker's mark: AJ: signed; JANESICH. Ca. 1925. H. 6.4 cm, W. 2.2 cm. Victoria and Albert Museum, London (M. 74–1979).

This pendant/pin, made in the Art Deco period in oriental style, shows a Chinese rather than a Japanese influence as in earlier examples. Because of their angular lines and bolder use of colour, Chinese styles and patterns of ornamentation seemed to lend themselves more easily to the design concepts of Art Deco.

This pendant is elaborately constructed, with pavé-set diamonds in platinum forming an openwork frame for the centre. The stem with tendrils and leaves is carved from black chalcedony, with additional leaves of carved sapphire and round buds of green jade. The pendant is suspended from a black moiré ribbon fastened on to platinum and diamond end-pieces.

59 Necklace with Pendant. White and yellow gold, platinum, silver, black lacquer and an aquamarine. French, by Jean Fouquet (b. 1899). Ca. 1925/1930 L. (chain) 58 cm, H. (pendant) 9 cm. Private Collection.

A fascinating and bold juxtaposition of circle, rectangle and straight line, the design of this necklace and its execution, as well as the choice of the materials, demonstrate a complete break with traditional concepts of jewellery.

Made of snake chain, the pendant is suspended from the centre of three links of white gold tubing by a straight section (half gold, half black lacquer) that ends in the middle of the grooved circle. A large rectangular-cut aquamarine is attached to this bar off-centre on the right-hand side, overlapping the circle.

Jean Fouquet was the third generation of Fouquets to make and design jewellery in the family business, and from the beginning, he was interested in jewellery as an art form. Soon Jean developed completely new forms, choosing the materials that would best underline the strong contours of his designs.

60 Earrings. Platinum, coral, diamonds and onyx. Dutch, by unknown maker. Ca. 1925/1930. L. 6.5 cm, W. 1.3 cm. Nederlands Kostuummuseum, The Hague (KS 22–1963 AB).

The long earrings popular in the 1920s, when ultra-short hairstyles and long necks were all the rage, took a little more time to become fashionable in Holland, according to C.H. de Jonge in *Sieraden* (published in 1924), but he admitted that the form had a most flattering effect, accentuating the face.

There is no doubt that these earrings are elegant: slim lines of black onyx, pavé-set diamonds in platinum in Chinese-inspired motifs, and large coral drops.

61 Brooch. White gold, coral, diamonds, onyx. Dutch, by unknown maker. Ca. 1925/1930. H. 3 cm, W. 4 cm. Nederlands Kostuummuseum, The Hague (KS 21–1963). Quite obviously conceived in the contemporary Art Deco style, the design of this brooch owes much to the concepts of Raymond Templier (see Pl. 57) but lacks his sure, decisive touch: the interpretation of the formal resolution is heavier. The strong red colour of the coral is set off to advantage by contrasting areas of polished white gold, and the lines of diamonds and curved onyx emphasize the alignment of the two semicircles.

62 Pendant. White and red gold, onyx and rock crystal. French, by Gérard Gustave Sandoz (b. 1902). Ca. 1928. H. 14.2 cm, W. 8.4 cm. Private Collection.

This unusually large pendant, vaguely resembling a banjo in shape, is suspended from a chain consisting of thirteen long, conical links

of drilled rock crystal. The centre bar, made of black onyx, cuts across a disc of rock crystal set in white gold and is crossed at the top by four horizontal sections of white gold and flanked by a narrow strip at either side that continues below the disc. A larger disc of red gold forms the backing.

Sandoz came from a family of provincial French watchmakers and jewellers, but he was more orientated towards the arts. Besides designing interesting and avant-garde jewellery for his father's workshop, Gérard was also a painter, poster designer and film-maker.

63 Ring. Gold, pearls, sapphire, star sapphires, moonstones and amethysts. German, by Elisabeth Treskow (b. 1898). 1928. L. 2.2 cm, W. 2.5 cm. Kunstgewerbemuseum, Cologne (G. 1085).

The rectangular bezel of this ring is slightly curved and set with a colourful assortment of pearls, a faceted sapphire and cabochon star sapphires, moonstones and amethysts. Some of the settings are surrounded by gold granules. Elisabeth Treskow is remarkable for her long career as an artist/jeweller and as a pioneer of contemporary design in jewellery. She first distinguished herself as a prominent member of a group who rediscovered in the early 1920s the ancient technique of granulation as practised by the Romans and Etruscans (see Pl. 56).

64 Brooch. Silver. German, by Richard Haizmann (1895–1963). 1928. L. 12.5 cm. Private Collection.

An abstract brooch of sober simplicity, this piece is a typical example of 'primitive' jewellery made by several well-known artists of the period in an attempt to provide 'alternative' jewellery. Cut from silver sheet, the shape seems to have been inspired by the most basic form of life: its fluid contours suggest an amoeba, or perhaps an animal in the early stages of its foetal development.

Haizmann was motivated by his search for the inner meaning of nature. He was a versatile artist and a member of a circle that included Brancusi, Klee, Ensor, Kandinsky, Léger and Nolde. Much of Haizmann's work, like the work of many others, was vandalized and destroyed by the Nazis in 1934; while other pieces, removed from museum collections, were exhibited in Germany in 1937 as prime examples of *entartete Kunst* ('decadent art').

57 Sheet of Designs. Pencil, crayon and ▷ gouache. French, by Raymond Templier (1891–1968). Ca. 1925. 64 × 49.5 cm. Private Collection.

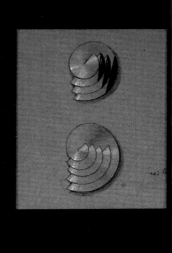

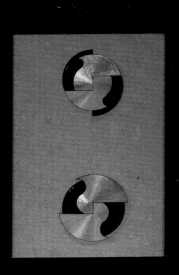

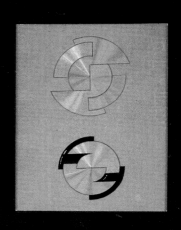

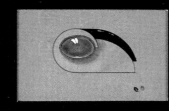

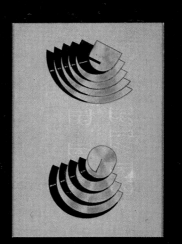

58 Pendant/Pin. Diamonds, sapphires, black chalcedony, jade, platinum and gold, ribbon. French maker's mark: AJ: signed; Janesich. Ca. 1925. H. 6.4 cm, W. 2.2 cm. Victoria and Albert Museum, London (M. 74–1979).

59 Necklace with Pendant. White and yellow gold, platinum, silver, black lacquer and an aquamarine. French, by Jean Fouquet (b. 1899). Ca. 1925/1930 L. (chain) 58 cm, H. (pendant) 9 cm. Private Collection.

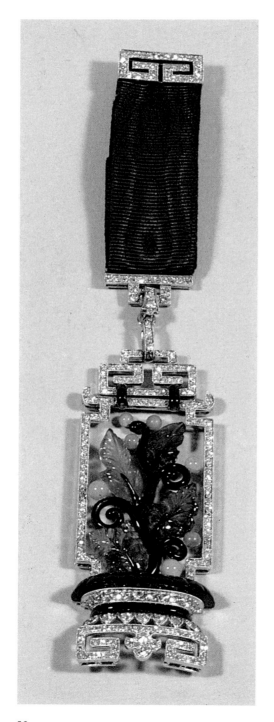

60 Earrings. Platinum, coral, diamonds and onyx. Dutch, by unknown maker. Ca. 1925/1930. L. 6.5 cm, W. 1.3 cm. Nederlands Kostuummuseum, The Hague (KS 22–1963 AB).

61 Brooch. White gold, coral diamonds, onyx. Dutch, by unknown maker. Ca. 1925/1930. H. 3 cm, W. 4 cm. Nederlands Kostuummuseum, The Hague (KS 21–1963).

62 Pendant. White and red gold, onyx and rock crystal. French, by Gérard Gustave Sandoz (b. 1902). Ca. 1928, H. 14.2 cm, W. 8.4 cm. Private Collection.

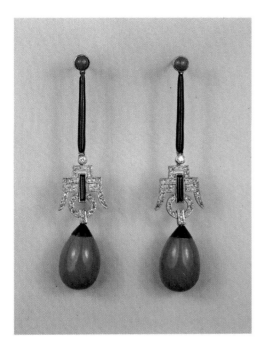

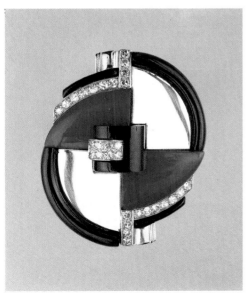

63 Ring. Gold, pearls, sapphire, star sapphires, moonstones and amethysts. German, by Elisabeth Treskow (b. 1898). 1928. L. 2.2 cm, W. 2.5 cm. Kunstgewerbemuseum, Cologne (G. 1085).

64 Brooch. Silver. German, by Richard Haizmann (1895–1963). 1928. L. 12.5 cm. Private Collection.

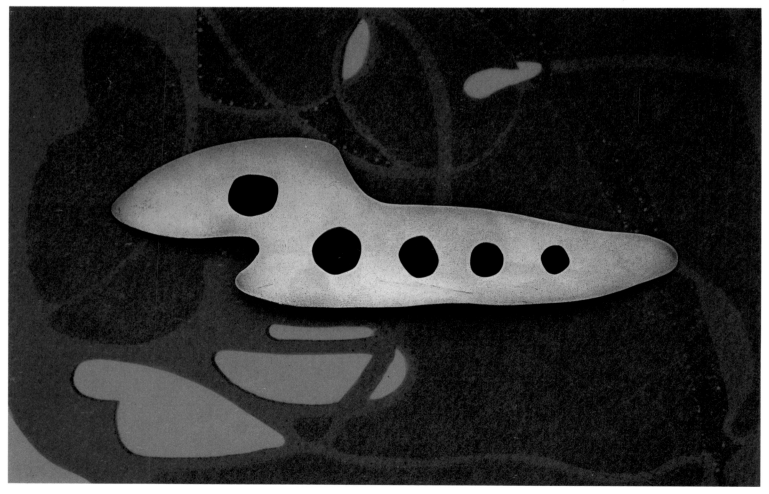

65 Brooch. Silver, gold and lapis lazulis. French, by Jean Després (1889–1980). Ca. 1929/1930. L. 8.1 cm. Private Collection.
Three semicircles of two-tone gold surround two cabochon lapis lazulis, connected by a base, textured in the centre, with plain edges. The brooch was made by Jean Després, a descendant of a famous family of glass-makers (Desprès de Loisy) and a prominent artist/jeweller of the period, who counted Georges Braque (see Pl. 116) and Jóan Miró among his friends. Desprès was fascinated by metals, geometry and technology, including aircraft construction.

66 Bracelet. Chromium-plated brass and haematite. German, by Naum Slutzki (1894–1965). 1929. L. 18 cm, W. 4.2 cm. Victoria and Albert Museum, London (Circ. 1235–1967).
The links of this bracelet are made from narrow strips of brass, chromium plated; a rectangular piece of haematite is set on a central plate, the same width as the links.
This kind of Art Deco design echoes the hard line and metallic colours popular then and also found in the furniture and sculpture of the period. The bracelet illustrated was designed when Slutzki was living and working in Hamburg, Germany, but was re-made by him in 1960 in England, where he had taken refuge in 1933.
Slutzki was a remarkable man, a versatile artist and teacher, who exerted an enormous influence on the many students who trained under his guidance.

67 Bracelet. Silver and blue stone. Danish, by A. Tillander. Ca. 1930/1940. Diam. 6.5 cm. John Jesse/Irina Lasky Gallery, London.
Demonstrating the wide differences that exist between the gem-set jewellery of the grand 'houses' and the modern concepts of Scandinavian design, this bracelet is composed of four silver bands that flank the blue stone, which is held in the curved front section by being riveted through squared-off silver prongs. The bracelet is hinged, with a snap fastening on the side, complete with safety chain. Despite its uncluttered simplicity, the overall effect of this design has a dramatic impact.

68 Bracelet and Ring. Platinum, rock crystal, amethyst and moonstone. French, by Jean Fouquet. Ca. 1930. W. (bracelet, front) 8.2 cm; (ring, front) 2.8 cm. Private Collection.
These two superb pieces of jewellery by Jean Fouquet have been shown many times over the years at exhibitions of Art Deco jewellery in Germany and France.
The bracelet is open-ended, cut from a single piece of rock crystal and set with five cabochon moonstones and five faceted amethysts in platinum mounts. The matching ring has three stones on either side of the centre ridge. Another version of the ring existed; it was made in white gold and without stones.

69 Bracelet. Gold, diamonds and sapphires. French, by Boucheron. Ca. 1930/1940. Diam. (inside) 6.3 cm, W. 2.5 cm. Private Collection.
The massive gold bracelet is hinged at the back and opens from the front, where both ends are decorated with twin scrolls set with calibré-cut sapphires bordered by pavé-set diamonds.
The overall format and design is one that recurs frequently in jewellery made by the high-quality craftsmen in Boucheron's workshops for their affluent customers, who often ordered whole 'suites': matching necklace, brooch, earrings, ring and bracelet. The piece is quite typical of the period, though rather uninspiring; its greatest worth lies in the intrinsic value of the materials and the fine workmanship with which it was constructed.

70 Brooch. Silver. Mexican, by Rebajes (dates unknown). Ca. 1930/1940. L. 6 cm, W. 4.5 cm. John Jesse/Irina Lasky Gallery, London.
Designs with stylized faces were used frequently by many artists of the period; they appear cut in stone or cast in cement on houses with Art Deco facades and in various other materials as ornamental details on furniture or on medallions and brooches.
This brooch by a Mexican artist/jeweller known only by his surname demonstrates beautifully the essence of this style. It exploits the contrast between two faces: a male profile in bright silver set against a female one in oxydized silver, the sex of the latter indicated merely by one sharply angled eyebrow and two bold wavy lines representing hair.

71 'Kanagu' (Metallic Ornamental Clasp for Lady's Handbag). Silver, copper and gold alloy (*kinkeshi*). Japanese, by Hideharu Oki (1895–1968). 1935. 2.6 cm × 5.3 cm × 8 cm. Private Collection.
Hideharu Oki was an important pioneer of contemporary jewellery design in Japan. A master-craftsman, highly skilled in the traditional Japanese techniques used to decorate the *tsuba* ('sword guard') and *tsuka* ('sword hilt'), he adapted these complex methods to his own, modern designs. Oki began to make a name for himself in the 1930s, when his beautiful jewellery became very popular among the ladies of Japanese high society. Inspired by nature, his earlier work consisted of flowers and leaves; the metallic ornamental clasp is an orchid of beautifully formed and textured silver leaves, which surround the gold ventricular centre that is just open enough to reveal tiny gold stamen. From 1940 onwards, Oki's favourite subjects included beetles and dragonflies and various kinds of fish and frogs.

72 Cigarette Cases, Bracelets, Necklaces, Brooches and Rings. French, by Jean Després (1889–1980); Jean Dunand (1877–1942); Georges Fouquet (1862–1957); Jean Fouquet (b. 1899); Gustave Miklos (1888–1967); Gérard Sandoz (b. 1902); Raymond Templier (1891–1968). Platinum, 18-carat gold, silver, enamel, aquamarine, diamonds, onyx, rock crystal, lapis lazuli, amethyst and moonstone. 1925–1930. Formerly Laurence and Barlach Heuer Collection.
This illustration provides a rare opportunity to see an entire collection: this group of jewellery and cigarette cases was acquired over the years by a discerning and caring collector. The photograph was taken just before the collection was dispersed and passed into the hands of new owners. It gives a view of many famous pieces that represent the essence of French Art Deco jewellery made by the most important artist/jewellers of the period (see Pls 59, 62, 65, 68, 79). Made from platinum, gold and silver, enamel and precious as well as semi-precious stones, the designs reflect various influences such as orientalism, technology, geometry and mechanics. Here we can see the sum total of the enormous change that occurred in jewellery in the period between the two World Wars.

73 Necklace. Platinum, diamonds and emeralds. French, by Cartier. Ca. 1930. L. 38 cm. Private Collection.
This is a design based on a classic style popular centuries ago (see Pl. 56). The necklace consists of platinum beads ornamented with pavé-set diamonds and strung on chain. Attached to every fourth bead is a tumble-polished baroque emerald bead, carefully graduated: the largest ones at the front.
This simple but quite spectacular necklace once belonged to Merle Oberon, the film star.

74 Bracelet. Platinum, rubies and diamonds. French, by Cartier. 1930. L. 18.5 cm. Private Collection.
A linked bracelet, set in platinum, on which sections with calibré-cut rubies and round diamonds alternate with sections of pavé-set and baguette diamonds. In the middle of one of the ruby links is the snap fastening, making it invisible when closed.
A bracelet of this kind and design is by no means unusual for the period, but the fine workmanship, for which Cartier was always renowned, lifts it well above the ordinary.

65 Brooch. Silver, gold and lapis lazulis. French, by Jean Desprès (1889–1980). Ca. 1929/1930. L. 8.1 cm. Private Collection.

66 Bracelet. Chromium-plated brass and haematite. German, by Naum Slutzki (1894–1965). 1929. L. 18 cm, W. 4.2 cm. Victoria and Albert Museum, London (Circ. 1235–1967).

67 Bracelet. Silver and blue stone. Danish, by ▷ A. Tillander. Ca. 1930/1940. Diam. 6.5 cm. John Jesse/Irina Lasky Gallery, London.

68 Bracelet and Ring. Platinum, rock crystal, amethyst and moonstone. French, by Jean Fouquet. Ca. 1930. W. (bracelet, front) 8.2 cm; (ring, front) 2.8 cm. Private Collection.

69 Bracelet. Gold, diamonds and sapphires. French, by Boucheron. Ca. 1930/1940. Diam. (inside) 6.3 cm, W. 2.5 cm. Private Collection.

70 Brooch. Silver. Mexican, by Rebajes (dates unknown). Ca. 1930/1940. L. 6 cm, W. 4.5 cm. John Jesse/Irina Lasky Gallery, London.

71 'Kanagu' (Metallic Ornamental Clasp for Lady's Handbag). Silver, copper and gold alloy (*kinkeshi*). Japanese, by Hideharu Oki (1895–1968). 1935. 2.6 cm × 5.3 cm × 8 cm. Private Collection.

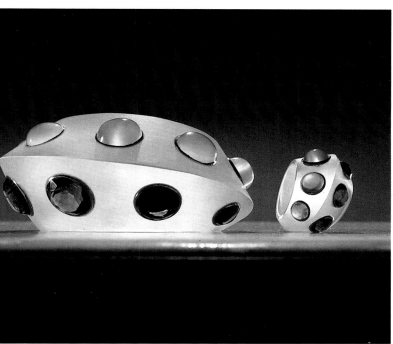

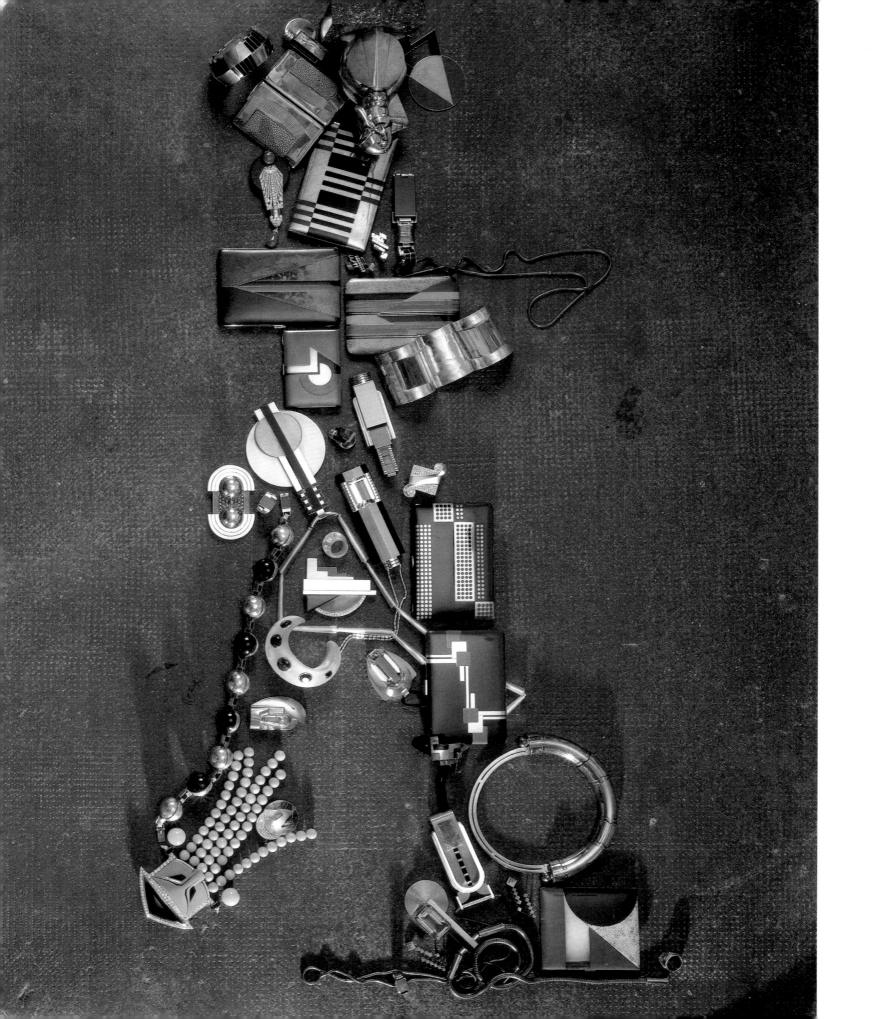

72 Cigarette Cases, Bracelets, Necklaces, Brooches and Rings. French, by Jean Desprès (1889–1980); Jean Dunand (1877–1942); Georges Fouquet (1862–1957); Jean Fouquet (b. 1899); Gustave Miklos (1888–1967); Gérard Sandoz (b. 1902); Raymond Templier (1891–1968). Platinum, 18-carat gold, silver, enamel, aquamarine, diamonds, onyx, rock crystal, lapis lazuli, amethyst and moonstone. 1925–1930. Formerly Laurence and Barlach Heuer Collection.

73 Necklace. Platinum, diamonds and emeralds. French, by Cartier. Ca. 1930. L. 38 cm. Private Collection.

74 Bracelet. Platinum, rubies and diamonds. French, by Cartier. 1930. L. 18.5 cm. Private Collection.

75 Bracelet and Two Pairs of Earrings. Platinum, white gold, diamonds and emeralds. (*Top left*) French, by Van Cleef & Arpels; (*bottom right*) signed: KOCH; (bracelet): unknown maker. Ca. 1930/1940. L. (bracelet) 18.5 cm; L. (clip earrings) 1.8 cm, W. 1.4 cm; L. (drop earrings) 6.2 cm. Private Collection.

The renowned Parisian jewellery firm Van Cleef & Arpels was established in 1906. One of its specialities is the so-called 'invisible' setting, a method of mounting calibré-cut gemstones on to a gold or platinum grid so close to one another that no metal protrudes between the stones. This requires a high standard of skill in mounting and cutting, and many of the firm's elaborate designs feature this method; however, it is quite unusual for emeralds to be used in this fashion. Sapphires and rubies are more suitable because the stones are harder.

The ear-clips (top left) are made in a convex shape, bordered by two lines of baguette diamonds that are mounted in platinum and white gold. The bracelet is made from the same materials: three large flat links with indented sides, encrusted with pavé-set diamonds and having a large cabochon emerald in the centre, are interconnected by cylindrical links, set with round and baguette-diamond bands and tipped at each end with cabochon emeralds. This is an important piece of jewellery, beautifully made, and it is quite surprising that it is unmarked and its maker therefore not known.

The drop earrings (bottom left) each feature a large drop-shaped emerald (ca. 6.5 cts); these stones are surrounded by a diamond-set loop suspended from a line of diamonds that is flexible and has a tulip motif at either end. The design suggests that these earrings might be dated a little earlier than the other two pieces, but it is difficult to be exact because jewellery was made in this style over a span of thirty years or more, starting from the early 1920s.

76 Necklace and Earrings. Silver, opals, rubies and stained chalcedony. British, by Sybil Dunlop (ca. 1889–1968). Ca. 1934. L. (necklace) 43.8 cm; (earrings) 3 cm. Victoria and Albert Museum, London (M. 27-d-1979).

A very late example of the Arts and Crafts style, this necklace with matching earrings was designed by Sybil Dunlop and made in her own workshop under the direction of W. Nathanson, who carried on the business after Dunlop's retirement at the end of World War II.

The design makes some concessions to Art Deco's geometric alignment with its angular adaption of floral motifs. Specially cut stained chalcedony provides a colourful foil for the large oval opals that are surrounded by blue chalcedony triangles. The connecting links are set with rubies, some of them star rubies. The earrings each have an opal at the top, from which is suspended a ruby-set form resembling a raspberry.

77 Design. Ink, poster paint and metallic paint. French, by Jean Lambert-Rucki, (1888–1967) for Fouquet. Ca. 1936/1937. Size unknown. Fouquet Archives.

This is a typical design by Lambert-Rucki, primarily a sculptor, for the 'Maison Fouquet' at a time when Jean Fouquet was playing a decisive role in the artistic decisions about works executed by its workshops.

These designs for bracelets and earrings exploit the interrelationship of repeated forms: the forms are reminiscent of radiator fins or cooling systems and were intended to be lit up by rows of diamonds on the edges.

78 Necklace with Pendant. Gold and aquamarine. German, by Theodor Wende (1883–1968). 1936. L. (pendant) 5.3 cm. Schmuckmuseum, Pforzheim (1966/11).

A complex construction in heavy, hand-wrought gold, the design of this necklace with pendant defies a clear definition of its style. The principles underlying Wende's design concept still show traces of earlier influences (he was one of the last artists invited to join the artists' colony at Darmstadt – in 1913). In consideration of the general trend towards streamlined contours and geometric shapes, Wende has transformed the floral motifs of Art Nouveau into abstract and angular forms with just a hint of a stylized flower on either side of the centre.

Extremely competent in execution, the links of the chain are structured from strips of gold, while the pendant supports an octagonal aquamarine surrounded by an elaborate, three-dimensional framework in a symmetrical pattern.

An individualist and creator of distinctive, original jewellery, Wende gained recognition at home and abroad as a 'leading member of a new generation of German goldsmiths' (*La Revue Moderne*, Paris, 1927).

79 Brooch (in Original Box with Design). Platinum and diamonds. French, by Raymond Templier (1891–1968). 1936. W. 3.8 cm. Private Collection.

This platinum brooch is rectangular in shape and encrusted with pavé-set diamonds; two platinum bands run diagonally across the base, ending in a swirl that protrudes over the edge of the rectangle. This piece can be worn as a brooch or taken apart to make two clips, a form of jewellery very popular at the time and usually worn on the edge of a neckline or lapel.

The design is extremely characteristic of Raymond Templier's approach to form: an exploration of the endless possibilities of stark contrast – in this case the brilliance of the stones against the smooth surface of the metal, and round shapes (swirls) against straight edges (rectangle).

80 Brooch. Gold, silver, ivory, mother-of-pearl, pearls, opals tourmalines, crystals, enamel. British, by George Hunt (1892–1960). Ca. 1936. H. 5.1 cm, W. 8.6 cm. Victoria and Albert Museum, London (Circ. 657–1969).

This fan-shaped brooch has a silver base and is ornamented at the top with a row of gold granules beneath which is a row of tiny pearls. An assortment of tourmalines, opals, crystals and other coloured stones of different shapes are set below these rows along with an ivory panel carved with a female face in relief. The face represents the Queen of Sheba. Two elongated triangles, set with mother-of-pearl, jut out from the sides of the ivory inset, and a triangular drop of ivory and crystal hangs from the top edge of the brooch on either side.

In style, this design is a typical cross-breed characteristic of the gentle transition from Art Nouveau to Art Deco: still somewhat romantic, idealized flora and a female face, but an outline that is much more restrained despite the overall ornamentation.

81 Necklace. Brass. U.S.A., by Alexander Calder (1898–1976). Ca. 1938. L. 9 cm, W. 3.7 cm. Victoria and Albert Museum, London (Circ. 19–1962).

An artist of international repute and standing, Alexander Calder made this necklace when he was living and working in Paris. Calder's fame rests mostly on his superb sculptures and on his renown as the 'father of the mobile'.

The necklace is made from brass wire, curled into domed spirals of graduated sizes, connected by small round links. Calder made quite a number of necklaces (see Pl. 90) and earrings, mostly for friends and people who moved in the international art circles of that time.

82 Necklace and Brooch. Gold. Italian or French, by unknown maker. Ca. 1938. L. (necklace) 42 cm; H. (pendant) 7 cm; (brooch) 8 cm. Private Collection.

This is a late 1930s' version of the perennial theme of ribbons and bows; the massive matching set is made in gold, skilfully wrought into large loops to form a triple bow. Three graduated circular links, with an off-centre cut-out, connect the pendant to the links at the back.

There was quite a vogue for plain but chunky gold jewellery made with real gold in the late 1930s, as well as versions of similar designs made from cheap base metal.

75 Bracelet and Two Pairs of Earrings. Platinum, white gold, diamonds and emeralds. (*Top left*) French, by Van Cleef & Arpels; (*bottom right*) signed: KOCH; (bracelet): unknown maker. Ca. 1930/1940. L. (bracelet) 18.5 cm; L. (clip earrings) 1.8 cm, W. 1.4 cm; L. (drop earrings) 6.2 cm. Private Collection. ▷

76 Necklace and Earrings. Silver, opals, rubies and stained chalcedony. British, by Sybil Dunlop (ca. 1889–1968). Ca. 1934. L. (necklace) 43.8 cm; (earrings) 3 cm. Victoria and Albert Museum, London (M. 27–d–1979).

77 Design. Ink, poster paint and metallic paint. French, by Jean Lambert-Rucki, (1888–1967) for Fouquet. Ca. 1936/1937. Size unknown. Fouquet Archives.

78 Necklace with Pendant. Gold and aquamarine. German, by Theodor Wende (1883–1968). 1936. L. (pendant) 5.3 cm. Schmuckmuseum, Pforzheim (1966/11).

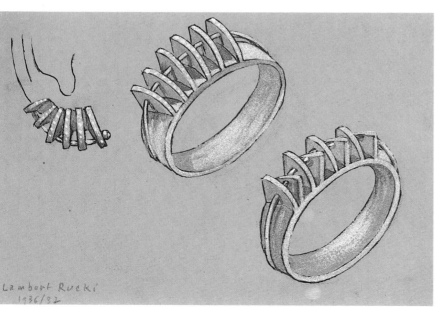

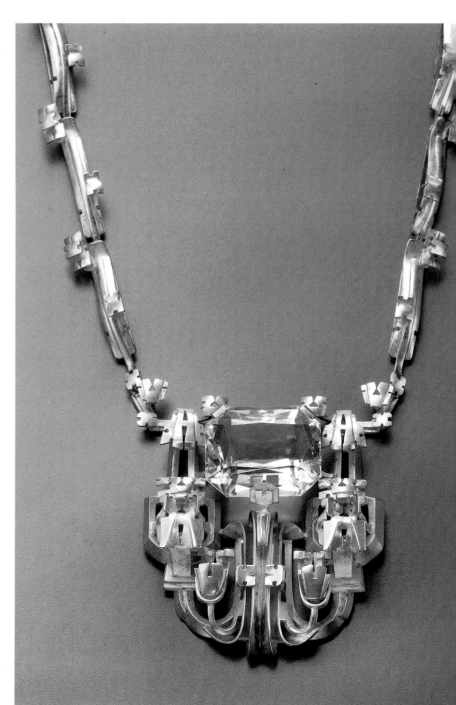

79 Brooch (in Original Box with Design).
Platinum and diamonds. French, by Raymond
Templier (1891–1968). 1936. W. 3.8 cm. Pri-
vate Collection.

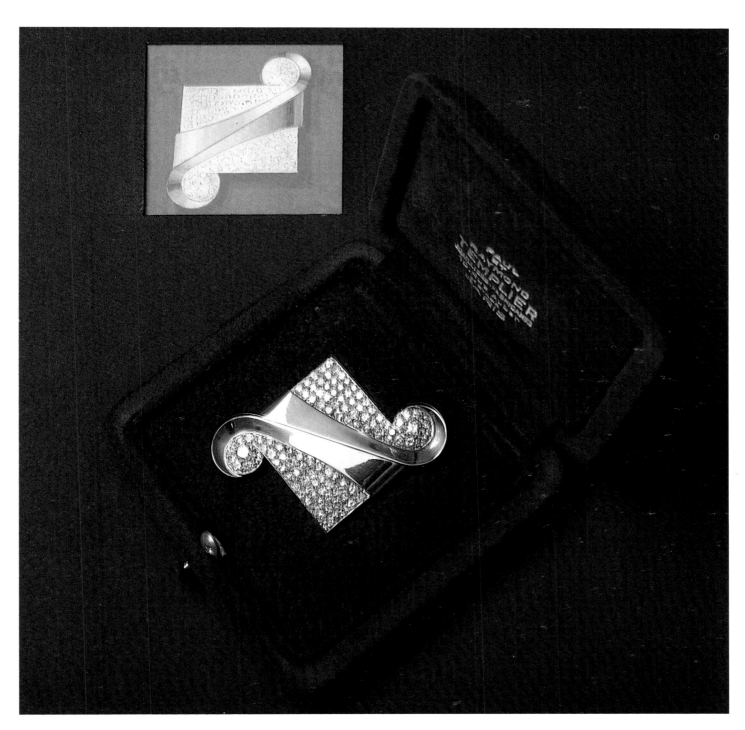

80 Brooch. Gold, silver, ivory, mother-of-pearl, pearls, opals tourmalines, crystals, enamel. British, by George Hunt (1892–1960). Ca. 1936. H. 5.1 cm, W. 8.6 cm. Victoria and Albert Museum, London (Circ. 657–1969).

81 Necklace. Brass. U.S.A., by Alexander Calder (1898–1976). Ca. 1938. L. 9 cm, W. 3.7 cm. Victoria and Albert Museum, London (Circ. 19–1962).

82 Necklace and Brooch. Gold. Italian or French, by unknown maker. Ca. 1938. L. (necklace) 42 cm; H. (pendant) 7 cm; (brooch) 8 cm. Private Collection.

83 **Two Rings.** Iron, gold and diamonds. German, by Hildegard Risch (b. 1903). (*Left*) 1958, Inside Diam. 1.8 cm, H. 3 cm; (*right*) 1959, Inside Diam. 2 cm, H. 2.7 cm. Kunstgewerbemuseum, Cologne (gift of Dr W. Richter, Genoa: G. 1259, gift of Elisabeth Treskow: G. 1336).

The ring illustrated on the left is shaped like a snake twisted around the finger; the shank, made of iron, is inlaid with gold, and the snake's head has two tiny diamond eyes.

The ring on the right is narrow at the back and has two trumpet-shaped ends in front, lined inside with gold. One end is set with a diamond in the centre; the other sprouts gold stamens.

It is characteristic of Hildegard Risch's approach to her work that she used the controversial combination of iron and gold in these rings and in many of her other pieces. Her constant search for new forms and for new ways of using old and new materials have served as a model and inspiration to successive generations of artist/jewellers.

84 **Ring.** Silver, tourmaline and garnet. U.S.A., by Sam Kramer (1914–1964). Ca. 1940. H. 4.5 cm, W. 4 cm. Private Collection.

The design of this silver ring owes nothing to either tradition or convention.

The oblong, irregular shape of the heavy silver bezel has an edged oval opening in the centre. Through it curls a silver wire (partially bound with another spiraling silver wire); at the side where it emerges, the end is adorned with a small cabochon garnet. The other end of the wire rests on the straight edge of the bezel and supports a tourmaline of an unusual cut that has only three facets.

Kramer, a former journalist, took up designing and making highly original jewellery in the early 1930s. He was a serious and committed artist, sensitive to the developments in contemporary art as a whole and to the need for changes in the traditional attitudes and concepts of jewellery.

85 **Necklace.** 18-carat gold, diamonds and rubies. French, by Van Cleef & Arpels. Ca. 1940. L. 55 cm. John Jesse/Irina Lasky Gallery, London.

The pendulum, which had swung from the figurative and complex motifs of Art Nouveau

to the stark, geometric forms of Art Deco, then came back to more intricate designs.

The five sections of this necklace from the renowned workshops of Van Cleef & Arpels each consist of one large and two smaller gold spheres, studded with small diamonds and separated from each other by gold discs edged with rubies. Each of these sections is connected to the next by a length of heavy gold rope chain. The clasp is cleverly concealed in one of the larger gold spheres.

86 **Earrings.** 14-carat gold, diamonds, rubies and sapphires. U.S.A., by unknown maker. Ca. 1940. L. 3 cm. Private Collection.

War effort and patriotism as themes for jewellery were bound to inspire some makers on both sides of the Atlantic. The fact that this pair of earrings was made in 14-carat gold suggests its American origin.

Two little men, each body set with a diamond, ruby and sapphire, are suspended by five tiny chains from fully opened parachutes. The colours of the stones (red, white and blue) correspond to the national colours of the three major partners in the Allied Forces: France, Great Britain and the United States of America.

87 **Pendant.** Gold. Swiss, by Max Fröhlich (b. 1908). 1940. H. 6.5 cm. Ruth Fröhlich Coll.

The pendant is made from red-gold wire, its spiraling curls twisted from one continuous length to fit inside the loop forming the frame. This design of deceptive simplicity relies heavily on the skill and exactitude with which the spirals have been made to fit with ease into the given form.

Max Fröhlich's long career as a master craftsman and designer, teacher and later Assistant Director at the Kunstgewerbeschule in Zürich have earned him well-deserved recognition as a leading exponent of contemporary jewellery. His constant search for and refinement of original design ideas have kept him in step with the times and exerted much influence on his many students, now masters in their own right.

88 **Ring.** 18-carat white and yellow gold and synthetic rubies. French, by unknown maker. Ca. 1940. W. 1.3 cm. John Jesse/Irina Lasky Gallery, London.

A typical design that was considered 'modern'

in 1940, this ring is still reminiscent of Art Deco styling, now modified into an asymmetric shape: narrow at one end but with widening contours culminating in a semicircular shape that crosses the shank at the other end. The upper strip of white gold is set with calibré-cut synthetic rubies and runs over the main body of the ring, made of solid yellow gold.

The shape of the ring suggests that it may have been designed to be worn on the little finger, possibly by a man, with the widest part on the outside of the hand, although massive rings were fashionable for ladies too and worn with jewellery to match.

89 **Necklace.** 18-carat gold, agates aquamarines. British, by Sah Oved (1900–1983). Ca. 1950. L. 39 cm. Victoria and Albert Museum, London (M. 138–1984).

Sah Oved was perhaps one of the most original artist/jewellers working in Britain from the 1930s to the 1950s. This necklace is a fine example of her subtle blend of the traditional and the thoroughly contemporary approaches to jewellery.

A colourful array of aquamarines and agates of varying sizes and cuts is set onto a semi-flexible gold structure, intended to lay at the base of the neck; the last seven links cascade off-centre in a downwards curve, five of them high-lighted by aquamarine drops.

90 **Necklace.** Brass, U.S.A., by Alexander Calder (1898–1976). Ca. 1940. Diam. 38.1 cm. Wadsworth Atheneum, Hartford, Conn.

The necklace is made from brass wire (see also Pl. 82), beaten into the form of large entwined loops that spread out to form a collar. It is fitted with a bar-fastener of twisted wire at the back.

The simple form, achieved by basic metal-working techniques, was one favoured by several famous artists, including Picasso (Pl. 158) and Max Ernst (Pl. 149). It was not only a deliberate move to avoid letting virtuosity of craftsmanship take precedence over design, but also a means of enhancing the concept and impact of their jewellery, which demands from the wearer an entirely different, and unconventional, attitude to the value of jewellery.

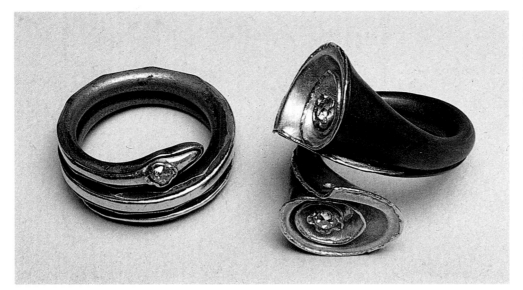

83 **Two Rings.** Iron, gold and diamonds. German, by Hildegard Risch (b. 1903). (*Left*) 1958, Inside Diam. 1.8 cm, H. 3 cm; (*right*) 1959, Inside Diam. 2 cm, H. 2.7 cm. Kunstgewerbemuseum, Cologne (gift of Dr W. Richter, Genoa: G. 1259; gift of Elisabeth Treskow, G. 1336).

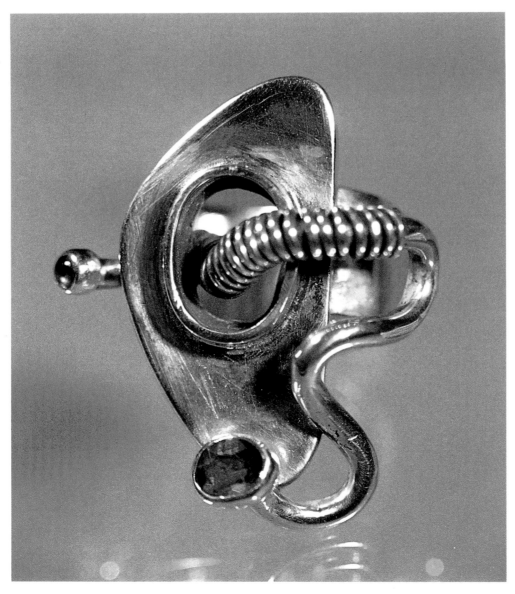

84 **Ring.** Silver, tourmaline and garnet. U.S.A., by Sam Kramer (1914–1964). Ca. 1940. H. 4.5 cm, W. 4 cm. Private Collection.

85 Necklace. 18-carat gold, diamonds and rubies. French, by Van Cleef & Arpels. Ca. 1940. L. 55 cm. John Jesse/Irina Lasky Gallery, London.

86 Earrings. 14-carat gold, diamonds, rubies and sapphires. U.S.A., by unknown maker. Ca. 1940. L. 3 cm. Private Collection.

87 Pendant. Gold. Swiss, by Max Fröhlich (b. 1908). 1940. H. 6.5 cm. Ruth Fröhlich Collection.

88 Ring. 18-carat white and yellow gold and synthetic rubies. French, by unknown maker. Ca. 1940. W. 1.3 cm. John Jesse/Irina Lasky Gallery, London.

89 **Necklace.** 18-carat gold, agates aquamarines. British, by Sah Oved (1900–1983). Ca. 1950. L. 39 cm. Victoria and Albert Museum, London (M. 138–1984).

90 **Necklace.** Brass, U.S.A., by Alexander Calder (1898–1976). Ca. 1940. Diam. 38.1 cm. Wadsworth Atheneum, Hartford, Conn.

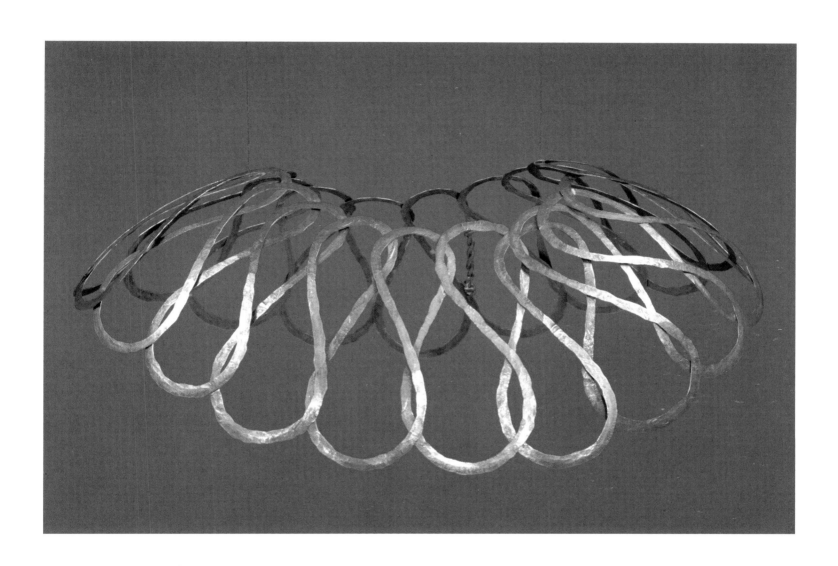

91 Earrings. 18-carat gold, turquoise and diamonds. Probably U.S.A., by unknown maker. Ca. 1940. L. 6 cm. John Jesse/Irina Lasky Gallery, London.

It is rather regrettable that so few firms producing jewellery mark their wares so they can be identified in later years. The assumption that these earrings were made in the United States rests mostly on their overall size. For although they were designed in a style that was equally popular on both sides of the Atlantic, the format of European jewellery tended to be smaller in scale, then as now.

These earrings in the popular ribbon motif are made to resemble four loops, edged with pavé-set diamonds and tied to a curved gold bar, closely set with rows of graduated turquoises. The earrings are fitted with clips, a kind of fitting frequently used during the 1930s and 1940s because large earrings were fashionable, and clips can hold more weight on the earlobe than the attachments generally supplied for pierced ears.

92 Necklace. Platinum and diamonds. U.S.A., by Harry Winston (1896–1978). 1946. L. 42 cm. Private Collection.

The design of this necklace is totally unassuming and conventional, though typical of the period; the diamond drop, however, is the kind of stone sure to have aroused passions over the centuries.

Known as the 'Briolette of India' (said to be the oldest diamond on record), it is reputed to have belonged to Eleanor of Aquitaine (1122?–1204), queen of France and then of England. Possibly she acquired it in Asia Minor during the Second Crusade, when she accompanied her first husband, King Louis VII of France. Eleanor is said to have given it to Richard Lion-Heart. In the sixteenth century, it was owned by King Henry II of France, who gave it to his mistress, Diane de Poitiers; it is shown on many of her portraits.

The rough stone was cut as a briolette, the name given to a drop shape cut with triangular facets, at Neuilly, France, in 1908 or 1909. The diamond is considered unique, not only be-

cause of its history, but also in view of its weight (90.38 cts), its unusual shape and cut.

Cartier sold it to the American philanthropist George Blumenthal in 1910; Harry Winston bought it from Blumenthal's widow in 1946. The transactions that followed were the kind that earned Winston the undisputed title of 'King of Diamonds': first, he sold it to an Indian maharajah, then bought it back (in 1956) and had it remounted as a pendant on the V-shaped necklace illustrated, composed of 157 marquise diamonds. This he sold to Mrs I.W. Killam, a Canadian. After her death in 1967, Winston bought her entire jewellery collection. In 1971, he sold the 'Briolette of India' as a loose stone to a titled European family.

93 Brooch/Watch. Platinum, diamonds, cabochon ruby and enamel. Spanish, by Salvador Dali (b. 1904). 1949. W. 8.7 cm. TAG Oeuvres d'Art S.A., copyright ©.

Salvador Dali, the famous Surrealist painter, has designed jewellery for many years, but none is as spectacular and revolutionary, in terms of concept, as the collection he created in the late 1940s and the 1950s. Comprising both wearable jewellery and sculptural jewellery objects, the collection was owned for many years by the Owen Cheatham Foundation in New York, who exhibited it worldwide for charity.

The piece illustrated is called 'The Eye of Time', a classic Dali concept; it incorporates a working watch movement and hands on the enamelled watch face, represented as the eye's pupil. The three shades of blue enamel on the eyeball are surrounded by rows of pavé-set diamonds that define the shape of the eye, which is shedding a diamond tear from its inside corner, set with a cabochon ruby.

Dali's jewellery has made an enormous impact by its sheer boldness, flamboyance and extravagance, as much as by its serious artistic statements, expressed in the characteristic symbolism of his designs.

94 Brooch. 18-carat gold, diamonds and lapis lazuli. French, by Boucheron. Ca. 1950. L. 5 cm, W. 6 cm. John Jesse/Irina Lasky Gallery, London.

Contemporary sculpture undoubtedly served to influence the design of this brooch. Shafts of gold and lapis lazuli are laid across two curved bars of gold, pavé-set with diamonds and pointed at each end. The irregular shape and alignment of the cross-sections contrast well with the clear-cut formal treatment of the supporting bars.

95 Brooch. Silver, white gold, amber, coral, malachite, onyx and moss agate. U.S.A., by Margaret de Patta (1903–1964). 1950. H. 4.3 cm, L. 8 cm. The Oakland Museum, Oakland, Cal. (gift of Eugene Bielawski: 67.21.12).

The designer of this brooch is one of the most important pioneers of contemporary jewellery in the United States, Margaret de Patta. The brooch demonstrates clearly her unique sense of form, colour and composition – way ahead of most her contemporaries.

De Patta's imaginative use of stone required specialized cutting. This brooch is made in silver; it consists of a flat vertical bar with a rectangular stone at either end; there is a round flat coral disc pivoting on a silver rod at the left, just below the top. The vertical bar is crossed by a narrow strip of silver that also has a rectangular stone at one end; at the other is a small round onyx, set at a right angle. A flat disc of amber with a silver surround has been set on top along the strip on the right.

This brooch contains movable elements in order to allow the colours to change. White gold has been used to reinforce the horizontal extension that holds the pin, thereby making the lines of the piece visually finer.

96 Earrings. 18-carat gold and amethysts. Danish, by unknown maker. Ca. 1950. L. 3.5 cm. John Jesse/Irina Lasky Gallery, London.

Cast in solid gold, these earrings are in the shape of a triangle, one side of which has three prongs tipped with cabochon amethysts. The smooth sculptured gold form is simple and dramatic, exemplifying the classic features of the 'Scandinavian Look', uncluttered by florid ornamentation, relying on the beauty of the inherent qualities of the materials.

91 Earrings. 18-carat gold, turquoise and diamonds. Probably U.S.A., by unknown maker. Ca. 1940. L. 6 cm. John Jesse/Irina Lasky Gallery, London.

92 Necklace. Platinum and diamonds. U.S.A., by Harry Winston (1896–1978). 1946. L. 42 cm. Private Collection.

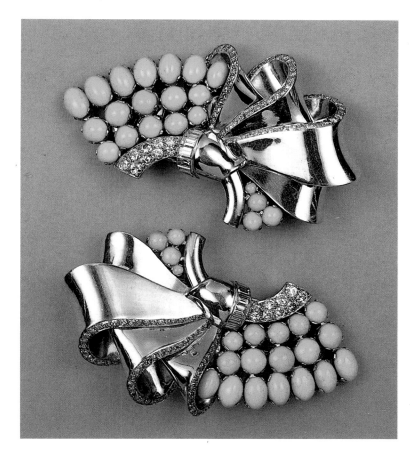

◁ **93 Brooch/Watch.** Platinum, diamonds, cabochon ruby and enamel. Spanish, by Salvador Dali (b. 1904). 1949. W. 8.7 cm. TAG Oeuvres d'Art S.A., copyright ©.

△

94 Brooch. 18-carat gold, diamonds and lapis lazuli. French, by Boucheron. Ca. 1950. L. 5 cm, W. 6 cm. John Jesse/Irina Lasky Gallery, London.

95 Brooch. Silver, white gold, amber, coral, malachite, onyx and moss agate. U.S.A., by Margaret de Patta (1903–1964). 1950. H. 4.3 cm, L. 8 cm. The Oakland Museum, Oakland, Cal. (gift of Eugene Bielawski: 67.21.12).

96 Earrings. 18-carat gold and amethysts. Danish, by unknown maker. Ca. 1950. L. 3.5 cm. John Jesse/Irina Lasky Gallery, London.

III 1950–1970

The relief at the end of six years of hostilities was enormous. Although the next few years of the immediate post-war period were still fraught with difficulties, there were also grounds for hope that the lessons of the past had been learnt. People were certain that future wars of such scale and violence, economic depressions like the collapse on Wall Street and the resulting mass unemployment, were all things of the past, avoidable catastrophies. In the light of the post-war boom that started in the early 1950s, this certainly seemed a realizable possibility.

In keeping with these hopes and aspirations, Dior had created the 'New Look' in fashion; he was later to be followed by Courrèges with the miniskirt. Other fashion designers turned to bold, futuristic patterns and bright contrasting colours.

Jewellery was slower to react to the new trends. Obviously the standard of living was improving everywhere, with full employment and higher wages as industry and trade went into top-gear to cope with rapidly growing consumer demands. As yet, competition was not a serious problem, and little thought was given to design as long as the production figures kept rising.

Scandinavia was the only exception; its abstract, free forms seemed to correspond best to the new climate—the 'Scandinavian' look was everywhere. Jensen employed a whole host of talented artists (Nana Ditzel, Torun Bülow-Hübe, Bent Gabrielsen, etc.) and in addition continued to produce the well-tried, classic jewellery of its pre-war designers.

It was during the late 1950s and early 1960s, that some great artists—Picasso, Max Ernst, Alexander Calder, Dali and Braque—involved themselves with jewellery, though never to any serious extent, except for Dali, whose jewellery designs were carried out by highly skilled craftsmen and whose excursion into the realm of jewellery represents an important part of his whole contribution to art. Dali's extraordinary Surrealist jewellery in gold and precious stones, with built-in mechanisms, for instance a pulsating heart, shocked the conventional world of jewellery with its boldness and extravagance. Such jewellery helped to pave the way for a new, younger generation of artist/jewellers to use the medium as an art form.

Education

The 1950s brought significant changes in education in both schools and colleges and, in a wider sense, via films and eventually television. A whole new world was opening up for millions of people who could now afford cars and take advantage, on an unprecedented scale, of cheap travel by train, boat and plane. Travel, formerly the privileged preserve of the scholar and the wealthy, was now available to almost everyone. By the 1960s and

1970s, even students went on intercontinental trips to areas of Africa, Asia and South America hitherto known only to explorers. Those who stayed at home learnt much about other cultures as well as their own with the aid of film and television documentaries, which stimulated the minds of broad sections of society in a way books never could.

Wider knowledge and broadened experience was bound to provide a fertile ground for interest in the arts and humanities. The trend even grew so strong that, later, education authorities deliberately made it harder to pursue such studies in order to channel more students into science and technology, which is always considered more practical and of greater use to the economy and commerce.

The impact of these dramatic changes on the education, outlook and patterns of income groups was impossible to ignore. The number of ultra-rich customers of established 'houses' of both fashion and jewellery had diminished to such an extent that drastic measures were necessary for their survival. They found the answer in producing lines of jewellery under their still-famous labels, which could be sold by other retail outlets besides their own. Moreover, every major city in the world now has branches of Cartier, Boucheron, Bulgari, Chaumet and Harry Winston. Like the days of 'couture' fashions, the days of *haute joaillerie* are almost, but not quite, gone. There will always be some people in this world who long to own a fabulous piece of jewellery of outstanding size, quality or beauty. There will always be someone who enjoys looking at and owning an outsize diamond or emerald, someone who wants to possess a historic jewel that once rested on the shoulders of an empress.

An example of changing attitudes is the story of the famous English model, Fiona Campbell-Walter, who married Baron Heinrich von Thyssen in 1964. On the occasion of their wedding, he showered his bride with presents, among which were a magnificent diamond necklace and a pair of earrings, each with a diamond weighing 27 carats. Twenty years later (they were divorced in 1973), in an interview on British television with Alan Whicker, the Baroness recalled the jewellery she had so proudly modelled for him during another interview shortly after her wedding. To Whicker's question as to the jewels' present whereabouts, she replied without regret that she no longer owned them, they were not the sort of jewellery she would want to wear now. Today, even those who can afford it, rarely flaunt such jewels, the exception being royalty on state occasions, where it seems right and proper to everyone for them to uphold time-honoured traditions.

Generally speaking, during the last thirty years, people who owned expensive jewellery tended to keep it in the safe, for fear of being robbed or mugged, or simply for fear of losing it.

Nowadays, the majority of customers for that type of jewellery are from the Middle East, where customs are still governed by rigid etiquette and where there exists a tradition of displaying status and wealth in that manner.

Since the 1950s, when jewellery began to play such a different role in people's lives, it started to divide itself gradually into three distinctly different mainstreams.

On the one hand were the designers and makers of 'fine' and 'precious' jewellery, who continued making 'one-of-a-kind' pieces or limited-production pieces for an established market with traditional ideas, perhaps occasionally adding a new model to their range. In complete contrast, on the other hand, was the costume-jewellery trade benefiting greatly from the discovery of plastics, a material with which one could not only imitate faceted or cabochon stones but also metals and pearls. Plastic was light, cheap and could be moulded into any shape or form; it could be assembled with glue and easily handled by unskilled labour or automated machinery. A third kind of jewellery also emerged: unique pieces made by individuals who may have trained as jewellers and/or in the fine arts; some were even self-taught.

The United States

In the United States, for instance, artists like Margaret de Patta, Margaret Craver and Sam Kramer made important jewellery that can hardly be classified merely as 'craft' jewellery. Sam Kramer studied journalism and graduated from the University of Southern California in 1936, before making jewellery (at first for his own personal satisfaction) while working as a reporter in Los Angeles and Hollywood. Kramer became more and more interested in gemstones, American Indian jewellery and experimentation with jewellery techniques. In 1939, he finally moved to New York and set up shop in Greenwich Village, where he became an integral part of 'the Village scene'. Kramer wrote about his work in the *Media Arts Magazine* in the late 1950s:

> ...Although I have no formal credo for jewelry-making, I have many loosely woven ideas which might possibly form a fabric for consideration by those who never thought of jewelry as a particular art form. Experimentation, for example, with metals, materials, gems, tools and techniques is doubtlessly the life flow of jewelry as a creative expression. Accident, aimless but recognized, which often suggests new directions an artist can take, is another important element. Working by trial and error in the fireplace (a convenient place for such experiments), I was trying to evolve a new casting technique. When silver is molten, it flares and dances like mercury. Suddenly a spluttering bubble of liquid silver squirmed out of the ingot-mold and cooled in an odd shape on the hearth. This piece, this accident of spilled metal, vaguely resembled a duck's head. And it started me thinking about how silver and gold could be blasted by flame until it ran almost fluid, then controlled, built upon and fused again until it resulted in small sculptures with the texture and all the flame-like movement of this kind of primal ordeal by fire.

Kramer's words describe pretty accurately what was also happening in other areas of art like painting and sculpture; the fine arts were given over to total abstraction; figurative representation was 'out'. Textures and rough-edged contours produced by 'controlled accidents' could serve well to express strong emotional concepts with great variety. The process and its resulting structure also allowed gemstones, precious and semi-precious, to appear in forms completely different from either faceted or cabochon cuts—the only two commonly in use until then. Crystal formations and cross-sections of tourmaline in their natural shape, cube-shaped pyrites and other geological specimens became exciting focal points of such jewellery.

Opportunities to learn the techniques of the jeweller, offered at art schools and colleges in Europe and America, attracted a new kind of student to the profession. Removed from the hide-bound traditional method of training, exposed to liberal studies and with close contact to other disciplines in art, such students became conscious of the immense possibilities and creative range offered by jewellery as an art form. Vital influences were exerted on them by many teachers who were not only—or above all—artists in their own right, but also people motivated by a deep commitment to society and who understood the true value of jewellery for the individual.

One such teacher was Margaret de Patta, who taught during the 1950s at the California Labor School in San Francisco, the California College of Arts and Crafts in Oakland and at the Oregon Ceramic Studio of the University of Oregon Extension Division. She also lectured and acted as an exhibition juror in other parts of the United States from 1941 to 1964, besides her continuous activities in craft organizations: Metal Arts Guild, Designer Craftsmen of California, American Crafts Council.

Born in 1903, she was trained originally in the traditions of painting and sculpture, until (in 1929) her interest turned to jewellery. An artist first and foremost, de Patta spent the following years acquiring and mastering many different skills and disciplines in order to free herself from technical limitations and to become able to carry out her concepts using jewellery as an art form. Margaret de Patta's innovative designs often required fastenings and settings that could not be produced with traditional jewellers' techniques. At all times she was concerned with liberating her work from inhibiting, conventional attitudes; this necessitated inventing new ways of setting stones, making special catches and earring fittings. Experimental from the start, de Patta worked with materials that were then completely new to jewellery: stainless steel and plastics, for instance. Fascinated by semi-precious stones, by 1941 she began to collaborate with a lapidary in San Francisco, Francis J. Sperisen, Sr, with whom she developed entirely new angles of cuts for gemstones. By 1946, when her output could not keep pace with demand and her prices were rising in consequence, Margaret de Patta felt that her situation had begun to contradict her social views and the method of working she preferred; therefore, she resolved at once to try and devote more time to creating prototypes that could be produced at lower prices. With the help of her husband, Eugene Bielawski, she set up a manufacturing business that competed successfully with producers of conventional costume-jewellery: her output at popular prices surpassed that of others in design and quality.

Involvement in a commerical venture did not, however, detract her from a constant concern with original work, which she continued until her untimely death in 1964.

The efforts of Margaret Craver, discussed in the previous chapter, provided the foundation for other training programmes, which began to be open to any applicant and were soon incorporated into the university structure for easier administration, although quite a few of the well-known schools are still run privately. Penland School of Arts and Crafts in North Carolina, for instance, was founded by Lucy Morgan in 1923 and is still very active, as is the Haystack Mountain School of Crafts at Deer Isle in Maine.

Australia and Japan

The period following the end of World War II was marked by a certain amount of isolation for artist/jewellers in Australia. It was not until the end of the 1950s and early 1960s, that a few individuals began to involve themselves in making jewellery different from the conventional sort. Just as in other countries, they came from different areas of the arts, such as sculpture or industrial design. Gordon Andrews, for instance, was an industrial and interior designer from Sydney who worked at some point for Olivetti and started to make very beautiful and unique contemporary jewellery for private clients after returning from Scandinavia in the 1950s. Although his work was hardly ever publicly exhibited, it made an impact, through being worn by many of his customers, sufficient to earn him a reputation in the circles that mattered. Similarly, during the 1950s, Clement Midmore, who was a sculptor, made jewellery as well in Melbourne, although he left Australia subsequently and has been living in the United States since 1963.

In complete contrast, Rod Edwards (born 1922 in Sydney) was a superlative craftsman who served his apprenticeship in a traditional manner under Lionel 'Nugget' Paton, one of Australia's master craftsmen in the firm of Angus and Coote. Edwards also had a strong interest in sculpture, which he practised at the National Art School in Sydney, where he eventually also taught jewellery and became Head of Department. He had a great passion for large and beautiful cabochon stones, which he set onto elevated bezels placed in concave, oval or round bases with highly polished surfaces that reflected the glowing colours of the tourmalines, emeralds, garnets or topazes. Edwards left Australia in 1951; he travelled over much of Europe and finally settled in England, where he continued to make jewellery and teach until the early 1980s, when he returned to his native land. Throughout his absence from Australia, he retained strong ties with it, exhibiting his work in Sydney. Rod Edwards has won a number of important commissions, including trophies for the Olympic Games in 1968 and 1972, and he made a superb gold sphere and medallion for the Worshipful Company of Goldsmiths, London, to commemorate the opening of the Sydney Opera House in 1973. The Australian contribution to the first International Contemporary Jewellery Exhibition (held at the Goldsmiths' Hall, London, in 1961) was composed of work by Rod Edwards, Helge Larsen and Darani Lewers. Helge Larsen was born in Copenhagen, Denmark, in 1929; he studied jewellery there at the College of Craft and Design and set up his own workshop/studio in the city in 1955. Darani Lewers (born 1936 in Sydney) joined him in 1959 after studying jewellery at the East Sydney Technical College and with an Estonian master

jeweller in Sydney. In 1961 they both went back to Australia, where Larsen became Senior Instructor in the Department of Industrial Arts at the University of New South Wales. Since those early days, Larsen and Lewers have continued to work separately and together, making distinctive and original jewellery as well as involving themselves in the wider issues of teaching by taking part in workshops and symposia and organizing exhibitions at home and abroad. Their work is represented in many public collections in Austria, Denmark, Germany, Czechoslovakia and, of course, in Australian museums. Darani Lewers was Chairperson of the Australian Crafts Board from 1976 to 1980.

A further influx of immigrant artist/jewellers did much to contribute to the growing interest in the making of contemporary jewellery in Australia. Wolf Wennrich (born 1922 in Germany) arrived in Melbourne in 1953. He was lecturer in Jewellery/Design in the Department of Gold and Silversmithing at the Royal Melbourne Institute of Technology from 1963 to 1980. An artist of great integrity and commitment, with much vision and determination, he exerted a tremendous influence on his students, among them Rex Keogh, Norman Creighton and Marion Hosking. Their joint exhibition, called '3 + 1', at the Georges Gallery in Melbourne in 1974 contributed greatly to the dramatic growth of interest in contemporary jewellery in Australia.

In Melbourne, the work of artist/jewellers demonstrated a certain cohesion as a group, perhaps as a result of the strong influence from contemporary German jewellery via Wennrich. Sydney's artists developed in more individual, separate ways. It was in Sydney, at the Marion Best Gallery in 1963, that Emanuel Raft had his first major exhibition of jewellery. Raft was born in Egypt in 1938 to Greek/Italian parents and went to Australia in 1956 to study painting at the Bissietta Art School in Sydney; he also studied sculpture for a year in Milan (1959–1960) with Luciano Minguzzi, after which he returned once more to Australia. In the early 1960s Raft began to make jewellery using design concepts, techniques and materials that were not only new to Australia but also made a great impact at international exhibitions elsewhere. With his sensitive blend of painterly and sculptural talents, he brought a new dimension into the field of jewellery, and his great qualities as an artist and a teacher did much to open the eyes of the public and fire the enthusiasm of his students.

Again as in Europe and the United States, the changing social pattern in Japan was reflected in a changing attitude towards jewellery and its design. Such design ran on lines fairly parallel with Western countries until the end of World War II. That dramatic experience and its horrible outcome brought about drastic change in Japan's social structure once more. In its wake, the younger generation of Japanese artist/jewellers began to create something different: jewellery that was contemporary, yet essentially based on their own cultural roots and images. Drawing on a rich artistic heritage, crystallizing an aesthetic typical of the very best in Japan—refining forms to their essence in a minimalist approach—the jewellery of Yasuki Hiramatsu (professor at Tokyo University), Aya Nakayama, Kazuhiro Itoh and Erico Nagai provides outstanding examples of this quality. Their work demonstrates vividly the finely tuned relationship between creative concept and functional aspect, so essential to the medium of jewellery.

Europe

In Britain, only a few art schools offered courses in metalcraft or jewellery-making, mainly to accommodate apprentices in trade workshops who, by law, had to attend a training college one day a week until they reached the age of eighteen. In the early 1950s, not many students took advantage of these courses for vocational purposes; most of those who did were mature students whose education had been interrupted by the war. At that time, these school workshops were unbelievably ill-equipped, having only the simplest tools and machinery imaginable. The Central School of Art and Design in London was perhaps the most important in those early days; its students were to make a name for themselves subsequently: among others, Nele, Gerda Flöckinger and, later, Susanna Heron. The principal at that time, Edward Johnson, asked artists like Mary Kessel and Alan Davie (both painters) to take an active interest in the Jewellery Department in order to stimulate among the students a more art-orientated attitude towards their subject. Mary Kessel made comparatively little jewellery herself, but Alan Davie became quite prolific and supplemented his income by making jewellery for private clients as well as shops like Aspreys and Harrods. Davie also made the jewellery worn by Vivien Leigh in the film 'Anthony and Cleopatra'.

Germany's training facilities for jewellers were unlike Britain's, and developed along entirely different lines in the post-war period. For one thing, the traditional apprenticeship method has remained much more strongly in force there to this day: the highly skilled and professionally schooled technician at his workbench is far more respected in Germany (and France) than elsewhere and therefore to qualify as such in these countries is still considered a desirable and worthwhile ambition. Furthermore, German students now had the possibility of learning the discipline at specialist schools that offered a highly technical training combined with tuition in the fine arts. These colleges were concentrated mainly in towns like Pforzheim and Hanau—both of which have traditionally strong links with the jewellery industry—and in Munich, Nuremberg, Düsseldorf and Schwäbisch-Gmünd. Within these training establishments, activities evolved and crystallized around the personalities of some of the teachers and professors whose individual approach to, and concept of, jewellery proved extremely influential and made a lasting impression on their students.

Franz Rickert (born 1905), for example, became professor at the Munich Akademie der bildenden Künste in its Jewellery Department. It was an unusual appointment in that he was the son of a well-known philosopher, who brought many of his father's views and his own philosophy of the crafts to his teaching programme which, in turn, proved highly influential to the development of his students: Hermann Jünger (who now holds the same post), Eberhard Hössle (professor at Nuremberg) and Sigurd Persson, one of Sweden's best-known artist/jewellers. One could almost speak of a 'German School' that would include the students of those people already mentioned and others who studied under Friedrich Becker (Düsseldorf) and Reinhold Reiling

(Pforzheim). The influence of this group is still recognizable in work by third-and fourth-generation students, now living in places as far apart as Australia, Japan and the United States.

During the 1960s, this new German jewellery became known as *neuer Schmuck* ('new jewellery'), its typical features consisting of a strong sculptural element achieved by a liberal use of solid gold, fused and encrusted in layers of different textures in asymmetrical formations. Sometimes offset against a background of blackened iron, frequently with groups of variously cut semi-precious stones, and/or a sprinkling of diamonds, these designs were based on abstractions of landscapes and body forms. Works of that period by Herbert Zeitner, Hildegard Risch, Klaus Ullrich and Hermann Jünger, among others, are strong examples of this new kind of jewellery, which represented an abrupt move away from the strict discipline of conventional form and technique. At the same time, such jewellery is also characterized by a very high standard of technical finish, entirely consistent with the traditional demands of quality craftsmanship. The growing appreciation in Germany for this new jewellery rested not only on the very high teaching standards in the various colleges but also on the great efforts made by the Schmuckmuseum, Pforzheim, to exhibit it and by a number of small but important private galleries.

The Schmuckmuseum, located in the Reuchlinhaus (named after Pforzheim's illustrious citizen, the Humanist Johann Reuchlin, 1455–1522) is entirely devoted to jewellery and probably owns one of the best and most extensive collections of both antique and modern jewellery in the world. Its present director, Dr Fritz Falk, is a recognized expert in the field of antique jewels and, at the same time, keenly aware of contemporary work. Pforzheim's modern collection ranks amongst the finest anywhere. The frequent exhibitions such as *'Tendenzen'* ('Trends'), often combined with competitions on chosen themes, have made an important contribution to the encouragement and flowering of the jewellers' art over the last fifteen years or so, and have attracted widespread international participation and recognition. After the large-scale destruction of the town in World War II, Pforzheim's town council, aided by the County Council of Baden-Württemberg and by private patronage, provided the funds for the custom-built museum, designed by the architect Manfred Lehmbruck. The museum serves as a vital link among artist/jewellers world-wide, often bringing jewellery exhibitions from many different countries to Germany and showing its own collections abroad. It publishes excellent catalogues, generously illustrated and containing detailed information on jewellery, ranging from ethnic to the most sophisticated antique and modern pieces.

The first German private gallery to deal entirely with contemporary jewellery was opened in 1968 in Cologne by Map Sauer. Within a year, Marie and Peter Hassenpflug opened Orfèvre in Düsseldorf, and today there are several more: Cardillac (Cornelia Rating) in Karlsruhe, Wilhelm Mattar in Cologne, and Spektrum in Munich.

The Craft Revival

Compared to the extent of the Arts and Crafts Movement in the early part of the century, the new enthusiasm for hand-made artifacts of all kinds has grown immensely everywhere since the end of World War II. It still had its roots, however, in the ideological conflict that pitted man against machines and preferred the imperfection of the human hand to the cold, mechanized and uniform finish of the machine. By the early 1960s, western Europe and America had had their fill of mass-produced articles for all aspects of life. No one would seriously consider acquiring a hand-made refrigerator or automobile, but the areas where personal individuality could be exercised were getting smaller and smaller in this new age. This feeling was undoubtedly one of the primary reasons underlying the craft revival. Other factors played an important part, for instance the enormous wave of interest among the younger generation for the cultures of Africa, India and South America, their art and religious cults.

In North America and Europe, there was a great yearning to return to a simpler way of life, to a closer contact with the basic necessities of growing one's own food, weaving cloth, baking bread and making pots. The 'flower children' were preaching universal love and the communal family; and the Beatles went to India to meditate with gurus. Ethnic jewellery began to be imported on a vast scale, and it became very fashionable to wear quantities of it, as was customary in tribal communities, although the fact that tribal jewellery was actually worn to display status and wealth was overlooked and ignored. Such jewellery was inexpensive, colourful and frequently made in the shape of ancient amulets that still seemed able to exert their inherent magic on sophisticated modern youth. All over the Western hemisphere, boutiques sprang up; Liberty's oriental department offered really superb examples of ethnic craftsmanship, and most street-markets had stalls festooned with garments and jewellery from the Third World.

The great popularity of 'ethnic' jewellery inspired quite a few Western makers to use primitive techniques and produce bold, sculptural pieces with tumble-polished, irregularly shaped semi-precious stones. The deliberate crudeness of finish and fastenings was at first heavily criticized by those involved in the regular jewellery business who were offended by the apparent disrespect for time-honoured precious materials and by the disregard of accepted standards in jewellers' techniques. But despite their criticism, contemporary jewellery had arrived, although it was not yet known by a specific name, and it developed in a variety of ways amid conflicts and arguments that are still flying back and forth to this day.

Within a couple of years, even the industry went to great trouble to adapt machinery to give their 'new' models similar textures or to incorporate the new ideas for lower-priced 'fashion' jewellery. Nevertheless, no industrial process could ever achieve the superb quality of textured metal as exemplified by the unique works of Reinhold Reiling or Gerda Flöckinger. Such perfection needs the touch of a creative artist, who knows exactly where and how to apply such a finish and is aware within which context form and texture combine to create the desired image.

This essential difference in the look of the finished product serves once more to high-light a fundamental distinction between the jewellery creators of the second half of this century and those of earlier times: today's artist/jewellers for the most part not only conceive but also make their own jewellery, their hands being actually involved in the work process from start to finish so that they have had to acquire highly complex skills and learn to handle small-scale machine-tools. While one or the other may employ the odd apprentice or assistant, the most interesting work in contemporary jewellery has almost always come from artists totally responsible for all the different stages of their work.

Is Jewellery Art?

In the 1960s, the question was again being asked—and is still being asked—is jewellery an art form? Can it ever reach the level of other media like painting and sculpture?

First of all, the definition of art is a subject on which many volumes have been written; it means different things to different people. Whether good or bad, no one would claim that all paintings and sculptures qualify automatically as works of art, nor would anyone make that claim for all jewellery. But art is not bound to any particular medium—it finds its own way of expression, and sometimes in unexpected areas. All art is a means of communication, and in jewellery, visual art can find the means of expressing intellectual and emotional concepts that no other art form can offer: jewellery makes an immediate, direct body contact; first, with one person—the wearer—and through her or him with a wider public—all those who see it on the wearer. Objects, life-size or larger, can often be intimidating or overpowering, whereas we are conditioned to relate easily to small things. A small item like jewellery must limit itself to the essentials in order to focus on the creative concept. Moreover, jewellery's ancient association with mystique and magic, and its powerful personal connotations, act as a pre-conditioner, making the mind more accessible and susceptible to visual language, which is then reinforced by the tactile quality of jewellery.

Throughout the ages, artists have been involved with jewellery, but it is typical of the second half of this century, that awareness and exploitation of jewellery as a serious art form took root then. Public collections have recognized this fact, and a growing number of people are now able to appreciate it.

Conversely, many people buying jewellery are still unduly concerned with the intrinsic value of the materials—a consideration that would never enter their minds when acquiring a painting or a sculpture: the price of a work of art by a well-known and skilful artist is never questioned on the grounds that it is only made of canvas, wood, paint, stone, paper or base metal.

Thanks to constant questioning of traditional values by artist/jewellers during the 1960s, today's jewellery has finally broken through the barriers of prejudice in terms of both materials and techniques, as well as on the wider issue of whether or not jewellery is an appropriate art form. The field has been extended to larger works of art, best seen in conjunction with the body, and to smaller objects made with jewellers' techniques, though not necessarily wearable as functional jewellery.

Quite a few artist/jewellers in different countries have made larger sculptural objects or three-dimensional wall-pieces that contain certain smaller, removable parts that can also be worn as jewellery. Claus Bury, Fritz Maierhofer, Kurt Neukomm and Roger Morris, among others, have all made such 'two-way' jewellery; others like Gerd Rothmann, Otto Künzli, Onno Boekhoudt and Martin Page have also made jewellery-like objects that have no function whatsoever, to hang on a wall or to display on a shelf.

Women in Gold- and Silversmithing

The greater scope within the profession and the wider training facilities available in the late 1950s and early 1960s, attracted a larger number of female students than ever before, and it was inevitable that some of them would rise to make a name in a profession that had been completely dominated by men in the past. There had always been a few women jewellers: Margaret MacDonald (wife of Charles Rennie Mackintosh, the Glasgow architect) and her sister, Frances MacNair (wife of Herbert MacNair), who belonged to the famous 'Glasgow Four'; Georgina Gaskin and Sybil Dunlop (England); Elisabeth Treskow and Hildegard Risch (Germany) and Margaret de Patta (U.S.A.). But until the end of the nineteenth century and early in the twentieth, women were employed for the menial tasks of polishing and cleaning in jewellers' workshops, or they worked at the sales counter in the retail trade.

In the City of London, the Worshipful Company of Goldsmiths is a time-honoured institution of great importance, which traces its origin uninterruptedly back to the Middle Ages. It acts as the guardian and patron of the professional interests of its members, Freemen of the Company and of the City of London. The 'freedom' is granted either after having served the prescribed apprenticeship with a Master Freeman, or it can be inherited by 'patrimony'. More importantly, it can also be awarded by the governing body of the Company (the Prime Warden and his Court of Liverymen) in recognition of services to the craft and/or the industry. By 1982, the Company counted among its several thousand Freemen, only nineteen 'lady Freemen' who were practising jewellers in their own right and seventy-seven who were unconnected with the craft. Nowadays, female students enrolled at jewellery classes in art colleges represent nearly 50 per cent of the total enrolment, so it is likely that, by the end of this century, the balance in the profession will change. But even as late as the 1950s and 1960s, the jewellery profession was so thoroughly male-orientated, that a woman buying silver or gold at one of the trade counters of the bullion dealers in London was served in a rather patronizing manner.

In the United States, Margaret de Patta, mentioned earlier, was one of the important pioneers of modern jewellery. Nowadays, the largest single collection of Margaret de Patta's work is in the Oakland Museum in Oakland, California, and she is also represented in the collection of the Museum of Modern Art in New York.

One of the first women to make a name for herself internationally was Torun Bülow-Hübe. Born in Sweden in 1927, she graduated from the Konstfakskolan ('Academy of Industrial Arts') in Stockholm in 1948. Torun, as she became known professionally, moved to France where she worked in Paris first, then in Biot, Provence, creating silver jewellery of exceptional beauty and classic simplicity of line. Its sheer elegance and innovative form created a sensation and emphasized the contours of the body with dramatic boldness. Exhibiting at many important international exhibitions, Torun won wide recognition and many awards and prizes over the years. A many-sided talent, she has also designed prototypes for other artifacts: cutlery, candle-holders and textile totebags (as well as jewellery) for Jensen and Dansk International Designs Ltd of New York,

Copenhagen and Tokyo. She has designed porcelain and ceramics for Hutschenreuther AG and glassware for Glashütte Löhnberg, both in Germany.

Of equal importance and distinction is the superb jewellery by Gerda Flöckinger, who was born in Austria but has lived in England since 1938. In 1971 she was the first woman and artist/jeweller to be honoured with a 'one-man' show at the Victoria and Albert Museum in London. Her work had already commanded attention at the 1961 Exhibition of Contemporary Jewellery at Goldsmiths' Hall in London. At that time, she made jewellery mostly out of silver and non-precious materials like copper, brass and, to a lesser extent, acrylic. In the mid-1960s, she developed a unique and original style that broke away from the traditional structure of jewellery: she evolved new techniques that included controlled fusion with gold and silver to obtain fine textures, broken surfaces and fluid lines. Many of her pieces incorporate opals, topazes or amethysts (that she cuts and polishes herself), as well as small diamonds and baroque pearls. Her overall concepts are a subtle blend of abstract form and Eastern jewels with a faint hint of the flowing movement found in Art Nouveau. Flöckinger also created the course for modern jewellery at the Hornsey College of Art in London, where she taught the subject from 1962 to 1968.

Galleries

In the 1950s and 1960s, artist/jewellers had a distinct problem marketing their work anywhere. In the wake of the growing popularity of all kinds of arts and crafts, a number of shops and galleries began to open, selling all different sorts of hand-made goods: weaving, pottery, glass and jewellery. In addition, a number of established galleries for fine art widened their horizons and started to sell jewellery of particularly high artistic merit.

But to handle modern jewellery of any kind in such retail outlets presented its own problems. It required a certain amount of specialized knowledge of gemmology and metals on the part of the sales staff. Art gallery owners found their clients receptive, particularly since the prices compared favourably with those for paintings and sculpture, though some owners feared they might be thought to have lowered their standards. For many clients, including works with any sort of practical application —however high its aesthetic and artistic standards—was still an act of arguable taste; the very term 'arts and crafts' carries with it an aura of inferiority for some people. The jewellery made by contemporary artists of standing and integrity, however, looked ill at ease displayed alongside the conventional kind, nor did it fit well among the other arts and crafts, because it needed such special handling and extra security to protect it from shoplifters.

In response to these problems, a number of galleries sprang up around the world, whose owners had both the understanding and drive needed to present contemporary jewellery to the public. These establishments became focal points for both artists and the public, and the relationship between artists and gallery owners provided a vital encouragement for the creation of jewellery that was both original and unique.

In Germany, the 1960s represented a period of great hope and idealism among the new generation of artist/jewellers. They were full of confidence in their ability to express new and original ideas within the discipline of jewellery, with both old and new techniques and concepts; but they also felt misunderstood and looked down upon by those engaged in the fine arts. They rose to this challenge by maintaining close contact with each other, collaborating in workshops and organizing exhibitions with other young goldsmiths in their own studios, sharing expenses for catalogues and publicity. At that time, Germany was enjoying an economic boom; the public had money to spend, and gold was incredibly cheap by present-day standards. The small band of 'new' artist/jewellers were able to make a decisive impact, getting their work shown on television and discussed in the daily newspapers.

In England, a number of well-established shops (Primavera, which dealt in very high-quality arts and crafts, Heals with their Craftsmen's Market, the Arnolfini Gallery in Bristol and the Ewan Phillips Gallery in London) were among the first to show individual and unique pieces of contemporary jewellery by named designer/makers. The Design Centre followed suit. Contemporary jewellery was featured in fashion magazines such as *Vogue* and *Harpers* and frequently reviewed in daily newspapers. By the late 1960s and early 1970s, the Victoria and Albert Museum had begun to acquire such jewellery for its permanent collection and, in fact, since that first show of Gerda Flöckinger's work in 1971, contemporary jewellery exhibitions have become a regular feature in the museum's special-exhibition programme.

From Royal Regalia to 'Op' Jewellery

In 1969, Louis Osman was commissioned to make the crown for the investiture of the Prince of Wales, which was presented to Her Majesty Queen Elizabeth II by the Worshipful Company of Goldsmiths. That gift represented a milestone in the history of contemporary jewellery: it is perhaps the only piece of royal regalia that can be described as truly contemporary. Made with all the symbols its historic significance demanded, the crown's design consists of a sculpted, textured, basic structure, electroformed from a wax original in 24-carat gold; it is the largest object ever to be constructed by this method. The added features of *crosses patées*, the four fleurs-de-lis and the orb at the top of the single arch are forged from pure gold, reinforced with iridium platinum and high-lighted by seventy-five tiny, square diamonds. Their shapes are strongly reflective of latter twentieth-century forms; the orb, especially, with its surrounding bands and complex, textured surface, resembles a space satellite.

In Europe and America, where the wave of interest in tribal and ethnic jewellery had accustomed the public to wearing such jewellery in great profusion, interest now extended to other kinds of jewellery as well. This readiness to accept new forms, new ideas and new functions coincided with a general relaxation in attitudes towards clothes which, in turn, reflected the far freer social structure and less rigid inter-personal relationships. By this time, the notion that on certain occasions a particular type of dress or suit—with the appropriate sort of jewellery—was required, had virtually disappeared. Every social strata was affected by the advent of jeans. In this climate, individuals could indulge their own personal preferences, and within this atmosphere of free choice, small trends of one kind or another could prosper; in the lower price bracket of costume-jewellery especially, fantasy knew no bounds.

First 'Op' jewellery appeared, derived from the 'Op Art' of Victor Vasarely and Bridget Riley. This was swiftly followed by an explosion of 'Pop' jewellery, made chiefly from plastic—brooches and earrings on representational themes that looked remarkably like real biscuits, slices of lemon or even pieces of half-chewed chocolate bars.

Even the style of jewellery made from precious metals changed from heavy sculptural forms with molten surface textures to more delicate structures with finer surfaces and increased technical refinements. Some of the designs were firmly inspired by space technology and science fiction, like the superb ring-sets (Pl. 152) by Wendy Ramshaw—groups of rings set with differently shaped and coloured stones, or with bezels consisting of circles, and that were designed to be worn in a cluster on one finger. Each set had its own, specially made stand of clear acrylic on which it could be displayed when not in use. Ramshaw's husband, David Watkins, experimented at that time with neckpieces and bracelets made from new materials like perspex, for which he invented special techniques to colour the rods and to bend them; he also used a lathe to cut grooves in it for shaping and inlaying.

Other artist/jewellers moved to more literal, figurative interpretations of their ideas: Noma Copley made a zipper brooch of 14-carat gold. Elton John, the singer, bought a ring made by Ros Conway with part of a tiny piano keyboard in ivory and ebony, set in gold. Paul Podolsky made a tiny pendant in 18-carat gold, a monkey-wrench gripping a diamond.

These two decades were an exciting span of time, within which important developments occurred from small beginnings. Great strides were made in the field of contemporary jewellery, though not in that field alone; similar developments took place during this period in other areas of the fine and decorative arts, in fashion design and graphic art—all of which flourished in the atmosphere of comparative peace and economic expansion and reached new levels of excellence.

97 **Necklace.** Silver and rock crystal. Swedish, by Torun Vivianna Bülow-Hübe (b. 1927). 1951. L. 80 cm, including drop. The artist's collection. ▷

97 Necklace. Silver and rock crystal. Swedish, by Torun Vivianna Bülow-Hübe (b. 1927). 1951. L. 80 cm, including drop. The artist's collection.

The necklace is open-ended, forged from a continuous piece of silver, beaten out to a wider section in the front before curling around the back; it comes over the shoulder as a narrow strip from which a large rock-crystal drop is suspended. Designed and made by Torun (as she is known professionally) in her first workshop in Stockholm, Sweden, this necklace represents a milestone in the history of modern jewellery: the complete break with the formal resolutions of jewellery shape was unique. Torun's enormous creative talent and deep understanding of the relationship between shape and body produced jewellery of such outstanding quality that it won her the U.S.A.-Lunning Prize (cf. Pl. 105) and a gold medal in Milan in the early 1960s, as well as the Grand Prix awarded by Sweden in 1965.

98 Tiara. Gold and diamonds. U.S.A., by Fulco di Verdura (1898–1978). Ca. 1950. Diam. 18.5 cm. Private Collection.

Inspired by the form of an American Indian headdress, this tiara is composed of gold 'feathers', pavé-set with diamonds and attached to a solid gold band that is open-ended at the back. It was designed and made for an American ambassador's wife (to wear for her presentation at the Court of St James) and is a typical example of the wit and ingenuity of Fulco di Verdura, or to give him his proper name – Fulco Santostefano della Cerda, Duke of Verdura.

Cultured and pleasure-loving, the highly successful Duke of Verdura counted famous artists and international socialites among his friends and clients in France and, later, in the United States, where he lived from 1957 to 1970. For over thirty years, di Verdura created fabulous and innovative jewellery for Lily Pons, Cole Porter, Elsa Maxwell and the Duchess of Windsor, among others.

99 Brooch. Platinum and diamonds. French, by Cartier. 1953. L. 9.8 cm, W. 5.3 cm. Her Majesty Queen Elizabeth II.

A conventional design of spectacular dimensions and quality, this brooch was made in the Cartier workshops by J.-J. Cartier and F. Mew for Queen Elizabeth. The platinum stem is set with baguette diamonds; two marquise diamonds represent the leaves. The five large flower petals with upturned ends are encrusted with pavé-set diamonds and set off the large pink diamond in the centre, which is surrounded by a circle of marquise diamonds. The pink diamond (23.52 cts)—the first to be found in South African mines—was given to H.R.H. Princess Elizabeth in 1947 as a wedding gift by Dr Williamson, a Canadian gemmologist.

100 Jewellery Object. Gold, diamonds, pearls, rubies and emeralds. Spanish, by Salvador Dali (b. 1904). 1953. H. 16.5 cm, W. 10 cm. TAG Oeuvres d'Art S.A. ©.

'The Royal Heart' is the title of this amazing bejewelled object, designed by the Surrealist painter, Salvador Dali. The heart is made from a nugget of solid gold. Inside a section has been cut out to form a recess, within which gold stalks tipped with rubies move in rhythm to the heart beat, driven by a built-in mechanical device. The heart is surmounted by a crown of gold, set with diamonds, pearls, rubies and emeralds.

Dali said of this creation that it was inspired by the coronation of Queen Elizabeth II in 1952: the gold nugget representing the people and the pulsating rubies symbolizing the queen whose heart beats constantly for her subjects.

101 Bracelet, Brooch and Hat-Pin. Platinum, diamonds, sapphires and emeralds. French, by Cartier. 1957. Inside diam. (bracelet) 7 cm; L. (brooch) 6.5 cm; W. (hat-pin) 7 cm. Private Collection.

The panther figure, adapted to various forms of jewellery, has been a continuous favourite of Cartier's clients since it was first made up to a design by Jeanne Toussaint in the mid-1920s. She created the figure to match the new fashion for furs made of the skins of big wild cats imported from Kenya. This set, or parure, comprises bracelet, brooch and hat-pin in platinum, pavé-set with diamonds and sapphire spots; the panthers' bright-green eyes are emeralds. The bracelet has a sprung hinge at the back and two panther heads facing each other at the open-ended front. The hat-pin has a diamond encrusted stopper. The set was made for Nina Dyer (1930–1965), a beautiful model with a passion for wild animals and jewellery, who was at one time the wife of Baron H. von Thyssen.

102 Brooch. Gold and silver. Italian, by Arnaldo Pomodoro (b. 1926). 1958. L. 7.3 cm. Victoria and Albert Museum, London (Circ. 63–1960).

Arnaldo Pomodoro is a universally acclaimed sculptor for whom the argument over jewellery's format and functional aspects versus its artistic validity does not exist; his jewellery is simply an extension of his larger works in sculpture, made with the same commitment and aesthetic principles.

This gold and silver brooch consists of elongated, irregular spears and granules bundled onto a concave rectangle with rounded sides. The contrast among the random forms is heightened by the protrusion of some of the components over the edges of the base.

103 Brooch. Gold, silver, ivory, garnet, tourmaline, coral and glass. U.S.A., by Sam Kramer (1914–1964). Ca. 1958. H. 8.8 cm. American Craft Museum, New York.

Kramer's fantasy and wit comes to the fore in this design of a mystical bird, a Surrealist image with an all-seeing glass eye of yellow and black set into a ring of ivory. The bird's large head is supported on a narrow neck that continues into a bulging, rounded body with tiny feet and a foreshortened tail. Appealing and amusing, it is a far cry from the fashionable and sentimental animals set with gemstones made by conventional jewellers of the time.

104 Pendant. White gold, ebony, quartz crystal. U.S.A., by Margaret de Patta (1903–1964). 1956. L. 9.5 cm, W. 6.3 cm. The Oakland Museum, Oakland, California (gift of Eugene Bielawski, 67.21.6).

An integral part of Margaret de Patta's design concepts were the effects of light and shadow, transparency and translucency, magnification and multiplication, which could be obtained by designing special cuts and settings for stones. She used to design complex stone cuts, make models of them in Lucite, and have them executed by Francis J. Sperisen Sr in San Francisco (who collaborated closely with her for many years, developing new experimental cuts for gemstones). Intent on making such stones appear to be floating freely in space, de Patta devised ingenious and unorthodox methods of setting them, as this pendant demonstrates.

The large rhomboid quartz crystal, faceted in opposing courses, is attached to an angle-iron form of ebony set in white gold, counterbalanced by a fine rod of white gold set at an angle in the opposite direction at the top. The metal structure holding the stone is hidden by the blind areas. The broken up lines of the ebony, seen through the faceted stone, change pattern constantly with the movement of the wearer.

98 Tiara. Gold and diamonds. U.S.A., by Fulco di Verdura (1898–1978). Ca. 1950. Diam. 18.5 cm. Private Collection.

99 Brooch. Platinum and diamonds. French, by Cartier. 1953. L. 9.8 cm, W. 5.3 cm. Her Majesty Queen Elizabeth II.

100 Jewellery Object. Gold, diamonds, pearls, rubies and emeralds. Spanish, by Salvador Dali (b. 1904). 1953. H. 16.5 cm, W. 10 cm. TAG Oeuvres d'Art S.A., copyright ©.

101 Bracelet, Brooch and Hat-Pin. Platinum, diamonds, sapphires and emeralds. French, by Cartier. 1957. Inside diam. (bracelet) 7 cm; L. (brooch) 6.5 cm; W. (hat-pin) 7 cm. Private Collection.

102 Brooch. Gold and silver. Italian, by Arnaldo Pomodoro (b. 1926). 1958. L. 7.3 cm. Victoria and Albert Museum, London (Circ. 63–1960).

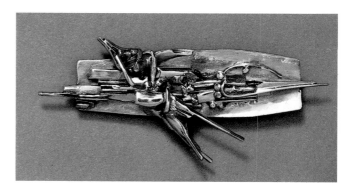

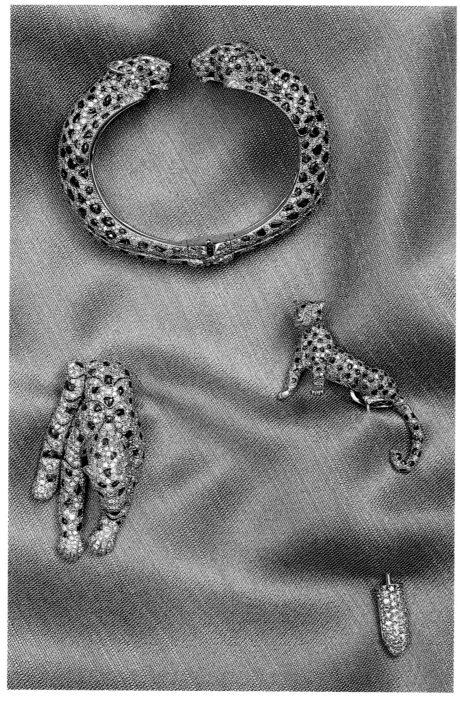

103 Brooch. Gold, silver, ivory, garnet, tourmaline, coral and glass. U.S.A., by Sam Kramer (1914–1964). Ca. 1958. H. 8.8 cm. American Craft Museum, New York.

104 Pendant. White gold, ebony, quartz crystal. U.S.A., by Margaret de Patta (1903–1964). 1956. L. 9.5 cm, W. 6.3 cm. The Oakland Museum, Oakland, California (gift of Eugene Bielawski, 67.21.6).

105 Necklace. Silver and glass. Norwegian, by Grete Prytz-Kittelsen (b. 1917). 1958. Diam. 17.5 cm. The artist's collection.

In 1952, Grete Prytz-Kittelsen was the first Norwegian artist/jeweller to win the coveted Lunning Prize (awarded annually from 1951 to 1969 to Scandinavian artists by Frederick Lunning, a director of Jensen, for the best work in arts and crafts, or for industrial design), and she won many other awards and gold medals in subsequent years. The artist designed this unusual necklace made of glass set into silver as part of a collection she produced for the *Formes Scandinaves* ('Scandinavian Shapes') Exhibition of 1958 in Paris. The specially designed forms of glass were made up for her at Murano, Italy, by the Italian glass artist Paolo Venini, and mounted in the necklace by the Tostrup workshops in Oslo. The necklace consists of four basic parts: two plain silver bands fit over the shoulders and are hinged to the front section, which is a curve of green-speckled glass, overlaid by a V-shape in pale beige. An arrow head of the same colour dangles from the tip of the V. The back section is a curve in the same green and beige as the front, but has a shorter V-shape suspended from the inner edge and crossed by a silver bar at its tip.

106 Ethnic Jewellery Collection. Silver, nickel, brass, agates, turquoise, garnets. International, by unknown makers. 1960. L. (cornelian-bead necklaces) 76 cm; (turquoise-bead necklace) 90 cm; (silver chain with Hand of Fatimah) 99 cm; Diam. (silver torque) 13 cm; L. (Indian bracelet with turquoise) 14.7 cm, W. 1 cm; L. (matching earrings) 2.2 cm; W. (matching ring) 1.3 cm; (2nd ring) 1.8 cm; L. (Indian drop earrings) 7.5 cm; Diam. (round silver earrings) 1.8 cm; L. (Mexican lizard brooch) 7.5 cm; H. (Egyptian necklace and pendant) 28 cm; L. (Mexican necklace) 45 cm; (round pendant with silver beads) 7.9 cm. Private Collection.

This collection of ethnic jewellery, some old and some made in the 1960s, illustrates examples of designs produced by native craftsmen in the Third World. The pieces illustrated come from such diverse locations as India, North Africa, Central Africa, Mexico and from North American Indians. The carved silver torque on the bottom right and the chain with the 'Hand of Fatimah' pendant from North and Central Africa are probably between fifty and a hundred years old. The agate-bead necklaces and the triangular earrings set with red glass and turquoise paste are recent reproductions of traditional patterns from India. Also modern 'traditional' is the large pendant of crescent-shaped filigree with dangling medallions, which originates in Egypt. The necklace and earrings on the bottom left are Mexican and made

in nickel. The set of bangle, ring and earrings at the centre right, in sterling silver with turquoise stones, is machine fabricated by American Indians. Jewellery of this kind was freely available in every boutique and street market – in fact, it still is – and, in the 1960s, became very fashionable both in Europe and the United States.

107 Pendant. Gold and enamel. U.S.A., by John Paul Miller (b. 1918). 1959. 1.6 cm × 5.4 cm. American Craft Museum, New York. Artist and master craftsman, John Paul Miller began making jewellery in 1936, after a school friend taught him how to solder silver and use a jeweller's saw. In his capacity as a teacher from 1946 to 1983 at his old college, the Cleveland Institute of Art, and as an artist/jeweller in his own right, Miller exerted an enormous influence on the development of contemporary jewellery in the United States. This pendant is in the form of a flounder, the complex pattern of its markings, beautifully executed on 18-carat gold with cloisonné enamel. An unusual feature are the gold lines that separate the enamels, here broken up into small sections, mosaic fashion.

108 Pendant. Gold, rock crystal and pearls. West German, by Herbert Zeitner (b. 1900). Ca. 1960. W. 5.3 cm. Schmuckmuseum, Pforzheim (1979/2).

The figure of a mermaid, complete with flowing hair and fish tail, holds two pearls in the centre of the pendant. She is surrounded by five irregularly shaped rock crystals, set on the outer edge with gold claws and having a pearl between each of them. Zeitner was a sculptor and goldsmith with a Masters' Degree from the Zeichenakademie of Hanau, Germany, who taught for many years in Berlin. Since 1946 he has worked free lance. His jewellery always has a strong sculptural quality as an integral part of the design concept.

109 Hair Ornament. Gold, *en resille* enamel. U.S.A., by Margaret Craver. 1959. L.14.6 cm, W. 6.3 cm. American Craft Museum, New York. Margaret Craver is a key figure in the development of contemporary jewellery in the United States, whose contribution lies not only in her innovative designs and techniques but also in her committed involvement with setting up educational programmes in the immediate post-war period.

In the early 1950s, Craver extended her already considerable expertise with metals to *en resille* enamel, an old technique she learnt to master and incorporate in her designs. The hair ornament illustrated shows an example of this technique in the centre, a semicircular, delicately enamelled section flanked by two gold 'wings', set at the top of a long flat pin.

110 Brooch. Gold, enamel and diamonds. U.S.A., by Tiffany & Co. Ca. 1960. L. 5 cm. John Jesse/Irina Lasky Gallery, London.

Animals have always provided appealing subjects for jewellery designers, and particular species enjoy popularity at different times: the butterfly and dragonfly in Art Nouveau, ladybirds and panthers in the 1930s, to name but a few. In the 1950s and 1960s, parrots were much in vogue, making this monkey brooch by Tiffany something rather unusual and special. With upheld arms ready to cling to a branch, the monkey's fur is simulated by enamel on the textured gold. Diamonds are used for eyes and two larger ones are set into the animal's posterior, one on each side of his tail.

111 Pendant on Chain. Gold, emerald and pearls. West German, by Hildegard Risch (b. 1903). 1961. W. 2.6 cm. Schmuckmuseum, Pforzheim (1961/62).

The large cabochon emerald is surrounded by three strings of pearls coming together in the front. The links of the chain resemble twigs, joined by several wire loops; every other one is strung with a small cluster of pearl beads to form small buds.

Always at pains to bring out the best in her materials and entirely unsentimental in approach, Risch has succeeded in this design without resorting to complex elaborations, in conveying a feeling of joy at nature's beauty and colours.

112 Bracelet. 18-carat gold and tourmalines. Danish, by Nanna Ditzel (b. 1923), for Georg Jensen. 1962. Diam. 7 cm, W. 2.5 cm. Production Design No. 1131, for Georg Jensen, Copenhagen.

The design of this bracelet is interesting, a classic of both Ditzel's work and the Scandinavian jewellery 'look' in the wider sense. With production in mind, Ditzel designed the bracelet so that it could be cut out from flat gold sheet in two identical halves with four narrow strips on either side of the band. After the two bands are bent round to form the bracelet, the strips are turned back and attached to the stone mounts, allowing the beautiful colour of the tourmalines to be reflected in the highly polished surface beneath them.

Another holder of the Lunning Prize (1956) (see Pl. 105), Nanna Ditzel was responsible for many of the outstanding designs produced by Jensen since 1954.

105 Necklace. Silver and glass. Norwegian, ▷ by Grete Prytz-Kittelsen (b. 1917). 1958. Diam. 17.5 cm. The artist's collection.

106 Ethnic Jewellery Collection. Silver, nickel, brass, agates, turquoise, garnets. International, by unknown makers. 1960. L. (cornelian-bead necklaces) 76 cm; (turquoise-bead necklace) 90 cm; (silver chain with Hand of Fatimah) 99 cm; Diam. (silver torque) 13 cm; L. (Indian bracelet with turquoise) 14.7 cm, W. 1 cm; L. (matching earrings) 2.2 cm; W. (matching ring) 1.3 cm; (2nd ring) 1.8 cm; L. (Indian drop earrings) 7.5 cm; Diam. (round silver earrings) 1.8 cm; L. (Mexican lizard brooch) 7.5 cm; H. (Egyptian necklace and pendant) 28 cm; L. (Mexican necklace) 45 cm; (round pendant with silver beads) 7.9 cm. Private Collection.

107 Pendant. Gold and enamel. U.S.A., by John Paul Miller (b. 1918). 1959. 1.6 cm × 5.4 cm. American Craft Museum, New York.

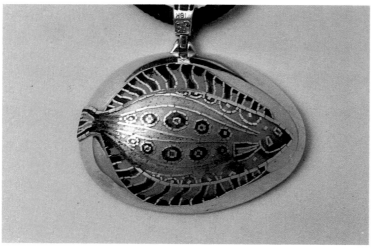

108 Pendant. Gold, rock crystal and pearls. West German, by Herbert Zeitner (b. 1900). Ca. 1960. W. 5.3 cm. Schmuckmuseum, Pforzheim (1979/2).

109 Hair Ornament. Gold, *en resille* enamel. U.S.A., by Margaret Craver. 1959. L. 14.6 cm, W. 6.3 cm. American Craft Museum, New York.

110 Brooch. Gold, enamel and diamonds. U.S.A., by Tiffany & Co. Ca. 1960. L. 5 cm. John Jesse/Irina Lasky Gallery, London.

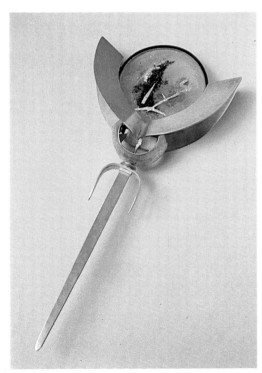

111 Pendant on Chain. Gold, emerald and pearls. West German, by Hildegard Risch (b. 1903). 1961. W. 2.6 cm. Schmuckmuseum, Pforzheim (1961/62).

112 Bracelet. 18-carat gold and tourmalines. Danish, by Nanna Ditzel (b. 1923), for Georg Jensen. 1962. Diam. 7 cm, W. 2.5 cm. Production Design No. 1131, for Georg Jensen, Copenhagen.

113 Bracelet. 18-carat gold, platinum, diamonds. U.S.A., by Jean Schlumberger (b. 1907). 1962. Diam. (bracelet). 7.6 cm. Private Collection.

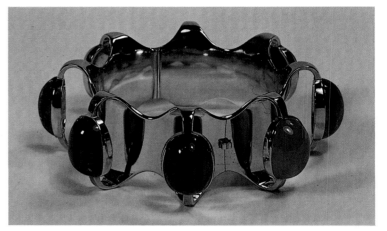

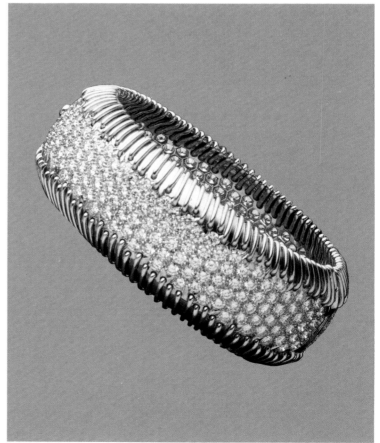

113 Bracelet. 18-carat gold, platinum, diamonds. U.S.A., by Jean Schlumberger (b. 1907). 1962. Diam. (bracelet). 7.6 cm. Private Collection.

The illustrious career of jewellery designer Jean Schlumberger began almost by accident: the fashion designer Elsa Schiaparelli saw some china flowers from the Parisian flea market that he had mounted into clip-brooches for friends. She promptly commissioned him to design costume-jewellery for her famous fashion house, an experience which encouraged him to employ gold and precious stones subsequently. After World War II, Schlumberger settled in the United States, where he eventually became top designer at Tiffany's and a vice-president of the famous jewellery store.

The bracelet is a hinged band of diamonds pavé-set in platinum, with gold-wire 'stitches' on the borders.

114 Pendant. Gold and pearls. West German, by Klaus Ullrich (b. 1927). 1963. W. 3.5 cm. Schmuckmuseum, Pforzheim (1970/9).

Suspended from a rigid gold neckband, this pendant consists of four horizontal gold bars, three of which have fringes of varying lengths composed of beaten gold strips. The lowest bar has five baroque pearls suspended at irregular intervals.

Klaus Ullrich, an artist/jeweller with a thorough traditional training as a goldsmith, has never considered the 'limiting' format of jewellery a hindrance to the expression of artistic concepts. He was one of the first important individuals in the 1950s and 1960s to develop a unique style of his own, which opened up new avenues of thought about formal structure and material combinations in jewellery. With several awards to his credit, Ullrich taught for many years as professor at the Akademie der bildenden Künste, Munich.

115 Pendant. 18-carat gold and diamond. British, by Paul Podolsky (b. 1923). 1962. L. 3.5 cm. Production Design.

By the 1960s, some jewellery design had turned very figurative and literal. Objects of all sorts became inspirations for reproduction in miniature, for instance this pendant in the form of a 'monkey-wrench'. Cast from 18-carat gold, the wrench's 'adjustable' grip is firmly clenched over a 12-point diamond set into an octagonal, white-gold 'nut'.

Paul Podolsky received his jeweller's training from his father, a Russian emigré and diamond cutter. Podolsky is reputedly the seventh generation of his family in the jewellery business; he took over his father's firm in 1947, re-naming it Albioncraft, and still runs it successfully, producing good quality jewellery for the retail trade. Podolsky is aware of new trends, sensitive to design and craftsmanship and concerned with the wider issues of training

programmes and job opportunities for the younger generation – an attitude that other 'commercial' jewellers could emulate.

116 Brooch. Gold, diamonds and jasper. French, by Georges Braque (1882–1963). 1962. H. 4.5 cm, W. 4.8 cm. Gimpel Fils Gallery, London.

Entitled 'Icaros', this brooch was made by Baron Heger de Lowenfeld to a design by Braque. The bird in 18-carat white gold, pavé-set with diamonds, rests on an oval red-jasper base mounted onto a textured yellow-gold cross.

It is interesting that even Braque, who ranks among the great painters of the twentieth century, should venture into the field of jewellery, if only briefly.

117 Fibula. 18-carat gold, sapphires and diamonds. Austrian, by Adolf (b. 1938) and Elsa Drobny (b. 1936). 1965. L. 18.2 cm, W. 7.5 cm. Private Collection.

This is an abstract composition composed of three textured gold plates (the third is hinged), interconnected by cross bars set with diamonds at the ends. Three long vertical bars protrude beyond the last section and are set with one faceted and two cabochon sapphires. Six diamonds have been mounted between the vertical bars on the top plate, and a larger diamond has been placed at the end of the long bar on the middle section.

This fibula was designed and made by a husband and wife team, both master goldsmiths: Since 1964, they have worked together, and this early example of their collaboration already shows the extent of their awareness of new forms and techniques, which has kept them abreast of the times and in the forefront of current trends.

118 Pendant on Chain. 18-carat gold and tourmalines. Finnish, by Björn Weckström (b. 1935). 1965. L. 7 cm. Private Collection.

Björn Weckström's first ambition was to become a sculptor but, for practical reasons, this urge was chanelled by his father into goldsmithing. Equipped with the necessary jewellers' skills, Weckström soon began to incorporate his sculptural talents into the designs of his jewellery in a unique manner that has earned him an international reputation and enormous commercial success over the years. Since 1965, he has been chief designer of the jewellery produced by the Lapponia Jewellery Co.

Weckström, a man of strict principles, is a firm believer in making his work accessible to a wide public by producing jewellery in limited editions. The pendant illustrated won him the Grand Prix in Rio de Janeiro in 1965. Inspired by landscapes and the natural formation of a gold nugget, the heavy texture and jagged edges of the rectangular pendant are high-lighted by

the luminous green of the tourmalines set into its crusty surface. The chain is made of rectangular links that match the pendant in texture.

119 Cufflinks. Silver. Danish, by Flemming Eskildsen (b. 1930). 1965. W. 1.6 cm. Production Design No. 113/90, for Georg Jensen, Copenhagen.

The surface of the silver rectangle, in a classic design in the 'Scandinavian' style, is cast into a relief of small squares, every other one oxidized black for colour contrast.

Flemming Eskildsen, who trained as a silversmith in the workshops of Georg Jensen, has been working for the firm continuously since 1958. His jewellery designs have contributed greatly to the continued high and reputation of the firm on an international level.

120 Brooch. Iron, steel, 22-carat gold and rock crystal. West German, by Hubertus von Skal (b. 1942). 1965. 6 cm × 6 cm. Private Collection.

Trained as a gold- and silversmith as well as at the Akademie der bildenden Künste in Munich, von Skal is versed in the most sophisticated techniques; he is a superb craftsman, but one who never allows his expert skills to take precedence over his artistic concepts. As an artist, his first consideration when creating a piece of jewellery is to determine its form and content – a focus to attract the attention of the eye and engage the observer's mind. His highly original ideas for jewellery often incorporate unexpected elements; they are always thought-provoking, frequently branch out into non-wearable jewellery and even into pure sculpture. In the centre of the brooch, is a golden fly with rock-crystal wings on steel mesh, attached to an outer frame of iron.

121 Brooch. 18-carat gold and diamonds. U.S.A., by Tiffany & Co. Ca. 1969. L. 10 cm. Private Collection.

It is often said that the high standards in manual skills and the supreme craftsmanship of the past have died out in the twentieth century—a statement which is, of course, patent nonsense. Sometimes it may be difficult for a layman to appreciate the demanding expertise required to execute what appears to be a comparatively simplelooking design, but the capability and talent (which was always rare) to do so, is certainly still with us.

This brooch made in the late 1960s is a perfect example. Based on a design that would have fitted easily into the nineteenth century (or even earlier) this 'lily of the valley' was made with meticulous attention to detail: set into white and yellow gold, encrusted with carefully graduated pavé-set diamonds, the flowers are mounted on flexible joints so that the wearer can change their position.

114 Pendant. Gold and pearls. West German, by Klaus Ullrich (b. 1927). 1963. W. 3.5 cm. Schmuckmuseum, Pforzheim (1970/9).

115 Pendant. 18-carat gold and diamond. British, by Paul Podolsky (b. 1923). 1962. L. 3.5 cm. Production Design.

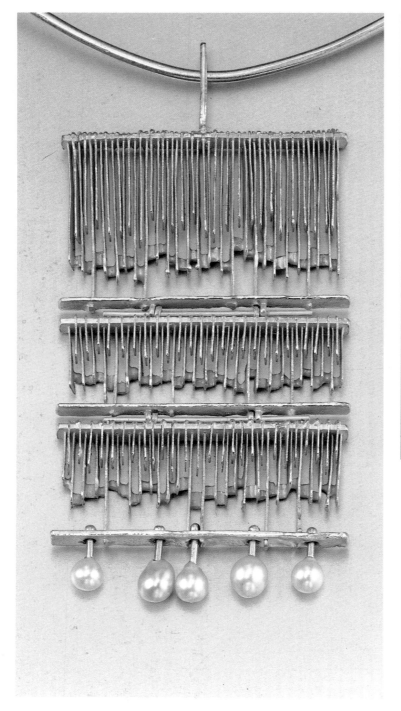

116 Brooch. Gold, diamonds and jasper. French, by Georges Braque (1882–1963). 1962. H. 4.5 cm, W. 4.8 cm. Gimpel Fils Gallery, London.

117 Fibula. 18-carat gold, sapphires and diamonds. Austrian, by Adolf (b. 1938) and Elsa Drobny (b. 1936). 1965. L. 18.2 cm, W. 7.5 cm. Private Collection.

118 Pendant on Chain. 18-carat gold and tourmalines. Finnish, by Björn Wekström (b. 1935). 1965. L. 7 cm. Private Collection.

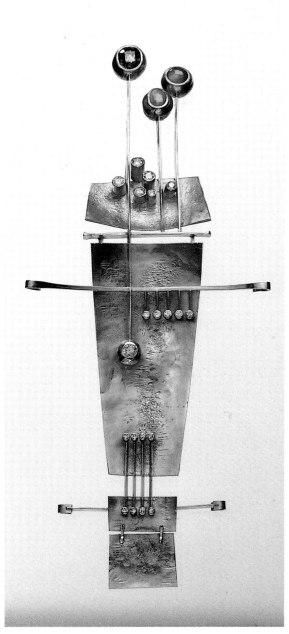

119 Cufflinks. Silver. Danish, by Flemming Eskildsen (b. 1930). 1965. W. 1.6 cm. Production Design No. 113/90, for Georg Jensen, Copenhagen.

120 Brooch. Iron, steel, 22-carat gold and rock crystal. West German, by Hubertus von Skal (b. 1942). 1965. 6 cm × 6 cm. Private Collection.

121 Brooch. 18-carat gold and diamonds. U.S.A., by Tiffany & Co. Ca. 1969. L. 10 cm. Private Collection.

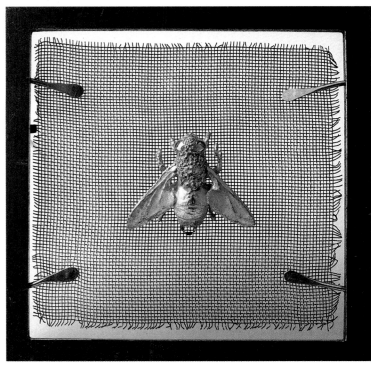

122/123 Brooch (Two Versions). White gold, diamonds, emeralds and sapphires. West German, by Friedrich Becker (b. 1922). 1965. (Each section) 2.2 cm. Private Collection.
'Inactivity is death; motion embodies life' might well be the motto for Friedrich Becker's design. Trained as a mechanical engineer and student of aeronautics, he also completed an apprenticeship as a gold- and silversmith. As a freelance artist/jeweller, teacher and finally professor at the Fachhochschule in Düsseldorf (until 1982), Becker can look back on countless exhibitions where his amazing and innovative jewellery design has earned him coveted prizes and awards.

Mobility and movement in one form or another has always held a fascination for him; this brooch is an early example in which the principle is used to allow one piece to assume a variety of different shapes. The basic structure consists of eight levers joined to each other by articulated axles and three rods of varying lengths, set with stones at the ends. All the movable parts can be fixed in the desired position by means of spring pressure.

124 Ear Ornaments. 14-carat gold, emeralds and lapis lazuli. Norwegian, by Grete Prytz-Kittelsen (b. 1917). 1966. H. 6 cm. Private Collection.
Although they are an unusual form of jewellery for the ears, the shape of these ear ornaments is in fact extremely comfortable and effective. The gold has been forged into an elongated curve of varied width and fits over the ear with the widest section covering the lobe; that part is set with a square emerald. The other end of the ornament, set with a flat, oval-shaped lapis lazuli, curls around the ear to rest against the cheek of the wearer.

125 Two Brooches. Silver, gold, moonstone, opal, emerald and enamel. West German, by Hermann Jünger (b. 1928). 1965. W. 4.8 cm. Private Collection.
A professor at the Akademie der bildenden Künste in Munich since 1971, Hermann Jünger has made a major contribution to the development of contemporary jewellery taken in the widest possible sense. Jünger was one of the first to break away from the traditional attitudes and concepts of jewellery; he brought an entirely new aesthetic into the field, and as an inspired teacher, he has influenced whole generations of young artist/jewellers to think beyond conventional limitations and to strike out towards individualism and originality.

Jünger's own work has always testified to the freedom of his spirit. With different shapes, textures and stones, he composes a unified image, creating his own harmony out of contrast. These two brooches, for instance, are abstract compositions made of silver and gold and set with precious and semi-precious stones.

126 Bracelet. 18-carat gold, tourmalines and diamonds. British, by David Thomas (b. 1938). 1967. L. 17.5 cm, W. 2.4 cm. The Worshipful Company of Goldsmiths, London.
In 1961, after winning scholarships to study in Italy, France and Scandinavia, David Thomas graduated from the Royal College of Art in London. Since then, he has run his own studio/workshop and exhibited at important international exhibitions.

Set with nine rectangular blue tourmalines, the design of this bracelet emphasizes the smooth, clean cut of the stones by contrasting them with the square gold bars of irregular lengths that form the links and are interspaced with twenty-eight baguette diamonds.

127 Necklace. 18-carat gold and diamonds. British, by Andrew Grima (b. 1921). 1968. Diam. 20.3 cm; L. (front) 10.2 cm. Private Collection (Japan).
Born in Italy but brought up in Britain, Grima entered his father-in-law's small jewellery business after World War II – an enterprise he proceeded to develop with enormous flair and success. In 1966, he opened his beautifully designed shop in Jermyn Street, London, which has been a mecca for all those in search of unusual gem-set jewellery for many years now. In the same year, Grima was awarded the Duke of Edinburgh's Prize for Elegant Design and the Queen's Award for Industry.

Totally natural forms like twigs and leaves became a favourite and characteristic element of inspiration in Andrew Grima's design in the 1960s. The necklace was made to Grima's design in his workshop by Fritz Maierhofer (see Pl. 167), a superlative craftsman from Vienna. It took 185 hours to make and consists of an intricate network of gold twigs, with 876 pavé-set diamonds. (Later, before it was sold in Japan in 1973, Grima added an additional 43 marquise emeralds [not illustrated], scattered over the necklace.)

128 Ring. Steel, gold and silver. British, by Malcolm Appleby (b. 1946). 1966/67. 3 cm × 4 cm. The artist's collection.
The shank and bezel of this ring unite to form a hawk's head, its features outlined in silver and gold inlay on the overall shape, which is made of steel. Designed and made by Malcolm Appleby, it demonstrates his highly individual talent as well as his superb skill as an engraver. Appleby lives in a disused rural railway station located in northern Scotland, where he is close to nature, which inspires his designs.

Among the farmers and local gentry, for whom he makes jewellery from old iron, gunmetal, gold and silver, Appleby has an appreciative following; but he has also been commissioned by members of the Royal family, as well as by the Worshipful Company of Goldsmiths and by the Victoria and Albert Museum. Both institutions have examples of his work in their collections.

129 Pendant. Gold. Italian, by Arnaldo Pomodoro (b. 1926). 1966/68. L. 17.5 cm. Schmuckmuseum, Pforzheim (1970/35).
A clear progression from the sculptured, random shapes of Arnaldo Pomodoro's earlier designs (see Pl. 102), the form of this pendant owes its inspiration more to mechanical devices and their components. The central feature is a yellow-gold cylinder, banded with sections of various textures and with extrusions, some of them in white gold. It hangs from a plain white-gold cylinder, which is in turn suspended from a round yellow-gold section, flanked on either side by two white-gold discs to which the chain is connected. A second, plain white-gold cylinder hangs from the lower end and has protruding yellow wire rods. The links of the chain are made of gold rods, 2 centimetres long.

130 Brooch. 18-carat gold, sapphires and fire opal. West German, by Elisabeth Treskow (b. 1898). 1967. 4.5 cm x 4.5 cm. Overstolzengesellschaft, on permanent loan to the Kunstgewerbemuseum, Cologne (Ov. 20).
Made forty years after she rediscovered the secret of granulation together with Wilm and Rosenberg, this brooch by Treskow demonstrates clearly her brilliant mastery of the art. The concave rounded shape of the brooch is divided by wavy lines into fields of graduated granulation, set at intervals with cabochon sapphires of various sizes; there is a large fire opal towards the centre, which serves as a focal point.

131 Earrings. Gold, onyx and diamonds. British, by Cartier, London. Ca. 1965. L. 7 cm. John Jesse/Irina Lasky Gallery, London.
In a dramatic and beautifully uncluttered design, these hoop-shaped earrings are set with rectangular black onyx that alternates with rows composed of three pavé-set diamonds; the hoop shapes are formed of gold semicircles.

This design is unusual and does not belong to a particular trend in the period; but its restrained, disciplined lines and geometric composition echo the earlier styles of Art Deco. The execution, consistent with Cartier's reputation, is impeccable.

122/123 Brooch (Two Versions). White gold, diamonds, emeralds and sapphires. West German, by Friedrich Becker (b. 1922). 1965. (Each section) 2.2 cm. Private Collection.

124 Ear Ornaments. 14-carat gold, emeralds and lapis lazuli. Norwegian, by Grete Prytz-Kittelsen (b. 1917). 1966. H. 6 cm. Private Collection.

125 Two Brooches. Silver, gold, moonstone, ▷ opal, emerald and enamel. West German, by Hermann Jünger (b. 1928). 1965. W. 4.8 cm. Private Collection.

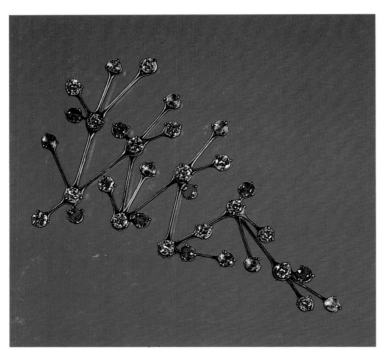

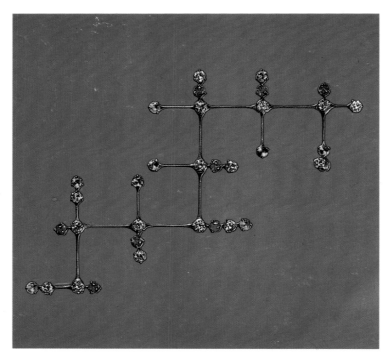

2 Broschen 1965

Silber
Gold
Email
Mondstein
Smaragde
Opal

126 Bracelet. 18-carat gold, tourmalines and diamonds. British, by David Thomas (b. 1938). 1967. L. 17.5 cm, W. 2.4 cm. The Worshipful Company of Goldsmiths, London.

127 Necklace. 18-carat gold and diamonds. British, by Andrew Grima (b. 1921). 1968. Diam. 20.3 cm; L. (front) 10.2 cm. Private Collection (Japan).

128 Ring. Steel, gold and silver. British, by Malcolm Appleby (b. 1946). 1966/67. 3 cm × 4 cm. The artist's collection.

129 Pendant. Gold. Italian, by Arnaldo Pomodoro (b. 1926). 1966/68. L. 17.5 cm. Schmuckmuseum, Pforzheim (1970/35).

130 Brooch. 18-carat gold, sapphires and fire opal. West German, by Elisabeth Treskow (b. 1898). 1967. 4.5 cm × 4.5 cm. Overstolzengesellschaft, on permanent loan to the Kunstgewerbemuseum, Cologne (Ov. 20).

131 Earrings. Gold, onyx and diamonds. British, by Cartier, London. Ca. 1965. L. 7 cm. John Jesse/Irina Lasky Gallery, London.

132 Ring, Bracelet and Comb. Aluminium. Vietnamese and Laotian, by unknown makers. Ca. 1968. (Ring) 2.2 cm × 2.1 cm; L. (bracelet) 20.5 cm; L. (comb) 15 cm. Private Collection.

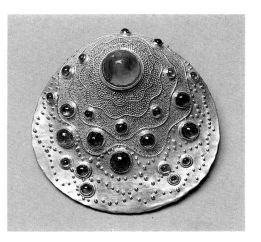

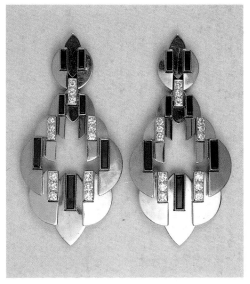

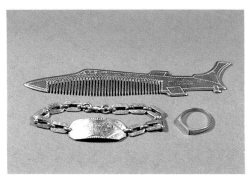

132 Ring, Bracelet and Comb. Aluminium. Vietnamese and Laotian, by unknown makers. Ca. 1968. (Ring) 2.2 cm × 2.1 cm; L. (bracelet) 20.5 cm; (comb) 15 cm. Private Collection.

Even in situations of great stress and privation, jewellery plays a part in people's lives that cannot be ignored. Although the prolonged period of war in South-East Asia brought untold misery and destruction to the population in these countries, yet they found time to make small ornamental objects and jewellery from the fragments of metal around them.

The comb is hand-engraved with zigzag lines, using primitive methods and hand-tools; its teeth were cut out with a fret-saw. The signet ring is hand-cut from tubing and filed to shape; the top of the bezel is stamped with the letters: F.L.N.S.V.M., the initials in French of the National Liberation Front Movement of Vietnam. The bracelet was made in Laos; it is also hand-forged and engraved. On the reverse of the centre section is stamped: FRONT PATRIO-TIQUE LAO, 1970 ('patriotic front, Laos, 1970').

133 Torque. Brass. Austrian, by Manfred Nisslmüller (b. 1940). 1969. L. 13.5 cm. The artist's collection.

A trained and fully qualified goldsmith who won a De Beers' Diamond International Award in 1969, Manfred Nisslmüller works to a strict formal discipline. His designs are governed by his declared principle: the true function of jewellery is to disturb the appearance or to alter its outline. Utmost economy should govern its final form.

This neckpiece made from gold-plated brass, demonstrates Nisslmüller's point perfectly: the bold, hard curve of the torque consists of a wide band folded back at the ends – once on the right, a double fold on the left. The asymmetric form of the torque provides a dramatic contrast to the softer contours of the wearer's neck and the texture of the skin.

134 Pendant. Gold and pyrite. Finnish, by Bertel Gardberg (b. 1916). 1969. H. 5 cm. Private Collection.

Of classic simplicity in the 'Scandinavian' style, this pendant features a large, cushion-shaped pyrite. Its metallic lustre is set off by the gold-wire frame: three bands radiating downwards over the stone, connected at the lower end by a curved section that forms a loop on each side at the outer edge. The pendant is suspended by two links from a rigid, gold-wire neckband.

Bertel Gardberg trained in Finland and Denmark; his designs won him an international reputation and many awards from the early 1950s. He has designed jewellery for Georg Jensen, was a designer for Galeries Lafayette in Paris (1953-54) and spent several years in Ireland, first as Design Director for Kilkenny Workshops and later for Rionore in Dublin.

135 Wrist-Watch. Stainless steel. Danish, designed by Torun Bülow-Hübe (b. 1927), for Georg Jensen. 1969. Diam. (face) 3 cm. Production design no. 327, for Georg Jensen, Copenhagen.

Stainless steel was becoming respectable in the 1960s, good enough even for jewellery. Its surfaces could be given the matt 'satin' finish, which was becoming very popular, with the added advantage that it would not wear off as easily as on the softer precious metals. The hardness of steel also makes stainless steel an eminently suitable material for wrist-watches, which need to be securely fastened since they are exposed to much wear and tear.

This stunning and ultra-simple design by Torun for Jensen has a totally plain dial. A rigid narrow strip on either side of the broad, satin-finished edge of the casing slots onto the bracelet.

136 Bracelet. 20-carat yellow and 18-carat white gold. Italian, by Bruno Martinazzi (b. 1923). 1969. H. 6.5 cm. Private Collection.

Martinazzi is an artist of deep commitment and concern: his design concepts are dictated by his research into the human condition and interpersonal relationships and by his own emotional and intellectual responses to the events of our time. In the late 1960s, he sought to express such concepts by representing parts of the human body: the mouth (a symbol of waste and greed in a society that eventually devours itself), the fist (encounters between forces, not necessarily violent ones). Next he chose the hand (creative, an instrument of knowledge and invention, meant to establish a relationship with others). The last concept – the contact between one person and another – is symbolized by this bracelet, entitled 'Goldfinger'. The five fingers that firmly grip the wearer's wrist are hollow, formed in yellow gold by the *repoussé* technique, and joined together at the back by a white gold band.

137 'Demi-Crown'. 24-carat gold, iridium platinum, enamel, diamonds, emeralds. British, by Louis Osman (b. 1914). 1969. Diam. 17.5 cm, H. 20 cm. Her Majesty Queen Elizabeth II.

Probably the only piece of royal regalia made in this century in an entirely contemporary design, this crown was commissioned by the Worshipful Company of Goldsmiths from Louis Osman and presented as their gift to Her Majesty Queen Elizabeth II on the occasion of the investiture of H.R.H. Prince Charles as Prince of Wales in 1969.

By tradition, the single-arch form (demi-crown) is appropriate for a Prince Paramount in his principality of Wales; this 'demi-crown' is the first of its kind to be designed and made since the fourteenth century. The body was electroformed from a wax original and is the largest piece ever to be made in gold by this method. The four *crosses patées* (representing protection) and the four fleurs-de-lis (for purity) were forged from a nugget of Welsh gold. Reinforced with iridium platinum and high-lighted by seventy-five tiny, square-cut diamonds, the symbols are attached to the crown with emerald (green for Wales) 'nails'. The gold content of the 'demi-crown' is 45 ounces. The crown is worn over a separate Cap of Estate made of hand-woven purple velvet, trimmed with ermine.

138 'Demi-Crown': detail of the orb in Pl. 137. Gold, platinum, diamonds and enamel. British, by Louis Osman (b. 1914). 1969. Diam. (orb) 3.2 cm. Her Majesty Queen Elizabeth II.

The single arch of the 'demi-crown' is surmounted by a 'pomum' (for original sin): a type of orb, with a cross above it, symbolic of good triumphant over evil. The orb is engraved with a free interpretation of heraldic references to the Prince of Wales: The Lion (England), Llywelyn ap Gruffydd (Rothsay), the Unicorn (Scotland, Rothsay and the Goldsmiths' Company), the Red Dragon (Wales), the Harp (Ireland), the feathers of the Prince of Wales, the Black Prince's Feathers, the fifteen bezants (a type of coin) of Cornwall and the three garbs (wheat-sheaves) of Chester. Also heraldic are the mottoes issuing from the mouths of the beasts: Y DDRAIG GOCH DDRYRY CYCHWYN, HONI SOIT QUI MAL Y PENSE and ICH DIEN.

The orb is ringed horizontally by a circle of platinum enamelled blue, set with seven diamonds on each side to represent the Seven Gifts of God and the Seven Deadly Sins respectively. The vertical arch atop the circle carrying the cross is set with thirteen diamonds in the pattern of the constellation Scorpio, for Prince Charles's birth date.

The enamelling was carried out by the artist's wife, Dilys Osman, and the engraving is by Malcolm Appleby (see also Pl. 128).

133 Torque. Brass. Austrian, by Manfred Nisslmüller (b. 1940). 1969. L. 13.5 cm. The artist's collection.

134 Pendant. Gold and pyrite. Finnish, by Bertel Gardberg (b. 1916). 1969. H. 5 cm. Private Collection.

135 Wrist-Watch. Stainless steel. Danish, designed by Torun Bülow-Hübe (b. 1927), for Georg Jensen. 1969. Diam. (face) 3 cm. Production Design No. 327, for Georg Jensen, Copenhagen.

136 Bracelet. 20-carat yellow and 18-carat white gold. Italian, by Bruno Martinazzi (b. 1923). 1969. H. 6.5 cm. Private Collection.

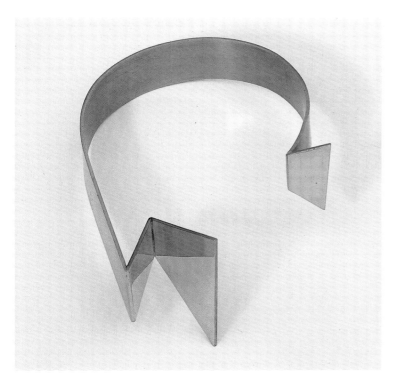

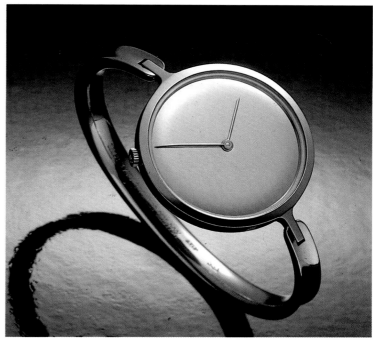

137 'Demi-Crown'. 24-carat gold, iridium platinum, enamel, diamonds, emeralds. British, by Louis Osman (b. 1914). 1969. Diam. 17.5 cm, H. 20 cm. Her Majesty Queen Elizabeth II.

138 'Demi-Crown': detail of the orb in Pl. 137. Gold, platinum, diamonds and enamel. British, by Louis Osman (b. 1914). 1969. Diam. (orb) 3.2 cm. Her Majesty Queen Elizabeth II.

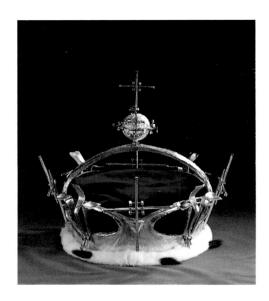

139 Bracelet. 18-carat gold, topaz, garnets and smoky quartz. Finnish, by Börje Rajalin (b. 1933). 1970. Diam. 6 cm. Museum of Applied Arts, Helsinki.

140 Four Brooches. Acrylic and 18-carat white gold. Dutch, by Robert Smit (b. 1941). 1970. W. 8 cm and 7 cm. Private Collection.

139 Bracelet. 18-carat gold, topaz, garnets and smoky quartz. Finnish, by Börje Rajalin (b. 1933). 1970. Diam. 6 cm. Museum of Applied Arts, Helsinki.

This openwork bracelet is entirely constructed of mounts joined together and set with variously sized and coloured semi-precious stones. The fifty-four stones that make up the bracelet are all indigenous to Finland, and the gold was mined there as well. Known as the 'Tokyo' bracelet, it is a unique piece designed by one of Finland's best-known artist/jewellers. It was made in the workshops of Kalevala Koru Oy of Helsinki, a jewellery manufacturing firm that specializes in the reproduction of ancient Finnish designs as well as in modern jewellery designed by Rajalin.

Rajalin was chief instructor at the Institute of Applied Arts in Helsinki from 1961 to 1971 and also director of that city's Trade School for Applied Arts from 1969 to 1971. His many awards and prizes include the Lunning Prize 1963 (see Pl. 105) and three Finnish State awards.

140 Four Brooches. Acrylic and 18-carat white gold. Dutch, by Robert Smit (b. 1941). 1970. W. 8 cm and 7 cm. Private Collection.

Trained as a goldsmith at the Staatliche Kunst-und Werkschule in Pforzheim, Germany, Smit was one of the first young rebels to reject the traditional form and treatment of jewellery. He looked for, and found, new materials, new forms, a whole new and mysterious code of symbols designed to provoke the complacent into thinking and to awaken responses other than the purely materialistic.

The rectangular brooches are made from pink acrylic backed with white gold, with a white gold 'handle' protruding on one side. A pattern of tiny numbers and drilled holes has been scattered over the acrylic.

141 Brooch. Gold and diamonds. West German, by Reinhold Reiling (1922–1983). 1970. W. 7.8 cm. Schmuckmuseum, Pforzheim (1970/40).

After serving a traditional apprenticeship as a steel engraver and chaser, Reiling, a pupil of Theodor Wende (see Pl. 78), qualified as a goldsmith. His long career as one of Germany's most influential teachers began in Pforzheim in 1954. Reiling managed at all times to maintain his identity as an outstanding artist/jeweller, which earned him the respect of his students; and his own design concepts underwent a constant process of refinement and re-evaluation.

Reiling was always interested in textures and abstract forms, which he had distilled into their subtler formulations by the late 1960s. As demonstrated by this brooch, he also introduced a human element, often in the shape of a stylized profile. Four diamonds are set to the left of the head within the two fields divided by a grid of uneven lines.

142 Pendant. Electrical wire, plastic coating. Swiss, by Max Fröhlich (b. 1908). 1970. 12 cm x 12 cm. Private Collection.

This pendant, typical of the open-minded approach Max Fröhlich has always exercised, is part of a whole series of jewellery made by him in the course of his experiments with non-precious materials. Commonplace electrical wire, which comes in bright colours and is firm yet flexible, has been shaped into a square of bold proportions for this pendant by simple coiling; it is suspended by a loop from a length of wire placed around the wearer's neck.

Audacious in its time, it was an early forerunner of many later experiments (by Fröhlich and by others) into the possibilities of using plastics within the context of jewellery.

143 Brooch. Silver, gold, garnet and lacquer. Czech, by Anton Cepka (b. 1936). 1970. W. 10.6 cm. Schmuckmuseum, Pforzheim (1970/37).

Cepka won early acclaim for his creative design concepts: the Bavarian Staatspreis and a gold medal at Munich in 1964. His unique blend of forms, which stem in part from geometric configurations and technical drawings, reflects a visual and tactile experience consistent with the period in which this brooch was made.

Two square silver panels are joined together by a shorter section of curved silver sheet, drilled with rows of holes. The untreated surface of the silver squares is broken up by horizontal and diagonal lines and by half circles punctuated by rivets. A semicircular sheet of gold is riveted onto the left square, which is traversed by a bright line of red lacquer. A garnet is set onto the edge of the engraved semicircle on the right square. Suspended by wire loops from the middle of the brooch is a rectangular piece of silver painted with red lacquer; it is surmounted by a smaller silver shape with a semicircular cut-out at the top.

144 Two Rings. 18-carat gold. French, by Pol Bury (b. 1922). 1970. W. 2 cm. Private Collection.

Pol Bury is first and foremost a sculptor, concerned in his designs with basic forms – cube, triangle and sphere – their relationship to each other in conjunction with mobile elements. These sculptural concepts, adapted to jewellery by a professional craftsman, lend themselves superbly to the smaller format and to precious metals.

The ring on the left has a square gold plate as a bezel to which cross-sections of thick gold wire have been attached by tiny springs, enabling them to vibrate when the wearer's hand moves. The hollow gold spheres on the open ring on the right are attached to its wide band by the same method.

145 Watch/Bracelet. 18-carat gold and smoky quartz. British, by Andrew Grima (b. 1921). 1970. W. 4 cm. Private Collection.

Commissioned by Omega Watches of Switzerland, this watch/bracelet is one piece from a stunning collection Andrew Grima designed for their exclusive, top-price range. Making a complete break with traditional watches, Grima has incorporated all the features so characteristic of his work at that time: the gold has been given a massive look, using a heavily grained texture and thick irregular edges. The watch-face, set under a specially cut slice of smoky quartz, is sunk into the surface of the bracelet, its jagged contours echoing the shape of the watch's outer edges.

146 Bracelet. 18-carat gold, silver, tourmaline, sapphires and diamond. Austrian, by Helfried Kodré (b. 1940). 1970. Diam. 6.5 cm, H. 5.5 cm. Private Collection.

This massive bracelet is constructed of irregularly shaped plates of silver, which sometimes overlap and sometimes leave gaps in the manner of layers of broken slate. Several sections have been oxidized black, for colour contrast, and the design is accentuated by a large, irregular slice of pink and green tourmaline at the lower edge. A cluster of sapphires and a diamond have been set in gold alongside the tourmaline.

Such random shapes and jagged contours offer endless possibilities for Kodré's imaginative use of diverse materials (see Pl. 184); they evoke images of rugged landscapes and rock formations.

147 Three Rings. 18-carat white gold. Dutch, by Emmy van Leersum (1930–1984). 1970. W. 1.9 cm. Private Collection.

Emmy van Leersum was one of the first important artist/jewellers to emerge in the post-war period in Holland; she played a vital part in shaping Dutch design over the years from the mid-1960s. Van Leersum was an exceptionally gifted and perceptive artist, whose underlying design principle was the use of a perfect geometric form, varied by the most subtle deviations in contour or line.

The concept is well illustrated by these three rings, each a perfect cylinder. The smooth surface is disturbed by a diagonal ridge on the left ring; a vertical, partially split one on the centre ring and a straight vertical one on the ring to the right. Versions of these designs as bracelets also exist in heavy-gauge stainless steel.

141 **Brooch.** Gold and diamonds. West German, by Reinhold Reiling (1922–1983). 1970. W. 7.8 cm. Schmuckmuseum, Pforzheim (1970/40).

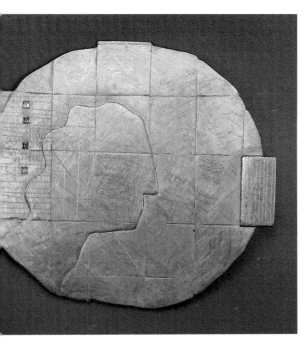

142 **Pendant.** Electrical wire, plastic coating. Swiss, by Max Fröhlich (b. 1908). 1970. 12 cm × 12 cm. Private Collection.

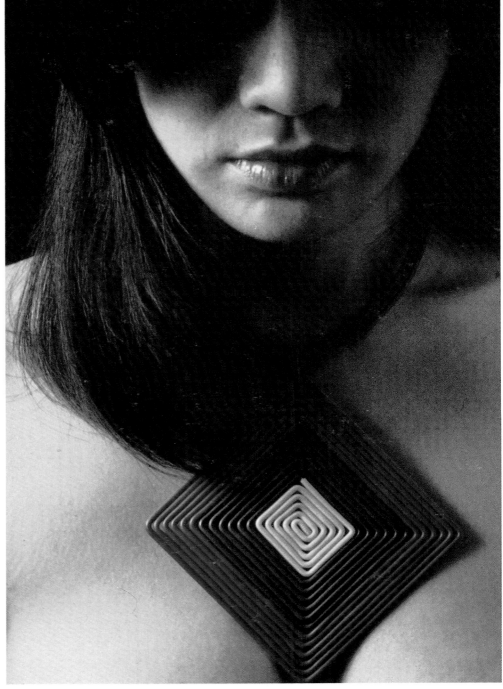

143 **Brooch.** Silver, gold, garnet and lacquer.
Czech, by Anton Cepka (b. 1936). 1970.
W. 10.6 cm. Schmuckmuseum, Pforzheim
(1970/37).

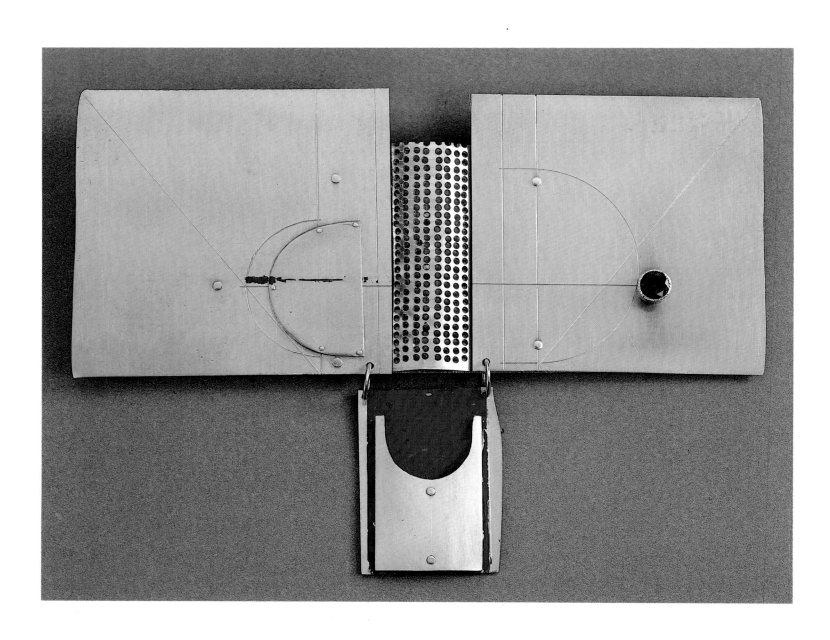

144 Two Rings. 18-carat gold. French, by Pol Bury (b. 1922). 1970. W. 2 cm. Private Collection.

145 Watch/Bracelet. 18-carat gold and smoky quartz. British, by Andrew Grima (b. 1921). 1970. W. 4 cm. Private Collection.

146 Bracelet. 18-carat gold, silver, tourmaline, sapphires and diamond. Austrian, by Helfried Kodré (b. 1940). 1970. Diam. 6.5 cm, H. 5.5 cm. Private Collection.

147 Three Rings. 18-carat white gold. Dutch, by Emmy van Leersum (1930–1984). 1970. W. 1.9 cm. Private Collection.

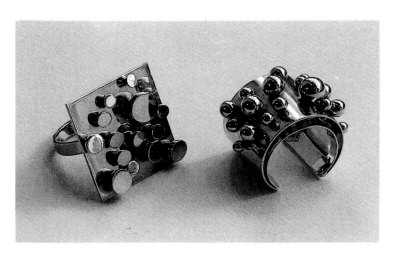

IV 1970–1984

With the arrival of the 1970s, the jewellery scene became truly international, with interconnecting links that proved to be of vital importance to the emergence of new talent in different countries and continents. By now, interest in the crafts as such, and in jewellery in particular, had grown to such an extent that governments began to fund special bodies which would administer grants to individuals, organize workshops and exhibitions and, in some instances, meetings and conferences all over the world.

Internationalism

The World Craft Council, based in the United States, has held its conferences in places as far apart as Mexico and Japan; they include lectures by invited artists, programmes for discussion, museum visits and study trips.

The Society of North American Goldsmiths (SNAG), the Crafts Council of Great Britain, the Handwerkskammer of Bavaria, Germany, have all been active in mounting exhibitions at home and abroad. With the Pforzheim Schmuckmuseum in the forefront, other museums like the Stedelijk Museum in Amsterdam, the National Gallery of Victoria, Australia, the Museum of Modern Art in New York, the Musée des Arts Décoratifs in Paris and the Kunstgewerbemuseum in Vienna have enlarged their permanent collections and continue to hold special shows of contemporary jewellery.

In Japan, the Japan Jewellery Designers' Association celebrated its twenty-eighth anniversary with two exhibitions, one at the Tokyo Central Museum and the other at the Nabio Gallery, Osaka, in September 1984. Since 1970, they also organize a 'Tokyo Triennale' at the Seibu Museum of Art, Tokyo, with an international jury and special awards and prizes for the best work among the several hundred exhibitors from all over the world.

A number of important exhibitions took place which helped much to encourage and promote contemporary jewellery. The town council of Nuremberg in conjunction with the Landesgewerbeanstalt Bavaria celebrated the five-hundredth anniversary of the birth of Albrecht Dürer with an exhibition entitled 'Gold + Silber, Schmuck + Gerät' ('Gold + Silver, Jewellery + Hollow Ware') in the Norrishalle, Nuremberg. It ran from March to August 1971 and showed a cross-section of jewellery and plate from Dürer's time to the present, a display that put contemporary jewellery firmly into the historical perspective. Among the one hundred and twenty exhibitors from twenty-four countries were Cepka, Torun, Ulrike Bahrs, Friedrich Becker, Hermann Jünger, Hubertus von Skal, Saara Hopea-Untracht, Björn Weckström, Braque, Robert Smit, Yasuki Hiramatsu, Bruno

Martinazzi, Lisa Kodré-Defner, Sigurd Persson and Stanley Lechtzin. A similar event was the exhibition 'Sieraad 1900–1972' ('Jewellery 1900–1972') at the Zonnehof, Amersfoort, Holland; not quite as extensive as the Nuremberg exhibition, it was organized by the Amersfoort Town Council in conjunction with the Dutch Ministry of Culture.

Exhibitions like these, and others since, helped to introduce new and often controversial jewellery to a wider public; yet it is still hard for all but a few artists in every country to make a reasonable living from the sale of their work. Like painters and sculptors, the individual artist/jewellers take years to mature to the point where they command wider public recognition. As with other artists, the only choices open to them are to supplement their income with part-time teaching or to be prepared to make more 'commercial' jewellery. Even the most courageous find it hard to accumulate sufficient capital for expensive materials. Especially in recent years, with the rise and fluctuation in the price of precious metal, only very established artists are able to use those materials in any experimental way.

Contemporary Views on the Old Argument

This circumstance has caused a whole gamut of new and cheaper materials to find their way into jewellery. With them, a passionate division in opinion has occurred amongst artist/jewellers between those working with gold and silver, and those who use base metals and other materials such as acrylics, wood, silk and paper. The Establishment has come down firmly in favour of platinum, gold, silver and precious stones, claiming that without those materials jewellery is not jewellery in the true sense of the word; the opponents of this view are convinced that the only new and meaningful jewellery of this day and age is made from non-precious or intrinsically worthless materials.

The dispute itself is not only unfortunate and painful for some, it is also confusing and quite destructive. Jewellery has always been made from all kinds of materials, frequently combinations of precious and non-precious ones; its merit or true worth has never been determined by its material content alone, though that may contribute to the monetary value. Gold and silver may have a greater chance of survival, but the Vikings and Anglo-Saxons used iron and bronze as well; the Egyptians employed coloured glass and faience and many of the great jewels of the Renaissance were embellished with enamel; thereafter the list grows endless.

Both sides of this argument are really quite untenable: the lasting property or monetary value of some material might be desirable, but it cannot be the determining factor when judging the quality of a work of art. A piece of jewellery may be intentionally designed to serve for a shorter period of time—perhaps just for one day—in order to achieve its desired effect. Surely it is valid for an artist to create jewellery that transforms the visual aspect of the wearer and thus makes him or her feel different, even for one evening? Such an experience can have a lasting effect. The crucial point is that jewellery can and does make a decisive impact on people—on the wearer and on the people with whom he or she is in contact. Quite apart from the emotional bond that may be expressed, certain shapes and forms demand a different posture from the wearer; others emphasize body movement or body form.

In 1974, the Dutch artist/jeweller Gijs Bakker made a stainless-steel plate, a semicircle with Fritz Maierhofer's profile cut out of the straight side. Worn in the middle of the face, strapped on with leather thongs at the top of the head and under the chin, this highly polished surface of metal mirrored half of the wearer's face on each side. Since no face has two identical sides, the fascinating result of this interesting experiment was to show, as it were, the two distinctly different faces of one and the same person—a revealing truth in itself perhaps.

The year before, in 1973, Gijs Bakker made a gold wire intended to be twisted tightly around the wrist to make an imprint on the skin. When the wire was taken off, the mark it left became 'invisible' jewellery. What interested Bakker here more than the jewellery itself was the effect of jewellery on the body. The exercise certainly alienated some people, since there was no tangible end-product that could be worn, but he did make his point by exhibiting the wire, presented in a silk-cushioned box, accompanied by a photograph of the imprint on the skin. The exhibit sparked off a host of discussions and thoughts on the purpose of jewellery, the experience of wearing and owning it, the moral issues of materialistic attitudes, and whether such an artistic statement on Bakker's part was valid within the realm of jewellery. He had used his awareness as an artist and his skills as a jeweller—however simply in this case—to disturb and to awaken responses not normally expected in the field.

The jewellery of Friedrich Becker, a German, moves (literally) in a different direction: accentuating the body's movements, his rings and bracelets are an extension of the techniques of mechanical construction and technology. Becker's jewellery is made of precision-turned steel or precious metals, with built-in mechanisms that allow parts of the structure to glide freely on or across the base. Every gesture of the wearer's arm or hand will alter the visual aspect of the piece, producing turning and spinning reflections on the glistening surface of the metal. Perhaps Becker's work is a personal celebration of the age of technology, making use of the machine's capacity for perfection, yet humanizing it in his own inventive ways. After seeing his jewellery, one can appreciate and view a complex piece of machinery in an entirely different light, as a magnificent piece of moving sculpture rather than as a cold, mechanical, functional necessity. That too, is one of the functions of a true artist: to open other people's eyes and mind, to teach them to see things in new ways, to enjoy and appreciate their environment.

For Claus Bury, another German, the involvement with jewellery has been a painstaking process of observations, drawings, construction of actual objects and pieces of jewellery—each carefully charted and documented through every stage. Starting with a more or less conventional training as a jeweller, he soon found himself hemmed in by the limitations of traditional materials and forms. Bury was one of the first artist/jewellers to use acrylics, often in conjunction with gold. His designs owe much to technology and the machine, but unlike Becker's, there is a certain abstraction: he incorporates forms inspired by engineering components within complex constructions of imaginary design. Although Bury already made a number of larger, purely sculptural objects at that time, he was still concerned that at least part of them could be worn as jewellery. When not being worn, such jewellery would become a part of the whole object, for instance attached within the frame of a wall-hanging together with related drawings and written explanations of how the form was arrived at and the precise details of the materials used. About as far removed as possible from the notion of jewellery depicted in glossy magazine advertising, Bury's fantastic 'machines' fire the imagination. Their shapes and colourful components seem to be juxtapositions of juke-boxes, car engines and plumbing spewing out stripy acrylic or giving us a glimpse of a mysterious, imaginary perspective that seems to lead straight into outer space. Unlike pretty baubles that never change, Bury's pieces (both the wearable ones and those for the wall) lead us constantly to new observations and angles of view: sometimes from the inside, about the piece itself; sometimes externally, when we rediscover the origin of his concepts in the surrounding environment.

Work of this kind by these artists and others like them, needed a special type of attention and environment: the kind a gallery rather than a shop could provide. In the early 1970s, a number of galleries opened to devote themselves either entirely, or at least to a large extent, to contemporary jewellery.

In London, Electrum Gallery opened in 1971, showing the work of some fifteen to twenty artist/jewellers, a small number that soon grew to more than fifty from all over the world. The gallery's declared policy was to bring contemporary jewellery into focus for a wider public, promoting unique and original work with one-person and group exhibitions, at least six or eight every year.

Elsewhere in Britain, the Arnolfini Gallery in Bristol and the Oxford Gallery in Oxford both devoted an important part of their activities to contemporary jewellery.

Other galleries opened in the United States: in New York, Sculpture to Wear and Artwear, in Philadelphia, Helen Drutt's gallery, and Concepts in Carmel, California; in Vienna, the Galerie am Graben, and Atrium in Basle. Finally, in Holland, there are Nouvelles Images in The Hague and the Galerie Ra in Amsterdam; and in Australia, the Makers' Mark Gallery in Melbourne. The clients of such galleries are as diverse as the price range of contemporary jewellery—and since its price ranges from a few pounds to several thousand, the work can attract all age and income groups.

Etiquette

By the early 1970s, the last vestiges of etiquette in clothing and jewellery had really disappeared: 'anything goes'. Although there were still social groups, it was hard to distinguish them by their jewellery. For some people, it will always be important to have very expensive, precious jewellery, but this is now a matter of personal choice (and of being able to afford it) rather than a social 'must'.

Perhaps the only jewellery being designed specifically for a 'social group' (and one that includes members of the working and middle classes at that) is punk jewellery: bicycle chains, razor blades, safety pins, reproductions of iron crosses and swastikas and the all-important studs in many different shapes, which can be riveted onto jackets, belts, armbands and caps. Part joke, part serious, they are all emblems of violence. Difficult to understand and shocking to the older generation, punk jewellery can none the less look remarkably good with the requisite hair-style, make-up and clothes. While it certainly does contain an element of threat, on a different level, it also dispels this sinister import by the facetious manner in which it is worn. However, at the same time, punk jewellery acts as a powerful reminder that we live in violent times—times in which violence is a frequent, personal experience, and in which the threat of unimaginable wholesale destruction hangs over us all like a dark cloud.

Strangely enough, the design of jewellery made under very real conditions of brutality and violence alludes to such dangers quite differently. Like the soldiers in the trenches during World War I and on battle-fields during World War II and the Korean War, people made jewellery in Vietnam and Laos throughout the 1960s and 1970s from the fragments of shot-down aircraft. Hundreds of thousands of signet rings stamped with the initials of 'National Liberation' movements were made, as were identity bracelets and combs in the shape of aircraft with engraved ornamentation. Many other items such as vases and dishes of complex pattern were also produced from the same raw materials by skilful craftsmen beating, embossing and engraving, usually by hand.

Other Original Ideas

It was not long before other and more original ideas for jewellery emerged, inspired by mundane and ordinary objects in our environment. In the early 1970s, Bernhard Schobinger, a Swiss, based a whole series of jewellery pieces on the theme of the 'throw-away society'; they included a necklace made of shampoo sachets, linked together with gold wire, and a bracelet constructed from rusty iron, like a park railing, and set with a piece of broken glass. Another of his bracelets, made of sheet gold, resembles the strip twisted off a newly opened sardine tin; it goes through the eye of the key at the end. In Britain, Tom Saddington took up a similar theme, using paper bags, tins cans and sachets, made in solid silver, and ranging in size from very tiny brooches and earrings to table-size sculptures.

In the United States, the artist/jeweller Mary Ann Scherr made very beautiful jewellery in a more practical manner; some of it incorporated features for disabled or hypersensitive people. She has specialized in designing jewellery that can hide physical defects, pendants that can monitor heart beats or that contain electronic sensors warning the wearer of toxic substances in the air as they release an oxygen mask.

New techniques have helped to develop certain kinds of jewellery that were simply not possible to create using traditional methods. Electroforming, a method similar to electroplating, is not new in itself. Invented in the mid-nineteenth century, it was used to reproduce perfect copies of three-dimensional art works in museum collections and has been used in industry for mass production. Its use for making original, 'one-of-a-kind' pieces of jewellery, however, is a new departure, practised with superb skill and effect by Stanley Lechtzin, another American artist. His application of the technique has not only resulted in beautiful work, but he has also generously shared his knowledge with many students in places as far apart as California and Israel.

The ever-inventive Arline Fisch, from San Diego, California, has adapted hand-knitting and weaving methods to metal; with them she created spectacular chokers, bracelets, brooches and belts. She knits and crochets wire of precious and non-precious metal—light-weight and flexible, yet strong and resilient—into intricate lacy patterns. A mistress of many different techniques with a great flair for design, she has played an important role in the development of contemporary jewellery in the United States. A professor at the San Diego State University and a former vice-president for North America of the World Crafts Council, Arline Fisch is currently president of the Society of North American Goldsmiths; and these are but a few of the many commitments that have taken her all over the world to exhibit, lecture, preside over workshops and participate in seminars.

The influence and inspiration of people like Arline Fisch, Claus Bury, Friedrich Becker, Hermann Jünger, Gerda Flöckinger, Wendy Ramshaw, David Watkins, Mario Pinton, Bruno Martinazzi and many more, was not lost on the new generation of aspiring artist/jewellers. Activity now spread to countries where, either little indigenous tradition of jewellery-making was present to draw on (for example, Japan and Australia), or the traditional process had been abruptly altered in its course by political events (for instance, in the Socialist countries).

Australia

By the early 1970s, the growing interest in the crafts as such had reached a level of recognition and appreciation in Australia which made the formation of a Crafts Council imperative. In 1971, the Crafts Council was founded with financial assistance from the Australian government; since then, it has consistently pursued an imaginative policy and promoted Australian crafts, on a national basis, at home and abroad. By co-ordinating the activities of different centres whose geographic location is often thousands of miles apart, organizing tours of visitors from many different countries, as well as exhibitions and teacher/ student exchanges abroad, the Crafts Council has been enormously successful in widening the horizons of Australian artist/ jewellers. It has provided them with the opportunity to unfold their own talents and given them a self-confidence that is clearly reflected in their work.

A second organization—the Crafts Board of the Australia Council—can also take credit for stimulating activities with an assistance programme for individuals and organizations that finances prestigious exhibitions, such as 'Australian Jewellery' and 'Objects to Human Scale'. With additional aid from the Department of Foreign Affairs, and selected by Dick Richards (curator of the Decorative Arts Gallery of South Australia), the 'Australian Jewellery' exhibition travelled extensively all over Europe and South-East Asia from 1982 to 1984. It demonstrated clearly the wide range, skilfulness and individuality of jewellery made by the various exhibitors, the rich potential of such progressive policies on the part of the powers that be and the growing cohesiveness of such work in terms of an Australian identity.

Firm contact with artist/jewellers elsewhere in the world has been a key factor in generating the current favourable conditions for contemporary jewellery in Australia, but it is well to remember that the ideas and stimuli fell on fertile ground. In this microcosm of different cultures (mostly European with a sprinkling of Asian, American and Aborigine), government assistance in addition to self-help succeeded in creating wider exposure for, and public understanding of, contemporary jewellery, which in turn proved a healthy catalyst for the jewellers.

Visiting artist/jewellers like Arline Fisch, Claus Bury, Wendy Ramshaw and David Watkins, David Poston, Elisabeth Holder, among others, found not only eager and receptive students but also gained inspiration and strength for themselves in the experience. Conversely, Jan and Ted Arundel, Frank Bauer, Ann Brownsworth, Rowena Gough, Rex Keogh and Dorothy Erickson, among others, made the trip to Europe, in some instances for prolonged periods of time.

Like artist/jewellers in other countries, those in Australia have lately concerned themselves with reassessing the meaning of jewellery and the demand to adapt its design and material to life in the final decade of the twentieth century.

As elsewhere, women have played an increasingly significant role in recognizing such needs, both as consumers and as creators of such jewellery. Over a period of two years (from 1982 to 1984), a group of about ten women artist/jewellers in Sydney combined their talents within a workshop to explore, in the context of their work, the theme 'the natural and human environment'. The participants included Darani Lewers, Lyn Tune, Jenny Toynbee-Wilson and Sieglinde Brennan. Made from materials taken out of the immediate environment—paper, feathers, wire, electronic components, plastics and steel—the products of the workshop experience were an exciting collection of unusual, unique and appealing jewellery. Under the title 'Worn Issues?' (and with financial assistance from the Crafts Board of the Australia Council), this collection was exhibited in Adelaide, Melbourne and Sydney, accompanied by an extensive catalogue containing full documentation on the work processes and individual statements from the participating artists. Such projects are immensely rewarding, as can be observed not only by the excellence of the work itself but also by its impact, which reaches far beyond the boundaries of Australia.

Canada

Canada has, alas, not enjoyed the same scale of development in contemporary jewellery, in spite of the fact that it has government-assisted and sponsored organizations to promote its artists, including its artist/jewellers. Perhaps its close proximity to the United States has had an intimidating effect on the artists, or perhaps the great distances within the country proved an inhibiting factor. Be that as it may, there too, interest in the crafts has grown, providing better training facilities. Visiting artists from America and Europe have succeeded in encouraging the forty or fifty Canadian artist/jewellers now working professionally. Within the last two years, a small group, mostly graduates from art schools (notably the Nova Scotia College of Art and Design) have begun to take part in international exhibitions of contemporary jewellery.

Europe

In design, the pronounced simplicity of line that characterizes the Japanese work described in the last chapter is also the keynote of the most interesting and beautiful jewellery from Italy. In complete contrast to Japan, Italy is a country where jewellery has always played an important role; it has always been recognized as an art form there. The great master painters and sculptors —Cellini, Mantegna, Verrocchio, Ghirlandaio and even Leonardo da Vinci—were all trained in, and exercised, the art of the goldsmith.

Bruno Martinazzi continues this tradition, working easily in both sculpture and jewellery without making one the diminutive format of the other. His superb sense of form has enabled him to create truly 'wearable sculpture', for example a magnificent 'goldfinger' bracelet, a piece of jewellery that is as effective when worn as it is in its own right as a table sculpture. Much of Martinazzi's jewellery during the 1970s consisted of different parts of the body—eye, mouth, finger, or buttocks—formed of 18-carat gold and made into rings, brooches or bracelets. More recent designs have included calibrated numbers and lines, like mysterious measuring devices, carved in marble or punched into silver.

Another Italian sculptor, Arnaldo Pomodoro, finds his inspiration in more technical shapes: columns, wheels or small, textured components that he casts from wax models.

Associated since mediaeval times with art and goldsmithing, Padua, in the north of Italy, is perhaps currently the most important town for Italian jewellery design. Artist/jewellers such as Giampaolo Babetto, Diego Piazza and Graziano Visintin, among others, were trained at the Istituto d'Arte 'Pietro Selvatico' and now teach a unique and special kind of jewellery design: although each artist maintains his originality within the overall concept, there are certain basic elements common to all their work, which enable us to qualify it as the 'Padua School'. The essence of this design lies in geometry—the fundamental forms of circle, triangle and square connected by straight lines. The perfection of construction and the finesse with which the matt gold is treated to bring out the sublety of the metal recall the masterly skill of the ancients. Demonstrating precision without machinery, hand-forged with superb accuracy and classically perfect in proportion, their jewellery expresses strongly the spirit of our day and age.

Whilst it obviously enjoys a certain amount of appreciation within Italy, it is nevertheless abroad, particularly in Japan and Holland, that the 'Padua School' artists have made their greatest impact. Babetto, in particular, won awards in Japan and spent several years working in Holland: the country where contemporary jewellery rose to its present renown with the work of Gijs Bakker, Robert Smit, Emmy van Leersum, Marion Herbst, Paul Derrez and Onno Boekhoudt, Lam de Wolf and Joke Brakman, among others.

Since the late 1970s and the early 1980s, the movement towards contemporary jewellery of importance, made from intrinsically cheap or worthless materials, achieved wider attention in Holland than elsewhere. Perhaps Holland's strong position as the centre of the diamond trade or the pronounced bourgeois element in the Dutch social structure were responsible for the violent Dutch reaction against traditional forms of jewellery, opulent, ornamented and materialistic in overtone. Gijs Bakker once said that, unlike his fellow students with degrees in the fine arts who were looking forward to being artists contributing to progress in culture, his years of training as a goldsmith had only made him fit to make expensive trinkets for rich elderly ladies—it seemed a poor goal for a life's work. This feeling was shared by many others and ultimately generated a drive to change the deeply entrenched attitudes of the Establishment, to shock it out of its materialism. As yet it is difficult to assess how far this has succeeded. Suffice it to say that Paul Derrez has managed to survive for some years now running Galerie Ra in Amsterdam, which is devoted exclusively to non-precious jewellery of most original and innovative design.

This movement, if it can be called that, has echoes elsewhere, for instance in Germany, Britain and the United States.

In Germany, Wilhelm Mattar owns a gallery in Cologne that specializes in this type of jewellery, which it displays in a very imaginative exhibition programme; and Marianne Schliwinski and Jürgen Eickhoff pursue a similar policy in their Galerie Spektrum in Munich.

In Britain, Aspects Gallery in London serves as the prime outlet for such work, but a major part of critical attention has centred on some of the Craft Council's touring exhibitions like 'Jewellery Redefined', held in the early 1980s. Apart from the jewellery world itself, arguments about the validity of making jewellery from non-precious materials have hardly touched a wider public in Britain. The national talent for tolerating any eccentricity makes it quite hard to shock the British Establishment to any serious extent; and the United States is even more open-minded and has always been far more ready to accept new ideas.

This trend was inevitable if we keep in mind the wider issues such as social change, the struggle for improvement and equality, and the complex difficulties of the individual in a mass-oriented environment. Throughout the twentieth century, such problems have become more universal and acute, and many people are aware of them, particularly the younger generation. Questions on the morality of materialistic attitudes, on the role of the individual in society at large, on freedom of expression, the economic climate and the political situation—all these are factors that change the role, form and material content of jewellery.

Developments in Eastern Europe

Seen in this context, the development of modern jewellery in the Socialist countries has been interesting to observe. In the Soviet Union, for instance, the advent of World War I and the Russian Revolution in 1917 had left the country in a colossal state of economic collapse, with nothing but the remains of a backward industry and an underdeveloped agriculture. The major part of the Tsar's priceless treasures and the possessions of wealthy aristocrats were confiscated by the Bolscheviks and placed in the Kremlin Museum where they can be seen by visitors to Moscow to this day. The austerity that followed the Revolution was not only necessitated by the widespread poverty but also a conscious reaction against all things bourgeois, which certainly included jewellery. Badges and military insignia were the only form of 'jewellery' produced. The state took over the refining of, and trading in precious metals and diamonds, mostly to export them in exchange for badly needed foreign goods. Throughout the period between the two World Wars, the situation in this respect remained fairly static.

It is common knowledge that World War II cost the Soviet Union more lives and economic sacrifice than any other country involved in that catastrophe. In consequence, its post-war recovery was much slower than the West's. However, by the early 1960s, with greater prosperity and a growing number of tourists visiting, mass production of inexpensive jewellery began to flourish. Made from base metal, much of it with amber from the Baltic, such jewellery was generally designed in all the traditional styles of the many different states of the U.S.S.R. and freely available from souvenir shops in hotels and airports. A tourist at that time, who asked an Intourist guide where he might be able to see and purchase modern jewellery, was shown a stamped-out, gilt maple-leaf brooch with the proud comment: 'we produced over two million of this model alone this year'. The same guide described some of the magnificent jewellery on display in a museum as 'hand-made and very crude'. As shocking as this remark may appear now, it is really not so hard to understand when the historical background is considered.

In Tsarist Russia, a country of extreme social differences, jewellery was regarded by most people as the exclusive privilege of the very rich. It is little wonder then that the new generation, born and brought up in years of extreme hardship, in a society with a completely different social structure, takes great pride in the emergence of jewellery that is available to everyone. Nor is it surprising that the designs for it were first and foremost traditional. Considerations of quality and discriminating taste can only prevail after a product becomes available. The pride in the industrial achievement, expressed by the guide above, is probably quite similar to that felt by people during the Industrial Revolution in the nineteenth century, when any machined article was considered superior to things made 'crudely' by hand.

Twenty years later—in the early 1980s—a new awareness and appreciation of unique, original work in jewellery has occurred in the Soviet Union. Because jewellery-making is considered once more an integral part of art and culture, the efforts of Soviet artist/jewellers are being recognized now. Since they live in many different parts of the Soviet Union, and almost all of them are cut off from any Western influence, it is remarkable how similar the development of contemporary jewellery has been to that in Western countries in terms of materials and design.

The only precious metal used is silver, most of the pieces are made from German silver or brass, and there is little evidence of diamonds; however, superb semi-precious stones are used, for the Soviet Union is also a rich source of them.

The most contemporary and exciting designs for jewellery come from Tallinn, capital of the Estonian Soviet Socialist Republic, where there is also an excellent art college that specializes in training jewellers. Individual artist/jewellers belong to the Artists' Union in the U.S.S.R. and work free lance in their own studios and workshops. The Union promotes their work by holding exhibitions all over the country and publishing catalogues and books with extensive information on the artists and their work as well as full-colour illustrations.

In other Socialist countries—Czechoslovakia, Hungary, Poland and the German Democratic Republic—the break with conventional jewellery was equally drastic if not quite as prolonged.

Czechoslovakia has always had a large jewellery industry with its centre in Jablonec, though not quite on the same scale as before World War II. While Czech artist/jewellers are also restricted in their use of precious materials, they continue to create individual jewellery of interesting design and good quality.

In Hungary, all 'precious' jewellery is made in state-owned workshops attached to the Mint, but young designers and artists are making exciting pieces from stainless steel, silver and acrylics. They have their own studios from which they can sell their work, or they offer it at state-run galleries for the crafts; an organization called Artex promotes their work at home and abroad in an imaginative way with exhibitions and publicity.

Artist/jewellers in the German Democratic Republic are fully recognized and accepted members of the Artists' Union, which includes all branches of the fine arts, arts and crafts as well as designers and graphic artists. An enormous amount of state aid is available to them in the form of individual grants, commissions, credit facilities to set up studios and workshops, to organize exhibitions, seminars and symposia. Museums in the German Democratic Republic are encouraged to enlarge their collections of contemporary jewellery, and there are a number of state-run galleries all over the country where the work of artist/jewellers is displayed and sold as a free service to artists. All members of the Artists' Union are eligible for election to the various administrative posts that distribute the resources allocated to them by the state on a five-year basis. This includes their own department for the supply of raw materials, wherein the state subsidizes the prices, since such materials are mostly imported and would otherwise be subject to constant fluctuations due to the varying prices abroad.

The result of this generous policy has been very interesting. Of course it has brought its own problems with it; but whatever these may be, the policy itself was obviously born out of a pronounced need on the part of both makers and consumers for a new kind of jewellery that reflected their personal life styles and expressed new, current values. Such encouragement on so many different levels has drawn lively young minds to the jewellers' ranks, who feel free to exercise their creative urges and who find contemporary jewellery an area where there is lots of room for making a contribution welcomed by a receptive public.

France: A Special Case

In France, the country that had reigned supreme in terms of jewellery for centuries and whose standards were always regarded as the pinnacle to which others aspired, the development of contemporary jewellery appears in complete contrast. It was in France that the finest, most sophisticated designs and techniques developed, that the best tools were made and, even to this day, many technical terms employed in the workshop and in the trade outside France are still in French.

France's artist/jewellers face problems not experienced by those in other countries. To begin with, there are few training facilities available outside the conventional apprenticeship structure. Traditional types of high-quality, gem-set jewellery are still being produced in France, but the purchase and use of precious metals are strictly controlled by a complex set of bureaucratic rules and regulations.

Nevertheless, to overcome such inhibiting factors, in 1982 a small group of creative artist/jewellers formed themselves into the Association française des Créateurs de Bijoux, known under the name of 'Hephaïstos'. Founded by Francine Sixou, Goudji, Catherine Noll, Bonny Anderson and Roland Schad, it now has some thirty-two members who work quite individually in many different regions of France. What brought them together was a common feeling that ordinary commercial jewellery production and its marketing are too conventional and narrow in approach. These artists are convinced that they have more to offer than can be adequately catered for within the confines of the traditional jewellery industry: a look at their work will bear this out. It ranges in style from pieces clearly inspired by the past and with ethnic roots to designs of emotive, tactile portent and strictly formal, almost geometric constructions. They are succeeding in breaking new ground despite the hindrance of lack of official support. Solely through their own efforts they have organized a number of exhibitions at home and abroad, which have earned them public recognition and, finally, even some government help.

The 1980s

By the late 1970s and early 1980s, significant changes in the design of jewellery began to be noticeable. Much experimentation with metal alloys of different composition and with laminating took place in many parts of the world in an effort to obtain more colours in metal with which artists could achieve interesting patterns. The 'German School' in particular made much use of the exciting possibilities and variations offered by these methods; some beautiful examples are Reinhold Reiling's necklace/pendant in 1977, and Hermann Schafran's brooch in 1980. Elsewhere too, combinations of precious and non-precious metals became popular, in preference to using stones of any kind, which often had to be the determining factor for the overall shape of the design. Many materials new to jewellery made their appearance—titanium, niobium and tantalum for their refractory properties (they can be anodized into rainbow colours), strands of dyed nylon and also silk, paper and cloth.

Jewellery is perhaps the only art medium within which women artists equal men in numbers, and their work can be judged and evaluated on the same terms as jewellery made by men. Now women are playing an important part in every aspect of the jewellery profession: retailing and manufacturing, designing for industry or working independently in their own studios. Quite a few of the more important galleries now dealing in contemporary jewellery were founded and are run by women.

Wonderful new shapes and patterns dominate the 1980s' look in jewellery—it is sufficient to cast a glance at the work of Caroline Broadhead, Lam de Wolf, Rowena Gough, Annie Holdsworth, Ivy Ross, Kai Chan, Antoinette Ricklin-Schelbert and many others illustrated hereafter to be enthralled by the infinite variety and the imaginative colours. As always, much of the inspiration was sparked by things in our everyday environment, then extended and built upon with fantasy into manifestations of an imagery that, in the case of jewellery, is tactile and tangible.

No one knows what the future has in store, but it is certainly bound to bring changes. In one form or another, jewellery will always remain a part of our personal environment, and changing circumstances and life styles will continue to provide the impetus for fertile and inventive minds to create the kind of jewellery that expresses the very essence of its time.

148 **Ring.** Gold, enamel and mother-of-pearl. ▷
Austrian, by Ulrike Zehetbauer (b. 1934). 1971.
L. 5.8 cm, W. 2.5 cm. The artist's collection.

148 Ring. Gold, enamel and mother-of-pearl. Austrian, by Ulrike Zehetbauer (b. 1934). 1971. L. 5.8 cm, W. 2.5 cm. The artist's collection.

The unusual form and structure of the design demonstrate very clearly how far individual artist/jewellers had removed themselves from traditional concepts by the early 1970s. With a vague reference to the paintings of Gustav Klimt, a bold and elegant sweep of curved gold sheet has been mounted to overlap the almost circular bezel of the ring, enamelled in pale blue. An irregular pattern of lines and squares in reddish-brown and black enamel adds interest to the gold surface, as do tiny squares and rectangles of mother-of-pearl in gold settings.

Ulrike Zehetbauer was a student of Franz Rickert at the Akademie der bildenden Künste, Munich. She opened her own studio/workshop in Vienna in 1958.

149 Pendant. 18-carat gold. French, by Max Ernst (1891–1976). 1971. Diam. 9.8 cm. Erica Brausen Collection .

Although predominantly a painter, Max Ernst, like many other famous artists (see Pls 100, 116, 158), made brief excursions into the field of jewellery. Throughout his life, Ernst was interested in many different disciplines and techniques of the fine arts. The design of this pendant, with its images of human figures and a bird achieved by casting, is characteristic of his *frottage* drawings (a method of rubbing textures through paper or onto paint).

150 Hair Ornament. Silver and resin. British, by Susanna Heron (b. 1949). 1971. H. 6 cm, L. 10 cm. The artist's collection.

Trained at the Central School of Art and Design, London, Susanna Heron developed her unique and original style within a short time of leaving college.

Here the multi-coloured resin has been poured into a silver frame, the surface of which is polished level with the edges. A smaller, plain silver disc has been mounted above on the silver grip fastening. Simple overall forms and subtle blends of coloured resins were the keynotes of Heron's jewellery at that time. Later variations using the same technique included more figurative elements, mainly birds in flight.

151 Necklace. Alloy of brass, nickel and gold with glass. Czech, by Svatopluk Kasalý (b. 1944). 1971. L. 42 cm. The artist's collection.

Excited by the immense possibilities of glass in various forms applied to jewellery, Kasalý has spent many years refining and crystallizing his concepts. This necklace was begun in 1971 but it took him twelve years, until 1983, to bring it to completion so that it satisfied his own criteria.

The shape and overall size alone are dramatic by any standards. The basic components are deceptively simple—a long forged strip of metal with a disc of glass at either end. Intended to be adjustable as the wearer desires, it is a great credit to Kasalý's craftsmanship to have discovered a secure, yet invisible means of attaching the glass to the metal and to have used an alloy that is flexible yet stays rigid when bent into shape. The necklace can be worn either curled around the neck, with the smaller disc jutting out close to the neck and the larger one resting low on the chest; or the metal strip can be bent in the centre, placing both discs at the same height in the front.

152 Ring-Set. 9-carat gold, enamel, acrylic, dyed cornelians, amethyst. British, by Wendy Ramshaw (b. 1939). 1971. L. 12 cm, W. 3 cm. The Worshipful Company of Goldsmiths, London.

An artist/jeweller whose work has made an important contribution to the development of contemporary jewellery, Wendy Ramshaw gained early recognition for her innovative design by being the first jeweller to win the Council of Industrial Design Award in 1972.

Ramshaw is perhaps best known for her stunning ring-sets. This early example consists of a group of five rings to be worn on one hand plus one to be worn on the other; they are shown mounted on a specially turned acrylic stand. The rings are set with circular and cabochon cornelians, dyed in different shades of green and blue, with one band of matching enamel stripes inlaid into the gold. Ramshaw's ring-sets have a special acrylic or nickel stand, which turns the set into a sculptural object when the rings are not being worn.

153 Necklace. 18-carat gold, opals, tourmaline, quartz, moonstones, pearls, Persian turquoise engraved with gold. British, by Gerda Flöckinger (b. 1927). 1971. L. 152.5 cm. Private Collection (U.S.A.).

A superb example of the artistry of Gerda Flöckinger is this delicate, sensitive structuring of gold links (each one individually formed), scattered with semi-precious stones and interspaced with baroque pearls. Flöckinger achieves these textured gold surfaces by carefully controlled fusion of gold, a technique she has developed and refined over many years, creating a style which is entirely her own.

Born in Austria, Gerda Flöckinger came to Britain in 1938 as a refugee; there she studied fine art and jewellery. She was one of the first in the early 1960s to see the potential of jewellery as an art form and created the course for modern jewellery at Hornsey College of Art, London, where she taught from 1962 to 1968.

154 Brooch. 18-carat gold, ivory, steel and plastic. West German, by Norbert Muerrle (b. 1948). 1972. W. 7 cm. G. Krauss Collection.

An accomplished draughtsman and painter, Norbert Muerrle is also a fully qualified goldsmith and probably one of Europe's best diamond-setters. A perfectionist as a craftsman, he has a remarkable talent and wit for design as this early piece of his work clearly demonstrates. Against a back-drop of precious metal (gold), a plastic cow (cut in half) has been set at the centre. Neat rows of steel staples have been clipped like fencing to the edges of the brooch on either side. Muerrle's design is incisive and explicit–characteristics he retained in his later work in more abstract forms.

155 Bracelet. Fine silver and 18-carat gold. West German, by Peter Hassenpflug (b. 1932). 1973. Diam. (inside) 6 cm. Private Collection. Half bangle, half bracelet, this unusual design in silver by Peter Hassenpflug consists of a rigid, hollow section connected to seven links that overlap like giant scales and are topped by circles in yellow gold.

Hassenpflug has also designed superb jewellery for the jewellery industry, particularly in platinum. Together with his wife, Marie Hassenpflug, he is the founder and director of the Orfèvre Gallery, Düsseldorf, which has been a leading centre for the exhibition and distribution of contemporary jewellery.

156 Ring. 18-carat gold, moonstone and ruby. Austrian, by Elisabeth Kodré-Defner (b. 1937). 1973. W. 6.5 cm, H. 2.5 cm. The artist's collection.

Elisabeth Kodré-Defner is an artist/jeweller of exceptional quality and imagination; her inspiration is the delicate structure and texture of nature itself, manifest in tiny shells, insects and small plants. Unlike the exponents of Art Nouveau, who sought to idealize and improve on nature, Kodré-Defner pays homage to nature's perfection by casting the natural forms directly and reassembling than within her own composition. This dramatic ring was cast from leaves; they now surround a cabochon moonstone. A ruby has been set on the left.

157 Brooch. 18-carat yellow and white gold. West German, by Claus Bury (b. 1946). 1973. W. 7.3 cm, H. 6.9 cm. Private Collection.

This brooch, by one of the undisputed leaders of the revolt against conventional jewellery in the early 1970s, illustrates vividly the extent of this rebellion. Apart from its function as a brooch and the gold from which it is made, the design owes absolutely nothing to tradition.

Using unpolished white gold that is almost black for the stripes and dotted lines, Bury has created a fantasy composition inspired by machinery and providing a fascinating perspective. Partly flat, but appearing three-dimensional, the form has been cleverly constructed on different levels that protrude over the flat sections.

149 Pendant. 18-carat gold. French, by Max Ernst (1891–1976). 1971. Diam. 9.8 cm. Erica Brausen Collection.

150 Hair Ornament. Silver and resin. British, by Susanna Heron (b. 1949). 1971. H. 6 cm, L. 10 cm. The artist's collection.

151 Necklace. Alloy of brass, nickel and gold with glass. Czech, by Svatopluk Kasalý (b. 1944). 1971. L. 42 cm. The artist's collection.

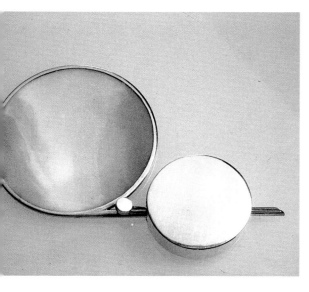

152 **Ring-Set.** 9-carat gold, enamel, acrylic, dyed cornelians, amethyst. British, by Wendy Ramshaw (b. 1939). 1971. L. 12 cm, W. 3 cm. The Worshipful Company of Goldsmiths, London.

153 **Necklace.** 18-carat gold, opals, tourmaline, quartz, moonstones, pearls, Persian turquoise engraved with gold. British, by Gerda Flöckinger (b. 1927). 1971. L. 152.5 cm. Private Collection (U.S.A).

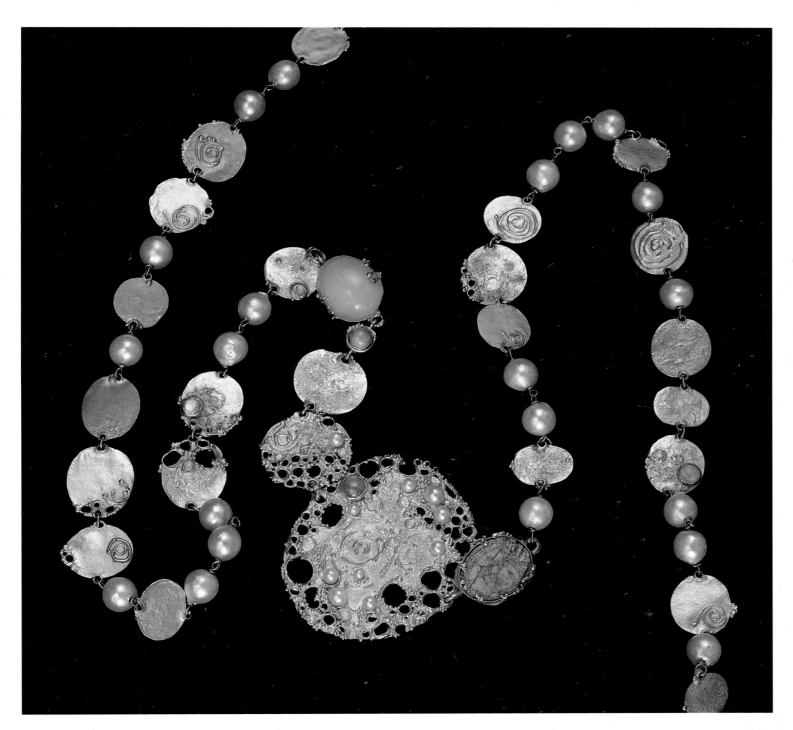

154 Brooch. 18-carat gold, ivory, steel and plastic. West German, by Norbert Muerrle (b. 1948). 1972. W. 7 cm. G. Krauss Collection.

155 Bracelet. Fine silver and 18-carat gold. West German, by Peter Hassenpflug (b. 1932). 1973. Diam. (inside) 6 cm. Private Collection.

156 Ring. 18-carat gold, moonstone and ruby. Austrian, by Elisabeth Kodré-Defner (b. 1937). 1973. W. 6.5 cm, H. 2.5 cm. The artist's collection.

157 Brooch. 18-carat yellow and white gold. West German, by Claus Bury (b. 1946). 1973. W. 7.3 cm, H. 6.9 cm. Private Collection.

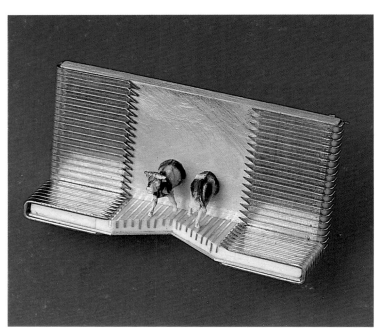

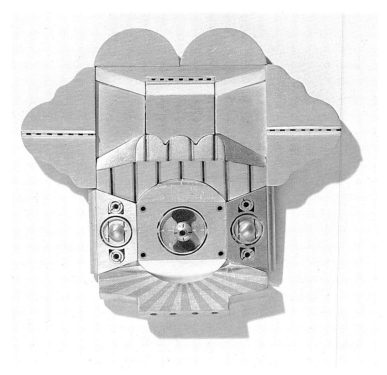

158 Brooch. Fine gold. French, by Pablo Picasso (1881–1973). 1973. W. 12.2 cm, H. 8.4 cm. Erica Brausen Collection.

Picasso's artistic genius knew how to breathe life into any material, as well as how to intrigue an audience. A friendly lion's head, or perhaps a smiling sun, this face surrounded by swirling edges bears the master's touch. Cast in fine gold, it was made in a limited edition of twenty in the year of Picasso's death.

159 Necklace. 18-carat gold, fresh-water pearls and a diamond. Swedish, by Sigurd Persson (b. 1914). 1973. L. 21 cm. Ulla Erikson Collection, Stockholm.

This necklace of classic Scandinavian design is made of forged gold; the neckband forms a V in the front from which the pendant is suspended. Three pearls are set along the vertical section on opposing sides; it ends in a curl that holds a gold ball, set with a single diamond.

An outstanding artist/jeweller and goldsmith, Sigurd Persson enjoys a well-deserved international reputation. He was trained by his father in the traditional techniques by making copies of Swedish folk-craft jewellery; later he studied in Munich with Franz Rickert. His superb designs for unique pieces as well as those he created for Georg Jensen have been of enormous importance in maintaining the high standing of Scandinavian design.

160 Necklace/Portable Cardiograph. Gold, silver and moonstones. U.S.A., by Mary Ann Scherr. 1973. L. 38.1 cm. Private Collection.

Mary Ann Scherr's talent is a unique blend of originality in design and practical applications of the most unusual kind. A woman of exceptional flair and drive, she has designed distinctive, one-of-a-kind jewellery and prototypes for multiple production.

This multiple-string necklace, composed of silver and gold beads, is joined by a cross-section that incorporates a portable electrocardiograph. Electrodes within monitor the wearer's heart, activating a liquid, crystal-colour display of the heart beat. With great ingenuity Scherr has made the functional object a part of the overall design. She has in fact designed a whole range of special jewellery, necklaces, belts and bracelets, with hidden sensors, warning of air pollution, incorrect posture, or simply with a buzz, indicating that the wearer has fallen accidentally asleep.

161 Bracelet. Silver and 18-carat gold. Italian, by Bruno Martinazzi (b. 1923). 1973. W. 5.1 cm. Private Collection.

By the early 1970s, Martinazzi's explorations into the symbolism of various parts of the body (see Pl. 136) had extended to include the symbols made by man—for instance measurement, representing the means by which man attempts to understand the universe of which he is a part. This bracelet is a wide band of silver, scored and notched with carefully distanced lines and dots. A gold 'marker' has been riveted from one edge into a slot, like the marker on a precision slide rule.

162 Brooch. Silver, gold and enamel. West German, by Hermann Jünger (b. 1928). 1973. W. 6 cm. Private Collection.

Although he still employs the traditional materials and the functional format of a brooch, Jünger nevertheless demonstrates the clear breaking away from conventional jewellery concepts by treating his forms like a painter treats his canvas. Moreover, in comparison with his earlier work (see Pl. 125), his shapes have become much stronger and bolder; they are more forceful expressions of his artistic convictions.

The silver base of the brooch, a rectangle of irregular sides, has been enamelled in white; onto it various forms and shapes constructed of sheet and wire have been soldered in an abstract composition. Jünger's maker's mark (in the shape of a bird) is stamped on the base at the bottom right.

163/164/165 Necklace. Black jade, 18-carat white gold, opal and rock crystal. British, by Charlotte de Syllas (b. 1946). 1974. L. 45 cm. Private Collection.

An artist/jeweller in a class of her own, Charlotte de Syllas sometimes spends several years working on one single piece of jewellery. She is a master of complex techniques such as metal inlay and stone carving; this necklace is a prime example of her intricate design and her keen awareness of the relationship of form to material.

Carefully graded and specially cut black jade, interspersed with bands of white gold, forms the links of the necklace. The pendant section was cut from opal to fit between the links in the front; its sides are in the shape of two heads in profile, looking outwards, and ending in a point at the centre below. The back of the pendant is surmounted by a face cut into rock crystal and set in white gold, which forms a scroll over the forehead. With the meticulous attention to detail typical of her work, de Syllas has made a delightful fastening in the shape of two hands gripping the two sections of the hinge clasp, which is topped by a cabochon stone at either end.

166 Pendant. Gold, silver, copper, stainless steel. Australian, by Wolf Wennrich (b. 1922). 1974. L. (including chain) 42 cm. National Gallery of Victoria, Melbourne (D141/1977).

Born in Germany and trained at the Hochschule für bildende Künste, Hamburg, as a goldsmith and jeweller, Wennrich emigrated to Melbourne in 1953. In his capacity as a lecturer at the Royal Melbourne Institute of Technology, he exerted an incredibly vital influence on the people who studied under him. The strong development in contemporary Australian jewellery over the last fifteen years, in Melbourne particularly, can be attributed to Wennrich's vision and determination.

This pendant illustrates very clearly a close affinity to Wennrich's artistic roots, though it is entirely his own interpretation. A composition of three scored circles has been broken up by three irregular lines on the right–vaguely suggestive of profiles or perhaps of the contours of a coast–and by the numbers of the year 1974, stamped in reverse between the scoring.

167 Brooch. 18-carat gold and acrylic. Austrian, by Fritz Maierhofer (b. 1941). 1974. 7 cm × 7 cm. Private Collection.

A craftsman of the highest standard, Fritz Maierhofer has always used his great expertise in a strict and disciplined manner, which has given him the freedom to express his own, very original ideas. Together with Claus Bury (Pl. 168) and Gerd Rothmann (Pl. 171), he was among the first to exploit the possibilities of acrylic in conjunction with jewellery.

This brooch is a typical example of his experimentation with acrylic and gold, a combination which upset many conventional people. With the finest precision, Maierhofer has constructed the brooch from a square sheet of gold, broken up into six fields by lines punctuated with minute 'screws'. The semicircular cut-out is filled with spokes radiating from the gold hub placed over a backing of white acrylic, edged with three wavy lines in purple, blue and red. The brooch is mounted on a box of matt white acrylic bordered by a grey stripe and bears the artist's signature; thus it can be hung on the wall like a picture when it is not being worn.

168 Bracelet. 18-carat gold, fine and sterling silver, copper, nickel and brass. West German, by Claus Bury (b. 1946). 1974. W. 6.2 cm, H. 7 cm. Private Collection.

This bracelet is part of the 'container-series', a format of presentation developed by Bury, whereby he documented the various thought and work processes leading to the final 'product': within one or more frames, or 'containers', because the pieces required a certain depth, Bury enclosed preliminary sketches, with explanatory notes and samples of metal, the final work drawing and the actual finished piece; the whole group could be hung on the wall, while the piece of jewellery could be removed for wear. This was a unique method of providing the owner/wearer with an intimate knowledge of the creative process, thereby bringing about a closer relationship to the artist and to the object–in this case a bracelet. The astounding colour effects Bury achieves with metals are the results of extensive researches into alloys (continued on p. 128).

158 Brooch. Fine gold. French, by Pablo Picasso (1881–1973). 1973. W. 12.2 cm, H. 8.4 cm. Erica Brausen Collection.

159 Necklace. 18-carat gold, fresh-water ▷ pearls and a diamond. Swedish, by Sigurd Persson (b. 1914). 1973. L. 21 cm. Ulla Erikson Collection, Stockholm.

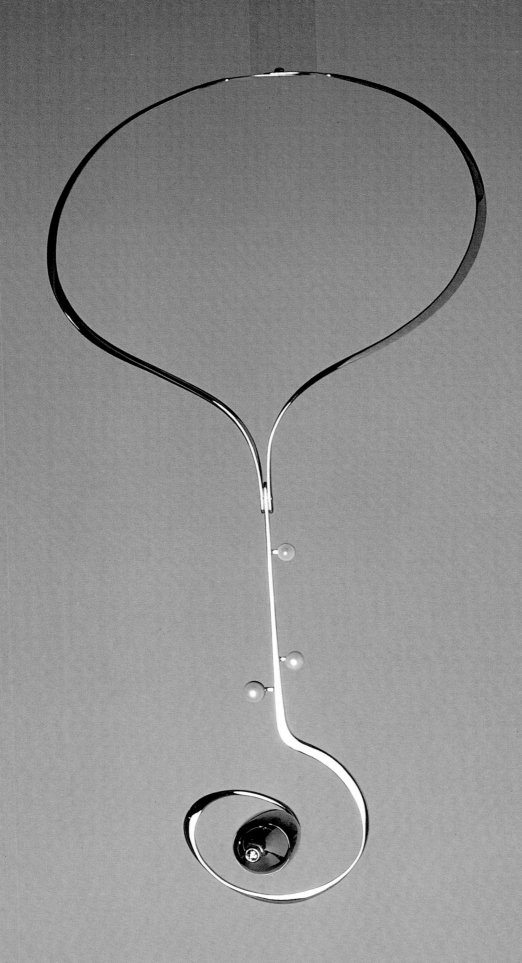

160 Necklace/Portable Cardiograph. Gold, silver and moonstones. U.S.A., by Mary Ann Scherr. 1973. L. 38.1 cm. Private Collection.

161 Bracelet. Silver and 18-carat gold. Italian, by Bruno Martinazzi (b. 1923). 1973. W. 5.1 cm. Private Collection.

162 Brooch. Silver, gold and enamel. West German, by Hermann Jünger (b. 1928). 1973. W. 6 cm. Private Collection.

163/164/165 Necklace. Black jade, 18-carat ▷ white gold, opal and rock crystal. British, by Charlotte de Syllas (b. 1946). 1974. L. 45 cm. Private Collection.

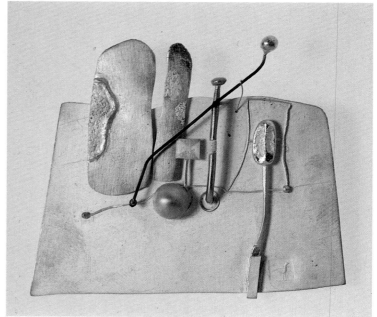

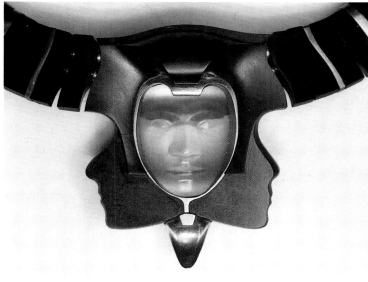

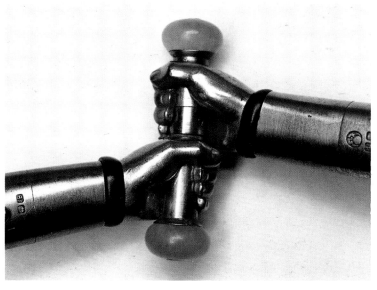

166 Pendant. Gold, silver, copper, stainless steel. Australian, by Wolf Wennrich (b. 1922). 1974. L. (including chain) 42 cm. National Gallery of Victoria, Melbourne (D141/1977).

167 Brooch. 18-carat gold and acrylic. Austrian, by Fritz Maierhofer (b. 1941). 1974. 7 cm × 7 cm. Private Collection.

168 Bracelet. 18-carat gold, fine and sterling ▷ silver, copper, nickel and brass. West German, by Claus Bury (b. 1946). 1974. W. 6.2 cm, H. 7 cm. Private Collection.

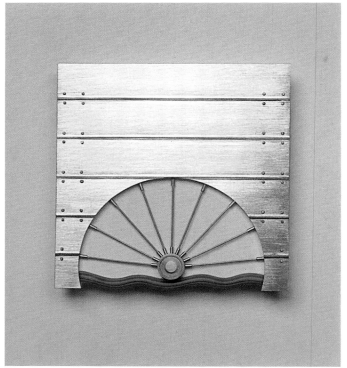

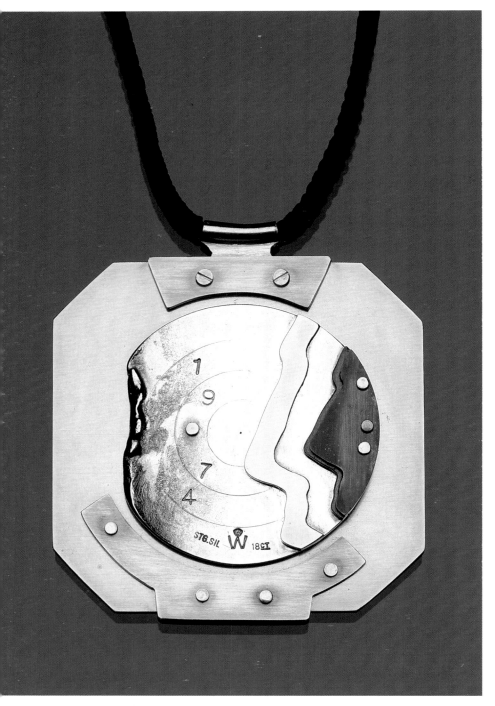

168 (**cont'd**). Here he has used them to inlay complex patterns on the sides of the bracelet as well as on the hollow form across its top. The downwards sloping form has been inlaid with straight and diagonal lines, interspersed with circles, holes and round protruberances. In direct contrast to the geometric lines in the rest of the bracelet, a softly draped shape sprawls across the top edge.

169 Pendant. Silver, perspex, leather and a photograph. Australian, by Helge Larsen (b. 1929) and Darani Lewers (b. 1936). 1974. H. 7 cm, W. 4.5 cm. Australian National Gallery Collection, Canberra.
A husband and wife team, Helge Larsen and Darani Lewers are both outstanding artist/jewellers in their own right who have earned a special place in the history of Australia's contemporary jewellery. They have played an important role in shaping training programmes and establishing workshops, promotions and exhibition projects. For Larsen and Lewers, jewellery is the ideal form of visual communication for expressing ideas and feelings on an intimate and personal basis.

This brooch, featuring 'Sydney Harbour', is one of a series they made at the time, focusing on national monuments in Australia and abroad; the series was inspired by several visits to Europe. A photograph of Sydney harbour has been mounted in a silver frame, suspended from a leather thong. The picture is protected by a corrugated sheet of perspex, which also serves to give the view greater depth and perspective.

170 Neckpiece. Silver and acrylic. British, by David Watkins (b. 1940). 1974. W. 14.6 cm, L. 30 cm. Private Collection (U.S.A.).
David Watkins, who is one of the most inventive and innovative artist/ jewellers in Britain, was trained as a sculptor, a background which no doubt provided some of the impetus for his revolutionary ideas in jewellery. Watkins adapted many techniques from other disciplines, including engineering, to jewellery so as to realize his designs; often he invented entirely new methods to achieve a shape or colour.

Inspired by technology and the space age, this neckpiece is made of two loops of acrylic rod in subtle shades of pale magenta, lilac, orange and yellow. The upper loop is fastened by hinges to the lower section, which is crossed by three horizontal bars. The rod has been grooved with a lathe and inlaid with bands of silver.

171 Six Pins. Steel, silver, nickel, copper and brass. West German, by Gerhard Rothmann (b. 1941). 1975. H. 10 cm; Diam. (disc) 6 cm. Private Collection.

These six pins were designed and made by Gerhard Rothmann, an artist/jeweller of exceptional originality. A fully qualified goldsmith and former student of Hermann Jünger (see Pls 125, 162, 203), Rothmann evolved his own characteristic approach to jewellery early in his career. His designs are the result of constant research into new and different ways of expressing his own thoughts on human relationships (see Pl. 243).

The pin on the left represents the planet Earth in the form of a steel disc engraved with three ovals to indicate a global shape. Five human heads are mounted on steel pins facing the 'globe': they are composed of different metals, the colours of which have been accentuated by heat. Rothmann has placed the pins into a glass-fronted wooden box (the type normally used by butterfly collectors to display their specimens) as an integral part of his design. The inspiration for the group and for its arrangement within the box came from a poem by the German poet Christian Morgenstern, about a planet ruled by flies who deal with people in the way that people treat flies–or in this case, butterflies.

172 Ring. 18-carat white gold and emeralds. U.S.A., by Noma Copley. 1975. Diam. (bezel) 2.3 cm. Thu Stern Collection.
Perhaps inspired by a keen interest in Surrealism and certainly encouraged by the tremendous broadening in outlook about jewellery in general, Noma Copley designed a whole range of jewellery concerned with the subject of fasteners–buttons and zippers. This ring, in the shape of a coat button, is made from white gold; the 'holes' are represented by four emeralds placed on a matt, textured background that has a thick polished edge.

173 Bangle. Silver. Danish, by K. Holst Andersen (b. 1935). 1974. L. 23 cm. Private Collection.
K. Holst Andersen is a gold- and silversmith in the classic Scandinavian tradition, a sensitive artist and master craftsman, who was named 'Artist-Craftsman of the Year' by the Danish Society in 1973. Andersen is also responsible for many of the beautiful designs produced by Georg Jensen.

This bangle is a characteristic piece of Andersen's work raised from silver sheet, turned and hollowed into a gently twisted curve that has been highly polished. Entitled 'Fable', it can be worn around the wrist or enjoyed as a sculptural object when placed on its plinth of shiny black acrylic.

174 Bracelet. 18-carat gold with niello. Italian, by Giampaolo Babetto (b. 1947). 1975. Diam. (inside) 6.5 cm. Private Collection.

A prominent member of the illustrious 'Padua School', Giampaolo Babetto makes superb jewellery which has won him international awards and recognition. The theme of circles within circles, pivoting at different angles to become global structures, fascinated Babetto at the time he made this bracelet. He constructed it of seven gold bands (given a black, crusty texture in parts with niello) made into a giro by placing rivets at different points.

175 Pendant. Silver and titanium. British, by Edward de Large (b. 1949). 1975. 5.5 cm × 5.5 cm. Private Collection.
Inevitably new materials brought with them new design possibilities. In the case of titanium, its greatest attraction lay in the brilliant colour range into which the metal could be anodized. The process, which involves applying electrical impulses to the metal, was refined by Edward de Large, among others, to allow for greater control of the actual areas to be treated.

This pendant is a typical example of the illusionist perspective effect used by de Large in a range of jewellery he made at the time; the effect is heightened by the refractory quality of the colouring. The titanium 'picture' has been riveted to a silver frame and is suspended from a rigid neckwire.

176 Three Brooches. Silver and gold. British, by Ros Conway (b. 1951). 1975. *(Top right)* H. 14.2 cm, W. 11 cm; *(top left)* H. 12.2 cm, W. 11.3 cm; *(bottom right)* H. 13.3 cm, W. 14 cm. Private Collection *(top two)*; Worshipful Company of Goldsmiths, London *(bottom)*.
Liberated from sweeping fashion dictates and universal trends, artist/jewellers of the 1970s followed their own chosen directions, producing a wide spectrum of designs which ranged from the totally abstract to the explicit and figurative. Ros Conway's work of that period was highly figurative as illustrated by these brooches, though in later years her designs became completely abstract.

The motif of these brooches is the manner in which a tarpaulin is fixed over the back of a truck: a study (in metal) of soft material placed against a rigid structure and held by the tension of a tightened rope. The tarpaulins are made from fine silver sheet 'draped' over the slatted body of the truck and held by ropes of twisted silver.

169 Pendant. Silver, perspex, leather and a photograph. Australian, by Helge Larsen (b. 1929) and Darani Lewers (b. 1936). 1974. H. 7 cm, W. 4.5 cm. Australian National Gallery Collection, Canberra.

170 Neckpiece. Silver and acrylic. British, by David Watkins (b. 1940). 1974. W. 14.6 cm, L. 30 cm. Private Collection (U.S.A.).

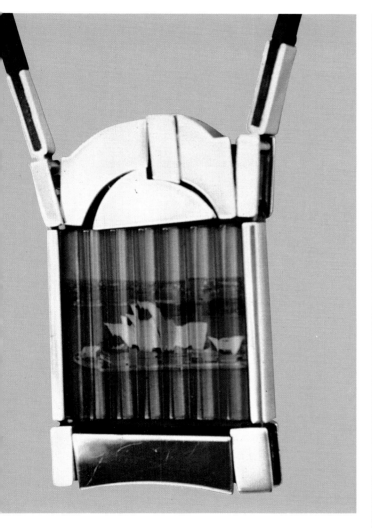

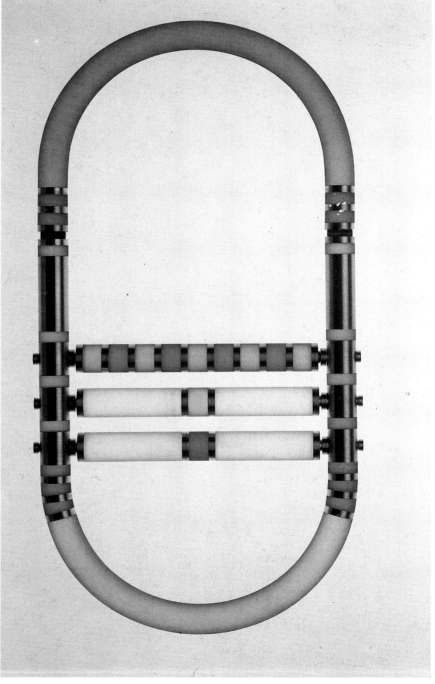

171 Six Pins. Steel, silver, nickel, copper and brass. West German, by Gerhard Rothmann (b. 1941). 1975. H. 10 cm; Diam. (disc) 6 cm. Private Collection.

172 Ring. 18-carat white gold and emeralds. U.S.A., by Noma Copley. 1975. Diam. (bezel) 2.3 cm. Thu Stern Collection.

173 Bangle. Silver. Danish, by K. Holst Andersen (b. 1935). 1974. L. 23 cm. Private Collection.

174 Bracelet. 18-carat gold with niello. Italian, by Giampaolo Babetto (b. 1947). 1975. Diam. (inside) 6.5 cm. Private Collection. ▷

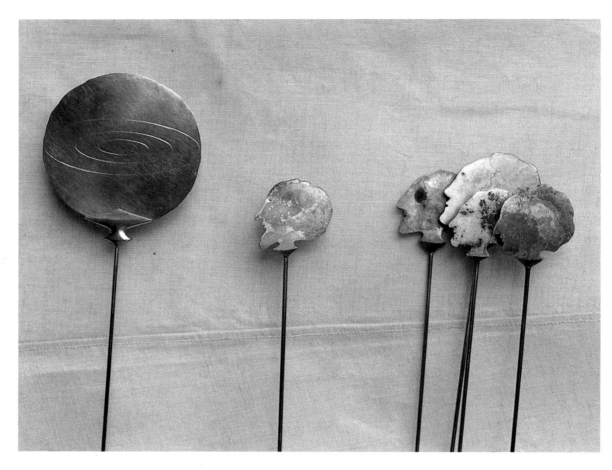

175 Pendant. Silver and titanium. British, by Edward de Large (b. 1949). 1975. 5.5 cm × 5.5 cm. Private Collection.

176 Three Brooches. Silver and gold. British, by Ros Conway (b. 1951). 1975. *(Top right)* H. 14.2 cm, W. 11 cm; *(top left)* H. 12.2 cm, W. 11.3 cm; *(bottom right)* H. 13.3 cm, W. 14 cm. Private Collection *(top two)*; Worshipful Company of Goldsmiths, London *(bottom)*.

177 Two Cigarette Lighters. Silver and 18-carat gold. British, by Karel Bartosik (b. 1942). 1975. H. 6.4 cm, W. 3.5 cm, D. 1.4 cm. Private Collection.

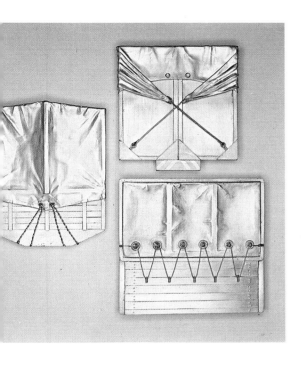

133

177 Two Cigarette Lighters. Silver and 18-carat gold. British, by Karel Bartosik (b. 1942). 1975. H. 6.4 cm, W. 3.5 cm, D. 1.4 cm. Private Collection.
Born in England of Dutch/Czech parentage, Bartosik has spent much of his working life in London, including a spell of several years in the workshop of Andrew Grima (see Pls 127, 145). A craftsman of exceptional talent and skill, Bartosik designed and made a whole range of lighters and jewellery on the theme of houses and office furniture. Many of them are now treasured collectors' items.

The lighter on the left represents a filing cabinet with gold handles on the drawers. The tiny gold telephone on top of the telephone directory is pressed down for the flame, which appears out of the golden ash-tray at its side.

The lighter on the right is a two-storey Victorian house with the shop front of a [Real] Estate Agent. The golden silhouette of a woman appears in the top left window, and the shop door opens to reveal the words: 'CAN I HELP YOU?' as if they came from within. The chimney-stack is pressed to release the flame at the top. The house has been textured to resemble bricks and mortar; the door knob and hinges as well as the chimney-stack and the 'sale' sign are in gold.

178 Necklace with Pendant. Platinum and diamonds. U.S.A., by Harry Winston (1896–1978). 1975. L. 44.7 cm; (pendant) 3.5 cm × 2.8 cm. Private Collection.
In 1975, Harry Winston purchased an extraordinary South African rough diamond, weighing 204 carats. After rolling the stone between his fingers for a few minutes, Winston, the 'King of Diamonds', quietly announced that it would produce a large, perfectly faceted stone. Indeed, the rough diamond was cut into a 75.52 carat, D-flawless pear-shaped diamond in spring, 1976, the year of the American Bicentennial; in its honour, his son, Ronald Winston, christened the stone the 'Star of Independence'. Within weeks after the faceting was completed, the stone was sold for four million dollars, making it the most expensive diamond sold up to that date. The 'Star of Independence' was set as a pendant to a V-shaped necklace containing 38 pear-shaped diamonds (totalling 29 cts) and 35 round diamonds (totalling 32 cts.).

179 Three Brooches. Silver, mother-of-pearl, ivory and acrylic. Polish, by Joachim Sokolsky (b. 1946). 1976. H. 5.2 cm, W. 4.6 cm. Private Collection.
The physiognomy of the human head has inspired artists and jewellers throughout the ages. Sokolsky designed a whole series of brooches in different materials with design variations, but based on the same profile, treating the subject almost like 'anatomical' drawings. The three brooches are all on silver bases. The

brooch on the top left has an ivory face and black acrylic 'hair' banded with strips of white acrylic, ivory and mother-of-pearl. The brooch on the top right has a silver face with the different 'areas' of the brain cut from mother-of-pearl and riveted to the base. The brooch in the centre has a black acrylic face and the 'brain area' is made of closely fitted sections of mother-of-pearl.

180 Two Brooches. Stainless steel, acrylic and fabric. Japanese, by Takeo Mitsuyasu (b. 1944). 1976. Diam. (round brooch) 6.5 cm; H. (triangular brooch) 6.3 cm. Private Collection.
One of the first of the younger generation of Japanese artist/jewellers, Mitsuyasu created designs that introduced a distinctly Japanese element into his concepts of form and material. Using traditional kimono fabric, he has stretched the material with tiny wires within an outer frame of acrylic (on the round brooch) or tubular rods of stainless steel having white acrylic curved corners (on the triangular one).

181 Bracelet. 18-carat gold and rubies. Italian, by Mario Pinton (b. 1919). 1976. Diam. 7 cm. Schmuckmuseum, Pforzheim (1977/21).
A qualified goldsmith and sculptor, Mario Pinton, director and a professor at the Istituto d'Arte in Padua is a superb craftsman, versed in all the ancient and modern techniques of goldsmithing and jewellery; he has been a key figure in the development of the design concepts practiced by the Padua 'School' of artist/jewellers. Fashioned with an enormous respect for the material–gold–and for the great art of the ancients, Pinton's bracelet in the shape of a snake (a timeless source of inspiration) smoothly curls itself around the arm and is embellished by two rubies.

182 Bracelet. 18-carat gold. U.S.A., by Arline Fisch (b. 1931). 1976. H. 10.1 cm, W. 6.8 cm. Private Collection.
An inspired and committed artist/jeweller, Arline Fisch has played a vital role in developing contemporary jewellery on an international scale. Her imaginative approach and ingenious adaptations of techniques like weaving, knitting and crochet have added a new dimension to the field. This bracelet is hand-knitted with gold wire in the form of a cuff, complete with hook and eye fastening; it is narrow at the wrist and widens out to a frilly edge.

183 Ring. 24-carat gold, plastic ducks, pearls and feathers. Israeli, by Bianca Eshel-Gershuni (b. 1932). 1976. W. 9 cm. Private Collection.
Bianca Eshel-Gershuni was born in Bulgaria and has lived in Israel since 1939. Her jewellery is an uninhibited mixture of precious and intrinsically worthless materials, assembled like collages to create vivid and colourful images. Eshel-Gershuni's exuberant fantasy and wit are

unhampered by material considerations or technical 'rules'; she finds practical solutions that suit her artistic concepts and lend her work a unique spontaneity, so often lacking in work made with more sophisticated techniques.

The underlying structure is made from fine gold, mounted on a wide shank and supporting a composition of baroque pearls, plastic ducks and feathers that spreads across the entire hand.

184 Pendant. 18-carat gold, steel, sapphire and rubies. Austrian, by Helfried Kodré (b. 1940). 1976. 6 cm × 1.8 cm. Private Collection (Vienna).
In complete contrast to the style of his earlier work (see Pl. 146), this pendant by Helfried Kodré, made in 1976, is composed of geometric forms, straight lines and circles. Suspended from a rigid neckwire, the pendant is made from yellow and white gold for colour variation and set with five rubies and a cabochon sapphire at the base.

185 Ring and Bracelet. Silver and acrylic. Dutch, by Paul Derrez (b. 1950). 1976. W. (bracelet) 6 cm; (ring) 2 cm. Multiple production by the artist.
As a qualified goldsmith, Paul Derrez began working with precious metals, but in the course of developing his own characteristic style of design he turned more and more towards less expensive materials, which also allowed him greater freedom for experimentation. Derrez's orientation in design was very much influenced by the trends current in Dutch jewellery at the time–a constant refining of geometric forms to their minimal shape, devoid of any decorative element. In the mid 1970s, Derrez was also very interested in the development of well-designed multiples, as illustrated by this set of matching bracelet and ring. The casing is made of silver wire bent into a double loop. Variously coloured acrylic cross-sections can be clamped between the loop; each item comes with a choice of four acrylic inserts.

186 Pendant/Brooch. Silver and gold. Australian, by Emanuel Raft (b. 1938). 1976. W. 7.7 cm, H. 7.7 cm. Private Collection.
Raft, who is of Greek/Italian parentage, went to Australia in 1956 and trained both there and in Italy in sculpture, architecture and industrial design. He is also an accomplished painter and applied a painterly approach to his jewellery in that period in contrast to the more sculptural feeling of his earlier work. Although this pendant, which can also be worn as a brooch, is in part a relief (the central broken ridge has been raised from the square silver sheet in uneven contour), the overall textures and inclusions have been applied almost like brushwork on canvas.

178 Necklace with Pendant. Platinum and diamonds. U.S.A., by Harry Winston (1896–1978). 1975. L. 44.7 cm; (pendant) 3.5 cm × 2.8 cm. Private Collection.

179 Three Brooches. Silver, mother-of-pearl, ivory and acrylic. Polish, by Joachim Sokolsky (b. 1946). 1976. H. 5.2 cm, W. 4.6 cm., Private Collection.

180 Two Brooches. Stainless steel, acrylic and fabric. Japanese, by Takeo Mitsuyasu (b. 1944). 1976. Diam. (round brooch) 6.5 cm; H. (triangular brooch) 6.3 cm. Private Collection.

181 Bracelet. 18-carat gold and rubies. Italian, by Mario Pinton (b. 1919). 1976. Diam. 7 cm. Schmuckmuseum, Pforzheim (1977/21).

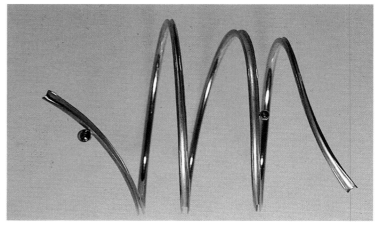

182 Bracelet. 18-carat gold. U.S.A., by Arline Fisch (b. 1931). 1976. H. 10.1 cm, W. 6.8 cm. Private Collection.

183 Ring. 24-carat gold, plastic ducks, pearls and feathers. Israeli, by Bianca Eshel-Gershuni (b. 1932). 1976. W. 9 cm. Private Collection.

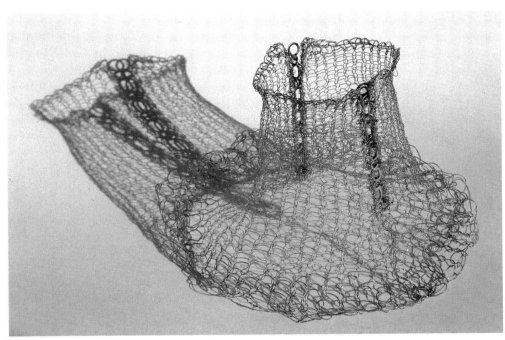

184 Pendant. 18-carat gold, steel, sapphire and rubies. Austrian, by Helfried Kodré (b. 1940). 1976. 6 cm × 1.8 cm. Private Collection (Vienna).

185 Ring and Bracelet. Silver and acrylic. Dutch, by Paul Derrez (b. 1950). 1976. W. (bracelet) 6 cm, (ring) 2 cm. Multiple production by the artist.

186 Pendant/Brooch. Silver and gold. Australian, by Emanuel Raft (b. 1938). 1976. W. 7.7 cm, H. 7.7 cm. Private Collection.

187 Necklace and Bracelet. Stainless steel. ▷ U.S.A., by Mary Ann Scherr. 1976. L. 43.3 cm. Private Collection.

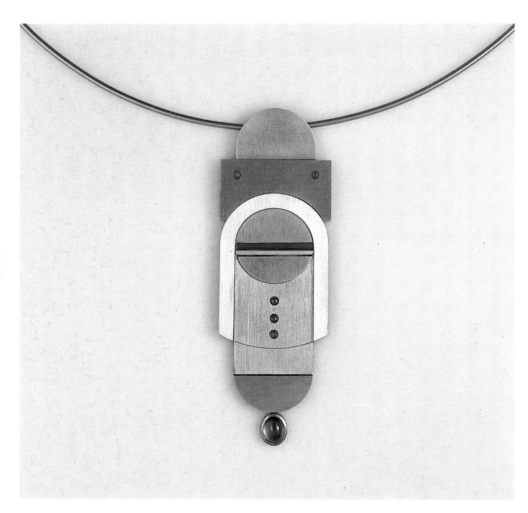

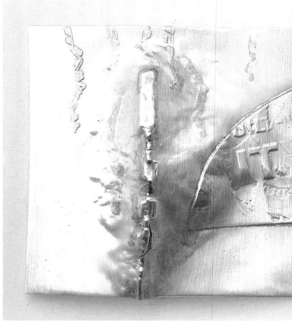

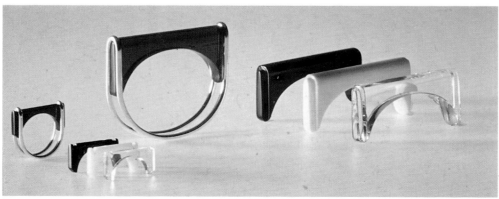

187 Necklace and Bracelet. Stainless steel. U.S.A., by Mary Ann Scherr. 1976. L. 43.3 cm. Private Collection.
This piece of jewellery by Mary Ann Scherr has no functional aspects (contrast with Pl. 160); it is a necklace of highly dramatic impact. Made from graduated sections of stainless-steel sheet, hinged together, it forms a light yet comfortable necklace of bold proportions. The broad bracelet is open-ended and also made of stainless steel, which underlines the simplicity of the design and has been used here with great flair to achieve a stunning effect.

188 Necklace. Copper, fine silver and silk. South African, by Daniel Kruger (b. 1951). 1976. 17 cm × 17 cm. Private Collection.
Daniel Kruger's designs, in common with those of several other artists/jewellers who left their native country to live and work in another, have been immensely enriched by the experience. Born and educated in South Africa, Kruger completed his studies in Munich under Hermann Jünger (Pl. 125). Many of Kruger's designs incorporate elements that are apparent opposites such as metal and silk in this necklace. The silver beads are partially gold-plated and connected to a crescent-shaped central cushion, made of crocheted silk in glowing colours, with cascading strands of silk hanging down from the lower edge.

189 Pendant. 18-carat gold. West German, by Reinhold Reiling (1922–1983). 1976/77. H. 7.9 cm. Schmuckmuseum, Pforzheim (1977/26).
A year or so before this pendant was made, Reinhold Reiling's design (see Pl. 141) underwent a complete change of direction. His forms began to be disciplined by strict and sober geometry and at the same time became much more three-dimensional than in any of his earlier works.
Made entirely of yellow and white gold, this rectangular pendant is suspended from the rigid neckpiece by two parallel wires attached to the open box frame, which has two shelves of yellow gold. The top section contains a 'cushioned' rectangle of matt yellow gold, engraved with two diagonal lines and inlaid with a short band of oxidized white gold on each side.

190 Earrings. 18-carat gold, diamonds and pearls. British, by Gerda Flöckinger (b. 1927). 1977. L. 10.3 cm, W. 2 cm. The artist's collection.
These earrings are another classic example of Gerda Flöckinger's great ability in bringing out the inherent beauty of gold (see also Pl. 153). The molten surface of the metal is accentuated with minute grains and swirled encrustations; tiny diamonds glisten as random spots within the texture. The circular tops of the earrings are set with pearls, while the drop consists of a rectangular shape connected to a square, from which a smaller rectangle is suspended.

191 Four Brooches. Silver and ivory. U.S.S.R., by Leili Kuldkepp (b. 1931). 1977. *(Top left)* 3.8 cm × 3.6 cm; *(top right)* 3.8 cm × 3.5 cm, *(bottom left)* 4.5 cm × 4.5 cm, *(bottom right)* 3.6 cm × 3.6 cm. The artist's collection.
A graduate of the Estonian State Art Institute in Tallinn, Leili Kuldkepp is Professor of the Metal Faculty at the Tallinn Institute and also has her own studio/workshop, where she works free lance on individual pieces only. Her widely exhibited jewellery has won her several gold and silver medals and is represented in public collections in the U.S.S.R. Both the high technical standard and artistic quality of her work and the wide-spread recognition Kuldkepp has gained in her own country bear witness to the dramatic change in the attitude to, and role of, contemporary jewellery in the Soviet Union over the last ten years.
The theme of these four brooches is the shape of softly draped fabrics, carved sensitively in ivory and set onto a silver base with raised edges.

192 Necklace. 18-carat gold and silk. Japanese, by Aya Nakayama (b. 1946). 1977. L. 38.2 cm, W. (pendant) 3.1 cm, D. 1.9 cm. Private Collection.
Aya Nakayama is a graduate of Tokyo University of Art (1969), and a talented, creative artist/jeweller of distinctive originality. She has designed jewellery for mass-production and made superb unique pieces that have won her international acclaim. Nakayama is also the Secretary General of the Japan Jewellery Designers' Association.
This necklace (a unique piece) is characteristic of Nakayama's work in the late 1970s, when she adapted an old Japanese technique called *kumihimo* for braiding silk cord. She dyes the silk strands herself before braiding them into an amazing range of patterns, gradually introducing fine gold wire that ends in a solid shape of beaten gold that forms the pendant.

193 Brooch. Gold and silver, cloisonné enamel on copper, sterling silver, 14- and 18-carat gold, bronze and pearls. U.S.A., by William Harper (b. 1944). 1978. 9.7 cm × 7 cm × 1.8 cm. The artist's collection.
William Harper is a renowned artist/jeweller whose supreme mastery of the art of cloisonné enamelling has provided his fantasy and imagination with an enviable freedom in expressing his artistic concepts. Harper's work is a diverse and colourful reflection of spiritual impressions and concepts, expressed in many different materials and varied forms that are full of symbolism and mystique.
The brooch illustrated consists of an outer wire frame, which has the fastening pin and catch across the top incorporated into the design. The centre features an abstract design between the crossed lines and circles in an explosion of colours. At the base, the frame has been twisted into coils and separated into two horizontal bars, each carrying a baroque-pearl bead of unusual shape and length.

194 Necklace. Silver. Finnish, by Saara Hopea-Untracht (1925–1984). 1978. 14 cm × 23 cm. Aki Hopea Collection.
Trained in interior design at the School of Arts and Crafts in Helsinki, Saara Hopea-Untracht devoted her talents to the design of furniture, lighting fixtures and glass before becoming one of Finland's distinguished jewellery designers. Her work has been widely exhibited and is represented in the permanent collections of several Finnish museums as well as in the Museum of Modern Art, New York, and the Newark Museum in New Jersey.
This necklace is made from three strands of silver- wire tubes, cross-knit by hand, with a fabricated semicircular pendant in a design of cones radiating from a hub of solid silver. Hopea-Untracht designed the piece and hand-knitted the wire; K. G. Ahlberg was responsible for the assembly.

195 Brooch. Silver and titanium. U.S.A./ Australian, by Jeanne Keefer (b. 1951). 1978. H. 6.3 cm, W. 12.7 cm. The artist's collection.
Born in the United States and educated in San Diego. Jeanne Keefer had already established herself as a notable artist/jeweller, a teacher and a distinguished member of the Society of North American Goldsmiths before becoming a lecturer at the School of Art of the Tasmanian College of Advanced Education in Australia in 1981. In the short time since her arrival in that country, both by her excellent work and her activities in the Crafts Councils of Tasmania and Australia, Keefer has contributed much to the general promotion and growth of Australian contemporary jewellery.
This brooch was made when Keefer was still working in the United States. Entitled 'Allegory 1', it is constructed of silver, inlaid with anodized titanium to give a blue-and-white cloud effect. Executed with precision and geometric in composition, it evokes an image of sky and bird, of space and flight.

196 Ring. 18-carat gold and diamonds. West German, by Friedrich Becker (b. 1922). 1978. W. 5 cm. Private Collection.
This ring by Becker, made in gold, consists of a slightly curved bar, pavé set with diamonds across the shank. The ultra-simple shape is given dramatic impact by the length of the bar, which stretches over three fingers when worn. The ring was originally made as a unique piece, but later produced in a limited series by the German firm Niessing (see Pl. 286).

188 Necklace. Copper, fine silver and silk. South African, by Daniel Kruger (b. 1951). 1976. 17 cm × 17 cm. Private Collection.

189 Pendant. 18-carat gold. West German, by Reinhold Reiling (1922–1983). 1976/77. H. 7.9 cm. Schmuckmuseum, Pforzheim (1977/26).

190 Earrings. 18-carat gold, diamonds and pearls. British, by Gerda Flöckinger (b. 1927). 1977. L. 10.3 cm, W. 2 cm. The artist's collection.

191 Four Brooches. Silver and ivory. U.S.S.R., by Leili Kuldkepp (b. 1931). 1977. *(Top left)* 3.8 cm × 3.6 cm, *(top right)* 3.8 cm × 3.5 cm, *(bottom left)* 4.5 cm × 4.5 cm, *(bottom right)* 3.6 cm × 3.6 cm. The artist's collection.

192 Necklace. 18-carat gold and silk. Japanese, by Aya Nakayama (b. 1946). 1977. L. 38.2 cm, W. (pendant) 3.1 cm, D. 1.9 cm. Private Collection.

193 Brooch. Gold and silver, cloisonné ▷ enamel on copper, sterling silver, 14- and 18-carat gold, bronze and pearls. U.S.A., by William Harper (b. 1944). 1978. 9.7 cm × 7 cm × 1.8 cm. The artist's collection.

194 Necklace. Silver. Finnish, by Saara Hopea-Untracht (1925–1984). 1978. 14 cm × 23 cm. Aki Hopea Collection.

195 Brooch. Silver and titanium. U.S.A./Australian, by Jeanne Keefer (b. 1951). 1978. H. 6.3 cm, W. 12.7 cm. The artist's collection.

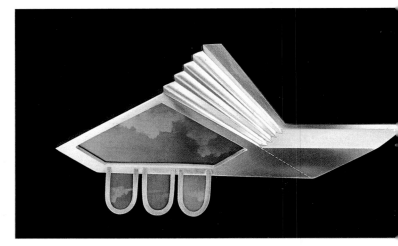

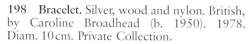

197 **Brooch/Wall-Hanging.** Fine silver, copper, kimono fabric, *shakudo*, sterling silver and acrylic. U.S.A., by Hiroko Sato Pijanowski (b. 1941) and Gene Pijanowski (b. 1938). 1978. 20.3 cm × 28 cm × 2.5 cm. Steve Murakishi Collection (U.S.A.).

198 **Bracelet.** Silver, wood and nylon. British, by Caroline Broadhead (b. 1950). 1978. Diam. 10 cm. Private Collection.

199 **Bracelet.** 18-carat gold, silver and alabaster. British, by Elisabeth Holder (b. 1950). 1978. Diam. 6 cm. Private Collection.

200 **Torque.** Silver gilt, acrylic and pearls. U.S.A., by Stanley Lechtzin (b. 1936). 1978. H. 27.3 cm, W. 26.7 cm. University of Tokyo: Permanent Collection (donated by K. Mikimoto & Co., Ltd).

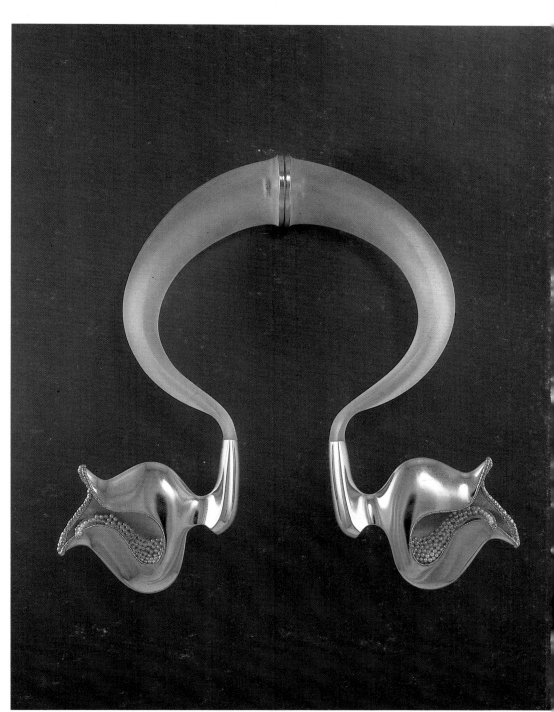

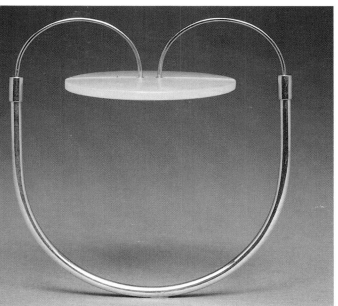

201 Necklace. Silver and copper alloy, moonstone, ivory, ruby and feathers. Austrian, by Elisabeth Kodré-Defner (b. 1937). 1979. L. (pendant) ca. 8 cm. The artist's collection.

202 Brooch. Gold, silver and acrylic. British, ▷ by Martin Page. (b. 1952). 1979. H. 6 cm. Private Collection.

203 Necklace. Gold, silver, enamel and ivory. West German, by Hermann Jünger (b. 1928). 1979. 11 cm × 7 cm. Private Collection.

204 Bracelet. 14-carat gold. Dutch, by Emmy van Leersum (1930–1984). 1979. Diam. 6 cm, L. 8 cm. Private Collection.

205 Three Brooches. Silver. Japanese, by Minato Nakamura (b. 1947). 1979. H. 2.5 cm, W. 6.5 cm. The artist's collection.

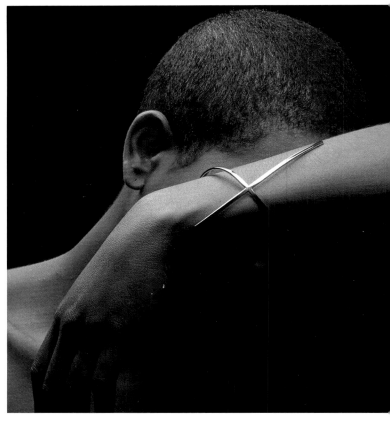

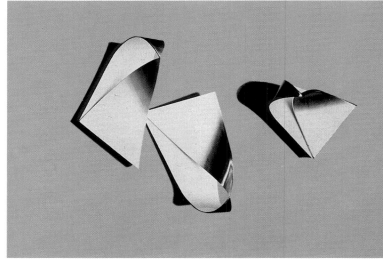

206 Brooch. Silver and silk. Dutch, by Marion Herbst (b. 1944). 1979. 9 cm × 5 cm. Private Collection.

In the late 1970s, the specific use of inexpensive materials in jewellery became far more important than a mere question of economy, particularly in Holland. There was a conscious and deliberate intent to relate to new conditions and social structures in order to identify with the aspirations of young people faced with the problems of the late twentieth century. In that endeavour, many young artist/jewellers discovered a completely new visual language and a new artistic integrity.

Marion Herbst belongs to that group of Dutch artist/jewellers of firm and committed principles that has produced such original work in the last eight years; they have made a decisive impact on the design of, as well as attitudes towards, contemporary jewellery all over the world. The brightly coloured silk in this brooch has been woven into a length of fabric and attached to a vertical rod by other strands of tightly wound silk.

207 Bracelet. 18-carat gold and iron. Dutch, by Jan Tempelman (b. 1943). 1979. H. 6 cm. Private Collection.

This hinged bracelet in textured, forged gold has a heavy strip of blackened iron cutting across the front. Tempelman's designs always aim to bring out the inherent quality of his material. He has a particular preference for iron, one of mankind's most commonly used metals. Tempelman is fascinated by its constant presence in rubbish dumps; there he gathers his material, refashioning it into jewellery and ennobling it with touches of gold.

This bracelet is one of a pair made for the exhibition 'Two-in-One', held at the Orfèvre Gallery in Düsseldorf in 1979. The companion piece is the exact reverse: a bracelet of iron with a strip of gold across the front.

208 Two Brooches. Steel and linen. Austrian, by Peter Skubic (b. 1935). (Top) 1980. 11.5 cm × 5.3 cm × 2 cm. Inge Asenbaum Collection (Vienna). (Bottom) 1979. 8 cm × 5.6 cm × 1.5 cm Beatrice Stähli Collection (Zurich).

Skubic qualified as a master gold- and silversmith in 1966 and has been professor at the Fachhochschule Kunst & Design in Cologne since 1979. His early work with precious metals was already inspired by technological shapes and by the massiveness of the metal. By the mid-1970s, he began to explore the potential of steel in jewellery, and continued by organizing an international symposium held in Austria in 1974.

These brooches are made of refined steel; the sections are held together by tension. The brooch on the top is bound with linen tape for contrast; while the inner sections of the brooch on the bottom incorporate four sprung steel bars on each side.

209 Brooch. 22- and 18-carat gold. British, by Paul Preston (b. 1943). 1979. 3.5 cm × 3.6 cm. Private Collection.

A fully qualified architect and a former professional salvage diver, Paul Preston finally settled down to making jewellery, finding it the best medium in which to express his creative urges. As a jeweller Preston is entirely self-taught, and it is perhaps this lack of traditional technical discipline which enables him to use his materials with such uninhibited freedom.

A keen observer of animals in their natural habitat, he 'draws' them in fine detail using his own gold alloys for colours. The motif on this brooch is a bee sitting on a small sunflower. Its wings have been pierced for transparency, while the body markings are in variously coloured shades of gold.

210 Two Rings. 18-carat gold and marble. Japanese, by Kazuhiro Itoh (b. 1948). 1979. (Left) 2 cm × 2.5 cm; (right) 2 cm × 2 cm. Private Collection.

Kazuhiro Itoh is a graduate in painting of the Tama Art University in Tokyo. He has also worked for many years as designer for the Mikimoto Pearl Company, but it is his individual work that best expresses the essence of his artistic concepts: in the manner of classic Japanese minimalists, Itoh reduces his forms to the absolutely essential, relying on a single contrasting colour or material to make his point.

The ring on the left is made of black marble, carved into a round shank that ends in a point traversed by a horizontal bar of gold. The ring on the right is completely square; on the inside it has been filled with an irregularly shaped piece of white marble.

211 Pendant. 18-carat gold, silver and fossil ammonite. West German, by E. R. Nele. 1979. H. 11.4 cm. Private Collection.

Nele was born in Berlin and studied sculpture at the Hochschule für bildende Künste there. She also spent some time studying in Paris, and later in London at the Central School of Art and Design, where she was a fellow student of Gerda Flöckinger (see Pls 153, 190) in the middle 1950s. Nele's highly original concepts for sculpture and jewellery bear a close affinity to Surrealism, as this superb pendant proves. Using an opalized fossil ammonite as a starting point, Nele has provided it with a beautiful pair of woman's legs, finely modelled in black oxidized silver; this is surmounted by a draped, flowing shape in textured gold.

212 Pendant. Silver and acrylic. Austrian, by Waltrud Viehböck (b. 1937). 1980. L. 15 cm. Mrs E. Linz Collection.

This pendant is made from silver rods alternating with black acrylic in a strict geometric design, its formal resolution reminiscent of Art Deco.

Born in Germany, Waltrud Viehböck studied sculpture in Linz and divides her time between making jewellery and large-scale sculpture, both successfully. For her jewellery she won the Herbert-Hoffmann Prize at Munich in 1975 and more recently (in 1984) the First Prize in the competition for a work of sculpture for the Neue Rathaus, Linz.

213 Brooch. Silver. Dutch, by Onno Boekhoudt (b. 1944). 1980. W. 4.5 cm. Whereabouts unknown (stolen).

This brooch is part of a series wherein Onno Boekhoudt experimented with altering a basic shape–a circle or square–by technical processes such as sawing and soldering. This brooch is made from a single sheet of silver in the given shape; Boekhoudt sawed it first into vertical strips, then soldered it back together before repeating the process in a horizontal direction. The resulting texture is fascinating, not unlike that found in certain types of rock formations.

Boekhoudt's concern with jewellery extends to objects that are not necessarily wearable as long as they are tactile and small enough to keep in one's pocket or within a person's close environment.

214 Ring. 18-carat gold, ivory, diamond, pearl, coral and feathers. Danish, by Birte Stenbak (b. 1938). 1980. W. 2.5 cm. The artist's collection.

Birte Stenbak's immense flair and total rejection of the 'Scandinavian' principles of design are well demonstrated by this example of her work. A sweeping curve of carved ivory, supported by a double loop of gold wire, forms the shank and bezel of this ring. A long stem of rounded-off coral has been attached to the gold wire loop, across the ivory, and set with a diamond over the junction. A single pearl is set into the ivory within the centre of the loop; and a cluster of black feathers emanates from underneath the shank.

215 Belt Buckle. Silver, *shakudo* and agate. U.S.A., by Arline Fisch (b. 1931). 1980. W. 13 cm. The artist's collection.

Most of Arline Fisch's design concepts have some reference to fabrics in their form or construction (see Pl. 182). This buckle is one of a whole range of jewellery devoted to the theme of ribbons, executed here in silver inlaid with *shakudo* to indicate a patterned woven edge. Both lengths of 'ribbon' are attached to rectangles with irregular sides, made of agate set in silver and clasped together in the centre.

206 Brooch. Silver and silk. Dutch, by Marion Herbst (b. 1944). 1979. 9 cm × 5 cm. Private Collection.

207 Bracelet. 18-carat gold and iron. Dutch, by Jan Tempelman (b. 1943). 1979. H. 6 cm. Private Collection.

208 Two Brooches. Steel and linen. Austrian, by Peter Skubic (b. 1935). *(Top)* 1980. 11.5 cm × 5.3 cm × 2 cm. Inge Asenbaum Collection (Vienna). *(Bottom)* 1979. 8 cm × 5.6 cm × 1.5 cm. Beatrice Stähli Collection (Zurich).

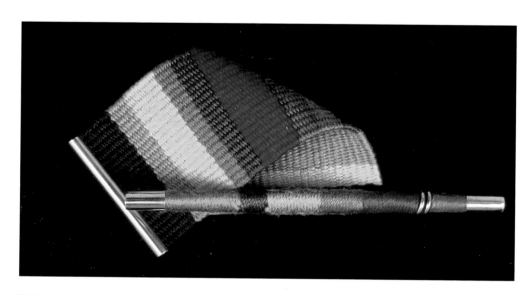

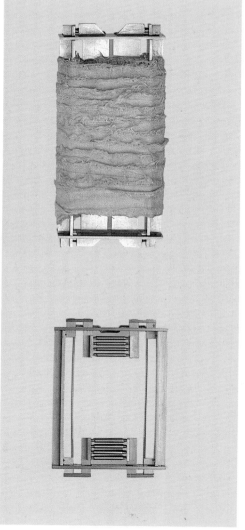

209 Brooch. 22- and 18-carat gold. British, by Paul Preston (b. 1943). 1979. 3.5 cm × 3.6 cm. Private Collection.

210 Two Rings. 18-carat gold and marble. Japanese, by Kazuhiro Itoh (b. 1948). 1979. *(Left)* 2 cm × 2.5 cm; *(right)* 2 cm × 2 cm. Private Collection.

211 Pendant. 18-carat gold, silver and fossil ammonite. West German, by E.R. Nele. 1979. H. 11.4 cm. Private Collection.

212 Pendant. Silver and acrylic. Austrian, by Waltrud Viehböck (b. 1937). 1980. L. 15 cm. Mrs. E. Linz Collection.

213 Brooch. Silver. Dutch, by Onno Boekhoudt (b. 1944). 1980. W. 4.5 cm. Whereabouts unknown (stolen).

214 Ring. 18-carat gold, ivory, diamond, pearl, coral and feathers. Danish, by Birte Stenbak (b. 1938). 1980. W. 2.5 cm. The artist's collection.

215 Belt Buckle. Silver, *shakudo* and agate. ▷ U.S.A., by Arline Fisch (b. 1931). 1980. W. 13 cm. The artist's collection.

216 Three Pendants. Silver and aluminium. ▷ Australian, by Johannes Kuhnen (b. 1952). 1980. (*Left to right*) 3.8 cm × 2.3 cm; 3.8 cm × 2.8 cm; 3 cm × 6.5 cm. Private collection and artist's collection.

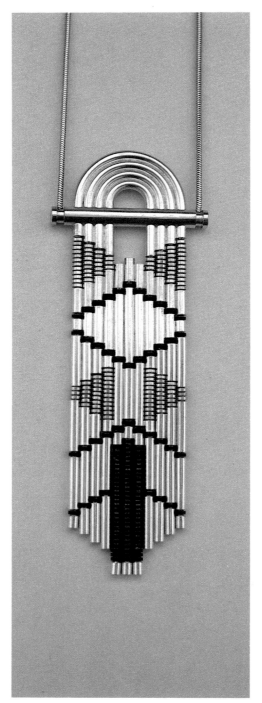

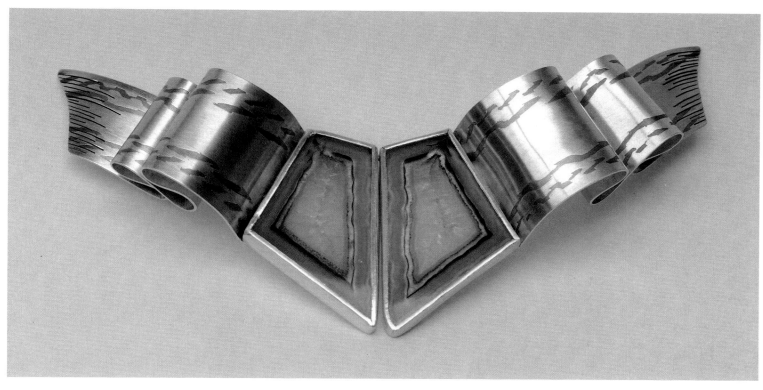

216 Three Pendants. Silver and aluminium. Australian, by Johannes Kuhnen (b. 1952). 1980. (*Left to right*) 3.8 cm × 2.3 cm; 3.8 cm × 2.8 cm; 3 cm × 6.5 cm. Private collection and artist's collection.

A comparative new-comer to the thriving community of Australian artist/jewellers (he has lived there since 1980), Johannes Kuhnen served a four-year apprenticeship in his native Germany with Friedrich Becker (see Pls 122/123, 196, 244) before graduating as a designer from the Fachhochschule, Düsseldorf, in 1978.

The ultra-simple, stark form of these pendants is characteristic of Kuhnen's style, which seeks to focus attention on the smooth contours of the overall shape. The pendants are hollow and made from anodized aluminium; they are held on either side by rigid wire, connected to a silver chain.

217 Pendant on Chain. Gold, silver, ruby and mirror-prism. West German, by Ulrike Bahrs (b. 1944). 1980. H. 7 cm, W. 4 cm. Rau Coll.

Each individual piece of jewellery by Ulrike Bahrs expresses her personal ethic with carefully researched symbols with which she is able to communicate complex thought processes. Deeply conscious of mankind's past and present, Bahrs seeks to re-establish new bonds with old traditional spiritual knowledge in a language understood by a contemporary society. This pendant is characteristic of her approach.

Bahrs is a firm believer in re-incarnation; the theme of this pendant is homage to our ancestry and past wisdom. The figure of a man in nineteenth-century attire represents a by-gone generation; the use of prisms and mirror symbolizes the instruments employed in the quest for knowledge in science. The golden head of the bearded man is reflected by a mirror through a prism onto a box below a triangle. His body, silk-screened onto metal, is contained within a circle under a domed prism; its centre magnifies his coat button. A cabochon ruby has been set onto the chain to the right of the pendant.

218 Necklace. 18-carat gold. Australian, by Frank Bauer (b. 1942). 1980. W. 7 cm. Private Collection.

Son of a Bauhaus architect, Frank Bauer was born in Germany and first studied architectural drawing and music before qualifying as a gold- and silversmith. Apart from a brief spell in London, he has been living in Australia since 1972. Crystallizing his fascinations with machinery and movement, his jewellery remains true to a certain purity and refinement, a careful working out of special relationships that echo his earlier involvement with architecture and movement. Much of the effect of his jewellery is based on his painstakingly accurate construction, as demonstrated by this pendant, a lattice of seventy-five cubes in step formation. Bauer's

infinite patience has helped him to achieve a mathematical equation, a rhythmic structure that can hold the observer spell-bound by its constant ability to change with movement.

219 Pendant. Gold and silver. Spanish, by Ana Font (b. 1945). 1980. H. 6.6 cm. Schmuckmuseum, Pforzheim (1982/20).

Partly trained in her native country of Spain and later in Germany at the Kunst + Werkschule, Pforzheim, Ana Font soon developed her own original style of design. The monolithic shape of the oxidized silver base, with its uneven texture, is broken up by a free organic form that seems to burst out from inside the pendant. The flat band of gold half-way across the base has been fitted with a tiny screw.

220 Two Rings. Silver and enamel paint. British, by Tom Saddington (b. 1952). (*Left*) 1980; Diam. 2 cm; (*right*) 1976; 4 cm × 5 cm. Private Collection.

Inspired by the distorted shapes of the worthless, discarded containers and wrappings that are part of our daily environment, Tom Saddington has explored the theme of throw-aways for several years in many different ways. The ring on the left is made in sterling silver and represents a faithfully reproduced, squeezed tube container, complete with screw top; the end has been twisted to form the shank. The ring on the right is composed of a group of bottle tops attached to a bar mounted on the shank.

221 Ring. Fine gold and quartz. West German, by Hubertus von Skal (b. 1942). 1980. Diam. 2 cm. The artist's collection.

The literal and figurative designs of Hubertus von Skal (see Pl. 120) have become less formalized and more spontaneous. For a time, von Skal explored spatial relationships in terms of large sculpture. When he returned to jewellery, the changing aspects of faces, indicated as it were by a few sketchy strokes of the pen, began to interest him; here he has carved them into quartz. The rounded shank of this ring is hand-forged and attached to the bezel by a loop to permit a swivel movement.

222 Necklace. Gold. Italian, by Francesco Pavan (b. 1937). 1980. L. 100 cm, W. 2 cm. The artist's collection.

Francesco Pavan is a prominent member of the 'Padua School' whose work is represented in the permanent collection of the Schmuckmuseum, Pforzheim, and has been widely exhibited in Europe and more recently in the United States. A graduate of the Istituto d'Arte, Padua, Pavan has been teaching there since 1961.

The classic simplicity of this necklace demonstrates an aspect typical of the 'Padua School': thin gold sheet has been cut into strips and twisted into a continuous spiral.

223 Ring. Copper. West German, by Walter Wittek (b. 1943). 1980/81. H. 8 cm, Diam. 1.4 cm. The artist's collection.

An interesting and imaginative artist/jeweller, Walter Wittek served an apprenticeship as a steel engraver and completed his studies at the Akademie der bildenden Künste, Nuremberg, in 1968. His designs (mainly for rings) exhibit a strong sense of individualism in a pronounced contemporary context.

Wittek has named this piece the 'President's Ring', and its design reflects very clearly Wittek's view of such an office. Defensive or aggressive (depending on your point of view), the heavy, massive shape and size of the ring evoke the commanding position of such power. Hand-forged in solid copper, the ring is gold-plated.

224 Brooch. Gold and silver. West German, by Hermann Schafran (b. 1949). 1981. Diam. 4.5 cm. Private Collection.

Designs by Schafran, a graduate of the Fachhochschule für Gestaltung, Pforzheim, are the sum total of his intensive research into the relationship between space and body, and of his superlative craftsmanship. With masterly precision, he expresses his concepts using symbols of geometric configurations to make his point.

This brooch was inspired by the map of Mannheim's inner city; the shape fits over the area containing its most important offices and buildings. The brooch is made in gold, the lines and dots are inlaid silver, oxidized black.

225 Two Pins. Aluminium and plastic. Dutch, by Paul Derrez (b. 1950). 1981. (*Left*) H. 7 cm; (*right*) 10 cm. The artist's collection.

In 1976 Paul Derrez founded the Gallery Ra in Amsterdam; in 1980 he was awarded the Françoise van den Bosch Prize for his efforts in the promotion of contemporary jewellery.

His own work, represented in several public collections in Holland, had become rather less severe in outline (see Pl. 185), as illustrated by these two pins made of aluminium; the colour is provided by pleated sheets of plastic slotted onto the framework of the pins.

217 Pendant on Chain. Gold, silver, ruby and ▷ mirror-prism. West-German, by Ulrike Bahrs (b. 1944). 1980. H. 7 cm, W. 4 cm. Rau Colletion.

218 Necklace. 18-carat gold. Australian, by Frank Bauer (b. 1942). 1980. W. 7 cm. Private Collection.

219 Pendant. Gold and silver. Spanish, by Ana Font (b. 1945). 1980. H. 6.6 cm. Schmuckmuseum, Pforzheim (1982/20).

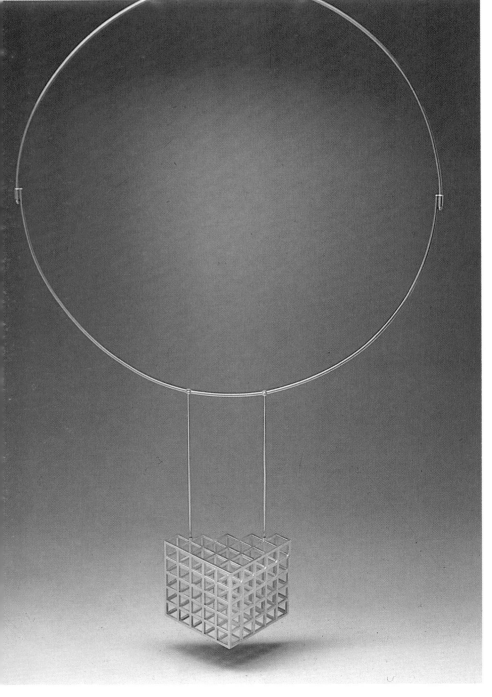

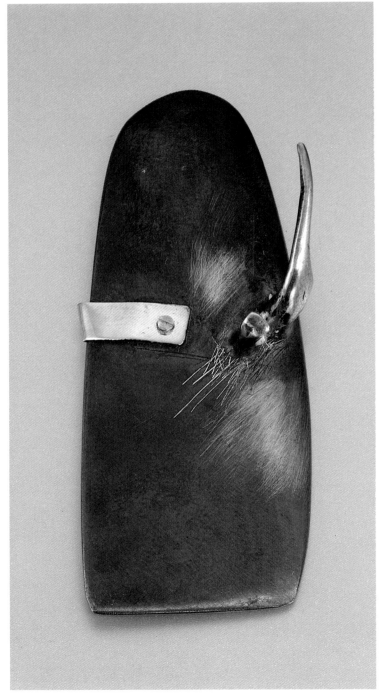

220 Two Rings. Silver and enamel paint. British, by Tom Saddington (b. 1952). *(Left)* 1980; Diam. 2 cm; *(right)* 1976; 4 cm × 5 cm. Private Collection.

221 Ring. Fine gold and quartz. West German, by Hubertus von Skal (b. 1942). 1980. Diam. 2 cm. The artist's collection.

222 Necklace. Gold. Italian, by Francesco Pavan (b. 1937). 1980. L. 100 cm, W. 2 cm. The artist's collection.

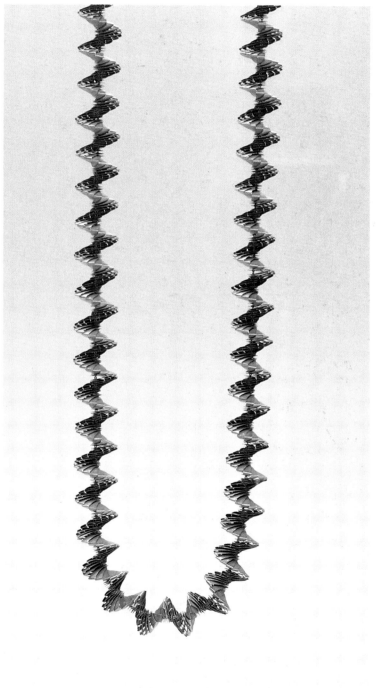

223 Ring. Copper. West German, by Walter Wittek (b. 1943). 1980/81. H. 8 cm, diam. 1.4 cm. The artist's collection.

224 Brooch. Gold and silver. West German, by Hermann Schafran (b. 1949). 1981. Diam. 4.5 cm. Private Collection.

225 Two Pins. Aluminium and plastic. Dutch, by Paul Derrez (b. 1950). 1981. *(Left)* H. 7 cm; *(right)* 10 cm. The artist's collection.

226 Bracelet. Iron and glass. Swiss, by Bernhard Schobinger (b. 1946). 1981. W. 6 cm. The artist's collection. ▷

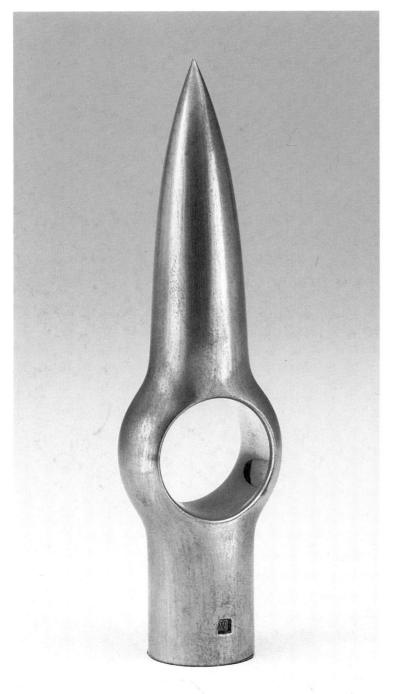

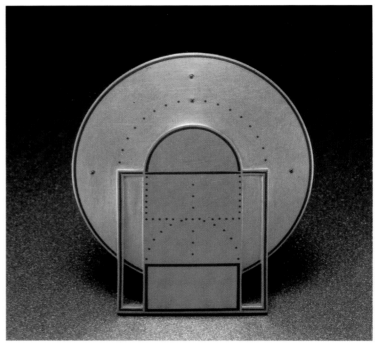

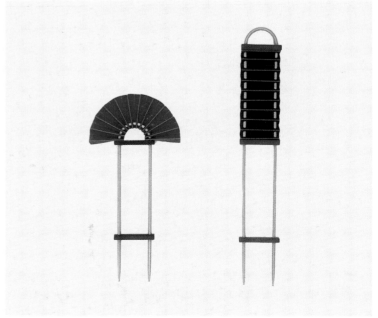

226 Bracelet. Iron and glass. Swiss, by Bernhard Schobinger (b. 1946). 1981. W. 6 cm. The artist's collection.

Schobinger's design concepts are always comments or reflections; he deliberately chooses his materials to make a specific point. This bracelet is made from iron with a weathered texture and shaped like a park railing. One end of it, overlapping the circular form, is buckled as if crushed by a car. There is a large spike of safety glass slotted through the vertical bars, which have been tightened around its uneven contours; its edges have been ground smooth.

227 Necklace. Silver, gold, steel and mother-of-pearl. Norwegian, by Tone Vigeland (b. 1938). 1981. L. (from shoulder in front) 24 cm, W. 22 cm. Private Collection.

The unique work of Tone Vigeland, one of Norway's foremost contemporary artist/jewellers, has won her an international reputation. She works predominantly with combinations of gold, silver and steel, and many of her designs are based on a kind of chain-mail–a technique she has ingeniously adapted to create astounding forms and textures.

The necklace illustrated has an underlying structure of chain-mail, made from thousands of silver links connected in different directions to form the pattern. The triangular sections on either side of the front have been covered by an extra layer of links attached to silver grains with gold tops and finished with a line of oblong, hollow gold dangles. The feathery look of the lower front sections has been achieved with blue-steel nails, hammered flat and suspended in rows from the mesh underneath. The centre piece in the front (which also acts as the clasp) consists of mother-of-pearl attached to a rectangle of beaten steel, held by a vertical gold wire that ends in a steel spike. The necklace is extremely flexible; its weight distributes itself comfortably on the shoulders.

228 Bracelet. 18-carat gold and steel. Swiss, by Bernhard Schobinger (b. 1946). 1981. L. 30.5 cm. Private Collection.

Made from a simple strip of gold sheet, twisted and attached to a steel key, the design of this bracelet was inspired by the strip that comes off when opening a tin can. A typical example of Bernhard Schobinger's wit and imagination, this bracelet expresses his rebellion against traditional values and attitudes and is reinforced by his irreverent treatment of the materials.

229 Five Rings. 10- and 14-carat gold, diamonds and enamel. U.S.A., by Balfour Inc. 1981. Sizes unavailable. Private collections of the teams mentioned.

Probably the most universal form of jewellery worn in the United States is the college ring, manufactured in great quantities by Balfour Inc. of Massachusetts. Similar in style though more elaborate are the rings Balfour makes for various professional sports teams. The top row (from left to right) shows the rings made for the Chicago Sting soccer team, the New York Islanders hockey team and the Boston Celtics basketball team. The ring on the bottom left was designed and made for the San Francisco 49'ers (an American football team) and the one on the right for the Los Angeles Dodgers (baseball).

All are shaped like signet rings and cast in gold, including the individual lettering around the outer edge of the bezel. Dark enamel has then been applied to the background of the lettering and either a single diamond or a group of pavé-set diamonds has been placed in the centre.

230 'Australian Arm Jewel, circa 1981'. Stainless steel, bamboo and linen, mounted on a satin background and framed. Australian, by Margaret West (b. 1936). 1981. H. (frame) 43 cm, W. 28 cm. The artist's collection.

Margaret West is an artist/jeweller whose work is represented in many public collections all over Australia; her designs and approach to jewellery have played an important role in the development of contemporary jewellery in her native country. Concerned with the metaphysical, psychological and social aspects of jewellery, she recognizes its ability to inform and transform. Her work deeply reflects her Australian roots as illustrated by these three arm ornaments that are wearable but have been deliberately made inaccessible by the glass-fronted frame in order to focus on their dualism: their aestheticism, and what the artist terms their 'lethality'.

231 Neckpiece and Bracelet. Nylon. British, by Caroline Broadhead (b. 1950). 1981. Diam. (necklace) 22.9 cm; (bracelet) 12.7 cm. Private Collection.

This exciting and dramatic neckpiece by Caroline Broadhead (see also Pl. 198) is made of nylon monofilament tinted in subtle shades of blue and yellow, entwined into a mesh. The loose ends have been fastened to toggles. The neckpiece can be worn bunched together or expanded like a hood. The spherical bracelet consists of a flat ring with nylon filament threaded through the perforations, which are flexible enough to allow a hand to slip through between them yet still maintain their rounded outer contour when placed on the lower arm.

232 Brooch. Cardboard, acetate, crayon, brass and flies. U.S.A., by Hugh Blind. 1982. H. 3.4 cm, W. 7.8 cm. Private Collection.

With perhaps a rather savage sense of humour, Hugh Blind made a series of brooches based on famous paintings by transposing them into quick drawings and substituting dead flies for the people. Entitled 'The Last Supper', this drawing was done on cardboard; flies caught in Blind's workshop have been placed around the table, preserved by the acetate lamination. The fly in the centre has a tiny metal halo.

233 Postcard-Brooch. Makrolon, Astrolon, rubber-band, brass pin and postcard. Swiss, by Otto Künzli (b. 1948). 1981. 14.8 cm × 10.8 cm. Edition of 200.

A qualified gold- and silversmith, born and trained in Zurich, Künzli completed his studies at the Akademie der bildenden Künste in Munich in 1978. Since then, he has lived and worked in Germany, searching for and finding many different and original ways of expressing his criticism of society in general and jewellery in particular.

In this example he has converted a picture-frame into a wearable brooch for postcards, interchangeable according to the mood and taste of the wearer. Künzli sees this as being in a direct progression from the earliest body ornamentation to pictorial representations (tattoos and later amulets, cameos and medallions portraying people, animals, landscapes, etc.). With postcards of great variety freely available everywhere, one can wear one's favourite view of a holiday location, change it for a much-loved painting after a visit to a museum or for a pretty picture of a bunch of roses on a birthday card.

227 Necklace. Silver, gold, steel and mother- ▷ of-pearl. Norwegian, by Tone Vigeland (b. 1938). 1981. L. (from shoulder in front) 24 cm, W. 22 cm. Private Collection.

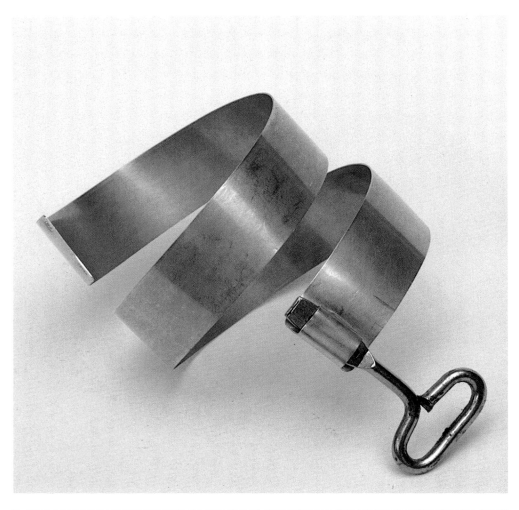

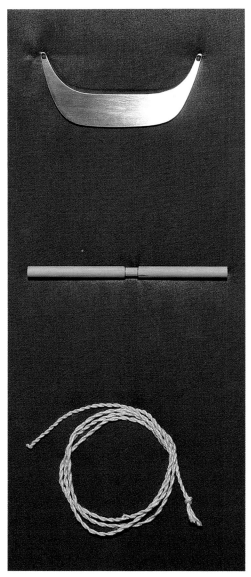

228 Bracelet. 18-carat gold and steel. Swiss, by Bernhard Schobinger (b. 1946). 1981. L. 30.5 cm. Private Collection.

229 Five Rings. 10- and 14-carat gold, diamonds and enamel. U.S.A., by Balfour Inc. 1981. Sizes unavailable. Private collections of the teams mentioned.

△

230 'Australian Arm Jewel, circa 1981'. Stainless steel, bamboo and linen, mounted on a satin background and framed. Australian, by Margaret West (b. 1936). 1981. H. (frame) 43 cm, W. 28 cm. The artist's collection.

231 Neckpiece and Bracelet. Nylon. British, by Caroline Broadhead (b. 1950). 1981. Diam. (necklace) 22.9 cm; (bracelet) 12.7 cm. Private Collection.

232 Brooch. Cardboard, acetate, crayon, brass and flies. U.S.A., by Hugh Blind. 1982. H. 3.4 cm, W. 7.8 cm. Private Collection.

233 Postcard-Brooch. Makrolon, Astrolon, rubber-band, brass pin and postcard. Swiss, by Otto Künzli (b. 1948). 1981. 14.8 cm × 10.8 cm. Edition of 200.

234 Necklace. Silver, beryl and mother-of-pearl. U.S.S.R., by Vladimir Alekseevich Zotov (b. 1934). 1982. 12 cm × 16 cm. The artist's collection.
Vladimir Zotov trained at the Moscow Surikov Art Institute; he is a member of the Artists' Union and works as a free-lance artist/jeweller in Moscow. His work is represented in several major museums in the U.S.S.R., and he has taken part in many exhibitions, winning awards and diplomas.

Zotov has called the design of this silver necklace 'Frozen Flower'. The icy colours of the beryls and mother-of-pearl blend well into the surrounding structure of textured silver sections, which echo the crystal formations of frost. The spiky central section with pendant is connected to a chain of long, straight links that has a clasp at the back.

235 Necklace. Silver and jet. French, by Catherine Noll (b. 1945). 1982. Diam. (bead) 1.5 cm, L. 35 cm. The artist's collection.
One of the five founder-members of Hephaïstos, a group of creative French artist/jewellers formed in 1982, Catherine Noll has designed whole collections of jewellery for Chanel, Dior and Nina Ricci. Her approach to jewellery is very sculptural, and she frequently carves an entire ring out of solid turquoise, or bracelets from rock crystal. For this necklace, Noll has hand-carved large beads from jet and set them off against silver beads, threaded onto the hollow silver sections at the back, which end in a simple hook-and-eye clasp.

236 Brooch. Silver and epoxy resin. U.S.A., by Robin L. Quigley (b. 1947). 1982. 5.1 cm × 7 cm × 0.6 cm. Ronald Abramson Collection, Washington, D.C.
Robin Quigley is Assistant Professor at the Rhode Island School of Design, a college from which she graduated herself in 1976 with an M.F.A. in sculpture, jewellery and metalsmithing. On a convex base of oval silver is a face composed of two dots, a circle, and two lines. The piece represents a simplified, minimal composition evolved from her earlier, more complex works, which included the use of varied patterns and shapes in a more two-dimensional setting.

237 Bracelet. German silver and resin. U.S.S.R., by Andrei Aleksandrovich Vasin, (b. 1952). 1982. 4.4 cm × 3.7 cm × 1 cm. The artist's collection.
A member of the Artists' Union of the U.S.S.R. since 1979, Andrei Vasin works free lance, creating one-of-a-kind jewellery that has been bought for public collections and exhibited at home and abroad.

German silver is an alloy of copper, zinc and nickel, widely used in the U.S.S.R. for jewellery. A little harder than silver, it is also cheaper, easy to work with and almost untarnishable. Entitled 'Mirror', probably in reference to a quotation from Ovid: 'the eye is the mirror of the soul', this bracelet is a flat band, inlaid with sections of translucent blue resin. The large open eye is connected to the band by hinges, one of which acts as the clasp.

238 'Two Wearables'. Cotton fabric and wire. British, by Susanna Heron (b. 1949). 1982. Diam. 45.7 cm. Stedelijk Museum, Amsterdam, and Crafts Council Collection, London.
By the late 1970s, Susanna Heron (see Pl. 150) had abandoned traditional materials and forms almost entirely. Experimenting with acrylics, plastics and even paper, she liberated her work from the formal restrictions imposed by the nature of metals and metalworking techniques. The result was an extraordinary collection of shapes and colours, conceived to work in conjunction with the body, and completely new in the context of jewellery. For example, the collection included a bracelet made of a square piece of brightly coloured polyester, with a diagonal cut for the hand to slip through.

Other pieces of Heron's work began to suggest a gradual movement away from functional jewellery as such. The two pieces illustrated, entitled 'Two Wearables', have a dual purpose: as 'jewellery' and as wall-hangings. The fabric has been stretched onto the circular wire frame and is held taut by a knot in the centre.

239 Neckpiece. Dyed nylon. Dutch, by Emmy van Leersum (1930–1984). 1982. W. 30 cm. Australian Crafts Council Collection, Sydney.
Synthetic materials have often played an important part in Emmy van Leersum's work (see Pls 147, 204)–she had a rare talent for recognizing their potential long before others discovered their value to jewellery.

This neckpiece is made of translucent, flexible nylon strips, dyed in two shades of blue. Similar to the design of her gold bracelet (Pl. 204), the basic shape of this neckpiece was evolved from a square. With minute variations of the right angle, four strips have been joined with mitred corners; one of them is twisted once, which causes the square to fold back on itself, forming a double oval with pointed ends. The neck divides the two shapes, slipped over the wearer's head, into one large loop in front and two corners pointing upwards at the back of the neck. Like the frame to a picture, the simple contours of this neckpiece emphasize the shape of the wearer's head and neck.

240 Brooch. Oxidized silver, formica, inlaid wood and titanium. U.S.A., by Ivy Ross (b. 1955). 1982. ca. 11 cm × 6 cm. Private Collection.
Ivy Ross won the 1981 Women in Design International Award for outstanding achievement in the field of design; her work is represented in important public and private collections. She has taught and lectured on many aspects of design and marketing, including on her own work, which encompasses one-of-a-kind jewellery as well as three-dimensional prototypes for production.

Ross's designs have a strong graphic quality and often a close affinity to textiles. In fact, they are frequently conceived in conjunction with garments, as a unified concept. This brooch is part of a suede scarf in two tones of blue, on which the brooch is to be pinned in a designated place. Within the triangular silver frame, the pattern is made up of inlaid formica shapes in ivory and dark and light blue; the remainder is filled with rows of brightly anodized titanium wires.

241 Brooch. Silver, steel, paper and polyester resins. Spanish, by Ramon Puig Cuyas (b. 1953). 1982. 10.5 cm × 1 cm. The artist's collection.
Shaped like a mysterious signalling device, the brooch is made in the form of a slightly tilted 'T' on a square base, inlaid with pale green resin and patterned with paper. The two vertical sections contain the pin fastening and meet just below the horizontal section, which carries a curved yellow rectangle on the right and a flat, shaped metal piece that resembles a profile on the left. The wire itself is steel, which allows it to vibrate with movement.

Puig Cuyas is a founder-member of a newly formed association of Catalonian artist/jewellers, called 'Grup Nou', and also professor at the Massana School of Jewellery Design, Barcelona.

242 Wearable Object. Wood and printed textile. Dutch, by Lam de Wolf (b. 1949). 1982. L. 85 cm, W. 45 cm. Australian Crafts Museum, Sydney.
Lam de Wolf's studies in textiles at the Gerrit Rietveld Academie in Amsterdam form the basis for her unusual designs and approach to jewellery. She works in large dimensions, winding and knotting small pieces of printed fabric around wooden links joined into multiple-stranded necklaces that are worn dramatically bunched over the shoulders and cover the entire back. Like many other pieces of her work, the one illustrated is also very effective as a wall hanging. It demonstrates well her intent–to make the wearer conscious of movement and posture as well as the need to exercise care in the choice of clothes to wear with the piece.

234 Necklace. Silver, beryl and mother-of- ▷ pearl. U.S.S.R., by Vladimir Alekseevich Zotov (b. 1934). 1982. 12 cm × 16 cm. The artist's collection.

235   Necklace. Silver and jet. French, by Catherine Noll (b. 1945). 1982. Diam. (bead) 1.5 cm, L. 35 cm. The artist's collection.

236 Brooch. Silver and epoxy resin. U.S.A., by Robin L. Quigley (b. 1947). 1982. 5.2 cm × 7 cm × 0.6 cm. Ronald Abramson Collection, Washington, D.C.

237 Bracelet. German silver and resin. U.S.S.R., by Andrei Aleksandrovich Vasin, (b. 1952). 1982. 4.4 cm × 3.7 cm × 1 cm. The artist's collection.

238 'Two Wearables'. Cotton fabric and wire. ▷ British, by Susanna Heron (b. 1949). 1982. Diam. 45.7 cm. Stedelijk Museum, Amsterdam, and Crafts Council Collection, London.

239 Neckpiece. Dyed nylon. Dutch, by Emmy van Leersum (1930–1984). 1982. W. 30 cm. Australian Crafts Council Collection, Sydney.

240 Brooch. Oxidized silver, formica, inlaid wood and titanium. U.S.A., by Ivy Ross (b. 1955). 1982. 11 cm × 6 cm. Private Collection.

241 Brooch. Silver, steel, paper and polyester resins. Spanish, by Ramon Puig Cuyas (b. 1953). 1982. 10.5 cm × 1 cm. The artist's collection.

242 Wearable Object. Wood and printed textile. Dutch, by Lam de Wolf (b. 1949). 1982. L. 85 cm, W. 45 cm. Australian Crafts Museum, Sydney.

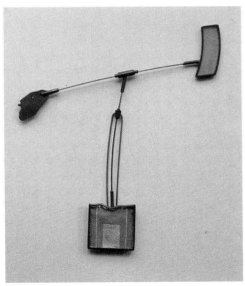

243 Brooch. Tin. West German, by Gerhard Rothmann (b. 1941). 1982. W. 7 cm. Private Collection.

Gerhard Rothmann's continuous research and experiments with many different forms and materials (see also Pl. 171), including gold, silver, steel and acrylics, drove him to look for the ultimate 'personal' aspect of jewellery, for a form of jewellery that would be as unique to the wearer as a finger-print and create a direct connection between the maker and the wearer. Rothmann found the answer in 'body-prints'. A client would chose a section of his/her body (or anyone else's of their choice); Rothmann would make an impression of the area in plaster and a cast from it in precious or base metal. The brooch is cast in tin, a soft metal that easily takes on every detail of skin texture, in this instance the fold of the right under-arm of a male body from the back.

244 Bracelet. 18-carat gold. West German, by Friedrich Becker (b. 1922). 1982. 6.5 cm × 7 cm. Private Collection.

Perhaps Friedrich Becker's greatest contribution to the development of modern jewellery is the introduction of kinetics (see also Pls 122/123, 196). An expert in fine mechanics, Becker built micro ball-bearings into the two bars mounted on the bracelet, which allow them to spin in every direction at the slightest movement of the wearer's arm. The effect is astounding and baffling since the mechanism is totally invisible and the bars, apparently unconnected, seem to swing and glide smoothly across each other. Becker has used this technique on many of his superb bracelets, rings and brooches with equal success, using all kinds of different forms (discs, cones and bars) that rotate and gyrate to achieve the kinetic effect.

245 Brooch. Ivory, mother-of-pearl, shale and silver. Australian, by Ann Brownsworth (b. 1950). 1982. 7 cm × 6.3 cm. Diamond Valley Shire Collection.

Ann Brownsworth is a graduate of the Royal Melbourne Institute of Technology (1973). She also spent a year at the Tyler School of Art in Philadelphia and has travelled as well as exhibited in Europe and the United States.

Brownsworth's jewellery demonstrates essentially her deep involvement with her environment–her inner perception of the landscapes of her native Australia, which she portrays with loving care and poetic sensitivity. This brooch, entitled 'Where to from Here', is made from organic materials–the ivory frame is inlaid with small pieces of silver and surrounds a landscape of shale with a mother-of-pearl sky.

246 Bracelet, Ring and Earrings. Gold and pure tin. Austrian, by Fritz Maierhofer (b. 1941). 1982. L. (bracelet) 22 cm; (ring) 7 cm; (earrings) 7 cm. Private Collection.

Fritz Maierhofer's constant quest for new forms and different ways with old or new materials has resulted in fascinating pieces of jewellery (see Pl. 167). In the course of many years, he has created original and unusual designs in traditional metals as well as in acrylics, steel and now tin. A remarkably soft and pliable metal, pure tin is also strong and holds its shape when used in a sufficiently heavy gauge. Maierhofer has used this property to great advantage in these pieces, all of which are fashioned from a pure tin strip that varies in thickness: the bracelet is 3 mm thick at the start, a rigid curve that fits around the wrist; the top edge is inlaid with solid gold. It narrows gradually towards the other end, where it has been beaten down to a 1/2 mm thickness that allows it to curl like a ribbon and is flexible enough to be bent into a variety of different shapes. The same applies to the ring, which has a triangular gold inlay on the top edge, and to the earrings, which have a gold bar at the top.

247 Brooch. Silver and granite. Japanese, by Kazuhiro Itoh (b. 1948). 1982. L. 15 cm. The artist's collection.

Itoh has carved the black stone in relief to look like a piece of paper rolled up diagonally. The fine lines go around the cylindrical shape that tapers to a sharp point at both ends. Two silver snap fasteners are affixed to the back.

The brooch is a typical example of Itoh's superb ability to express the essence of a concept with the stark simplicity inherent in Japanese art (see also Pl. 210).

248 Necklace and Pendant. Silver and ivory beads. Hungarian, by Vladimir Péter (b. 1947). 1982. L. 37 cm; (pendant) 3 cm × 4 cm. The artist's collection.

Péter is a graduate of the Academy of Applied Arts in Budapest where he is now professor. He has exhibited widely and in 1981 designed a collection of jewellery for Hans Hausen Sølvsmedie, Denmark.

This necklace and pendant by Vladimir Péter shows clearly a strong influence of traditional folk art, both south-east European and Indian, but with distinct contemporary overtones, as demonstrated by the centaur-like figures on wheels. The necklace is made of round ivory beads; the pendant is suspended from the central bead by several strands of green cord.

249 Neckpieces. Steel and neoprene. British, by David Watkins (b. 1940). 1982. Diam. 45 cm. Private Collection.

By the early 1980s, Watkins (see also Pl. 170) began to look for a certain reduction of material content in his jewellery, in order to form specific shapes with large, sweeping contours without having the distraction of solid areas in between. The result was an astonishingly effective range of neckpieces that could be worn singly or in groups and were contructed from steel wire coated with neoprene. Light in weight yet strong enough to hold its shape, this neckpiece consists of three separate parts that describe a series of arcs around the neck and shoulders. The title of the piece, inspired by the exploration of space, is 'Russian Orbits'; each section is in a different colour–red, black and grey respectively.

250 Collar. Bronze. French, by Dominique Favey (b. 1953). 1982. W. 7 cm. The artist's collection.

Trained in sculpture at the Ecole Nationale des Beaux-Arts in Paris, Dominique Favey sees sculpture and the creation of jewellery as two complimentary and closely connected activities. Fascinated by the contrast between materials–in this instance bronze and lace–Favey has made this collar by the process of lost-wax casting. The complex pattern of lace has been faithfully reproduced in golden-coloured metal, with every detail of its fragile construction. The collar is open-ended at the back.

251 Brooch. Silver, German silver, paper, crayon and pencil. West German, by Jens-Rüdiger Lorenzen (b. 1942). 1982/1983. 8 cm × 8 cm. The artist's collection.

Lorenzen's sensitive treatment of subject matter and material has been the keynote of his work, reflecting his ability to interpret his views and observations in a visual and tactile manner. Influenced to some extent by Far Eastern aesthetic and the work/thoughts of the late sculptor Eva Hesse, he creates his own images with a total lack of regard for jewellery in the traditional sense; this leaves the eventual possessor to decide whether to wear it or not.

This brooch puts the 'picture' outside the frame: part drawing, part collage on the metal base, and lacquered for protection. The 'picture' surrounds an inner frame of silver, unevenly oxidized. The central square has been textured like a blank canvas.

252 Necklace. Silver. Japanese, by Hajime Kimata (b. 1938). 1983. H. 23 cm. The artist's collection.

Since the early 1970s, Hajime Kimata's work has been represented in many international jewellery exhibitions touring Europe and the United States. Kimata is Assistant Professor at the Tokyo National University of Education and a prominent member of the Japan Jewellery Designers' Association; his designs exemplify the progression of Japanese contemporary jewellery towards its own specific formal concepts.

Kimata's approach is sculptural, as demonstrated by the pendant of this necklace. Three silver platforms, attached to a rigid neckwire, are suspended from one another and each supports small sculptural shapes.

243 **Brooch.** Tin. West German, by Gerhard Rothmann (b. 1941). 1982. W. 7 cm. Private Collection.

244 **Bracelet.** 18-carat gold. West German, by Friedrich Becker (b. 1922). 1982. 6.5 cm × 7 cm. Private Collection.

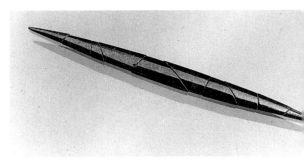

245 **Brooch.** Ivory, mother-of-pearl, shale and silver. Australian, by Ann Brownsworth (b. 1950). 1982. 7 cm × 6.3 cm Diamond Valley Shire Collection.

246 **Bracelet, Ring and Earrings.** Gold and pure tin. Austrian, by Fritz Maierhofer (b. 1941). 1982. L. (bracelet) 22 cm; (ring) 7 cm; (earrings) 7 cm. Private Collection.

247 **Brooch.** Silver and granite. Japanese, by Kazuhiro Itoh (b. 1948). 1982. L. 15 cm. The artist's collection.

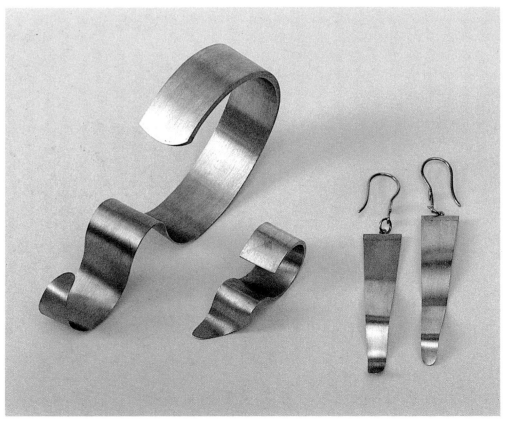

248 **Necklace and Pendant.** Silver and ivory beads. Hungarian, by Vladimir Péter (b. 1947). 1982. L. 37 cm; (pendant) 3 cm × 4 cm. The artist's collection.

◁ **250 Collar.** Bronze. French, by Dominique Favey (b. 1953). 1982. W. 7 cm. The artist's collection.

251 Brooch. Silver, German silver, paper, crayon and pencil. West German, by Jens-Rüdiger Lorenzen (b. 1942). 1982/1983. 8 cm × 8 cm. The artist's collection.

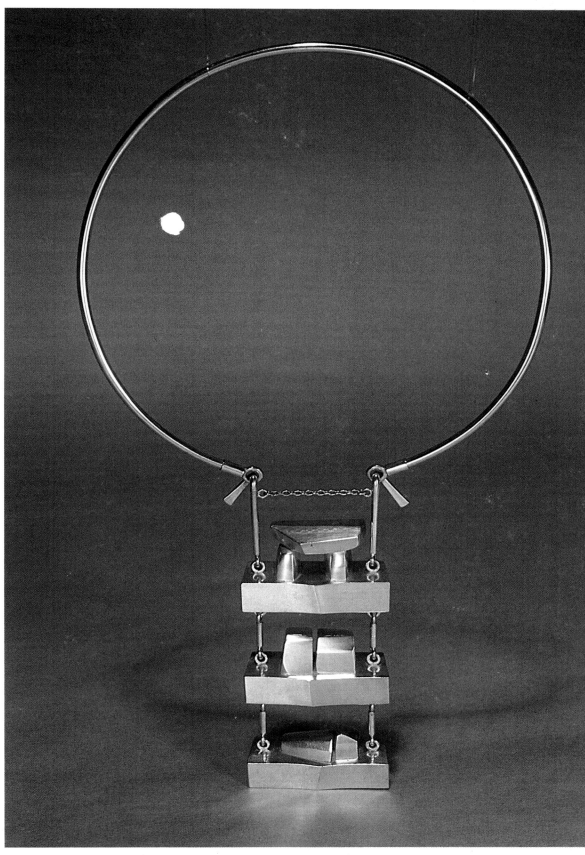

252 Necklace. Silver. Japanese, by Hajime Kimata (b. 1938). 1983. H. 23 cm. The artist's collection.

253 Necklace and Earrings. 18-carat gold and lapis lazuli. British, by Bryan Illsley (b. 1937). 1983. L. (necklace) 50 cm; (earrings) 3 cm. (Necklace) the artist's collection; (earrings) Private Collection.

Originally trained as a carver and stone-mason, Illsley turned to painting in the early 1960s. He then began making jewellery, after working part-time with Breon O'Casey, who taught Illsley the rudiments of the craft and later became his partner. Their designs, at that time, were much inspired by ancient and ethnic jewellery; and although that influence is still noticeable in Illsley's work today, he has developed an original style of his own, particularly in the last few years since his partnership with O'Casey was dissolved.

Illsley makes his own beads (fabricated in gold for this necklace); the large ones are carved from lapis lazuli. The earrings are made from thin, flat sheet gold, in a three-pronged shape, and have two gold wire links around the vertical section.

254 Three Rings. Stainless steel. Hungarian, by István Schuszter (b. 1953). 1983. Diam. 2 cm. The artist's collection.

In common with several other contemporary artist/jewellers, Schuszter's designs are inspired by technology and fine mechanics. Although entirely self-taught, he has mastered sophisticated engineering skills, which are crucial to the success of his design concepts.

Made with superb precision in stainless steel, the rings illustrated use screws (top right) and machined metal sections to form the bezels.

255 Necklace. 18-carat gold, emu feathers, cornelian, enamel and stoneware. British, by Wendy Ramshaw (b. 1939). 1983. L. 30 cm, W. 12.5 cm. The artist's collection.

At the beginning of 1978, Wendy Ramshaw (see Pl. 152) and her husband, David Watkins (see Pls 170, 249), were invited to spend six months as artists-in-residence in western Australia. Then, in 1981, Wendy Ramshaw was invited by the Josiah Wedgwood Company to design jewellery incorporating their famous porcelain and jasper ware made into beads to her design in their workshops. The two experiences sparked a new departure for Ramshaw's designs, which now became much freer in form and included complex interchangeable components.

This necklace has a rigid gold neckwire threaded with tubular beads that act as spacers to keep the pendants apart; some of them are banded with sapphire-blue enamel. The pendants are composed of blue and purple emu feathers, blue cornelian set in gold, cone-shaped beads made of blue and dark pink, fine-grain stoneware and one long gold tube, inlaid with several bands of blue enamel, with a gold bead drop at the end.

256 Neckpiece. Brass, steel, PVC and lacquer. Swiss, by Therese Hilbert (b. 1948). 1983. ca. 44 cm × 42 cm. The artist's collection.

The neckpiece consists of ten brass rods of equal length and diameter, lacquered matt black and threaded through a hole drilled in the centre onto the black, PVC-coated steel wire. Thus, they are adjustable and can be worn bunched together, or formed into crosses. Whilst no specific symbolism was consciously intended, the design does evoke certain associations with spikes and thorns–aggressive or defensive.

Therese Hilbert's work is represented in museums in Pforzheim, and Amsterdam, among others. Originally trained at the Kunstgewerbeschule in Zurich, she completed her studies at the Akademie der bildenden Künste in Munich.

257 Neckpiece. Stainless steel and acrylic. Hungarian, by Maria Lugossy (b. 1950). 1983. 25.5 cm × 30 cm. The artist's collection.

Maria Lugossy graduated as an artist/goldsmith from the Academy of Applied Arts in Budapest in 1973. Besides working as a sculptor making metal and glass constructions, Lugossy has also produced an impressive amount of original jewellery. Since 1977, her work in both fields has been exhibited in Hungary and in many other European countries.

This neckpiece is very typical of Lugossy's massive, monumental approach, apparent even in her jewellery design. The large rigid metal frame supports a square shape divided on the diagonal into a cross and set with four raised triangles of clear acrylic; a fifth triangle is attached to the outside of the square.

258 Necklace, Ring and Two Brooches. 18-carat gold. Italian, by Graziano Visintin (b. 1954). 1983. (Necklace) 15 cm × 15 cm; H. (ring) 3 cm; (brooches) 6.5 cm. The artist's collection.

A graduate of the Istituto d'Arte 'Pietro Selvatico' in Padua (1973), Visintin has been a teacher there since 1976. The superb jewellery illustrated, based entirely on geometric figures, won him the International Jewellery Art Prize at the 5th Tokyo Triennale in 1983. The square necklace is made of white gold, with a yellow gold triangle slotted over one section, which can be moved to a different angle or position. The ring is in the shape of a cone in yellow gold. The two brooches are constructed with parallel white gold bars surmounted by yellow gold triangles.

259 Brooch. Gold, moonstone, ivory, acrylic, kiln-hardened stone. British, by Kevin Coates (b. 1950). 1983. 4.3 cm × 3.2 cm. Private Collection.

An accomplished musician who specializes in baroque music, Kevin Coates graduated as a goldsmith from the Royal College of Art, London, wrote a thesis on 'Geometry and Proportion and the Art of Lutherie' for his Ph.D., and became a Freeman of the Worshipful Company of Goldsmiths (in 1980). The many facets of his creative mind are well reflected in the imaginative jewellery he has made over the years on themes as diverse as legends, mythical beasts, operas and the circus.

This brooch depicts the figure of Harlequin set into a niche carved from stone. Harlequin's face and hands are finely modelled and cast in gold. His mask and his costume are made of ivory, patterned with inlays of coloured acrylic. His hands are clasped around a moonstone.

260 Torque. Gold, lapis lazuli and rock crystal. French, by Goudji (b. 1941). 1983. 13.5 cm × 14 cm. Musée des Arts décoratifs, Paris (depôt de l'Etat français, F.N.A.C.).

A graduate of the Academy of Fine Arts at Tbilisi in his native Georgia, U.S.S.R., Goudji became the youngest member of the Artists' Union at the age of twenty-three and worked on metal sculptures. He left the Soviet Union in 1974 and settled in France where he turned his imaginative talents to jewellery and precious metals for the first time.

Though heavily influenced by the jewellery of antiquity, Goudji has adapted its forms in an original manner to bring them into a contemporary context. This necklace is a typical example–the gold section is hollow, hand-forged and encrusted with lapis lazuli; in the front are two curved rods of rock crystal with tourmaline inclusions. The back is hinged and the front clasp contains a magnet. The gold centre section can be removed entirely and worn as a ring. The torque has an additional pendant (not illustrated) that can be attached to the magnet in the centre when the ring is being worn.

261 Neckpiece. Steel and paper. Japanese, by Shuhei Miyata (b. 1933). 1983. W. 10 cm. The artists' collection.

Miyata is a prominent member of the Japanese Jewellery Designers' Association and currently professor at Mie University. Trained in industrial design at the Tokyo University of Arts, he has been responsible for such diverse projects as designs for cars and sight-seeing buses as well as for porcelain and jewellery, all of which have won him awards and recognition including representation in several public collections.

The necklace is made from wire that holds a pendant in the shape of an open fan, which is composed of moulded, hand-made, wood-pulp paper.

253 Necklace and Earrings. 18-carat gold and lapis lazuli. British, by Bryan Illsley (b. 1937). 1983. L. (necklace) 50 cm; (earrings) 3 cm. (Necklace) the artist's collection; (earrings) Private Collection.

254 Three Rings. Stainless steel. Hungarian, by István Schuszter (b. 1953). 1983. Diam. 2 cm. The artist's collection.

255 Necklace. 18-carat gold, emu feathers, cornelian, enamel and stoneware. British, by Wendy Ramshaw (b. 1939). 1983. L. 30 cm, W. 12.5 cm. The artist's collection.

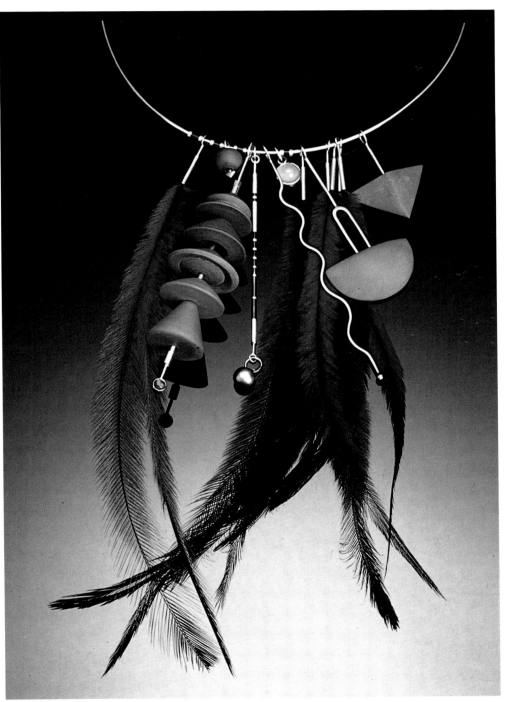

256 Neckpiece. Brass, steel, PVC and lacquer. Swiss, by Therese Hilbert (b. 1948). 1983. ca. 44 cm × 42 cm. The artist's collection.

257 Neckpiece. Stainless steel and acrylic. Hungarian, by Maria Lugossy (b. 1950). 1983. 25.5 cm × 30 cm. The artist's collection.

258 Necklace, Ring and Two Brooches. 18-carat gold. Italian, by Graziano Visintin (b. 1954). 1983. (Necklace) 15 cm × 15 cm; H. (ring) 3 cm; (brooches) 6.5 cm. The artist's collection.

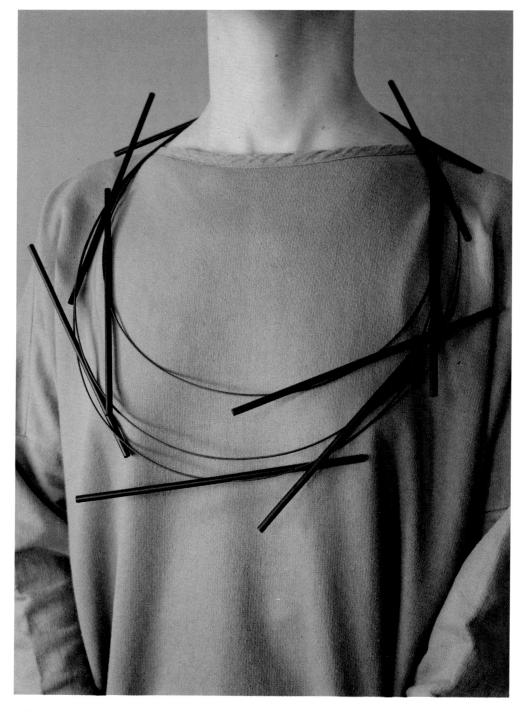

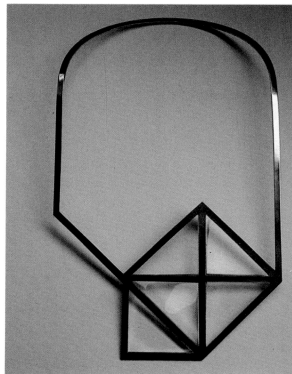

259 Brooch. Gold, moonstone, ivory, acrylic, kiln-hardened stone. British, by Kevin Coates (b. 1950). 1983. 4.3 cm × 3.2 cm. Private Collection.

260 Torque. Gold, lapis lazuli and rock crystal. French, by Goudji (b. 1941). 1983. 13.5 cm × 14 cm. Musée des Arts décoratifs, Paris (depôt de l'Etat français F.N.A.C.).

261 Neckpiece. Steel and paper. Japanese, by Shuhei Miyata (b. 1933). 1983. W. 10 cm. The artists' collection.

262 Pendant. 18-carat gold, ebony and a ruby. Swiss, by Othmar Zschaler (b. 1930). 1983. 10 cm × 4.5 cm. Private Collection.

Zschaler's superb jewellery has won him well-deserved acclaim over the years, well beyond his native Switzerland. A craftsman par excellence, he has developed an original style that owes much to the rugged mountain landscape around him.

The pendant demonstrates the characteristic manner by which Zschaler sensitively transforms his visual experiences into abstract compositions of textured gold, to which he often adds various kinds of wood, slate and precious stones. Suspended from a fine gold chain, the pendant has a square ruby at the top, set in gold, followed by two carved sections of black ebony fitted into formations of heavy, textured gold.

263 Brooch. Silver and acrylic. U.S.A., by Christina Y. Smith. 1983. 11.4 cm × 8.9 cm × 1.2 cm. The artist's collection.

Entitled 'Street Music', this brooch is constructed from silver and pigmented opaque acrylics. The image of the top of the record player and the patterned strip across the top of the brooch have been roller-printed on the surface of the silver using different cuts of silicon-carbide sandpaper. This brooch is one of a series of six, inspired by Christina Smith's personal observations of city life in Los Angeles during 1982–1983. Smith, who has several awards and prestigious exhibitions to her credit, was artist-in-residence and assistant professor at the University of Oklahoma in 1983 and 1984.

264 Collar. Gold leaf between two layers of plastic. Dutch, by Gijs Bakker (b. 1942). 1983. Diam. 35 cm. Ministry of Culture Collection, Amsterdam.

Gijs Bakker is one of Holland's foremost innovative artist/jewellers; over the past fifteen years or so, his unusual, avant-garde concepts have been crucial to the development of contemporary jewellery in Holland. Originally working in traditional materials like silver and gold, he was one of the first (in the late 1960s and early 1970s) to develop jewellery made from synthetic materials. A versatile and creative artist who has also ventured successfully into furniture and theatrical costume design, Bakker made this dramatic piece in the shape of a large collar from square sections of clear plastic, applying gold leaf between two layers of plastic sheet.

265 Three Rings. Gold, water opal and emerald. British, by Paul Preston (b. 1943). 1983. H. *(left)* 3 cm; *(centre)* 2.3 cm; *(right)* 2.8 cm. *(Left)* the artist's collection; *(centre and right)* Private Collection.

Most of Paul Preston's jewellery (see also Pl. 209) reflects his love of nature, with appealing small animals either engraved or carved in metal, using a whole range of his own gold alloys for colouring. The ring on the left has a bezel in the shape of a tiny crested duck; it is carved in yellow gold, with fine details of features and plumage in white gold, and sitting on a flat shank with a beaten texture. The ring in the centre is engraved around the shank and set in yellow gold with a square emerald. Also in yellow gold, the ring on the right has a minute figure of a mole drinking from a 'pool', consisting of a water opal; the shank is engraved with a leafy pattern.

266 Bracelet. Silver and enamel. Australian, by Helen Aitken-Kuhnen (b. 1952). 1983. 9 cm × 7.2 cm. Kunstgewerbemuseum, Staatliche Museen Preussischer Kulturbesitz, Berlin. Australian born, Helen Aitken-Kuhnen trained at the Royal Melbourne Institute of Technology as well as at the Fachhochschule Düsseldorf and the Middlesex Polytechnic in London. Both she and her husband Johannes Kuhnen (see Pl. 216) have been regular exhibitors at the Makers' Mark Gallery in Melbourne and have participated in publicly sponsored Australian jewellery exhibitions in Europe and Japan. Their work is represented in several public collections at home and abroad.

The bracelet is beautifully enamelled in delicate shades of green cloisonné and champlevé enamel that are surrounded on the outer edge by a wide band of silver.

267 Brooch. Mild steel and 24-carat gold. Australian, by Viliama Grakalic (b. 1942). 1983. Private Collection.

Born and partially trained in Yugoslavia, Grakalic arrived in Australia in 1963; in 1978 she completed her training as an artist/jeweller with a diploma from the Royal Melbourne Institute of Technology. Her figurative concepts border on the Surrealist as demonstrated by a series of wearable sculptures she created under the title 'The Dream of Flight', of which the illustrated brooch is an example. The lower part of a steel torso with diagonal stripes of fine gold inlaid across the stomach is attached to aeroplane-like struts, also constructed of mild steel.

268 Bracelet. Anodized aluminium, 14-carat gold, a mosaic stone of onyx and tiger's eye. U.S.A., by David Tisdale (b. 1956). 1983. 8.9 cm × 5.6 cm × 3.2 cm. The artist's collection.

The bracelet is constructed from anodized aluminium strip in the form of a double hoop: the plain oval inner one fits around the wrist; the outer hoop stands away from it and is angled to give a flat surface across the top. The triangular stone has been set across the top on a golden base.

Tisdale finds it stimulating to use industrial materials and processes for jewellery; he enjoys the challenge to prevailing attitudes created by their combination with precious and more traditional materials like gold, silver and stones. His work has been featured in many international shows and is represented in public as well as private collections.

269 Brooch. Silver and copper. East German, by Renata Ahrens (b. 1929). 1983. 11 cm × 4.5 cm. Kulturfond Collection, GDR. A member of the Executive Council of the Artists' Union of the German Democratic Republic since 1978, Renata Ahrens served her apprenticeship as a goldsmith in her father's workshop, gaining her Master's degree in 1959. Since 1970, Ahrens has worked free lance, creating jewellery in her own studio and exhibiting widely in Socialist countries. Her work, and that of a considerable number of her fellow artist/jewellers (see Pls 270–272), illustrates the strong and clear break with the traditional jewellery concepts formerly so popular in Socialist nations.

This four-sided brooch, with patterns of copper inlaid in silver, is traversed by a gently curved silver rod inlaid with copper swirls.

270 Earring. Silver, coral and leather. East German, by Christina Brade (b. 1936). 1983. L. 8.5 cm. The artist's collection.

An exciting composition of mixed materials, this earring by Christina Brade is made from silver-sheet brackets riveted over pieces of coloured leather and coral twigs. Although it owes nothing to tradition, it has a strong amulet-like quality, full of personal imagery and intriguing associations.

Brade was trained as a steel engraver and also studied at the Institut für künstlerische Werkgestaltung in Halle before establishing herself as a free-lance artist in 1959.

271 Brooch. Silver and enamel. East German, by Ute Feiler (b. 1941). 1983. 5.5 cm × 4 cm. The artist's collection.

Feiler won a silver medal at the 5th International Jewellery Exhibition in Jablonec in 1977. Her approach to jewellery design is fresh and entirely in a contemporary context. This brooch has a painterly quality, giving expression to the shape and contours of imaginary landscapes abstracted into gentle patterns, random shapes and subtle colours. The irregular outer edges of this brooch underline its sensitive design.

262 Pendant. 18-carat gold, ebony and a ruby. Swiss, by Othmar Zschaler (b. 1930). 1983. 10 cm × 4.5 cm. Private Collection.

263 Brooch. Silver and acrylic. U.S.A., by Christina Y. Smith. 1983. 11.4 cm × 8.9 cm × 1.2 cm. The artist's collection.

264 Collar. Gold leaf between two layers of plastic. Dutch, by Gijs Bakker (b. 1942). 1983. Diam. 35 cm. Ministry of Culture Collection, Amsterdam.

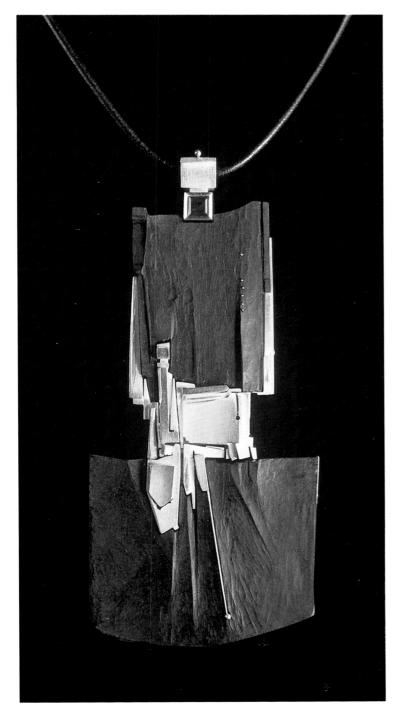

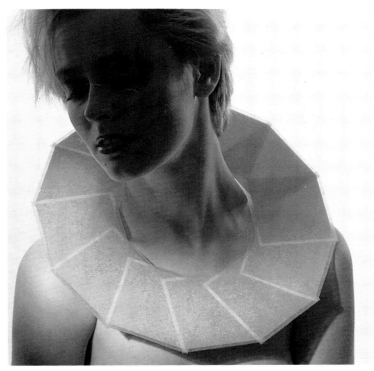

265 Three Rings. Gold, water opal and emerald. British, by Paul Preston (b. 1943). 1983. H. *(left)* 3 cm; *(centre)* 2.3 cm; *(right)* 2.8 cm. *(Left)* the artist's collection; *(centre and right)* Private Collection.

266 Bracelet. Silver and enamel. Australian, by Helen Aitken-Kuhnen (b. 1952). 1983. 9 cm × 7.2 cm. Kunstgewerbemuseum, Staatliche Museen Preussischer Kulturbesitz, Berlin.

267 Brooch. Mild steel and 24-carat gold. Australian, by Viliama Grakalic (b. 1942). 1983. Private Collection.

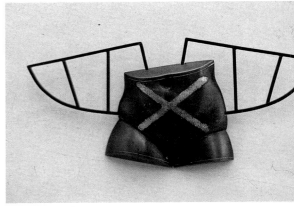

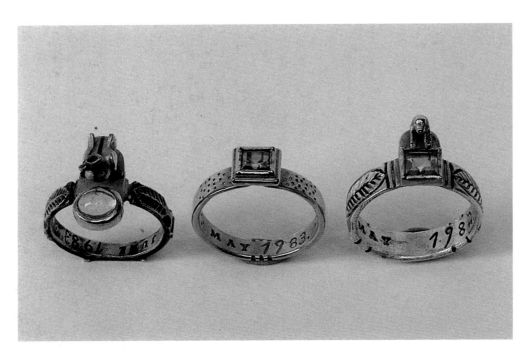

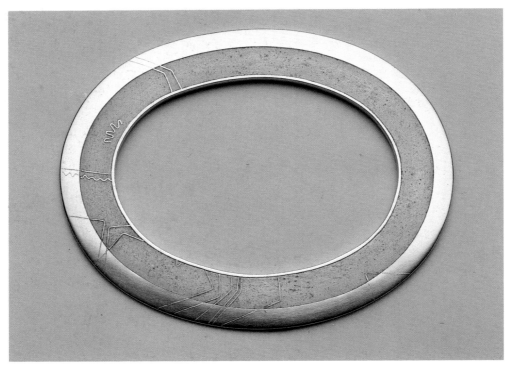

268 Bracelet. Anodized aluminium, 14-carat gold, a mosaic stone of onyx and tiger's eye. U.S.A., by David Tisdale (b. 1956). 1983. 8.9 cm × 5.6 cm × 3.2 cm. The artist's collection.

269 Brooch. Silver and copper. East German, by Renata Ahrens (b. 1929). 1983. 11 cm × 4.5 cm. Kulturfond Collection, GDR.

270 Earring. Silver, coral and leather. East German, by Christina Brade (b. 1936). 1983. L. 8.5 cm. The artist's collection.

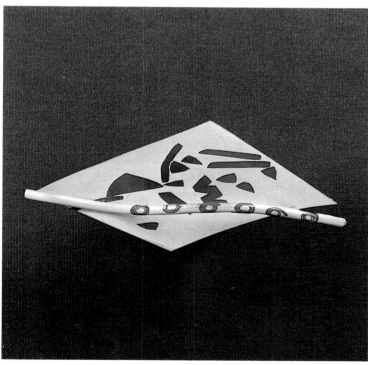

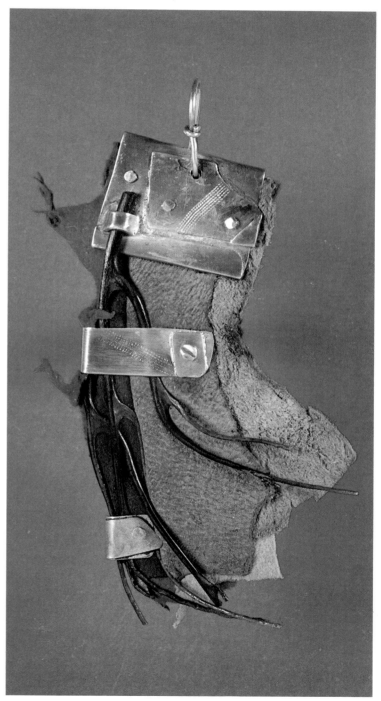

272 Brooch. Steel, tin and lacquer. East German, by Rolf Lindner (b. 1946). 1983. 9.5 cm × 4.5 cm. The artist's collection.
Lindner served a four-year jeweller's apprenticeship before continuing his studies at the Fachschule für angewandte Kunst in Heiligendamm, where he obtained his Master's degree as a goldsmith in 1976. Since 1977, he has been working free lance and has participated in several international exhibitions (at Jablonec, in Great Britain and in France).

The design and execution of this brooch bears a certain affinity to work by Saddington (Pl. 220) and by Schobinger (Pls 226, 228), although it is highly unlikely that Lindner ever saw the work of either artist. The trapezoid brooch is made of refined steel to which Lindner has applied dots punched out of a printed tin can. The large cross in the centre was applied with red lacquer.

273 Two Brooches and a Ring. 18-carat gold and acrylic resin. Italian, by Giampaolo Babetto (b. 1947). 1983. L. (brooches) 12.5 cm; outside diam. (ring) 3.8 cm. The artist's collection.
Classic and elegant simplicity of line coupled with superb craftsmanship have always been a keynote of Babetto's jewellery (see also Pl. 174). Pieces similar to the ones illustrated won him the International Jewellery Art Grand Prize at the 5th Tokyo Triennale in 1983.

The ring is hollow–a perfect circle with concave sides and a circular opening in the centre. It is intended to be worn on the little finger and has a segment cut out to enable the adjacent finger to move freely. The coloured sections are acrylic resin, inlaid into yellow gold, leaving a fine gold edge visible. Made with the same materials and according to the same principle, the brooches are elongated bars with triangular profiles, slightly bent in the centre.

274 Four Bracelets. Aluminium and vinyl tape. Australian, by Susan Cohn (b. 1952). 1983/1984. Diam. (top two) 13 cm; (bottom two) 9 cm. The artist's collection.
Susan Cohn originally trained and worked as a graphic designer before gaining a diploma in gold- and silversmithing from the Royal Melbourne Institute of Technology in 1980. Her interest in designing extends from jewellery to accessories and costume, activities which, in turn, have had a bearing on her approach to jewellery.

The concept behind these bracelets is based on the repetition of a simple, basic shape with a pristine, industrial finish. Each bracelet then achieves individuality through its decoration. Made by putting together two halves of pressed aluminium, the bracelets have been decorated with plastic-coated wire, coloured pop rivets, copper wire and coloured vinyl tape. The aluminium has been anodized in various shades of green, pale blue, pink and lilac.

275 Pendant on Chain. Gold, beetle, diamonds and black pearl. Swiss, by Gilbert Albert (b. 1930). 1983. 7.5 cm × 3 cm. The artist's collection.
Nine times a winner of Diamond International (awards 1958–79), Gilbert Albert enjoys an international reputation for the luxurious jewellery he creates in Geneva.

Although he works predominantly with precious metals and stones, his individual pieces of jewellery–mostly inspired by nature and organic forms–often incorporate shells and beetles into the designs, as demonstrated by this pendant. Albert has mounted an actual beetle as the pendant's central feature; it has been set on tatu (armadillo) skin and mounted on yellow gold on top of a concave, pointed oval in drop shape. The upper edges surrounding the beetle are encrusted with gold granules of varying sizes; one large and one small diamond are set above the beetle's head. A graduated strip of pavé-set diamonds with an oblong, black pearl forms the lower part of the pendant, which is suspended from a chain of half-round wire links accentuated by gold granules to match the upper edges of the pendant.

276 Four Brooches. Stainless steel and enamel paint. Canadian, by James Evans (b. 1952). 1984. L. (left to right) 19.5 cm, 23.4 cm, 16.5 cm, 17.5 cm. Private Collection.
James Evans belongs to a small but growing group of Canadian artist/jewellers whose original ideas have been making an impact at international jewellery exhibitions in the last few years. Influenced to a certain extent by David Watkins's linear concepts (see Pl. 249), Evans has used stainless steel rod coloured black and red (with automobile primer, two coats of enamel and sealed with polyurethane) for a collection of brooches, bracelets and neckpieces. The brooches illustrated are, from left to right, a triangle, two oblique crosses and a curve crossed by two lines. Evans feels strongly that the cheap material he uses affords him a spontaneity in his work that would be extremely difficult to achieve in precious metals.

277 Head Ornament. Silver. Japanese, by Wahei Ikezawa (b. 1946). 1984. L. (sides of triangle) 40 cm. The artist's collection.
Ikezawa is a graduate of the Kanazawa Arts and Crafts University and worked for eight years at the Hiramatsu Design Institute during the 1970s. Winner of the Japanese Jewellery Art Prize in 1974, he has exhibited widely at home and abroad and is a member of the Japan Jewellery Designers' Association.

Made from heavy-gauge silver wire, this head ornament is constructed in the form of an equilateral triangle attached, by three spokes, to an oval that fits over the head.

278 Ring. 18-carat gold and stainless-steel wire. Japanese, by Okinari Kurokawa (b. 1946). 1984. 3 cm × 2.5 cm × 2.5 cm. The artist's collection.
Kurokawa was born in China but lives in Japan; he graduated from the Musashino Art University in Tokyo (1971) and spent two years at the Fachhochschule für Gestaltung in Pforzheim, Germany.

The flat, rounded bezel of this ring almost forms a figure eight. The shank is composed of a double square, made of wire, and attached to the bezel on either side by grains of gold. Two gold wires attached to the grains cross at the centre of the bezel.

279 Brooch. Gold, silver, copper and nickel. Italian, by Francesco Pavan (b. 1937). 1984. 6 cm × 6 cm × 1.5 cm. The artist's collection.
This brooch is in the shape of an open-sided cube in a foreshortened perspective; the pattern of the bars has been achieved by a complex technique: twisting wires of gold, silver, copper and nickel and putting them through a rolling mill. The design and execution constitute a progression of Pavan's earlier work (see Pl. 222), although the overall shape is still governed by a strict geometric concept, which was the basic principle underlying the designs generally associated with the 'Padua School'.

280 Brooch. Bronze, enamel paint, silver, stainless-steel wire. Australian, by Carlier Makigawa (b. 1952). 1984. 8 cm × 6.5 cm × 5 cm. The artist's collection.
Makigawa is a graduate of the Western Australian Institute of Technology at Perth, which she attended from 1978 to 1980; her designs have been much concerned with the exploration of spatial relationships and the potential of linear concepts in three-dimensional form.

This brooch consists of different sections of bronze and silver tubing: some are shaped into zigzags; some are decorated with bands of yellow and blue enamel paint. The sections are connected to each other at varied angles, and two zigzag sections protrude outwards, held by the tension of stainless-steel wires attached to opposite corners.

271 Brooch. Silver and enamel. East German, by Ute Feiler (b. 1941). 1983. 5.5 cm × 4 cm. The artist's collection.

272 Brooch. Steel, tin and lacquer. East German, by Rolf Lindner (b. 1946). 1983. 9.5 cm × 4.5 cm. The artist's collection.

273 Two Brooches and a Ring. 18-carat gold and acrylic resin. Italian, by Giampaolo Babetto (b. 1947). 1983. L. (brooches) 12.5 cm; outside diam. (ring) 3.8 cm. The artist's collection.

274 Four Bracelets. Aluminium and vinyl tape. Australian, by Susan Cohn (b. 1952). 1983/1984. Diam. *(top two)* 13 cm; *(bottom two)* 9 cm. The artist's collection.

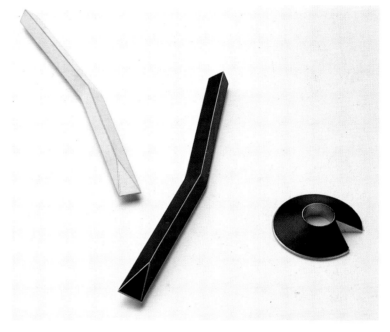

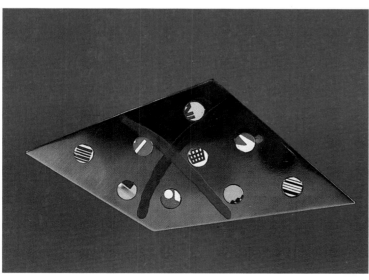

275 Pendant on Chain. Gold, beetle, diamonds and black pearl. Swiss, by Gilbert Albert (b. 1930). 1983. 7.5 cm × 3 cm. The artist's collection.

276 Four Brooches. Stainless steel and enamel paint. Canadian, by James Evans (b. 1952). 1984. L. (*left to right*) 19.5 cm, 23.4 cm, 16.5 cm, 17.5 cm. Private Collection.

277 Head Ornament. Silver. Japanese, by Wahei Ikezawa (b. 1946). 1984. L. (sides of triangle) 40 cm. The artist's collection.

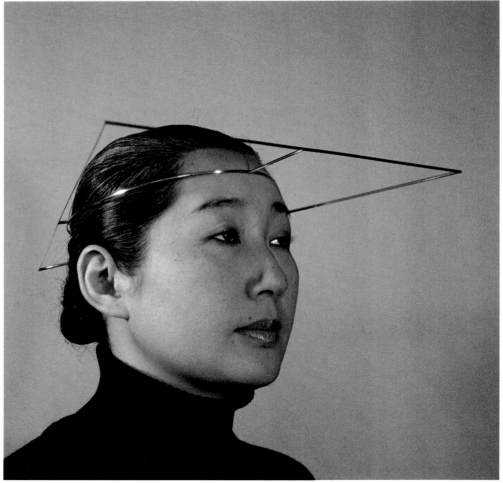

188

278 Ring. 18-carat gold and stainless-steel wire. Japanese, by Okinari Kurokawa (b. 1946). 1984. 3 cm × 2.5 cm × 2.5 cm. The artist's collection.

279 Brooch. Gold, silver, copper and nickel. Italian, by Francesco Pavan (b. 1937). 1984. 6 cm × 6 cm x1.5 cm. The artist's collection.

280 Brooch. Bronze, enamel paint, silver stainless-steel wire. Australian, by Carlier Makigawa (b. 1952). 1984. 8 cm × 6.5 cm × 5 cm. The artist's collection.

281 Ring and Bracelet. Silver and gold. Japanese, by Yasuki Hiramatsu (b. 1926). 1984. Diam. (ring) 2 cm, W. 1.5 cm; diam. (bracelet) 6 cm, W. 5.5 cm. Private Collections.

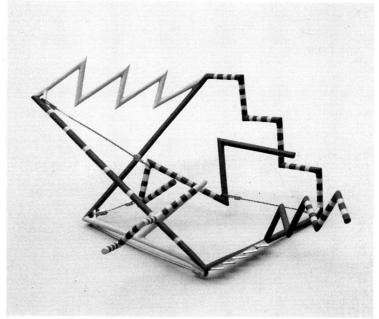

281 Ring and Bracelet. Silver and gold. Japanese, by Yasuki Hiramatsu (b. 1926). 1984. Diam. (ring) 2 cm, W. 1.5 cm; diam. (bracelet) 6 cm, W. 5.5 cm. Private Collections.

Perhaps Japan's best-known artist/jeweller, Yasuki Hiramatsu has exerted a crucial influence on the development of contemporary jewellery in Japan, both by his superb jewellery designs and by his untiring efforts as professor at Tokyo University of Fine Arts, as permanent director of the Japan Jewellery Designers' Institute and as chairman of the directors of the Japan Craft Design Association.

This bracelet and ring are classic examples of Hiramatsu's sensitive and imaginative approach to jewellery. Both pieces are made according to the same principle: separate layers of very thin sheet metal with a fine, matt texture are soldered together at one end. The bracelet is in fine silver; the top two layers have been cut along the centre line. The ring is in gold and has three cuts through the top two layers.

282 Bracelet. Fine and sterling silver, and 14-carat gold. U.S.A., by Mary Lee Hu (b. 1943). 1984. 10.2 cm × 8.9 cm × 1.2 cm. Leanette Bassetti Collection, (U.S.A.).

This bracelet is a fine example of the masterly skills Mary Lee Hu has achieved over the years in the adaptation of textile techniques to metalwork. Her exquisite jewellery is the result of painstaking research and experimentation (including a prolonged stay working in Taiwan) that have enabled her to create new forms and textures in an entirely contemporary context.

The bracelet is made of tubular sections joined at the corners and constructed from silver and 14-carat gold wire, entwined to form a woven pattern.

283 Bracelet. Aluminium, titanium and silk. Canadian, by Louis Tortell (b. 1954). 1984. W. 14 cm. The artist's collection.

Born and educated in part in Malta, Louis Tortell completed his studies at the Sheridan College, Oakville, Ontario in 1979. His exciting designs reflect the brightness and colouring of Mediterranean landscapes.

This bracelet is made from aluminium rod and tube, placed across the top and held at each end by wires twisted around the arm. Bright red silk has been tied in the centre of the top part over a semicircular piece of patterned titanium.

284 Brooch. Copper and silver. Austrian, by Edith Mostböck-Huber (b. 1947). 1984. 11 cm × 7 cm. The artist's collection.

The sensitive jewellery of Edith Mostböck-Huber reflects her strong involvement with textiles, an element she has incorporated into this unusual brooch with tufts of fine copper wire emanating from one corner. Shaped and textured to look like a piece of cloth, the irregular triangle is made from copper sheet with a smaller silver one placed along one corner.

285 Bracelet and Brooch. Silver and obsidian. U.S.S.R. by Jaan Pärn (b. 1953). 1984. Diam. (bracelet) 6 cm. Collection of the Ministry of Culture of the Estonian Republic; (brooch) 11 cm × 4 cm. The artist's collection.

In the short time since Pärn graduated from the Estonian State Art Institute at Tallinn (1982), his excellent design and craftsmanship have already won him a gold metal at Jablonec (in 1983). He works free lance in his own studio, creating only one-of-a-kind pieces, which have been exhibited in the Soviet Union and abroad.

The design of this brooch and bracelet is based on parallelograms. The rectangular, silver bracelet has rounded corners; the top is a juxtaposition of wire forms with a slice of obsidian set on the diagonal. The brooch is composed entirely of silver wire in a modern version of filigree; again a slanted rectangular slice of obsidian has been set across the centre.

286 Six Rings. Platinum, gold, copper, diamonds. West German, by Norbert Muerrle (b. 1948) for Niessing & Co. 1984. W. *(back row)* 1.7 cm; *(front row)* 3 mm. Limited series in production.

These six unusual rings were designed by Norbert Muerrle (see Pls 154, 298) for production by Niessing & Co., a West German firm of manufacturers specializing in wedding and engagement rings. In the late 1970s, Niessing took the unusual step of commissioning artists like Muerrle, Friedrich Becker (see Pls 122/123, 196, 244) and Walter Wittek (see Pl. 223), among others, to design special ranges of jewellery for them. The result has been spectacular, both in terms of exciting visual effects and of techniques for diamond settings, precious metal alloys and texturing.

The two rings in the back row are small versions of the bracelet by Muerrle (Pl.298). Made of platinum with a matt, sand-blasted finish, the shanks are cone-shaped and have uneven edges. All around the shank, coloured diamonds in different shapes and sizes have been set deep into the metal, along with small flecks of inlay in copper and gold. The two rings in the front row on the left are of yellow and red gold respectively with a crystallized texture, inlaid with spots of copper and white gold. The third ring, made of platinum, has a matt texture and is set with tiny diamonds. A large solitaire diamond has been set by tension between the open-ended platinum shank of the ring on the right. On the latter model, the shank has been polished and also inlaid with an abstract pattern in copper and gold.

287 Necklace. 24-carat gold. Swedish, by Sigurd Persson (b. 1914). 1984. 11.5 cm × 10 cm × 18 cm. The artist's collection.

Sigurd Persson's design for this necklace demonstrates a distinct change of direction from his earlier work (see Pl. 159). The forged, rigid neckband dramatically sprouts a sheaf of nine gold leaves that stand upright on the wearer's left shoulder. The introduction of such organic elements into the smooth, disciplined form of the metal represents an entirely new trend in Scandinavian design, also noticable in the work of Birte Stenbak (see Pl. 214) and Tone Vigeland (see Pl. 227).

288 Brooch. Ebony, paint, paper and sea shells. U.S.A., by Robert Ebendorf (b. 1938). 1984. 5.7 cm × 5.7 cm. The artist's collection.

Robert Ebendorf is currently professor of art at the State University of New York at New Paltz; his work and teaching activities have played an important part in the development of contemporary jewellery as an art form in the United States. He is a founder-member and past president of the Society of North American Goldsmiths.

The brooch is constructed of ebony. The triangular lower section is patterned with paper and paint, while the square inner area is textured by the application of small broken sea shells.

289 Bracelet. Mild steel, gold and diamonds. British, by Barbara Tipple (b. 1951). 1984. Outside diam. 10.8 cm. Private Collection.

Barbara Tipple won her first Diamond International Award in the De Beer's International Competition of 1972, while she was still a student at the Middlesex Polytechnic in London, from which she graduated in 1974.

This beautiful bracelet won her a second Diamond International Award in 1984. Made from blackened mild steel–hollow and hinged –the bracelet is inlaid with wriggly lines of gold, some of them widening out to surround 'pools' of pavé-set diamonds.

282 Bracelet. Fine and sterling silver, and ▷ 14-carat gold. U.S.A., by Mary Lee Hu (b. 1943). 1984. 10.2 cm × 8.9 cm × 1.2 cm. Leanette Bassetti Collection (U.S.A.).

283 Bracelet. Aluminium, titanium and silk. Canadian, by Louis Tortell (b. 1954). 1984. W. 14 cm. The artist's collection.

284 Brooch. Copper and silver. Austrian, by Edith Mostböck-Huber (b. 1947). 1984. 11 cm × 7 cm. The artist's collection.

285 Bracelet and Brooch. Silver and obsidian. U.S.S.R. by Jaan Pärn (b. 1953). 1984. Diam. (bracelet) 6 cm. Collection of the Ministry of Culture of the Estonian Republic; (brooch) 11 cm × 4 cm. The artist's collection.

286 Six Rings. Platinum, gold, copper, diamonds. West German, by Norbert Muerrle (b. 1948) for Niessing & Co. 1984. W. *(back row)* 1.7 cm; *(front row)* 3 mm. Limited series in production.

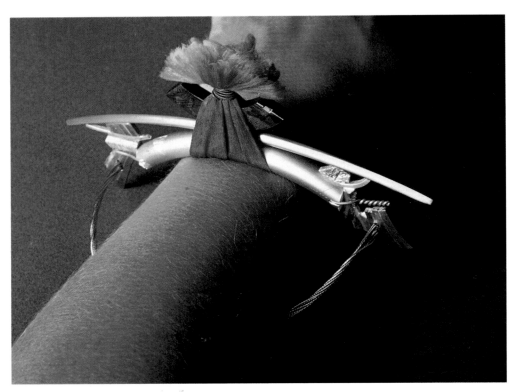

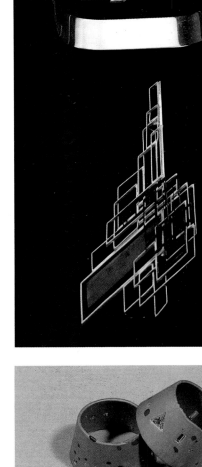

287 Necklace. 24-carat gold. Swedish, by Sigurd Persson (b. 1914). 1984. 11.5 cm × 10 cm × 18 cm. The artist's collection.

288 Brooch. Ebony, paint, paper and sea shells. U.S.A., by Robert Ebendorf (b. 1938). 1984. 5.7 cm × 5.7 cm. The artist's collection.

289 Bracelet. Mild steel, gold and diamonds. British, by Barbara Tipple (b. 1951). 1984. Outside diam. 10.8 cm. Private Collection.

290 Stick-Pins on Stand. Silver, nickel, 14-carat and 18-carat gold. U.S.A., by Randy Long (b. 1951). 1984. H. *(from left to right)* 17.8 cm; 17.8 cm; 15.2 cm. The artist's collection.

Entitled 'Pahos', this group of three stick-pins was inspired by Randy Long's interest in native American Indian culture, the word *paho* being Hopi, a south-western American Indian word for a 'prayer stick'. Unlike the native product (which is made from natural materials like wood, corn husks, pollen, feathers and cotton thread), Long has made these in gold and silver. The silver cones at the top are textured with small wriggly lines and crosses; the pointed ends are attached to a silver crescent, a disc and a spiral respectively. The pins are patterned with a gold twist and gold triangles at the top.

Currently assistant professor for art-jewellery design and metalsmithing at Indiana University at Bloomington, Randy Long is a graduate of the University of San Diego and California State University.

291 Bracelet. Bronze and silver. Swiss, by Antoinette Riklin-Schelbert (b. 1920). 1984. Diam. 15 cm. The artist's collection.

Antoinette Riklin-Schelbert trained as a gold- and silversmith at the Kunstgewerbeschule in Zurich (1939–1943); her early work in precious materials already demonstrated her keen awareness of the potential of jewellery as an art form. Rejecting traditional values and materialistic overtones, her later work is made of non-precious materials, which allow her the freedom to experiment with a greater variety of textures and forms.

This bracelet is made with a rigid inner ring of silver, to which Riklin-Schelbert has attached several layers of fine bronze mesh curling up at the edges.

292 Collar. Steel, palm-fibre flyscreen material. Australian, by Darani Lewers (b. 1936). 1984. 30 cm × 32 cm × 16 cm. Private Collection.

In 1983, Darani Lewers (see Pl. 169) played a leading part in forming a group of women artist/jewellers for the purpose of organizing a series of workshops in Sydney, which would lead to a touring exhibition in the eastern states of Australia during 1984. They chose 'the natural and the human environment' as their theme. Great emphasis was laid on the importance of making the jewellery accessible to a wide public, and the group decided to limit their prices to the $20 to $100 range. Under the title 'Worn Issues?', the exciting results of the group's work did much to stimulate interest in and discussion on the meaning and purpose of jewellery.

The illustrated collar is part of a series Lewers made expressing her observations on the environment seen in an industrial and urban context. Entitled 'Balance', it is about the need to create a balance between natural and human forces.

293 Torque. Silver gilt, quartz crystal and baroque pearls. U.S.A., by Stanley Lechtzin (b. 1936). 1984. 20.3 cm × 19 cm × 5.1 cm. Private Collection.

A classic example of Stanley Lechtzin's superb skills and sensitive feeling for organic forms (see also Pl. 200), this torque is called '83E' and was made by the process of electroforming silver gilt. Using the dramatic natural formation of quartz crystal as his starting point, Lechtzin has underlined its structure with the contours of the metal that loop and curl around the wearer's neck, and incorporate three large baroque pearls. The torque is hinged in the centre of the back.

294 Zigzag for the Breast. Huon pine, silver, steel. Australian, by Rowena Gough (b. 1958). 1984. 31 cm × 5 cm × 1.4 cm. The artist's collection.

In the short span of time since she graduated from the Royal Melbourne Institute of Technology in 1978, Rowena Gough's fresh and innovative approach to jewellery has demanded attention. This piece, carved from Huon pine, bold in dimensions and outline, makes a dramatic impact worn on a plain garment. It is fastened to the fabric by several steel pinch-clips.

295 'Black-Slat and Perforated Thigh Pockets'. Mild steel, rubber, brass and plastic tubing. Australian, by Annie Holdsworth (b. 1953). 1984. 26 cm × 8.5 cm × 4 cm. The artist's collection.

Paying homage to the universal 'jeans culture', these unusual thigh ornaments are designed to high-light people's attachment to and preoccupation with pockets. Although in some people they may evoke images of knives or daggers in sheaths, these ornaments are, in fact, shaped and functional as pockets. The upper one is textured with perforations, while the lower one has strips of black rubber slotted across it, which feel rather like a venetian blind when the hand runs down the form. They are fitted with steel pinch-clips that hook onto the trouser leg.

Annie Holdsworth is a graduate of the Royal Melbourne Institute of Technology (1980), and her designs reflect very much the spirit and vitality of Australian contemporary jewellery.

290 Stick-Pins on Stand. Silver, nickel, 14-carat and 18-carat gold. U.S.A., by Randy Long (b. 1951). 1984. H. *(from left to right)* 17.8 cm; 17.8 cm; 15.2 cm. The artist's collection.

291 Bracelet. Bronze and silver. Swiss, by Antoinette Riklin-Schelbert (b. 1920). 1984. Diam. 15 cm. The artist's collection.

292 Collar. Steel, palm-fibre flyscreen material. Australian, by Darani Lewers (b. 1936). 1984. 30 cm × 32 cm × 16 cm. Private Collection.

293 Torque. Silver gilt, quartz crystal and baroque pearls. U.S.A., by Stanley Lechtzin (b. 1936). 1984. 20.3 cm × 19 cm × 5.1 cm. Private Collection.

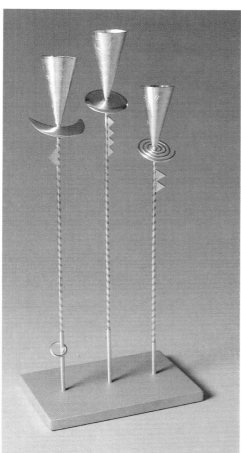

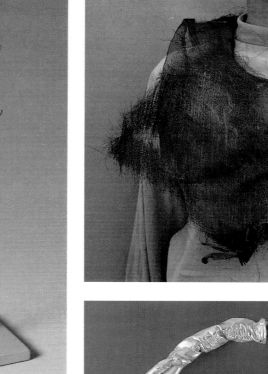

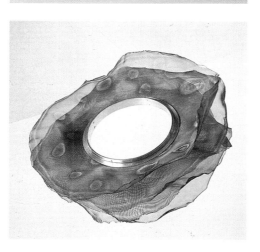

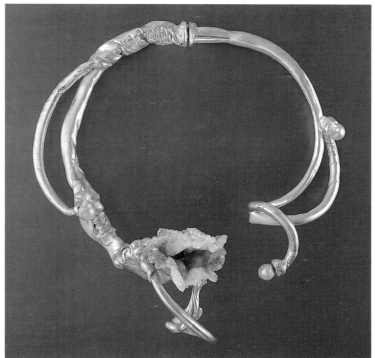

◁ **294 Zigzag for the Breast.** Huon pine, silver, steel. Australian, by Rowena Gough (b. 1958). 1984. 31 cm × 5 cm × 1.4 cm. The artist's collection.

295 'Black-Slat and Perforated Thigh Pockets'. Mild steel, rubber, brass and plastic tubing. Australian, by Annie Holdsworth (b. 1953). 1984. 26 cm × 8.5 cm × 4 cm. The artist's collection.

296 Collar. Recycled paper pulp, grass stems and linen thread. Australian, by Jenny Toynbee-Wilson (b. 1942). 1984. 60 cm × 30 cm. The artist's collection.

297 Ring. Gold. Dutch, by Robert Smit (b. 1941). 1984. H. 4 cm. Private Collection, Amsterdam.

298 Bracelet. Platinum, gold, copper, diamonds. West German, by Norbert Muerrle (b. 1948). 1984. Lower diam. 7.5 cm, W. 6.5 cm. De Beers International Jewellery Collection, London. ▷

299 Brooch. Silver, 18-carat gold and rutilated quartz. U.S.A., by Eleanor Moty (b. 1945). 1984. 7 cm × 6.4 cm × 2.5 cm. The artist's collection. ▷▷

300 Arm Ornament. Palm fibre. Canadian, by Kai Chan (b. 1940). 1984. 7.7 cm × 23 cm. The artist's collection. ▷

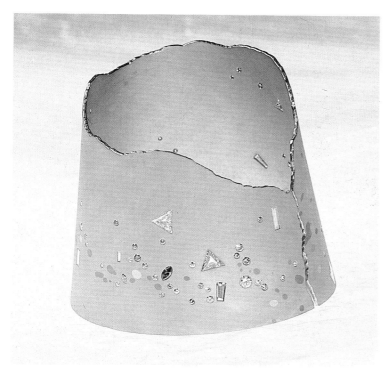

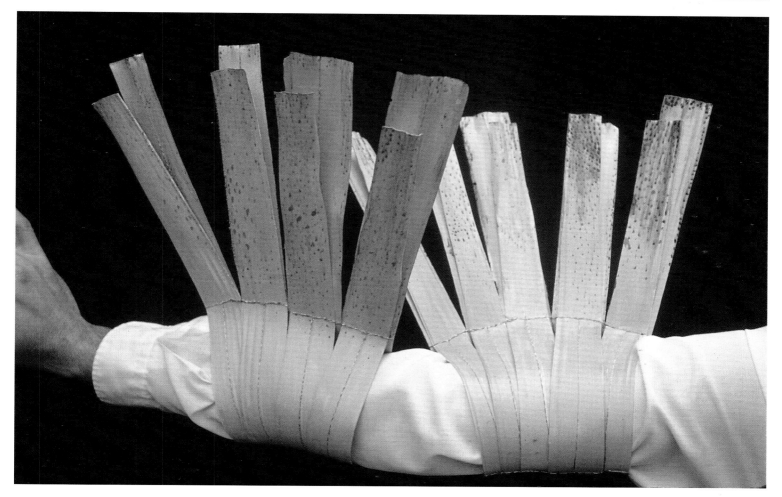

296 Collar. Recycled paper pulp, grass stems and linen thread. Australian, by Jenny Toynbee-Wilson (b. 1942). 1984. 60 cm × 30 cm. The artist's collection.

Born and educated in Edinburgh, Scotland, Jenny Toynbee-Wilson now lives and works in Sydney. Her involvement with jewellery came about accidentally when she was asked to photograph the work of a jewellery-workshop group in 1982. As a professional graphic designer and lecturer in visual communications at Sydney College of the Arts, Toynbee-Wilson's investigations into paper as a medium led her to a growing awareness of the uses and abuses of the material. The jewellery-workshop group's theme of jewellery related to environmental issues (see Pl. 292) inspired her to make paper wearable, in an attempt to make people re-evaluate their attitude to it in the light of the ecological problems that may soon make paper a luxury item.

Fashioned of hand-made paper, tinted in hues of beige and brown going into red, the broad collar (made of thick strips overlaid by a stiff mesh of grass stems at the shoulders) is sewn together.

297 Ring. Gold. Dutch, by Robert Smit (b. 1941). 1984. H. 4 cm. Private Collection, Amsterdam.

Textured all over with a small criss-cross pattern on a matt background, this ring is made from gold sheet that has been turned into a wide shank with a protuding pointed edge at the top and bottom. Designed and made by Smit (see Pl. 140), the ring marks a significant change in his concepts about jewellery. One of the first artist/jewellers to rebel against traditional attitudes, forms and materials, Smit spent many years refining and crystallizing his ideas by working with non-precious materials, which led eventually to Conceptualism and a total break with jewellery. Since 1984 he has come full circle; he now sees gold in a new light and finds appeal in its archaic associations.

298 Bracelet. Platinum, gold, copper, diamonds. West German, by Norbert Muerrle (b. 1948). 1984. Lower diam. 7.5 cm, W. 6.5 cm. De Beers International Jewellery Collection, London.

This superb bracelet by Norbert Muerrle (see Pls 154, 286) won him the Diamond International Award (1984) in the De Beers competition. Cone-shaped and open-ended, the bracelet is made of platinum with a matt, grey texture, patterned with inlaid flecks of gold and copper. The irregular contour of the upper part of the bracelet is underlined by the jagged edges. Diamonds of different shapes and many colours are scattered all over. Brilliantly demonstrating Muerrle's extraordinary skill as a diamond-setter, the stones are set deep into the metal like windows, without collets or claws.

299 Brooch. Silver, 18-carat gold and rutilated quartz. U.S.A., by Eleanor Moty (b. 1945). 1984. 7 cm × 6.4 cm × 2.5 cm. The artist's collection.

Eleanor Moty's innovative jewellery designs and extensive teaching activities have earned her many awards and a firm place as one of the outstanding artist/jewellers in the United States. Professor at the University of Wisconsin at Madison since 1981, she has participated in many prestigious exhibitions at home and abroad, and her work is in the collections of several museums in the U.S.A.

A life-long admirer of Margaret de Patta's work (see Pls 95, 104), Moty feels that her latest work is directly influenced by de Patta's aesthetics and sensitivity. Called 'Origami', this brooch is designed in geometric shapes and features a rutilated quartz specially cut, faceted and polished to Moty's specifications. The silver surrounding it has been shaped to emphasize the contours of the stone and patterned with strips of gold.

300 Arm Ornament. Palm fibre. Canadian, by Kai Chan (b. 1940). 1984. 7.7 cm × 23 cm. The artist's collection.

Palm fibres, bright yellow in colour, are stitched together to go around the arm, the stiff ends spreading outwards. Kai Chan has called this simple, strong and dramatic piece 'Sunshine, White Sand–Blue', like the memory of a sunny, tropical beach. The design and structure reflect Chan's sculptural approach to jewellery, an aspect of his work that is evident not only in his jewellery's overall dimensions but also in the way it dominates the wearer's appearance.

Artists' Biographies

Under each artist/jeweller the reader will find a selection of the exhibitions in which he or she participated; for full titles of the exhibitions consult the List of Exhibitions, pp. 219–230. The Central School of Arts and Crafts, London, is now known as the Central School of Art and Design; the Museum of Contemporary Crafts, New York, has changed its name to the American Craft Museum. The information below, for living artists, was made available to us by the artist/jewellers themselves.

Ahrens, Renata (Pl. 269) Born 1929 in Elbing, East Prussia (now Elblag, Poland). Served apprenticeship as goldsmith in father's workshop (1947–50). Attended Arbeitsschule für Güte und Form, Wismar, GDR (1950–53). Taught in Dept. of Jewellery/Metalwork/Enamel at Fachschule für angewandte Kunst, Heiligendamm (1954–70). Studied for master's degree (goldsmithing) (1957–59). Member of the Artists' Union of the GDR since 1965; freelance gold- and metalsmith since 1970. Awarded Pestalozzi medal; silver medal at the 4th International Jewellery Exhibition, Jablonec, 1974. Member of the Executive Committee of the Artists' Union since 1978. Won Art Prize of the GDR, 1982; Bavarian Staatspreis for Handicrafts, 1984.
Exhibitions: 284, 285, 336, 422, 424, 425, 426, 427, 739

Aitken-Kuhnen, Helen (Pl. 266) Born 1952 in Australia. Attended Frankston Technical College (1970); Royal Melbourne Institute of Technology (1975); Fachhochschule, Düsseldorf, (1977); Middlesex Polytechnic (1978).
Exhibitions: 259, 264 (with Frank Bauer), 305, 673, 675, 678, 898, 1038
Works in public collections: Victoria State Collection, Meat Market Craft Centre, Melbourne; National Art Gallery of Victoria, Melbourne; State Art Gallery of South Australia, Adelaide; Kunstgewerbemuseum, Staatliche Museen Preussischer Kulturbesitz, Berlin.

Albert, Gilbert (Pl. 275) Born in Switzerland. Served apprenticeship as jewellery designer and attended Collège de Dessin industriel (1945). Received Galland Scholarship for young jewellery designers (1949, 1952). Worked for Patek-Philippe, Geneva, as chief jeweller (1955–62). Designed silver mace and chain of office for Rector of Geneva University as gift for its 4th centenary (1958–59). Won Diamond International awards, New York, 1958–60; Prix de la Ville de Genève (only laureate), Geneva, 1960. Collaborated with French master tapestry-maker Jean Lurçat to produce jewellery collection for Patek-Philippe (1960). Opened his own workshop (1962). Won Diamond International awards, New York, 1963; 1st prize for jewellery watches without stones for Omega at Swiss National Exhibition, Lausanne, 1964. Named member of Diamond International Academy, New York (1965); 'Associate honoris causa' of the Worshipful Company of Goldsmiths, London (1966). Served as jury member of the Diamond International Academy Exhibition (1968–69). Lectured on 'Art and Jewellery' at the Musée de l'Athénée, Geneva (1970). Opened jewellery shop in Geneva (1972); opened boutique at Geneva airport (1980); opened jewellery shop in Zurich (1982).
Exhibitions: 95, 159, 216, 310, 312, 435, 489*, 749

Andersen, K. Holst (Pl. 173) Born 1935 in Copenhagen. Silversmith in Copenhagen since 1961. Attended Tokyo University of Arts (1961–64) and studied in Kyoto (1970–71). Director-designer at Royal Court Jeweller Frantz Hingelberg Ltd (1965–66). Designed mayor's chain for the town of Ribe (1966). Worked as artist for Georg Jensen Silversmithy from 1973. Received Artist-Craftsman of the Year award from Danish Society of Arts and Crafts, 1973. Further research at Royal College of Art, London (1975).
Exhibitions: 83, 111, 217, 219, 220, 223, 226, 240, 254, 322, 609, 827, 853, 988, 1000, 1001

Appleby, Malcolm (Pl. 128) Born 1946 in Beckenham, England. Attended Beckenham School of Art, Ravensbourne College of Art and Design, Central School of Arts and Crafts, London; Sir John Cass College, and the Royal College of Art, London. Set up a workshop in Kent in 1968 and designed and executed the engraving on the crown for H.R.H. the Prince of Wales. Moved to Scotland (1969). Commissioned by De Beers to make Diamond-Day Ascot Trophy (1978). Commissioned by London Assay Office to make 500th Anniversary silver and medals (1978). Awarded Victoria and Albert Medal at Sotheby's, 1980. Designed seal for Board of Trustees of the Victoria and Albert Museum, London (1985).
Works in public collections: Worshipful Company of Goldsmiths, London; British Museum, London; Victoria and Albert Museum, London; Aberdeen Art Gallery; East Midlands Arts and Crafts Council Collection, Nottingham; Scottish Crafts Council; Contemporary Arts Society, London; Royal Scottish Museum, Edinburgh.

Ashbee, Charles Robert (Pls 10, 14) Born 1863 in England (died 1942). Trained as an architect; also a designer and writer. Founded the famous School and Guild of Handicrafts in London's East End (1887–88), which served as the model for the Wiener Werkstätte in Vienna. Had no formal training for making jewellery, but gained much of his metalworking techniques from translating Benvenuto Cellini's *Treatises* (published in 1898). Exhibited regularly at shows organized by the Arts and Crafts Society, London (from 1888); also took part in the Vienna Secession exhibitions.

Babetto, Giampaolo (Pls 174, 273) Born 1947 in Padua, Italy. Attended Istituto d'Arte, Padua and Accademia d'Arte, Venice. Taught at Istituto d'Arte, Padua (1969). Guest teacher at Gerrit Rietveld Academy, Amsterdam (1979–80, 1983). Won Herbert Hoffmann Prize at the International Jewellery Show, Munich, 1975; Grand Prix, Japan Jewellery Designers' Association, Tokyo, 1982. Professor at Fachhochschule, Düsseldorf (succeeding Friedrich Becker) (1985).
Exhibitions: 32, 61, 135, 198*, 263*, 344, 346*, 349, 350, 355, 457, 547*, 604, 709, 782, 799, 891, 900, 903, 925, 929, 1039, 1120, 1135*

Bahrs, Ulrike (Pl. 217) Born 1944 in Grevesmühlen, GDR. Graduated from the Goldschmiedeschule, Neu Gablonz (1963). Attended the Akademie der bildenden Künste, Munich. Won 1st prize from the Dannerstiftung, Munich, 1969; Staatspreis, Hamburg, 1970; Bavarian Staatspreis, Munich, 1972.
Exhibitions: 15, 96, 107, 165, 244, 245, 260, 261, 272, 301, 363, 465, 553, 712, 808, 883, 887, 891, 922, 1030, 1035, 1119, 1120
Works in public collections: Museum für Kunst und Gewerbe, Hamburg; Schmuckmuseum, Pforzheim.

Bakker, Gijs (Pl. 264) Born 1942 in Amersfoort, Holland. Attended the Instituut voor Kunstnijverheidsonderwijs (Jewellery Dept.), Amsterdam (1958–62) and the Konstfackskolan, Stockholm (1962–63). Won Van de Rijn Prize for sculpture, 1965 and gold and silver medals at Jablonec, Czechoslovakia, 1968. *Exhibitions:* 16, 21, 22* and 24*, (with Emmy van Leersum), 48, 60, 61, 275, 516*, (with Emmy van Leersum), 545, 575, 996, 1011 *Works in public collections:* Stedelijk Museum, Amsterdam; State Collection, The Hague; Gemeentelijke Van Reekum Museum, Apeldoorn; Nederlands Kostuummuseum, The Hague; The Cleveland County Collection, Middlesbrough, (Yorkshire).

L.G. Balfour & Co. (Pl. 229) Company situated in Attleboro, Massachusetts and founded in 1913 by Lloyd G. Balfour (b. 1884). Largest producer of scholastic and fraternal jewellery in the United States.

Bartosik, Karel (Pl. 177) Born 1942 in Tamworth, England (Czech father and Dutch mother). Lived and studied in Czechoslovakia (1946–67) and worked in costume-jewellery industry there. Won 1st prize in 'The Gold Jewel 1960'; silver medal at 'Jablonec '65'; 1st prize at 'Czechoslovak Souvenir Expo '67'. On returning to England, worked with Andrew Grima in London. Free-lance jeweller since 1973. Commissioned by English Chamber Orchestra to make wedding gift for H.R.H. the Prince of Wales and Lady Diana (1981). *Exhibitions:* 257, 546*, 1031* *Works in public collection:* Victoria and Albert Museum, London.

Bauer, Frank (Pl. 218) Born 1942 in Hanover, FRG. Trained in architectural draughtsmanship (1958). Attended the Hanover Music Conservatorium (1959). Served apprenticeship with Carl Van Dornick, Hildesheim (1962). Studied silversmithing and enamelling with Walter Cohausz (1965). Further study at Kilkenny Design Workshop, Ireland (1966) and art schools in Kassel and Hamburg (1967). Worked with architects in Hamburg and with Institute of Light Space Constructions in Stuttgart (1970). Opened workshop in Sydney, Australia (1972); moved it to Adelaide (1975). Moved to London (1979). Returned to Australia (1983). *Exhibitions:* 7, 8*, 81, 388, 408, 587, 596, 891, 898, 976, 1004, 1005 *Works in public collections:* Craft Council, Sydney; Australian National Gallery, Canberra; National Gallery of Victoria, Melbourne; State Art Gallery of South Australia, Adelaide; Bauhaus – Museum für Gestaltung, West Berlin.

Becker, Friedrich (Pls 122/123, 196, 244) Born 1922 in Ende, FRG. Served apprenticeship as mechanical fitter in Düsseldorf. Studied aeronautical engineering in Thorn. Served apprenticeship as gold- and silversmith. Attended the Werkkunstschule, Düsseldorf (graduated, 1951; qualified as master, 1952). Opened workshop (1952). Won Bavarian Staatspreis, 1959; 1st prize in international competition 'for silver candlesticks', 1960. Headed Group for Metal Design (gold and silver, 1964). Won Nordrhein-Westfalen Staatspreis, 1965; 2nd prize in international competition at Schmuckmuseum, Pforzheim, 1969; 1st prize in competition for designing 'Prix Jeunesse' trophy, Munich, 1970. Professor at the Fachhochschule, Düsseldorf: director of studies and pedagogic director (1970). Named Associate Member of the Worshipful Company of Goldsmiths, London, 1971; bearer of the Ehrenring of the Gesellschaft für Goldschmiedekunst, 1972. Awarded Federal Cross of Merit, 1st class, 1973. Retired from teaching (1982). Won Rosenthal Studiopreis, 1982. *Exhibitions:* 269, 375*, 437*, 475, 499, 1118* *Works in public collections:* Goldsmiths' Hall, London; Schmuckmuseum, Pforzheim; Deutsches Goldschmiedehaus, Hanau; Österreichisches Museum für angewandte Kunst, Vienna; Kunstgewerbemuseum, Staatliche Museen Preussischer Kulturbesitz, Berlin.

Boekhoudt, Onno (Pl. 213) Born 1944 in Hellendoorn, Holland. Attended the Vakschool, Schoonhoven (1963–66); the Kunst- und Werkkschule, Pforzheim (1966–68). *Exhibitions:* 14, 16, 31, 33, 37, 48, 163, 279, 341, 347, 352, 353, 522, 534, 599* (with Jan Tempelman), 799, 883, 891, 900, 1011, 1026, 1030, 1035, 1039, 1120 *Works in public collections:* Centraal Museum, Utrecht; Schmuckmuseum, Pforzheim; State Collection, The Hague.

Boucheron (Pls 52, 69, 94) Firm famous for high-quality, gem-set jewellery; founded in Paris in 1858 by Frédéric Boucheron (1830–1902). Like Cartier, has been run, by a continuous line of his successors: Louis (1874–1959), followed by his son Gérard (b. 1910), whose son Alan (b. 1948) now also works in the business. Has branches all over the world.

Brade, Christina (Pl 270) Born 1936 in Leisnig, GDR. Served apprenticeship as steel engraver (ended 1954). Attended Institut für künstlerische Werkgestaltung, Halle/Burg Giebichenstein (Metal Dept. under Karl Müller) (1954–59). Began to work free lance in 1959. Member of the Artists' Union of the GDR. Won award at 5th International Jewellery Exhibition, Jablonec, 1977; diploma at the 2nd Quadriennale des Kunsthandwerks sozialistischer Länder, Erfurt, 1978. *Exhibitions:* 282* (with Helmut Brade), 283, 284, 285, 335, 336, 394, 422, 424, 425, 426

Braque, Georges (Pl. 116) Born 1882 in France (died 1963). Famous French painter and colleague of Picasso; a leading exponent of Cubism and collage. A large bird in flight is a recurrent theme in some of his later paintings.

Broadhead, Caroline (Pls 198, 231) Born 1950 in England. Attended Central School of Art and Design, London (jewellery) (1969–72). Awarded Crafts Council Bursary to work in Amsterdam, 1982. *Exhibitions:* 3, 17, 44*, 46, 62, 154, 315, 457, 458, 586* (with Michael Brennand-Wood), 634, 639, 747* (with S. Heron), 784, 793, 798

Brownsworth Ann (Pl. 245) Born 1950 in Australia. Studied at the Royal Melbourne Institute of Technology (1970–1973); Tyler School of Art, Temple University, Philadelphia (1974). Exhibited at international exhibitions in Australia, Europe and the U.S.A. *Works in public collections:* Australian National Gallery, Canberra; Victoria State Craft Collection, Melbourne; Queensland Art Gallery, Brisbane; Museum and Art Gallery of the Northern Territories, Darwin; State Art Gallery of South Australia, Adelaide.

Bülow-Hübe, Torun Vivianna (Pls 97, 135) Born 1927 in Sweden. Won silver medal at 10th Triennale, Milan, 1954; gold medal at 12th Triennale, Milan, 1960; Frederick Lunning Prize, USA-Scandinavia, 1960; Swedish State's Grand Prix for Artists, 1965. Has lived and worked in Indonesia since 1978. *Exhibitions:* 19, 55*, 212, 225, 491, 658*, 684, 693, 753*, 845, 847*, 848, 852*, 960, 978, 980, 1153 *Works in public collections:* Nationalmuseum, Stockholm; Malmö Museum, Malmö; Röhsska Konstslöjdmuseet, Göteborg; Det Danske Kunstindustrimuseum, Copenhagen; Vestlandske Kunstindustrimuseum, Bergen; Kunstindustrimuseet, Oslo; Juleum, Helmstedt, FRG.

Bury, Claus (Pls 157, 168) Born 1946 in Meerholz, FRG. Graduated from Kunst- und Werkschule, Pforzheim (1968). Lived and worked in London (1969–70). Taught at Kunst- und Werkschule, Pforzheim (1971). Guest teacher at Royal College of Art, London and at Hornsey School of Art, London (1972–73). Visiting artist at Nova Scotia Festival of the Arts, Halifax (1975). Guest teacher at Bezalel Academy of Arts and Design, Jerusalem (1975–76). Received grant from the Cultural Committee of the Federal Association of German Industry for 'artists working in industry,' at Degussa Factory, Hanau, FRG, 1976. Visiting professor at Bezalel Academy of Arts and Design, Jerusalem (1978). Visiting artist sent by Goethe Institut to Australia (1979). Guest teacher at Rhode Island School of Design, Providence, Rhode Island (1980).

Exhibitions: 3, 16, 231, 248, 253, 328, 340, 344, 364*, 378*, 465, 509, 518, 545, 671*, 808, 815, 883, 889, 890*, 1008
Works in public collections: Artothek Berlin, West Berlin; Deutsches Goldschmiedehaus, Hanau; Kunstgewerbemuseum, Staatliche Museen Preussischer Kulturbesitz, Berlin; Kunsthalle, Nürnberg; Landesmuseum für Kunst und Kulturgeschichte, Oldenburg; National Gallery of Victoria, Melbourne; Schmuckmuseum Pforzheim; Städtische Kunstsammlung – Historisches Museum, Hanau; Victoria and Albert Museum, London.

Bury, Pol (Pl. 144) Born 1922 in Haine-Saint-Pierre, Belgium; son of a garage proprietor. Family moved to France (1929). Attended School of Art in Mons, Belgium. Participated in the 'International Surrealist Exhibition', Brussels (1945) with paintings. Abandoned painting for sculpture (1955), exhibiting with Calder, Tinguely, Vasarely, Soto and Duchamp at the Galerie Denise René, Paris. Won international acclaim for mobile sculptures closely related to his jewellery.

Calder, Alexander (Pls 81, 90) Born 1898 in Philadelphia (died 1976). An important American sculptor; studied engineering before turning to fine art in the early 1920s. Spent some years living in Paris; met Mondrian, Arp and Duchamp there. (It was Duchamp who gave the name 'mobiles' to Calder's sculptures in 1932).

Cartier (Pls 26, 34, 46, 47, 48, 54, 73, 74, 99, 101, 131) Firm with indisputable position in the world of jewellery. Founded in 1859; four successive generations of the family presided over the business until it passed into public ownership (early 1960s). By the early part of the 20th century, holder of no less than 13 Royal Warrants. The firm was founded by Louis-François Cartier (1819–1904); his son Alfred (1841–1925) succeeded him in 1874. Running of the business passed to his sons, Louis-Joseph Cartier, Pierre Cartier and Jacques Cartier in the early part of the 20th century, who expanded it to London and New York. Louis-Joseph's son Claude (d. 1975) was the last member of the family to head the company.
In 1972, Robert Hocq (1917–79) was chairman of the company that acquired the Paris branch of Cartier; in 1974 he added Cartier-London and in 1976 Cartier-New York. Until his death in 1979, Hocq was managing director of the enterprise; he was succeeded by his daughter Nathalie (b. 1951).

Cassandre [pseudonym of **Adolphe Mouron**] (Pl. 51) Born 1901 in Russia (died 1968). A talented artist; studied (painting with Lucien

Simon) at the Ecole des Beaux-Arts, Paris, and at the Academie Jullian. Won the Grand Prix at the Exposition Internationale des Arts Décoratifs et Industriels Modernes, Paris, 1925, for his poster design. Interested in graphics and printing (designed new typefaces); eventually, after World War II, concentrated on stage design and painting. Designed jewellery for Georges Fouquet (mid–1920s).

Castellani (Pl. 56) Famous dynasty of Italian goldsmiths and jewellers. The founder, Fortunato Pio Castellani (1793–1865), began research into secrets of techniques of granulation after seeing excavated Etruscan metalwork (early 1820s). Although the family did not discover real method of granulation, successive generations of Castellanis (Alessandro [1824–83], Augusto [1829–1914] and Alfredo [1853–1930]) built up a thriving business; produced high-quality jewellery in the antique styles at workshops in Rome, Naples, Paris and London. London branch was eventually taken over by Carlo Giuliano (see Pl. 5). Examples of Castellani's work are in many major museum collections, including the Victoria and Albert Museum, London.

Cepka, Anton (Pl. 143) Born 1936 in Šulekovo, Czechoslovakia. Studied at the School of Applied Arts, Bratislava and at the College of Decorative Arts, Prague. Won Bavarian Staatspreis; gold medal, Munich, 1964; Cyprian Majerník Prize, Bratislava, 1967; gold medal, Jablonec, 1977; silver medal, Jablonec, 1980.
Exhibitions: 246, 260, 273, 297, 457, 693, 704, 808, 883, 889, 1030, 1114* (with Václav Cígler), 1120

Chan, Kai (Pl. 300) Born 1940 in China. Graduated in biology from Chung Chi College, Hong Kong (1963). Moved to Toronto (1966). Graduated from Ontario College of Art, Toronto, in interior design (1970). Attended the Banff Centre, School of Fine Arts, Alberta (1981).
Exhibitions: 138, 457, 624, 644, 1046, 1049, 1056, 1057, 1060, 1061*

Coates, Kevin (Pl. 259) Born 1950 in Kingston, England. Studied music with Antonio di Palma, Adelaide, Australia, while working in bank (1966–68). Return to U.K.; continued to study music with Margaret Radmall. Trained and worked as a computer operator (Seeboard, Worthing). Attended West Sussex College of Design. Graduated in jewellery design from the Central School of Art and Design, London (1973). Received 1st Marlow Award from Society of Designer-Craftsmen, 1973. Received M.A. R.C.A. in jewellery design from the Royal College of Art, London (1976). 1st musical instrument analysis (Baroque violin). Designed 8-course lute according to Golden-

Section (made by the luthier Julian Emery [1974]). Won the Society of Designer-Craftsmen's annual Medal of Excellence, 1974. Granted Freedom of the Worshipful Company of Goldsmiths and of the City of London (1980). Commissioned by De Beers to make Diamond Stakes Ascot Trophy (1982). Commissioned to make brooch 'Athene Noctua' by Victoria and Albert Museum (1982). Tutor at School of Silversmithing and Jewellery, Royal College of Art (1982). Judge in De Beers 'Diamonds Today' competition (1983). Ring 'Harlequin Mask' purchased by Goldsmiths' Company for permanent collection (1983). Book on *Geometry, Proportion, and the Art of Lutherie*, published (1984).

Cohn, Susan (Pl. 274) Born 1952 in Australia. Trained and worked as a graphic designer (1971–77). Diploma in gold- and silversmithing from the Royal Melbourne Institute of Technology (1980). Currently Director of Workshop 3000.
Exhibitions: 12, 234, 294, 670, 676, 677, 739, 746
Works in public collections: Australian National Gallery, Canberra; Queensland Art Gallery Collection, Brisbane; Queen Victoria Museum & Art Gallery Collection, Launceston; Shire of Diamond Valley Collection, Melbourne; National Gallery of Victoria, Melbourne.

Conway, Ros (Pl. 176) Born 1951 in Bristol, England. Attended Somerset College of Art (1969–70). Graduated from Central School of Art and Design, London (1973). Received M.A.R.C.A from the Royal College of Art, London (1975). Won Worshipful Company of Goldsmiths' Award, 1975; Sandersons Art in Industry Award to travel in Japan, 1975; British Craft Award, 1977. Received Northern Arts Fellowship, 1977–79. Crafts Council Grant to train in enamel techniques with Jane Short, 1982–83. Served on the Crafts Council of Great Britain (1981–82).
Exhibitions: 136, 141, 152*, 308*, 471, 563, 589, 642*, 736, 891
Works in public collections: Worshipful Company of Goldsmiths, London; Crafts Council, London; Leeds City Art Gallery; Birmingham City Art Gallery; Victoria and Albert Museum, London; Castle Museum, Nottingham.

Cooper, John Paul (Pls 24, 25) Born 1869 in England (died 1933). At death of J.D. Sedding, to whom he was apprenticed, completed his architectural training under Henry Wilson (see Pl. 29), Sedding's assistant (1891). Wilson's enthusiasm for metalwork awakened Cooper's interest in the craft, which he took up seriously (end of the 1890s). Cooper was one of the first to use shagreen (a type of leather covering for metal having an artificially granulated surface, usually dyed green), which became very fashionable much later (1920s and 1930s). Taught at Birmingham School of Art (head of the Metalwork Dept. from 1904-7).

Copley, Noma (Pl. 172)   Born in Minneapolis, Minnesota. Attended New York University; University of California at Los Angeles and the Ecole du Louvre, Paris. Lived abroad for 20 years; now residing in New York city. President of Noma Copley and Jean Stark Inc.: Jewels; consultant to Kristin Moore, Ltd.
Exhibitions: 170, 460, 507, 761*, 764, 765, 770*, 777*, 792* (with Jean Stark), 941, 1045, 1149, 1160

Cranach, Wilhelm Lucas von (Pl. 44)   Born 1861 in Germany (died 1928). Predominantly a portrait and landscape painter. Lived in Berlin from 1893. Spectacular jewellery designs won a gold medal at the Exposition Internationale, Paris, 1900, and were also shown at the Berlin Exhibition, 1906.

Craver, Margaret (Pl. 109)   Born in Kansas, Missouri. Studied at the Art School, University of Kansas and later with private teachers for her technical work. Has taken part in many exhibitions and one-woman shows.
Works in public collections: Museum of Contemporary Crafts, New York; Minnesota Museum of Art, St. Paul; The Metropolitan Museum of Art, New York; Newark Museum of Art, Newark, New Jersey; National Museum of American Art, Smithsonian Institution, Washington, D.C.; Museum of the Wichita Art Association, Wichita, Kansas.

Czeschka, Carl Otto (Pl. 38)   Born 1878 (died 1960). Taught at the Kunstgewerbeschule, Vienna (1920-7) and was professor at the Kunstgewerbeschule, Hamburg (1907-43). Important member of the Wiener Werkstätte; besides making jewellery, designed for the stage and was a brillant graphic artist. Also designed stained glass windows and embroidery cartoons.

Dali, Salvador (Pls 93, 100)   Born 1904 in Figueras, Spain. One of the great Surrealist masters, both painter and sculptor. Has also designed furniture, jewellery and textiles. Spent some time in the United States but returned to his birthplace, where he still lives today. Renowned for his flamboyance and extravagant behaviour, always attracted much publicity.

Dawson, Nelson (Pl. 32)   Born 1859 (died 1942) and **Dawson, Edith Robinson** (dates unknown). Nelson: studied painting at the South Kensington Schools, London; also an apprentice in his uncle's architectural practice. Met Edith in Yorkshire; the couple returned to London and married (1893). Lectures by Alex-ander Fisher awakened Nelson's interest in metalworking and enamelling; he taught Edith, who practiced enamelling much to the detriment of her health. Set up their own workshop in London; were prolific and successful artist/jewellers. Took part in many exhibitions and worked on commissions that, at times, required employing up to 20 craftsmen. Retired in 1914.

De Large, Edward (Pl. 175)   Born 1949 in Lincoln, England. Attended Grimsby and Camberwell Schools of Art, diploma A.D. (1966-71), and the Royal College of Art, London, M.A., R.C.A. (1972-75). Won Sanderson Art in Industry Award, 1975 and UK-USA Bicentennial Arts Fellowship from the National Endowment for the Arts and the British Council, 1979.
Exhibitions: 99, 150, 164, 173, 176, 277, 411, 549, 561, 564, 574, 584, 724, 834, 844, 891, 957, 958, 1169
Works in public collections: Victoria and Albert Museum, London; National Gallery of Victoria, Melbourne; Schmuckmuseum, Pforzheim; The Worshipful Company of Goldsmiths, London; Gemeentelijke Van Reekum Museum, Apeldoorn; Crafts Council, London.

De Patta, Margaret (Pls 95, 104)   Born 1903 in Tacoma, Washington (died 1964). Attended Academy of Fine Arts, San Diego (1921-23); California School of Fine Arts, San Francisco (1923-25); Art Students League, New York (1926-29), winning two Art Students League Scholarships. Completed formal studies in painting and sculpture (1929). Studied metalwork with Armin Hairenian, San Francisco (1929). Began work in jewellery (1930). Studied enamelling and engraving, San Francisco (1932). Transition from painting to jewellery; established studio (1934-35). Association with Amberg-Hirth Gallery, San Francisco (1936). Attended Mills College summer session; worked with guest artist, Moholy-Nagy (1940). Studied at School of Design, Chicago; worked with Moholy-Nagy (1940-41). Began lapidary projects; stone cutting from models by Francis J. Sperisen, Sr, San Francisco (1941). Taught at California Labor School, San Francisco; California College of Arts and Crafts, Oakland; Oregon Ceramic Studio, University of Oregon Extension Division. Design work with Edith Heath Ceramics, Sausalito (1957). Associated with Metal Arts Guild, with Designer Craftsmen of California and American Crafts Council. Participated in numerous exhibitions and competitions (1935-64).

Derrez, Paul (Pls 185, 225)   Born 1950 in Sittard, Holland. Studied at Vakschool, Schoonhoven (1972-75). Lives and works in Amsterdam. Won Françoise van den Bosch Prize, Amsterdam, 1980.

Exhibitions: 17, 31, 37, 43, 46, 151, 634, 900, 1011, 1120
Works in public collections: Stedelijk Museum, Amsterdam; City of Amsterdam; State Collection, The Hague; Centraal Museum, Utrecht; Gemeentemuseum, Arnhem; Nederlands Kostuummuseum, The Hague; Gemeentelijke Van Reekum Museum, Apeldoorn; The Cleveland County Collection, Middlesbrough (Yorkshire).

Desprès, Jean (Pls 65, 72)   Born 1889 in Souvigny-Allier, France (died 1980). Gold- and silversmith from a famous family of glassmakers (Desprès de Loisy): parents had an art and jewellery shop in Paris. Trained as a goldsmith in Avallon and Paris; studied drawing in Paris. Friend of many artists such as Braque and Miró. Served in French army (working in aeroplane construction), became fascinated with metal, geometry and technology (1914-18). Participated in the Exposition Internationale des Arts Décoratifs, et Industriels Modernes, Paris (1925), and in Salon des Indépendants (1926). Studied and restored works by antique gold- and silversmiths. Worked closely with Etienne Cournault making Surrealist jewels (1930). Exhibited jewellery inspired by aeroplanes at the Salon de Marsan (1930); participated in 'Artistes de ce temps' at the Petit Palais, Paris (1936). Won gold medal of Aéro Club of France, 1936; honorary diploma at Exposition Internationale, Paris, 1937. Named member of the French Légion d'Honneur (1937). Won gold medal at World Fair, Brussels, 1958. Managed Galerie l'Art et la Mode, Paris, for many years, as well as his own shop near the Champs Elysées. His workshop was in Avallon.

De Syllas, Charlotte (Pls 163, 164, 165)   Born 1946 in Barbados, West Indies. Trained at Hornsey College of Art, London, under Gerda Flöckinger (1963-66). Won Hornsey College of Art travel scholarship, 1966. Hitch-hiked round Nigeria studying beads and their symbolic meanings. Won Craft Advisory Committee Bursary, 1976. Taught at Royal College of Art, London, as part-time staff (1972-76). Visiting lecturer at many art schools (1966-85).
Exhibitions: 497, 531, 583, 623, 1023
Works in public collections: Goldsmiths' Hall, London; Craft Advisory Committee; Victoria and Albert Museum, London.

De Wolf, Lam (Pl. 242)   Born 1949 in Badhoevedorp, Holland. Studied at the Gerrit Rietveld Academie (Textile Dept.), Amsterdam (1978-81).
Exhibitions: 17, 37, 40, 43, 45, 46, 48, 50, 237, 238, 239, 359, 632, 634, 1011
Works in public collections: City of Amsterdam; Centraal Museum, Utrecht; Gementelijke Van Reekum Museum, Apeldoorn.

Ditzel, Nanna (Pl. 112)   Born 1923 in Copenhagen, Denmark. Industrial designer. Graduated from Aurehoj Gymnasium, Copenhagen (1942); then from Kunsthaandvaerkerskolen (1946). Opened own office for industrial design (together with Jorgen Ditzel) same year. Published *Danish Chairs* (1954). Awarded Frederick Lunning Prize, 1956; gold medal at Triennale, Milan, 1960. Study tours: Greece (1957), Mexico and U.S.A. (1959), the Far East (1972, 1973). Exhibited in London (1962), New York (1963), Berlin and Vienna (1964), Copenhagen (1965) and at Lerchenborg Castle, Denmark (1972). Chairman of Danish Design and Industries Association (1981).

Di Verdura, Fulco [Santostefano della Cerda, Duc) (Pl. 98)   Born 1898 in Sicily (died 1978). Son of distinguished but impoverished Sicilian landowners; went to Paris (1927), intending to become a painter but becoming a jewellery designer for Chanel instead. Moved to the United States (1937), managing shop in California for the New York jeweller Paul Flato and designing jewellery for film stars (including Katherine Hepburn's jewels in 'Philadelphia Story'). Moved back to New York; opened own business on Fifth Avenue, (sold it in 1973 to his former associate, Joseph G. Alfano, who still runs it). Retired to London, where he died.

Drobny, Adolf (b. 1938 in Linz, Austria) and **Elsa** (b. 1936 in Gevelsberg, Germany). (Pl. 117) Adolf: studied at Kunst- und Werkschule, Pforzheim (1958–61). Master's degree (jewellery) in Linz (1962). Worked as a gold- and silversmith and watchmaker. Elsa: served apprenticeship as goldsmith; studied at the Kunstschule, Schwäbisch-Gmünd, and the Kunst- und Werkschule, Pforzheim. Gained master's degree (1963). In 1964 they opened a workshop, in Linz, and 4 years later a silver gallery. Have worked and exhibited together since then, in Vienna, Salzburg, Graz, Bregenz, Munich, Jablonec and Pforzheim.

Dunand, Jean [John] (Pl. 72)   Born 1877 in Lancy, near Geneva, Switzerland (died 1942). Sculptor, craftsman and furniture designer. Studied sculpture and drawing at Ecole des Arts Industriels, Geneva. Received grant from the city of Geneva to study in Paris with Jean Dampt (1897). Participated in Exposition Internationale in Paris (1900). From 1903, regularly exhibited at the salons of the Société Nationale des Beaux-Arts. Participated regularly in Expositions des Artistes Décorateurs (1908–42). Began using lacquer (1912), a technique he learned from Sugawara, a Japanese specialist. Became French citizen (1922). Participated in Exposition Internationale des Arts Décoratifs et Industriels Modernes, Paris (1925) with a smoking room in black lacquer, designed for a French embassy. Named vice-president

of the Société des Artistes Décorateurs (1927). Received commissions as interior designer for luxury liners (1928, 1931, 1935). Named knight (1919) and officer (1926) of the French Légion d'Honneur. A retrospective exhibition of his work 'Jean Dunand – Jean Goulden' was held in the Galerie Luxembourg, Paris (1973).

Dunlop, Sybil (Pl. 76)   Born of Scottish parentage ca. 1889 (died 1968). Sent to school in Brussels to learn French; also learnt the basic techniques of jewellery-making there. Opened a shop and workshop in Kensington Church Street, London (early 1920s). W. Nathanson was in charge of the workshop which produced unusual jewellery using stones specially cut by a firm of lapidaries in Idar-Oberstein, Germany, and enamelwork by a Belgian craftsman, de Konningh, who also worked for Omar Ramsden. Firm closed at the outbreak of World War II, but Nathanson reopened it after the war; he retired in 1971.

Ebendorf, Robert (Pl. 288)   Born 1938 in Topeka, Kansas. Educated at the University of Kansas. Studied in Norway at the State School for Applied Arts and Crafts (1963) while on a Fulbright grant. Received a Louis Comfort Tiffany grant (1965–66), returned to Norway to work at Norway Silver Designs, Fredrikstad. Received a National Endowment for the Arts grant, 1970. Taught at Stetson University, Florida; the University of Georgia at Athens; Haystack Mountain School of Crafts, Maine; Penland School of Arts and Crafts, North Carolina. Currently Professor of Art at the State University of New York, New Paltz. Founding member and past president of the Society of North American Goldsmiths. Honoured as a Distinguished Member of that society (1982). Designed jewellery for the Tane Silver Company, Mexico City. Became a staff designer and consultant to a leading Norwegian gold and silver firm – David-Andersen, Oslo (1978); designed and executed a special collection of gold jewellery for the firm. Presently design consultant for David-Andersen. One of the top award winners in the Color Core 'Surface and Ornament' Design Competition II, 1984.
Exhibitions: 127, 306, 457, 682, 748, 750, 772, 779, 796, 970, 971, 972, 973, 975, 1034, 1041, 1136, 1149
Works in public collections: The Metropolitan Museum of Art (20th Century Decorative Arts Collection), New York; Renwick Gallery of Art, National Museum of American Art, Smithsonian Institution, Washington, D.C.; Cooper-Hewitt Museum, The Smithsonian Institution's National Museum of Design, New York; Kunststindustrimuseet, Oslo; Cleveland Museum of Art, Cleveland; Schmuckmuseum, Pforzheim; Nordenfjeldske Kunstindustrimuseum, Trondheim; Yale University Art Gallery, New Haven, Connecticut.

Eisenloeffel, Jan (Pl. 27)   Born 1876 in Holland (died 1957). Trained at an art school in Amsterdam; completed studies in St Petersburg and Moscow, where he learnt the art of enamelling. Director of a metal workshop in Amstelhoek (1896); worked as designer for a jewellery manufacturer in Utrecht (1904–7). In charge of the Vereinigten Werkstätten für Kunst, Munich (1908). A highly competent and skilful gold- and silversmith, who produced many superb pieces of tableware – decorative plates, tea sets and cutlery – in addition to jewellery.

Ernst, Max (Pl. 149)   Born 1891 in Germany (died 1976). Became a naturalized French citizen (1958). Surrealist painter of world renown. Had intended to study philosophy and psychology in his youth, but changed his mind after meeting the painter August Macke (1911). A friend and sometime collaborator of the sculptor Jean Arp; also active in the German Dada movement. Among the techniques used in his work were collage and *frottage*, with which he achieved poetic images of birds, cities, etc.

Eshel-Gershuni, Bianca (Pl. 183)   Born 1932 in Sofia, Bulgaria. Emigrated to Israel (1939). Studied (painting and sculpture) at the Avni Institute, Tel Aviv. During her studies, created her first pieces of jewellery for her own use. Eastern folklore influences evident in the hammering and welding techniques, and in the insertion of coloured beads that characterized her early bronze jewellery. Created silver jewellery (early 1960s), and (from 1967 onwards) used gold as the main material in her works. Awarded gold medal, Munich, 1971. Recipient of the 1st prize in a bracelet competition sponsored by the Israel Export Institute, 1967.
Exhibitions: 713, 882, 889, 891, 896, 900, 902, 1015
Works in public collection: Schmuckmuseum, Pforzheim (Permanent Collection).

Evans, James (Pl. 276)   Born 1952 in Kingston, Ontario. Attended George Brown College of Applied Art and Technology (diploma in Jewellery Arts) (1978–80); Nova Scotia College of Art and Design (diploma in Fine Art) (1980–82). Won design award for innovation from the Metal Arts Guild, Toronto, 1981; award of merit from Ontario Crafts Council, 1982; award of merit and John Nather Design Award, 1983.
Exhibitions: 334, 457, 644, 695, 799, 1051, 1052, 1053, 1054, 1055, 1056, 1059, 1062

Fabergé, Carl (Pls 11, 13)   Born 1846 in Russia (died 1920). Perhaps the greatest master jeweller of all time; his superlative skills – and that of his workmasters and their assistants – are still legendary at the end of the 20th century. Carl took control of the St Petersburg firm

(1870) at the age of 24; won a gold medal at the firm's first participation in the Pan-Russian Exhibition, Moscow (1882). Famous for his creation of Imperial Easter Eggs (made for Tsars Alexander III and Nicholas II). Firm quickly expanded to Moscow, Odessa, Kiev and London. In addition to the Royal Warrant from Alexander III (1884 or 1885), was granted the Royal Warrant from the Courts of Sweden and Norway (1897). Exhibited the Imperial Easter Eggs for the first time at the Exposition Internationale Universelle, Paris; acclaimed *maître* and decorated with the French Légion d'Honneur. London branch closed (1915); firm finally closed down as a result of the Russian Revolution (1918). Carl escaped to Wiesbaden, Germany, as a courier attached to the British Embassy (September, 1918); went to Lausanne, Switzerland (1920).

Fahrner, Theodor (Pl. 6) Born 1868 in Germany (died 1928). A manufacturing jeweller in Pforzheim, Germany, of inexpensive jewellery using low-carat gold and silver with semi-precious stones in mass-production. Designs for his output frequently the work of members of the artists' colony at Darmstadt, including Patriz Huber and J.M. Olbrich. His jewellery was sold all over Europe, supplied to Liberty's in London, and exported to customers in the United States. A famous Belgian artist, Henry van de Velde, designed several pieces for Fahrner's at the turn of the century (exhibited in Paris at the time).

Favey, Dominique (Pl. 250) Born 1953 in Baden-Baden, FRG. Studied at the Ecole Nationale des Beaux-Arts, Paris (sculpture) (1973–78). Worked on the Spring/Summer collection for Paco Rabanne (1979). Sculpture purchased by the Musée National d'Art Moderne, Paris (1980).
Exhibitions: 630, 867*, 868*

Feiler, Ute (Pl. 271) Born 1941 in Erfurt, GDR. Served apprenticeship as engraver (1955–58). Studied at Fachschule für angewandte Kunst, Heiligendamm (Jewellery/Metal/Enamel Dept.) (1959–62). Master's degree as engraver (1965). Member of the Artists' Union of the GDR since 1969. Further study with Lothar Zitzmann at the Hochschule für industrielle Formgestaltung, Halle/Burg Giebichenstein (1976). Won silver medal at 5th Internationale Schmuckausstellung, Jablonec (1977).
Exhibitions: 116*, 276*, 281, 284, 285, 286, 307, 333*, 336, 337*, 338*, 422, 424, 425, 426, 427, 431*, 997*, 1157*

Fisch, Arline (Pls 182, 215) Born 1931 in Brooklyn, New York. Received B.S. in art from Skidmore College, Saratoga Springs, New York (1952); M.A. in art, University of Illinois, Urbana (1954); Fulbright grant for study in Denmark at Kunsthaandvaerkerskolen, Copenhagen, 1956. Assistant Professor, San Diego State University (started jewellery program in Art Dept.) (1961). Founder Member, Society of North American Goldsmiths (SNAG) (1970). Worshipful Company of Goldsmiths, London, purchased work (1971). Published *Textile Techniques in Metal* (1975). Vice-President for North America, World Craft Council [5 year term] (1976). Received Fulbright lecture grant to Austria, 1982. Guest Professor for Metallgestaltung at the Hochschule für angewandte Kunst, Vienna (1982). Gave lecture at the Gerrit Rietveld Academie, Amsterdam (1982); seminar at the Sir John Cass College, London (1982). President, Society of North American Goldsmiths (1982).
Exhibitions: 215*, 460, 513*, 521, 548, 591*, 629*, 752, 759*, 763*, 773*, 877, 878, 889, 891, 947*, 1035, 1041, 1120, 1128*, 1149, 1156*, 1167

Flöckinger, Gerda (Pls 153, 190) Born 1927 in Innsbruck, Austria. Studied fine arts at St Martin's School, London (1945–50); etching, jewellery, enamelling at the Central School of Art and Design, London (1950–55). Taught at Hornsey College of Art, London, and created jewellery course there (1962–68).
Exhibitions: 16, 142, 146*, 162, 229, 233*, 504*, 509, 511, 512*, 514, 517, 522, 530, 532, 552, 560, 566, 574, 597, 602, 604, 625, 833, 850, 882, 891, 906, 1022, 1119, 1120
Works in public collections: Worshipful Company of Goldsmiths, London; Victoria and Albert Museum, London; Schmuckmuseum, Pforzheim; City Art Gallery, Bristol; Royal Scottish Museum, Edinburgh; Crafts Council, London; East Midland Arts and Crafts Council Collection, Nottingham.

Font, Ana (Pl. 219) Born 1945 in Barcelona, Spain. Goldsmith. Studied at Escuela Massana, Barcelona, and at the Kunst- und Werkschule, Pforzheim. Received grant from city of Barcelona, 1966. Won Leistungspreis at the Salzburg Summer Academy, 1972; grant from the Ministry of Culture, Barcelona, 1981. Has participated in exhibitions in Madrid, Toulouse, Castellón de la Plana, Antwerp, Barcelona, Kyoto, Paris, Vienna, Tenerif, Pforzheim, Saragossa, Santander and Seville (since 1966) and had solo exhibitions in Boston, Sabadell and Hamburg.
Works in public collection: Schmuckmuseum Pforzheim.

Fouquet, Georges (Pls. 12, 33, 50) Born 1862 in Paris (died 1957). Took over father Alphonse's jewellery shop in Paris (1890) after studying the humanities. Shop, designed by Alphonse Mucha, was in the Rue Royale (1900–36). Together with Jules René Lalique (Pls 1, 23), one of the pioneers of Art Nouveau jewellery. Won wide acclaim at the International Exhibition, Paris, 1900. Participated in the International Exhibition, Milan, 1906, with a snake bracelet that Mucha designed for Sarah Bernhardt. Firm's jewellery was designed by Georges, by his son Jean (worked for the firm from 1919), by the architect Eric Bagge, the poster designer Cassandre, by the painter and sculptor Lambert-Rucki and by C. Desrosiers. Chairman of the Admissions Comittee (1924) and president of the Jewellery Section for the Exposition Internationale des Arts Décoratifs et Industriels Modernes, Paris, 1925; and for the Exposition Internationale, Paris, 1937. Exhibited widely in France and abroad.

Fouquet, Jean (Pls 59, 68, 72) Born 1899 in Paris. After studying the humanities and intending to become a writer, entered his father Georges's firm instead (1919). Decisively responsible for the design of Fouquet's jewellery (until 1964). Designed starkly geometric jewellery that was made in his father's workshop (1920s). Participated in the Exposition Internationale des Arts Décoratifs et Industriels Modernes, Paris, 1925, and (since 1926) regularly in the salons d'Automne. Published *Bijoux et Orfevrerie* (1928). Founding member of the Union des Artistes Modernes, Paris (1930). Designed jewellery given by the president of France to the Empress of Ethiopia (1936). Participated in the Exposition Internationale, Paris, 1937, and the World Fair, Brussels, 1958. Stopped working (1974) and turned his customers over to Raymond Templier (Pls 57, 72, 79). Many of his design sketches now in the Cabinet des Dessins, Musée des Arts Décoratifs, Paris.

Fröhlich, Max (Pls 87, 142) Born 1908 in Ennenda, Switzerland. Attended Ecole des Arts Industriels, Geneva (1924–25); Kunstgewerbeschule Zurich (1925–28). Worked as silversmith in Lucerne, Brussels and Zurich (1928–34). Assistant at the Kunstgewerbeschule, Zurich (1933). Had own workshop in Zurich (1934–45). In charge of metalworking class at Kunstgewerbeschule, Zurich (1945–66). Principal of the Kunstgewerbeschule, Zurich (1948–72). Guest professor at the Ecole Nationale Supérieure d'Architecture et des Arts Décoratifs, Brussels (1964, 1969). Gave lectures and seminars at five universities in the U.S.A. (1976). External assessor for final exams in silversmithing at the Ecole de Métiers d'Arts, Abbey de Maredsous, Belgium (1963, 1965). Awarded Ehrenring from the Gesellschaft für Goldschmiedekunst, 1964. External assessor for final exams in gold- and silversmithing and ceramics at the University of Science and Technology, Kumasi, Ghana (1966, 1967, 1968, 1970). Won Staatspreis (gold medal) awarded at the Internationale Handwerksksmesse, Munich, 1966. External

assessor for final exams for art teachers at the Institut Sainte-Marie, Brussels (1969).
Exhibitions: 125*, 468*, 470*, 1069*, 1124*, 1165*, 1166
Works in public collections: Kunstgewerbemuseum, Zurich; Schmuckmuseum Pforzheim.

Froment–Meurice, Emile (Pl. 3)   Born 1837 in France (died 1913). Goldsmith and jeweller; inherited his father's business. For most of his working life, made jewellery in the romantic neo-Gothic style, which was popular towards the end of the 19th century; influenced by Art Nouveau in his later works.

Gaillard, Lucien (Pl. 15)   Born 1861 in France (date of death unknown). A third-generation jeweller; succeeded his father Ernest (1892). Encouraged by Lalique, a friend and contemporary, to turn his talents from silversmithing to jewellery-making. Very interested in Japanese techniques of working with mixed metals in order to achieve different colours and patinas of metal; Japanese design exerted a strong influence on him.

Gardberg, Bertel (Pl. 134)   Born 1916 in Tammisaari, Finland. Attended Institute of Industrial Arts and the School for Goldsmiths, Helsinki (1938–41). Studied in Copenhagen (1946–49). Had workshop in Helsinki (1949–66); moved to Pohjankuru (1973). Taught metal-art at the Institute of Industrial Arts, Helsinki (1951–53). Designed for Galeries Lafayette, Paris (1953–54). Won gold and silver medals at the Milan Triennale, 1954, 1957, 1960; four awards (National Industrial Design Council), Toronto, 1960; Gold Ehrenring from the Gesellschaft für Goldschmiedekunst, FRG, 1960; two gold medals (California state exhibition), Sacramento, 1961; the Lunning Prize, U.S.A., 1961; Pro Finlandia medal, 1962; Gulden Vorm (two awards), Utrecht, 1967. Design director of Kilkenny Design Workshop, Ireland (1966–68). Design director of Rionore, Dublin (1968–71). State Art Industry Prize, Finland, 1975. Awarded title of Academician (1982). Solo exhibitions in Finland, Ireland, Great Britain, FRG, France and U.S.A.
Works in public collections: Museum of Applied Arts, Helsinki; Nationalmuseum, Stockholm; Röhsska Konstslöjmuseet, Göteborg; Malmø Museum, Malmø; Det Danske Kunstindustrimuseum, Copenhagen; Staatliches Museum für angewandte Kunst, Munich; Kunstgewerbemuseum, Nürnberg and Stuttgart; Schmuckmuseum, Pforzheim; The Worshipful Company of Goldsmiths, London; The Museum of Modern Art, New York; Muzej '25. Mai', Belgrade; Victoria and Albert Museum, London.

Gaskin, Georgina Cave (Pls 30, 45)   Born 1868 in England (died 1934). Met husband, Arthur Gaskin (1862–1928), at Birmingham School of Art, where both studied and he later taught. After marriage (1889), set up a joint workshop in Birmingham (1894). Made jewellery and exhibited work at Arts and Crafts exhibitions (until 1909–10). Commissioned by city of Birmingham to make a necklace as a gift for Queen Alexandra.

Giuliano (Pl. 5)   Carlo Giuliano (1831–1895) moved to London from Naples (1860); established branch of Casa Castellani there on behalf of Alessandro Castellani. Set up own workshop and retail outlet in Piccadilly, London (1874), which produced antique and Renaissance-style jewellery of exceptional quality. After his death (1895), his sons Carlo Joseph and Arthur (1864–1914) inherited business, which they continued (until 1914).

Goudji (Pl. 260)   Born 1941 in Georgia, U.S.S.R. Studied at Academy of Fine Arts, Tbilisi, Georgia (1958–62). Left the U.S.S.R. (aged 33) and settled in Paris (1974). Commissioned to design and make the presentation sword for Academician Félicien Marceau (1976). Designed collection of jewellery for men for Yves Saint Laurent (1977). Won Oscar d'or at the Salon International, 1980; Palme d'or at the Salon International, 1982. Exhibited mainly abroad, often with 'Hephaïstos', the French Association of Creative Jewellers, of which he is founder member and Secretary General (1983).
Exhibitions: 630, 799, 875, 876
Works in public collections: see caption to Pl. 260

Gough, Rowena (Pl. 294)   Born 1958 in Maryborough, Australia. Attended Royal Melbourne Institute of Technology (diploma of art in gold- and silversmithing) (1976–78)
Exhibitions: 293, 430, 745, 898, 1011, 1039, 1158
Works in public collections: Australian National Gallery, Canberra; National Gallery of Victoria, Melbourne; Power House Museum, Sydney; Queen Victoria Museum and Art Gallery, Launceston; Victoria State Craft Collection, Melbourne; Meat Market Craft Centre, Melbourne.

Grakalic, Viliama (Pl. 267)   Born 1942 in Zagreb, Yugoslavia. Attended School of Applied Art, Zagreb (diploma of art) (1962). Moved to Australia (1963). Received diploma of art in gold- and silversmithing from the Royal Melbourne Institute of Technology (1978). Exhibited in Australia, South-East Asia and Europe. Represented in Australian state and national collections.

Grima, Andrew (Pls 127, 145)   Born 1921 in England. Trained in art before studying mechanical engineering, finally turned to jewellery. Joined father-in-law's jewellery manufacturing business after World War II. Became manager in 1947. Between 1963 and 1967 won 11 De Beers Diamond International awards. Won the Queen's Award for Export and the Duke of Edinburgh Prize for Elegant Design (1966). Given the Royal Warrant by H.M. The Queen (1970); has made jewellery for the Queen and the Royal Family personally, as well as for State gifts. First Grima shop opened in London (1966); Grima Galleries in Sydney, New York, Zurich, and three Grima shops in Tokyo (in the Seibu stores). Specializes in unusual stones and colour juxtapositions, mostly with highly textured metals. Possibly his most revolutionary designs: a collection of watches for Omega.

Haizmann, Richard (Pl. 64)   Born 1895 in Villingen, Germany (died 1963). Father was director of factory that made watch springs. Haizmann served in World War I, was prisoner-of-war in France (from 1917), where he met Herbert von Garvens-Garvensburg, a collector and gallery owner with whom he worked after their release (1920). Worked as sculptor, painter and with ceramics all his life. Earlier work was destroyed by the Nazis (May, 1934) or exhibited in the 'Entartete Kunst' exhibition (1937).

Harper, William (Pl. 193)   Born 1944 in Bucyrus, Ohio. Attended Case Western Reserve University, B.S., M.S., Cleveland (1966, 1967). Studied advanced enamelling at Cleveland Institute of Art (1967). Won crafts award, Cleveland Museum of Art May Show, 1973; merit award, Goldsmiths Competition, Renwick Gallery of Art, Washington, D.C., and Minnesota Museum of Art, St. Paul, 1974; city medal from Limoges, France, at the Biennale internationale: *l'Art de l'Email,* Limoges, 1975; 2nd prize, International Festival of Enamels, Laguna Beach Museum, California, 1976.
Exhibitions: 70*, 71*, 127*, 128*, 179, 181, 182, 183, 206, 207, 208, 227, 324*, 415, 483*, 573, 581*, 768, 908*, 966, 1079, 1152
Works in public collections: Cleveland Museum of Art, Ohio; Columbus Gallery of Fine Art, Ohio; Minnesota Museum of Art, St. Paul; Butler Institute of American Art, Youngstown, Ohio; Museum of Contemporary Crafts, New York; Vatican Museum, Vatican City, Italy.

Hassenpflug, Peter (Pl. 155)   Born 1932 in Germany. Attended the Meisterschule, Hildesheim (studying drawing). Studied forestry in Munich; trained at the Werkkunstschule, Krefeld (metalworking) and (with Friedrich Becker), Düsseldorf. Owns and runs Galerie Orfèvre, Düsseldorf, with his wife Marie.
Exhibitions: 186*, 362*, 693, 709, 808, 1045, 1162
Works in public collections: Norrishalle, Nürnberg; Schmuckmuseum, Pforzheim.

Herbst, Marion (Pl. 206) Born 1944 in Lingen an der Ems, FRG. Studied at the Instituut voor Kunstnijverheidsonderwijs (Jewellery Dept.), Amsterdam (1962–68). Won Françoise van den Bosch Prize, Apeldoorn, 1982.
Exhibitions: 14, 16, 17, 30, 33, 35, 37, 40, 46, 48, 63*, 534, 634, 1011
Works in public collections: Stedelijk Museum, Amsterdam; State Collection, The Hague; Gemeentemuseum, Arnhem; Centraal Museum, Utrecht; Nederlands Kostuum-museum, The Hague; Museum Boymans-van Beuningen, Rotterdam; P.T.T.-Collection, The Hague; University Museum, Mexico City; Françoise van den Bosch Foundation, Naarden.

Heron, Susanna (Pls 150, 238) Born 1949 in England. Studied jewellery at the Central School of Art and Design, London (1968–71). Awarded Bicentennial Arts Fellowship, 1977, to work in U.S.A. for 1978–79. Works in public collections in Australia, Britain and Holland.
Exhibitions: 16, 38*, 44*, 46, 51*, 64*, 143, 144, 145, 148*, 149, 154, 315, 457, 519*, 530, 537*, 595*, 621, 631, 634, 639, 738*, 747* (with C. Broadhead), 793, 889

Hilbert, Therese (Pl. 256) Born 1948 in Zurich, Switzerland. Trained as a goldsmith at Kunstgewerbeschule, Zurich (1964–69). Attended Akademie der bildenden Künste, Munich (1972–78). Won Herbert Hoffmann Prize at the Internationale Handwerksmesse, Munich, 1974. Awarded Leistungspreis from the Kunstgewerbeschule Zurich, 1975.
Exhibitions: 43, 46, 97, 134, 328, 330, 332, 354, 383*, 391, 457, 542, 624, 728, 729, 740, 741, 743, 799, 891, 895*, 1011, 1070, 1075, 1120, 1173
Works in public collections: Schmuckmuseum, Pforzheim; Deutsches Goldschmiedehaus, Ha-nau; Israel Museum, Jerusalem; Stadtmuseum, Munich; Stedelijk Museum, Amsterdam.

Hiramatsu, Yasuki (Pl. 281) Born 1926 in Osaka, Japan. Graduated from Tokyo University of Fine Art (1952). Regular exhibitor at Imperial Academy, Modern Living Industrial Arts Institute, Japan New Craft exhibitions and Japan Jewellery exhibitions (1950–70). Professor at Tokyo University of Fine Arts. Chairman of Directors at Japan Craft Designers' Association. Permanent Director of Japan Jewellery Designers' Institute.
Exhibitions: 3, 45, 67, 203, 297, 356, 436, 598, 604, 739, 799, 808, 882, 900, 1035, 1041, 1112*, 1120

Hoffmann, Josef (Pl. 28) Born in Austria (died 1956). Together with Koloman Moser (1868–1918), co-founder and key figure in the formation of the Wiener Werkstätte, Vienna (1903). Had great social awareness and was an admirer of C.R. Ashbee's Guild of Handicrafts, which served as a model for the Wiener Werkstätte. But unlike Ashbee, he insisted that all the craftsmen he employed be fully qualified. Own work included designs for tableware, furniture, textiles, glass and ceramics in addition to jewellery. Artistic director of the Wiener Werkstätte exhibitions (1903–31).

Holder, Elizabeth (Pl. 199) Born 1950 in Sindelfingen, FRG. Served apprenticeship in jewellery (1967–70). Attended Staatliche Zeichenakademie, Hanau (1972–74); Fach-hochschule, Düsseldorf (1974–78); Royal College of Art, London. Set up workshop in London (1980). Won 'Ring' competition at the Goldschmiedehaus, Hanau; awarded Preis der Deutschen Handwerker, 1978.
Exhibitions: 34* (with Johannes Kuhnen), 69, 129, 153* (with Frank Bauer), 243, 259, 301, 305, 457, 602, 603, 610* (with Frank Bauer), 612, 623, 632, 647, 900

Holdsworth, Annie (Pl. 295) Born 1953 in Melbourne, Australia. Attended Royal Melbourne Institute of Technology (diploma of art in gold and silversmithing) (1978–80).
Exhibitions: 293, 624, 662, 739, 1010, 1011, 1039
Works in public collections: Australian National Gallery, Canberra; National Gallery of Victoria, Melbourne; Power House Museum, Sydney.

Hopea-Untracht, Saara (Pl. 194) Born 1925 in Porvoo, Finland (died 1984). Trained at the School of Arts and Crafts, Helsinki, in interior design (1943–46). Designed furniture for Majander Oy (1946–48); lighting fixtures for Taito Oy (1948–52); art and utility glassware for Notsjoe Glassworks (1952–59). Since 1959 jewellery designer for family-owned goldsmith shop, Kultasepänliike Ossian Hopea in Porvoo. Lived for 7 years in U.S.A., Nepal and India (after 1960). Returned to Porvoo (1967) and continued jewellery designing and enamelling on metal. Awarded Finland's State Prize in Arts and Crafts (1981, 1982) and Porvoo Cultural Prize, 1981. Established the Hopea-Untracht Fund in Porvoo (1983), which is awarded to a Porvoo artist, craftsman or cultural organization; first award made in spring, 1984.
Exhibitions: 72, 403, 404, 406, 407, 489, 685, 686, 687, 694, 808, 1035, 1071, 1120
Works in public collections: Finnish Art and Craft Museum, Helsinki; Newark Museum of Art, Newark. New Jersey; The Museum of Modern Art, New York; Porvoon Museo, Porvoo; Finnish Glass Museum, Riihimäki.

Hu, Mary Lee (Pl. 282) Born 1943 in Lake-wood, Ohio. Attended Cranbrook Academy of Art, Bloomfield Hills, Michigan, B.F.A. (1965) and Southern Illinois University, Carbondale, M.F.A. (1967). Won exceptional quality award at National Arts and Crafts Exhibition, 1970, Jackson, Mississippi. Lived in Taipei, Taiwan, studying Chinese language, music, art and folk art (1971–73). Won Best in Show, Best in Metals award at the Exhibition 'Beaux Arts Designer/Craftsman 75', Columbus, Ohio. Taught at the University of Wisconsin, Madison (1976–77). Presently associate professor at the University of Washington, Seattle.
Exhibitions: 209, 241, 772, 941, 1073
Works in public collections: Goldsmiths' Hall, London; American Craft Museum, New York; Columbus Museum of Fine Arts, Columbus, Ohio; Yale University Art Gallery, New Haven, Connecticut; Illinois State University, Normal, Illinois; Southern Illinois University, Carbon-dale, Illinois; University of Indiana Art Gallery, Bloomington, Indiana.

Huber, Patriz (Pl. 8) Born 1878 in Germany (died 1902). Trained as architect and interior designer. Studied at colleges of arts and crafts, Mainz and Munich. Joined artists' colony, Darmstadt (1899), where jewellery was designed for the workshops of Theodor Fahrner that was far ahead of its time and quite demanding in technical terms. Committed suicide in Berlin at age 24 (1902), after having been dismissed by Grand Duke Ernst Ludwig of Hessen, who founded colony.

Hunt, George (Pl. 80) Born 1892 in England (died 1960). Trained at Margaret Street School of Art, Birmingham. Was pupil of Bernard Cuzner. Set up own workshop in Birmingham (1915).

Ikezawa, Wahei (Pl. 277) Born 1946 in Shimane, Japan. Trained at the Kanazawa Arts and Crafts University. Assistant at the Hirama-tsu Design Institute (1970–78). Won Jewellery-Art Prize, Tokyo, 1974, and award at the 'Japan Craft Exhibition', 1976, 1979.
Exhibitions: 68, 1026, 1030

Illsley, Bryan (Pl. 253) Born 1937 in Surbiton, England. Served apprenticeship as stonemason (1953). Attended evening classes at Kingston Art School (1954–57). Moved to St Ives, Cornwall (1963); worked part-time at Bernard Leach's pottery. Worked with Breon O'Casey making jewellery; then went into partnership with O'Casey (1966). Dissolved partnership with O'Casey (1982); continues making jewellery independently.
Exhibitions: 472, 496, 503, 562, 607, 608, 611, 619, 622, 626, 640, 641, 646, 659, 830, 837, 933, 934, 935, 936, 1138
Works in public collections: Contemporary Art Society, London; Kettles Yard, Cambridge; Plymouth City Art Gallery; Education Committees of Camden, Cornwall, Devon, Reading; Arts Council of Great Britain, London.

Itoh, Kazuhiro (Pls 210, 247) Born 1948 in Shikoku, Japan. Attended Tama Art University, Tokyo (degree in painting) (1968–71). Worked in design studio of Mikimoto Pearl Co., Tokyo (1971).
Exhibitions: 203, 205, 557, 602, 604, 638, 739, 745, 746, 781, 799, 891, 1027, 1040*, 1120
Works in public collection: Schmuckmuseum, Pforzheim.

Jensen, Georg (Pl. 17) Born 1866 in Denmark (died 1935). Man of remarkable character; as working-class boy, he struggled to become a sculptor, but after serving an apprenticeship in brazier's workshop of a foundry, was apprenticed to a goldsmith. After qualifying, still studied sculpture for a few years in the evenings; won a travel award to Paris. Family responsibilities turned him back to gold- and silversmithing. Opened own workshop in Copenhagen (1904). Commercial flowering of Jensen's enterprise was due to his partner, Niels Wendel, and to his associates Thorolf Møller (his brother-in-law), P.A. Pedersen (later a director in the company) and to the sales chief, Frederick Lunning.
  Deeply concerned with the artistic content of his jewellery's designs, Jensen gave each artist who designed for the firm full credit and remained committed to a deliberate policy of creating inexpensive jewellery of high standard.

Jünger, Hermann (Pls 125, 162, 203) Born 1928 in Hanau, FRG. Trained at the Staatliche Zeichenakademie, Hanau, and the Fachschule für Gold- und Silberschmiede (1947–49). Studied (with Franz Rickert) at the Akademie der bildenden Künste, Munich (1953–56). Won gold medal at the Internationale Handwerksmesse, Munich, 1962. Represented the FRG at the 1st International Symposium for silver jewellery in Jablonec, Czechoslovakia, and won silver medal (1968). Awarded Ehrenring from the Gesellschaft für Goldschmiedekunst, 1968. Professor for goldsmithing at the Akademie der bildenden Künste, Munich (1972). Invited by the Japan Foundation to Kyoto and Tokyo (1978).
Exhibitions: 16, 78, 107, 134, 139, 159, 177, 185, 200, 229, 230, 231, 260, 328, 391, 420, 465, 542, 545, 693, 705, 728, 729, 808, 809, 889, 891, 928, 989, 1023, 1026, 1030, 1035, 1173

Kasalý, Svatopluk (Pl. 151) Born 1944 in Pelhrimov, Czechoslovakia. Studied glazing, leading, glass cutting and picture-frame design. Won 1st prize from Železnýbrodské sklo Company for collection of costume-jewellery pendants, Železný Brode, 1965, and 1st prize in the costume-jewellery section at the International Costume Jewellery Exhibition, Jablonec, 1965. Awarded gold medal at the International Exhibition at Jablonec, 1971, 1974, and prize, Los Angeles, 1984.

Exhibitions: 149, 272, 317, 397, 419, 434*, 553, 661, 715, 727, 799, 889, 898, 917*, 964*, 1078, 1120, 1124*, 1143
Works in public collections: Museum of Industrial Art, Prague; North Bohemian Museum, Liberec; Museum of Glass and Costume Jewellery, Jablonec nad Nisou; Schmuckmuseum, Pforzheim; The Corning Museum of Glass, Corning, New York.

Keefer, Jeanne (Pl. 195) Born 1951 in the United States. Attended San Diego State University, awarded B.A. and M.A. with distinction in art (1975, 1979). Taught at Mesa College, San Diego (1979–81); now teaching at School of Art, Tasmanian College of Advanced Education, Launceston, Australia (lecturer in jewellery and silversmithing).
Exhibitions: 9, 234, 278, 294, 457, 459, 681, 692, 774, 783, 801, 1041, 1155
Works in public collections: Crafts Board of the Australia Council; Tasmanian Museum and Art Gallery, Hobart; Crafts Council of Tasmania, Hobart; Georgia State Museum and Art Gallery, Atlanta, Georgia; Queen Victoria Museum and Art Gallery, Launceston.

Kimata, Hajime (Pl. 252) Born 1938 in Aichi Prefecture, Japan. Graduated from Tokyo National University of Arts (1963). Member of Japan Craft Designers' Association; member of Japan Jewellery Designers' Association; Assistant Professor at Tokyo National University of Education. Won Japan Craft Prize from the Japan Craft Exhibition (1979).
Exhibitions: 68, 356, 438, 714, 901, 1023, 1026, 1030, 1035, 1039, 1120

Koch, Max Friedrich (Pl. 9) Born 1859 in Germany (died 1930). An artist/jeweller who – along with Robert Koch and W.L. von Cranach – produced work of high quality and originality comparable to that of Lalique, Fouquet and other major designers; in their lifetimes, however, these artists never received the same public recognition accorded their French counterparts.

Kodré, Helfried (Pls 146, 184) Born 1940 in Graz, Austria. Self-taught. Since 1961 free-lance artist exhibiting with Elisabeth Kodré-Defner. Won Bavarian Staatspreis, Munich, 1967; prize from the Vienna Art Fund, 1968.
Exhibitions: 23*, 97, 177, 188*, 190*, 251, 318, 325*, 326*, 327*, 328, 420, 465, 522, 688*, 710, 712, 717*, 771, 882, 883, 886, 889, 916, 942*, 993, 1023, 1026, 1030, 1063, 1083*, 1084, 1089*, 1097*, 1101, 1139*

Kodré-Defner, Elisabeth (Pls 156, 201) Born 1937 in Innsbruck, Austria. Attended Hochschule für angewandte Kunst, Vienna (1961) and opened her own studio. Won Bavarian Staatspreis, Munich, 1967; prize from

the Vienna Art Fund, 1968; Diamond International Award, New York, 1970.
Exhibitions: 23*, 97, 101*, 177, 188*, 190*, 192*, 251, 256*, 265*, 318*, 325*, 326*, 327*, 328, 420, 465, 522, 590, 688*, 710, 712, 717, 725, 733, 771, 794, 795*, 818*, 882, 883, 886, 889, 916, 942*, 949, 993, 1023, 1026, 1030, 1063, 1083*, 1084, 1089*, 1097*, 1101, 1103, 1116, 1139*

Kramer, Sam (Pls 84, 103) Born 1913 in Pittsburgh, Pennsylvania (died 1964). Started learning jewellery-making there in high school and worked in the machine shop. Studied journalism at the University of Pittsburgh; literature, art and psychology at the University of Southern California. Graduated with B.A. (1936). Began making jewellery on his own while working as a reporter in Hollywood (1938). Moved to Greenwich Village in New York city, (1939); worked there until his death. A colourful personality, as unconventional in his appearance as in his jewellery design. Took part in many important exhibitions all over the United States (1941–59) at the American Museum of Natural History, New York; the Walker Art Center, Minneapolis; Princeton University, Princeton, New Jersey – as well as in Mexico and Cuba. His work was featured several times in *Design Quarterly*.

Kruger, Daniel (Pl. 188) Born 1951 in Cape Town, South Africa. Attended Stellenbosch University (goldsmithing and graphic art) (1971–72). Studied painting at the Michaelis School of Fine Art, University of Cape Town (1973–74). Attended the Akademie der bildenden Künste, Munich (under Hermann Jünger) (1974–80).
Exhibitions: 51*, 74, 75, 76, 77, 112, 113*, 134, 197, 205, 260, 263*, 329, 387*, 391, 412, 443*, 458, 542, 728, 729, 747*, 891, 900, 904*, 969*, 1011, 1035, 1041, 1120, 1135*, 1173

Künzli, Otto (Pl. 233) Born 1948 in Zurich, Switzerland. Trained as a goldsmith at the Kunstgewerbeschule, Zurich (1965–70). Studied at the Akademie der bildenden Künste, Munich (1972–78). Graduated in 1978. Received grants from the Interior Dept., Berne, 1972, 1978, 1981; and prize from the Kunstgewerbeschule, Zurich, 1976.
Exhibitions: 40, 46, 47, 49, 134, 391, 448, 457, 542, 545, 624, 634, 729, 738, 741, 742, 743, 799, 889, 893*, 1011, 1070, 1075, 1098, 1120, 1125, 1173
Works in public collections: Schmuckmuseum, Pforzheim; Deutsches Goldschmiedehaus, Hanau; Victoria and Albert Museum, London; Israel Museum, Jerusalem; Stadtmuseum, Munich; Stedelijk Museum, Amsterdam; National Gallery of Victoria, Melbourne; Gemeentelijk Van Reekum Museum, Apeldoorn; The Cleveland County Collection, Middlesbrough (Yorkshire).

Kuhnen, Johannes (Pl. 216) Born 1952 in Essen, FRG. Served apprenticeship in private workshop of Friedrich Becker, Düsseldorf (1969–73). Attended Fachoberschule für Gestaltung, Düsseldorf (1973–74); Fachhochschule Düsseldorf (1974–78). Taught design at Fachhochschule Düsseldorf (1980–81), then silversmithing at Royal Melbourne Institute of Technology, Melbourne (1982). Head jeweller/designer for Hardy Brothers Group Ltd (1983–84). Won 1st prize in international competition: 10 Gramm Gold, 1976; and State Award Nordrhein-Westfalen, FRG, 1981.
Exhibitions: 9, 37, 129, 900, 1039, 1120
Works in public collections: Badisches Landesmuseum, Karlsruhe; Galerie Orfèvre, Düsseldorf; Boymans-van Beuningen Museum, Rotterdam; Victoria State Collection, Meat Market Craft Centre, Melbourne; National Gallery of Victoria, Melbourne; South Australia Art Gallery, Perth; The National Australian Gallery, Canberra.

Kuldkepp, Leili Petrovna (Pl. 191) Born 1931 in Vilnius, Lithuania. Graduated from the Estonian State Art Institute in Tallinn (1959). Member of the Artists' Union since 1972. Professor at the Metal Faculty, Tallinn Art Institute and has her own studio. Executes only unique works, many of which are in museums in the U.S.S.R. Participates regularly in exhibitions in the U.S.S.R. and in Bulgaria, Mongolia, GDR, Belgium, Japan, Hungary, FRG, and France. Won several gold and silver medals at the International Jewellery exhibitions, Jablonec.

Kurokawa, Okinari (Pl. 278) Born 1946 in Harbin, China. Graduated from Musashino Art University, Tokyo (1971). Attended the Fachhochschule für Gestaltung, Pforzheim (1972–73). Teaches at the Institute of Gemmology and Jewelry Arts, Yamanashi (1981–).
Exhibitions: 457, 901, 1120

Lalique, René Jules (Pls 1, 23) Born 1860 in France (died 1954). Trained as jeweller; served apprenticeship with well-known Parisian jeweller, Louis Aucoc; studied at the Ecole des Arts décoratifs, Paris, and after a spell in London (1879–80), opened own workshop, Paris (1884). Began by designing and making jewellery for Cartier, Boucheron and Aucoc, among others; won great acclaim for his innovative design and superb craftsmanship at the Paris Salon (1884) and Paris International Exhibition (1900). Also created exquisite jewellery for the legendary actress Sarah Bernhardt. Produced 145 of his best pieces over a period of years on commission from Calouste Gulbenkian: now housed in the Fundaçao Calouste Gulbenkian, Lisbon. Decided to abandon jewellery-making for glass (1914), and once again won acclaim for his superb designs.

Lambert-Rucki, Jean (Pl. 77) Born 1888 in Poland (died 1967). Sculptor, painter of frescos and mosaicist. Attended art school in Cracow. Emigrated to France (1911); settled in Paris and became friends with the artists of Montparnasse, including Modigliani and Soutine. Regular exhibitor in the Salon des Indépendants and the Salons d'Automne at the Tuileries; member of the Union des Artistes Modernes (from 1930). Became a naturalized French citizen (1932); designed jewellery for Georges Fouquet (1936–37).

Larsen, Helge (Pl. 169) Born 1929 in Copenhagen, Denmark. Served 4 year apprenticeship in jewellery. Received national diploma from the College of Craft and Design, Copenhagen. Set up workshop/studio in Copenhagen (1955). Emigrated to Australia (1961). Participated in the International Symposium on Steel, Austria (1974). Visiting Professor at the Sommerakademie für bildende Kunst, Salzburg (1975). Appointed head of Jewellery and Silversmithing Dept. at the Sydney College of the Arts, Sydney (1977). Participated in International Tin Symposium, Vienna (1980). Joint curator (with Darani Lewers) of touring exhibition 'Australian Jewellery to Europe' (1982).
Exhibitions: 246, 293, 294, 489, 491, 693, 891, 1038, 1105, 1120
Works in public collections: The Australian National Gallery, Canberra; Museum für angewandte Kunst, Vienna; Museum of Decorative Arts, Prague; Det Danske Kunstindustrimuseum, Copenhagen; Schmuckmuseum, Pforzheim; Museum of Applied Arts and Sciences, Sydney.

Lechtzin, Stanley (Pls 200, 293) Born 1936 in Detroit, Michigan. Studied at Wayne State University, B.F.A., Detroit (1960) and Cranbrook Academy of Art, M.F.A., Bloomfield Hills, Michigan (1962). Teaches at Tyler School of Art, Temple University, Philadelphia, where he is Professor of Crafts. Chairman of Crafts Department (1965–79). Chairman of Metals Department (1962–83). Won highest award for the creation of the most outstanding design at the First Annual Cultured Pearl Jewelry Design Contest, New York, 1966; Good Design award in American Jewelry Today, 1967; award for Excellence in Design at the Annual Cultured Pearl Jewelry Design Contest, New York, 1968, 1969, 1970; award in the Johnson Matthey Platinum Jewelry Design Competition, 1980; Governor's Award for Excellence in the Arts in Pennsylvania, 1984.
Exhibitions: 529*, 758*, 760*, 911, 915*
Works in public collections: Tokyo University of Fine Arts and Music, Tokyo; Goldsmiths' Hall, London; Schmuckmuseum, Pforzheim; American Craft Museum, New York.

Leersum, Emmy van (Pls 147, 204, 239) Born 1930 in Hilversum, Holland (died 1984).

Studied at the Instituut voor Kunstnijverheidsonderwijs (Jewellery Dept.), Amsterdam (1958–62) and at the Kunstfackskolan, Stockholm (1962–63). Won gold and silver medals at Jablonec, Czechoslovakia, 1968; Herbert Hoffmann Prize, Munich, 1983.
Exhibitions: 16, 20*, 22*, 24*, 25*, 29*, 36, 43, 46, 64, 275, 516, 545, 634, 1011
Works in public collections: Stedelijk Museum, Amsterdam; State Collection, The Hague; Nederlands Kostuummuseum, The Hague; Centraal Museum, Utrecht; Gemeentelijke Van Reekum Museum, Apeldoorn; Victoria and Albert Museum, London; The Cleveland County Collection, Middlesbrough (Yorkshire).

Lewers, Darani (Pls 169, 292) Born 1936 in Sydney, Australia. Took jewellery apprenticeship course at the East Sydney Technical College (1957). Studied with Estonian master jeweller, Sydney (1958). Worked in Helge Larsen's workshop, Copenhagen (1959). Formed partnership with Helge Larsen in Sydney (1961). Awarded the Moya Dyring Studio in the Cité Internationale des Arts, Paris, 1972. Chairperson of the Crafts Board of the Australia Council (1976–80). Part-time lecturer at the City Art Institute, Sydney (1980). Trustee of the Museum of Applied Arts and Sciences, Sydney (1981). Member of Artworks Advisory Committee for the Parliament House Construction Authority (1982). Appointed member in the General Division of the Order of Australia (1982). Joint curator (with Helge Larsen) of the touring exhibition 'Australian Jewellery to Europe' (1982).

Lindner, Rolf (Pl. 272) Born 1946 in Ichtershausen, GDR. Served apprenticeship as goldsmith (1965–67). Studied at the Fachschule für angewandte Kunst, Heiligendamm (Jewellery Dept.) (1969–72). Member of Artists' Union of the GDR since 1973. Worked in the 'Erfurt-Schmuck' Cooperative (1973–77). Master's degree in goldsmithing (1976). Works as free-lance goldsmith (since 1977). Won diploma at 3rd Quadriennale des Kunsthandwerks sozialistischer Länder, Erfurt, 1982.
Exhibitions: 114, 115, 117*, 156, 244, 245, 283, 284, 285, 287, 307, 336, 422, 424, 425, 426, 427, 477, 1014

Long, Randy (Pl. 290) Born 1951 in the United States. Won award of distinction at California Metals Invitational, Long Beach, California, 1978; craft award the Iowa Annual Arts Exhibition, Des Moines Art Center, Iowa, 1982; Award of Excellence at Artforms '84, Museum of Art, Lafayette, Indiana, 1984.
Exhibitions: 53, 132*, 242*, 306, 456, 461, 648*, 776, 783, 800, 912, 918, 1034, 1150

Lorenzen, Jens-Rüdiger (Pl. 251) Born 1942 in Hagen, FRG. Apprenticed as goldsmith

(1961–64). Attended Kunst + Werkschule, Pforzheim (1965–68). Master's degree in goldsmithing (1968). Had own workshop in Wuppertal (1968–74). Taught at Staatliche Zeichenakademie, Hanau (from 1974). Professor at the Fachhochschule für Gestaltung, Pforzheim (since 1984). Won 1st prize in International Watch Competition, Pforzheim, 1966; Bavarian Staatspreis, Munich, 1973, and Herbert Hoffmann Prize, Munich, 1973.
Exhibitions: 3, 16, 189*, 273, 304, 339*, 371*, 375*, 384*, 465, 522, 527, 660*, 808, 811*, 816*, 883, 884*, 889, 891, 900, 1026, 1035, 1041, 1112*, 1120, 1129, 1175*
Works in public collections: Schmuckmuseum, Pforzheim; Victoria and Albert Museum, London; Museum für angewandte Kunst: 'Die neue Sammlung', Munich; Deutsches Goldschmiedehaus, Hanau; Museum für Kunsthandwerk, Frankfurt; Museum für Kunst und Gewerbe, Hamburg.

Lugossy, Maria (Pl. 257) Born 1950 in Budapest, Hungary. Graduated with a degree as artist/goldsmith from the Academy of Applied Arts, Budapest (1973). Attended Master's School (1973–75).
Exhibitions: 169*, 262, 288, 360, 361, 370, 447, 690, 841, 924, 1013*, 1146*

Maierhofer, Fritz (Pls 167, 246) Born 1941 in Vienna, Austria. Lived in London (1967–70). Won prize from the Vienna Art Fund, 1972, prize in International Jewellery Competition, Schmuckmuseum, Pforzheim, 1972, Received grant from the Education and Art Dept. (1976).
Exhibitions: 3, 5, 84, 89, 121, 147, 171, 252, 318*, 328, 346*, 366, 381, 439, 467, 478*, 509, 518, 539*, 545, 604, 771, 856, 886, 889, 891, 892, 897, 900, 943, 995, 1026, 1035, 1063, 1084, 1090*, 1091*, 1094, 1095, 1099*, 1106*, 1115*, 1120, 1124*
Works in public collections: Österreichisches Museum für angewandte Kunst, Vienna; The Worshipful Company of Goldsmiths, London; Victoria and Albert Museum, London; Schmuckmuseum Pforzheim; and the museums of Lower Austria.

Makigawa, Carlier (Pl. 280) Born 1952 in Perth, Australia. Lived in Western Australia (1977–80). Attended Royal Melbourne Institute of Technology, B.A.
Exhibitions: 293, 457, 624, 739, 799, 1011, 1039, 1158
Works in public collections: State Art Gallery of South Australia, Adelaide; Art Gallery of Western Australia, Perth; The Australian National Gallery, Canberra; National Gallery of Victoria, Melbourne; Power House Museum, Sydney.

Martinazzi, Bruno (Pls 136, 161) Born 1923 in Turin, Italy, where he studied and took degrees in chemistry and psychology. Taught at the Accademia di Belle Arte, Turin, where first solo exhibition was held (1954). Other solo exhibitions in Geneva, London, New York, Boston, Monaco, Düsseldorf, Cologne, Vienna, Milan, Rome and Venice. Participated in all the important group exhibitions in Europe, America and Asia, and won many prizes.
Exhibitions: 457, 798, 1042

Masriera, Louis (Pl. 35) Born 1872 in Spain (died 1958). Belonged to family of goldsmiths and jewellers; inherited, with his brother, business their grandfather founded in Barcelona (1839). Also an accomplished painter. Studied at the Ecole des Beaux-Arts, Geneva (1889), where he learnt technique of enamelling from Lossier. So impressed with what he saw at the International Exhibition in Paris (1900) that he melted down his entire stock of jewellery on returning to Barcelona and made a complete break with traditional designs. Re-opened 6 months later with an entirely new stock in Art Nouveau style: so overwhelmingly successful that his reputation went beyond Spain. Commissioned to make a diadem for Queen Victoria (1906). Won the Grand Prize for Jewellery at the Saragossa Exhibition, 1908, and another prize in Ghent, Belgium, 1913.

Mikimoto, Kokichi (Pls 20, 39) Born 1858 in Toba (Shima), Japan (died 1954). Father ran noodle shop called 'Awako', a business that had been handed down through generations. Kokichi started to work in the family trade at 14. Decided to enter the pearl trade (1881). Established his first pearl oyster farm in the Shinmei inlet in Shima (1888). Then decided to determine whether pearls could be grown artificially, since in several thousand oysters only one or two natural pearls are found. Years of painstaking experimentation and research were crowned with success (1893); final fool-proof method for producing cultured pearls was not perfected and patented until 1908. Opened first overseas branch in Hatton Garden, London (1911). First round cultured pearls were marketed in London (1919). Appointed to the Japanese House of Peers by Imperial Decree. Since then, K. Mikimoto & Company have opened branches all over the world. Their founder became known as 'The Pearl King' and was awarded Japan's First Order of Merit posthumously.

Miklos, Gustave (Pl. 72) Born 1888 in Budapest, Hungary (died 1967 in France). Studied painting with Ladislas Kimnach at the Royal School of Applied Art, Budapest. Moved to Paris (1909); attended several art schools and exhibited at the Salon d'Automne. Spent World War I in Greece as member of the French Foreign Legion and became acquainted with Byzantine art. Returned to Paris (1919). Became a French citizen (1923). Friend of the fashion designer and collector Jacques Doucet, for whom he designed silverware, tapestries and other home furnishings. Devoted himself to sculpture, particularly copper reliefs, and jewellery design (from 1923). Participated in the Exposition Internationale des Arts Décoratifs et Industriels Modernes, Paris (1925); solo exhibition of his sculpture held in the Galerie de la Renaissance, Paris (1928); participated in Exposition Internationale, Paris (1937) as member of the Union des Artistes Modernes. Left Paris (1940) and moved to a small French town. Retrospective exhibition 'Gustav Miklos' held in the Galerie 'L'Enseigne du Cerceau', Paris (1972).

Miller, John Paul (Pl. 107) Born 1918 in Huntingdon, Pennsylvania. Graduated from the Cleveland Institute of Art (industrial design) (1940). Instructor in design and other subjects at the Cleveland Institute of Art (1946–83). Began teaching jewellery design (about 1970). Produced 3 films: one on the technique of stretching in silversmithing with Fred Miller (1950–51); another on making a piece of gold jewellery showing the techiques of granulation and enamelling (1953); and a third showing Fred Miller making a free-form sterling bottle (1962).
Exhibitions: 157, 178*, 179, 180, 489, 751, 756, 757*, 797, 940, 952, 961, 963, 1079, 1159, 1167
Works in public collections: Fleischmann Collection, Detroit; The Cleveland Museum of Art, Ohio; The Huntington Library, San Marino, California; Minnesota Museum of Art, St. Paul; Museum of Contemporary Crafts, New York.

Mitsuyasu, Takeo (Pl. 180) Born 1944 in Tokyo, Japan. Attended Musashino Art University (industrial design) (1964–68).
Exhibitions: 557, 781, 891, 1120

Miyata, Shuhei (Pl. 261) Born 1933 on Sado island, Japan. Trained at the Dept. of Industrial Art, Fine Art Faculty, Tokyo University of Arts (1952); graduate project 'Craft Relief on the Wall' purchased by Ministry of Education, now property of Tokyo University of Arts (1956). Postgraduate work at Tokyo University of Arts (1958). Won highest honours at design contest with a sight-seeing bus for foreigners. Received prize for 'Excellent Work' at the Japan Jewellery Art Exhibition, 1975. Professor at Mie University, Tsu (1975). 1st metal art exhibition by the brothers Kouhei, Shuhei and Ryouhei Miyata held, Atasaka (1980).
Exhibitions: 438, 1030, 1038

Morris, May (Pl. 18) Born 1862 in England (died 1938). Daughter of pioneer and champion of Arts and Crafts Movement, William Morris (1834–1906). An accomplished designer, embroideress and jewellery-maker; learnt her craft from her father. Staunch supporter of her father's ideals; one of the founders of the Women's Guild of Arts (1907). Also travelled to the United States, where she lectured on embroidery, jewellery and design.

Moser, Koloman (Pl. 16)   Born 1868 in Austria (died 1918). With Josef Hoffmann and Friedrich Waerndorfer, co-founder of Wiener Werkstätte (1903). A remarkably talented artist and craftsman, whose creative urges found expression in diverse areas in the arts and crafts: furniture, metal- and silversmithing, jewellery, textiles, graphic and stage design, among others. Completed his studies in fine arts at the Akademie der bildenden Künste, Vienna; trained at the Hochschule für angewandte Kunst, Vienna (1893–95). Later became teacher and professor there until his death.

Mostböck-Huber, Edith (Pl. 284)   Born 1947 in Vienna, Austria. Graduated from the Hochschule für angewandte Kunst, Vienna (1965). Studied textile design (1967–71) and metalwork (1971–76), and received master's diplomas in both. Free-lance member of the Austrian Crafts Council (since 1971). Member of the Berufsvereinigung Bildender Künstler and of the Künstlerhaus, Vienna. Won prize from the Theodor Körner Foundation, 1981.
Exhibitions: 54, 771, 897, 1014, 1082, 1099, 1111, 1119, 1122, 1164, 1170

Moty, Eleanor H. (Pl. 299)   Born 1945 in the United States. Attended the University of Illinois, B.F.A. (1968); Tyler School of Art, Temple University, Philadelphia, M.F.A. (1971). Won Purchase Award at the Contemporary Jewelry and Metalwork Exhibition, Georgia State University, Atlanta, 1974; 1st prize medals at the Contemporary Crafts of the Americas Exhibition, Colorado State University, Fort Collins. Professor at the University of Wisconsin, Madison (1981); member of the Board of Trustees of Haystack Mountain School of Crafts, Deer Isle, Maine (1982).
Exhibitions: 4, 155, 179, 457, 548, 768, 800, 804, 894, 912, 967, 968, 1162,
Works in public collections: Minnesota Museum of Art, St. Paul; Temple University, Tyler School of Art, Philadelphia; Georgia State University, Atlanta; The Lannan Foundation, Palm Beach, Florida.

Muerrle, Norbert (Pls 154, 286, 298)   Born 1948 in Pforzheim, FRG. Served apprenticeship as goldsmith and diamond setter (1962–65). Studied at the Kunst- und Werkschule, Pforzheim (1967–71). Received Master's degree at the Goldschmiedeschule, Pforzheim (1969). Opened his own studio/workshop (1971). Worked as free-lance designer for Messrs Niessing (1975–80). Free-lance chief designer for Niessing (since 1982). Frequent exhibitor at group exhibitions and had several one-man shows in Germany and abroad (since 1971). Won De Beers Diamond International Award, 1974; commendation and purchase of entry in the competition 'Armschmuck' at the Schmuckmuseum, Pforzheim, 1980; 1st prize at the International Competition for platinum rings (tension rings), 1983; De Beers Diamond International Award (bracelet), 1984.
Works in public collection: Schmuckmuseum, Pforzheim.

Murrle, Bennet & Co. (Pl. 6)   A London firm of manufacturing jewellers that existed from around the turn of the century. Produced large quantities of jewellery similar to that of Liberty's and to the German *Jugendstil* jewellery by T. Fahrner. Their products were advertized as 'Jewels by Artists of the Modern School'; premises were at 13 Charterhouse St., London.

Nakamura, Minato (Pl. 205)   Born 1947 in Tokyo, Japan. Attended Musashino Art University under Takashi Shimizu (1965–70); graduated with major in sculpture. Began studying jewellery under Yasuhiko Hishida (1971). Member of the Japan Jewellery Designers' Association and the Japan Craft Designers' Association. Won De Beers Diamond International Award, 1975; special mention in International Jewellery Art Exhibition, Tokyo, 1976; superior award in Craft Design Exhibition, Japan and Taiwan, 1984.
Exhibitions: 68, 457, 954, 1026, 1030, 1032, 1035, 1039

Nakayama, Aya (Pl. 192)   Born 1946 in Tokyo. Graduated with B.A. from Tokyo University of Fine Art (1969). Worked as industrial designer for GK Industrial Design Association. Opened her own studio (1973). Won Japan Craft Exhibition Award, 1974; GP Award at International Jewellery Arts Exhibition, Tokyo 1976. Director of Studio AYA. Secretary-General of Japan Jewellery Designers' Association.
Exhibitions: 454*, 579*, 638, 649*, 891, 1036*, 1041, 1120

Nele, E.R. (Pl. 211)   Born in Berlin, Germany. Studied at the Central School of Arts and Crafts, London (1950–55); with Professor Uhlmann in Berlin at the Hochschule für bildende Künste, and at Studio La Courière, Paris. Associate member of Goldsmith's Hall, London. Won gold medal at the Triennale in Milan, 1957; and Dantesca Award, 1975.
Exhibitions: 18*, 56, 94, 123*, 124*, 133*, 160, 172*, 186*, 193*, 214, 229, 299*, 300*, 302*, 309, 445, 446, 484, 485, 492*, 493, 495, 500*, 511, 550*, 686, 701*, 702*, 703, 708*, 719*, 728, 732*, 735, 737, 808, 838, 839, 840, 891, 914, 927, 1080, 1168

Nienhuis, Lambert (Pl. 31)   Born 1873 in Holland (died 1960). Trained in ceramics at the 'Minerva' Academie in Groningen. Further study at the Rijksschool voor Kunstnijverheid near Amsterdam. Soon demonstrated his original and innovative mind: introduced a matt glaze of his own invention, and developed a type of geometric design based on stylized naturalistic forms (1901). Taught enamelling at several schools, including the Rijksakademie van Beeldende Kunsten, Amsterdam.

Niessing & Co. (Pl. 286)   Founded in 1873 in Vreden, FRG, by the goldsmith Hermann Niessing (d. 1914). Soon began to specialize in the manufacture of wedding rings. Hermann's two sons, one of whom was killed in World War I, inherited the business. The second son, Franz Niessing (1868–1949), was succeeded by his widow Bernhardine (1897–1971) and by their two daughters, Ursula (b. 1921) and Lore (b. 1925), who were joined by Ursula's husband, Fritz Exner (1907–82). Niessing broadened its range of wedding rings to include diamond rings (1968). Further expansion, including other forms of jewellery (1971); began to use platinum as well as gold, inventing a special technique for combining the two metals (1977); developed the tension setting for diamonds (1980). Jochen Exner (b. 1951) became managing director, succeeding his father Fritz (1982).

Nisslmüller, Manfred (Pl. 133)   Born 1940 in Vienna, Austria. Worked as journeyman goldsmith (1958). Designed his first jewellery (1967). Won Diamond International Award (1969). Periodically designed jewellery (1975–1984). Participated in international and national exhibitions.

Noll, Catherine (Pl. 235)   Born 1945 in Bourg-la-Reine, France. Graduated (diploma in arts and crafts), Paris (1970). Vice-President of 'Hephaïstos'. Regular exhibitor at the Salon de Bijhorca, Paris (since 1975); worked on collection for Christian Dior (1975). Won gold medal at Jablonec, 1977. Worked on collections for Nina Ricci (since 1978); on collection for Chanel (1980).
Exhibitions: 85, 104, 196, 630, 699, 802, 803, 860, 861, 864, 865*, 869*, 950

Osman, Louis (Pls 137, 138)   Born 1914 in Exeter, England. Trained as an architect, studied drawing at the Slade School of Art, London. A man of many talents: practises as an architect, created sculpture and jewellery designs for private and pubic commissions – 'demi-crown' for H.R.H. the Prince of Wales (1969); the Golden Gift of the Magna Carta, presented by the British Government to the United States of America on the occasion of its bicentennial (1976). One-man show at Goldsmiths' Hall, London, with a large range of jewellery, ecclesiastical regalia and medals (May, 1974). Responsible, as architect, for the restoration of the north side of Cavendish Square, London, and for the contemporary building of the Principal's Lodging, Newnham College, Cambridge.

Oved, Sah (Pl. 89) Born 1900 in Devonport, England [as **Gwendolen Ethel Rendle**] (died 1983). Second daughter of country doctor; received grant for metalwork training (1918) after two years medical research work during World War I. First training and apprenticeship with John Paul Cooper (until 1923). Met and began working for Mosheh Oved in his shop, Cameo Corner, close to the British Museum, London (1927). Shop had wonderful supply of raw materials for Sah's original and inventive designs, and Mosheh's Polish/Jewish background provided enriching cultural stimulus to Sah's English upbringing. Studied silversmithing at the Central School of Arts and Crafts, London (during 1950s). (Proud to discover later that she was a descendant of the English silversmith Gabriel Sleath.) Published *The Book of Necklaces* (1953). Almost last work was necklace on the tomb of Queen Elizabeth I in Westminster Abbey, London.

Page, Martin (Pl. 202) Born 1952 at Pembroke Dock, South Wales. Attended Shrewsbury School of Art (1968–70); Central School of Art and Design, London, A.D. diploma (1970–73); Royal College of Art, M.A., R.C.A (1973–76). Won Melchett Award from British Steel, 1976, and New Craftsman Grant from the Crafts Council, 1977. Set up his own workshop (1977).
Exhibitions: 372, 373, 377, 527, 565, 576*, 588, 602, 616, 623, 724, 817, 837, 1035
Works in public collections: Victoria and Albert Museum, London; The Worshipful Company of Goldsmiths, London.

Pärn, Jaan (Pl. 285) Born 1953 in Sindi, Estonia. Graduated from the Estonian Art Institute (1982). Member of the Union of Young Artists (since 1983). Works as design editor for *Estinformkino*. Has own studio where he makes only individual pieces. Won a gold medal at Jablonec, 1983. Participates in exhibitions in the U.S.S.R. and abroad.

Partridge, May Hart (Pl. 37) Born in England (died 1917). Married to Fred T. Partridge, a chemist's son from Devon who had worked for several years with C.R. Ashbee in the Guild of Handicrafts, Chipping Campden, and had exhibited his work alongside Ashbee's at the Arts and Crafts Society (1903).

Pavan, Francesco (Pls. 222, 279) Born 1937 in Padua, Italy. Graduated from the Istituto d'Arte 'Pietro Selvatico', Padua (1955). Teaches goldsmithing at the Istituto d'Arte (since 1961). Won gold medal at Munich, 1963; Herbert Hoffmann Prize at the International Goldschmiede Ausstellung, Munich, 1973.
Exhibitions: 58, 101, 323, 343, 353,, 385, 706, 799, 808, 884, 891, 898, 903, 930, 931, 1081, 1120, 1122, 1176
Works in public collection: Schmuckmuseum, Pforzheim.

Peche, Dagobert (Pls. 40, 43) Born 1886 near Salzburg, Austria (died 1923). Attended the Akademie der bildenden Künste, Vienna, before joining the Wiener Werkstätte (1915); managed their Zurich branch (1917–18). He took part in many exhibitions, including the Secession Exhibition, Vienna (1913); International Art Exhibition, Rome (1914) and 'Kunstschau 1920' at the Künstlerhaus, Vienna (1921). Also designed an enormous variety of artifacts: furniture, posters, ceramics, glass, stationery, bookbindings, graphics, toys and even Christmas decorations.

Persson, Sigurd (Pls. 159, 287) Born 1914 in Hälsingborg, Sweden. Trained in his father's workshop. Passed journeyman's exam (1937). Studied at the Akademie der bildenden Künste, Munich, with J. Schneider and F. Rickert, and at the Konstfackskolan in Stockholm. Opened his own workshop in Stockholm (1942) and passed master's degree (1943). Won silver medal at Triennale, Milan, 1954, 1957, 1960; Ehrenring from the Gesellschaft für Goldschmiedekunst, FRG, 1955; gold medal and two honorary awards at the Biennale, Ljubljana, 1964. Made associate member of the Worshipful Company of Goldsmiths, London (1964). Member of the Cultural Commission of the Swedish government (1963–68), and of the committee responsible for planning advanced art training in Sweden (1967). Awarded St. Eligius Prize from the Union of Swedish Jewellers and Goldsmiths, 1969; Eugen Medal by the king of Sweden, 1970.
Exhibitions: 396*, 490*, 506*, 755*, 979*, 981*, 983*, 984*, 985*, 987*, 990*, 998*

Péter, Vladimir (Pl. 248) Born 1947 in Budapest, Hungary. Graduated from the Academy of Applied Arts, Budapest (1973). Participated in group exhibitions in Austria, Belgium, Czechoslovakia, Finland, France, Greece, The Netherlands, Yugoslavia, Mexico, FRG, GDR, U.S.S.R. Designed jewellery collection for Hans Hausen Sølvsmedie, Denmark (1981).

Picasso, Pablo (Pl. 158) Born 1881 in Spain (died 1973). Probably the most famous artist of the 20th century; lived most of his life in France. A prolific painter and sculptor, who created Cubism (with Braque). Became a legend in his lifetime, and extended his talents into other fields such as designing ballet sets and costumes (for Diaghilev in 1917) and later ceramics.

Pijanowski, Eugene M. (Pl. 197) Born 1938 in Detroit, Michigan. Attended Wayne State University, Detroit, M.I., B.F.A. in metalcraft (1959–64); M.A. in metalcraft, minor in printmaking (1965–67). Cranbrook Academy of Art, Bloomfield Hills, Michigan, M.F.A. in metalsmithing, minor in printmaking (1967–69); Tokyo University of Art (traditional metalworking techniques) (1959–71). Associate Professor of Metalwork/Jewelry/3-Dimensional Design in the Dept. of Creative Arts at Purdue University, West Lafayette, Indiana (since 1973).
Exhibitions: 4, 210, 414*, 417, 548, 772, 879, 912, 938, 974, 1021, 1035, 1120

Pijanowski, Hiroko Sato (Pl. 197) Born 1942 in Tokyo, Japan. Attended Rikkyo University, Tokyo, B.A. in Japanese history (1960–64); California State University, Northridge (fine arts) (1965–66); Cranbrook Academy of Art, Bloomfield Hills, Michigan, M.F.A. in metalsmithing, minor in weaving (1966–68). Received Gemstone Identification Certificate from the Gemmological Association of Japan (1971). Designs jewellery and metalwork for Hiro Ltd, West Lafayette, Indiana (1972). Assistant professor of art at the University of Michigan, Ann Arbor (1978).
Exhibitions: 4, 73, 209, 306, 414*, 776, 912, 938, 1016, 1018, 1019, 1021, 1025, 1032, 1034, 1120, 1150

Pinton, Mario (Pl. 181) Born 1919 in Padua, Italy. Learned engraving in his father's workshop. Attended Istituto d'Arte 'Pietro Selvatico' (gold- and silversmithing), Padua; Istituto d'Arte (goldsmithing and sculpture), Venice; Istituto superiore delle Arti decorative (silversmithing), Monza, and Accademia di Belle Arti di Brera (sculpture), Milan. Works as free-lance goldsmith and sculptor. Won 1st prize for jewellery at the Mostra nazionale, Venice, 1955, and 2nd prize for silversmithing, 1955; jewellery award from the Galleria Montenapoleone, Milan, 1955, and gold medal from the Istituto Veneto, Venice, 1955; gold medal at the Triennale, Milan, 1957; gold medal, Gubbio, 1961; 1st prize at the Biennale, Venice, 1963. Taught 5 years as director of goldsmithing class at the Istituto Statale d'Arte, Padua, and also taught geometry and design there. Director of the Istituto d'Arte 'Pietro Selvatico', Padua (since 1969).
Exhibitions: 187, 421, 464, 489, 704, 846, 955, 1020
Works in public collections: Victoria and Albert Museum, London; Schmuckmuseum, Pforzheim.

Pomodoro, Arnaldo (Pls 102, 129) Born 1926 in Morciano die Romagna, Italy. A sculptor; also studied architecture, as well as stage and jewellery design, partly in the United States, where he was awarded a scholarship (1959).

Winner of several art awards in Italy and in the United States for sculpture. 'Artist in Residence' at Stanford University, California (1966).

Preston, Paul (Pls 209, 265)   Born 1943 in Leeds, England. Attended school of architecture in Leeds (1962–65) and Oxford (1968–70). Qualified as architect. Entirely self-taught, worked with jewellery (from 1964). Supplemented income from jewellery by professional diving (until 1978), when he began to work full time in jewellery. Won award from Crafts Advisory Council, 1975, and Sotheby's first Jewellery Award, 1982.
Exhibitions: 198*, 261*, 314, 449, 582*, 794, 832, 873, 900

Prytz-Kittelsen, Grete (Pls 105, 124)   Born 1917 in Oslo, Norway. Studied at Arts and Crafts College, Oslo (1936–37), then in France (1937–38); continued studies at the Arts and Crafts College, Oslo (1938–41). Worked as designer for J. Tostrup & Co., Oslo (1945). Attended the Institute of Design, Chicago, as Fulbright Scholar (1949–50). Awarded the Lunning Prize, 1952; Grand Prix at the Triennale, Milan, 1954, and gold medals, 1957, 1961; won gold medal at the Internationale Handwerksmesse, Munich, 1960. President of the Landsforbundet Norsk Brukskunst (1975–78).
Exhibitions: 211, 685, 686, 693, 700, 754, 1067

Puig Cuyas, Ramon (Pl. 241)   Born 1953 in Barcelona, Spain. Studied at Massana School of Jewellery Design, Barcelona (jewellery and metal) and at Bellas Artes University 'Sant Jordi', Barcelona. Professor at the Massana School of Jewellery Design, Barcelona (1977). Founder member of Group Orfebres F.A.D. (1979) and founder member of 'Grup Nou'. Participated in World Crafts Council Conference, Vienna (1980). Won 'Fi de Carrera' Prize from the Fundación General Mediterránea, Barcelona, 1975; Herbert Hoffmann Prize at the Internationale Schmuckschau, Munich, 1981. Participated in exhibitions in Spain and many other European countries from 1973.
Exhibitions: 57, 84, 88, 89, 90, 91, 92, 93, 165, 316, 451, 628, 653, 654, 740, 862, 900, 1037, 1118

Quigley, Robin L. (Pl. 236)   Born 1947 in New York city. Attended Rhode Island School of Design, Providence, M.F.A. in sculpture, jewellery and metalsmithing (1976); Tyler School of Art, Temple University, Philadelphia, B.F.A. in jewellery and metalsmithing (1974). Assistant professor in the Light-Metal Dept. at the Rhode Island School of Design, Providence (since 1981).

Exhibitions: 48, 775, 786, 791, 800, 908*, 909*, 1034, 1039, 1120, 1155

Raft, Emanuel (Pl. 186)   Born 1938 in Suez, Egypt. Attended Bissietta Art School, Sydney (painting) (1956–59); Accademia di Belle Arte di Brera, Milan (studied sculpture under Luciano Minguzzi) (1959–60). Part-time lecturer in Dept. of Architecture, University of Sydney (1963–66); full-time lecturer, Birmingham College of Art and Design [now Birmingham Polytechnic] (1967–69); part-time lecturer at Sutton College of Liberal Arts, London (1971–78); visiting lecturer, West Sussex College of Design (1975–76); School of Textiles and Soft Forms (1977–78); part-time lecturer, Alexander Mackie College of Advanced Education (in painting, jewellery and graphics) (1978–80); and part-time lecturer, Dept. of Architecture, University of Sydney. Full-time lecturer at City Art Institute, Sydney (1981–84) and head of 3-D Studies at City Art Institute (since 1984).
Exhibitions: 6*, 8*, 16, 294, 411, 501, 502, 538, 561, 663, 669*, 986, 1002, 1003*, 1007*

Rajalin, Börje (Pl. 139)   Born in 1933 in Finland. Graduated from the Institute of Applied Arts, Helsinki (1955). Opened his own design office (1956). Chief instructor (metal arts section) at the Institute of Applied Arts, Helsinki (1961–71). Director of the Trade School of Applied Arts, Helsinki (1969–71). Member of the administrative board of ORNAMO, the Finnish Association of Applied Arts (1967–69); member of the Finnish State Committee of Applied Arts (1968–70). Designer for Kalevala Koru Oy (from 1956) and artistic manager (from 1975). A prominent designer whose activities include handicrafts, applied art as well as industrial and technical products. Organized several exhibitions in different countries for the Finnish Association of Applied Arts. Won gold medal at the 12th Triennale, Milan, 1960; design award from the American Institute of Decorators, 1961; gold medal at the Internationale Handwerksmesse, Munich, 1963; the Lunning Prize, 1963; Pro Finlandia award, 1968; State of Finland Artistic Award, 1972–74; State of Finland award for Applied Arts 1977; State of Finland Long-Term Artistic Award, 1984. Since then Rajalin has worked for Kalevala Koru Oy on a free-lance basis.

Ramsden, Omar (Pl. 36)   Born 1873 in Sheffield – an English town famous for its long-standing tradition of silversmithing and cutlery-making – (died 1939). Son of a manufacturer of silver and electroplate ware. Served his apprenticeship with a Sheffield silversmith; also attended evening classes at the local art school; eventually won a Corporation Scholarship. Commissioned to make the mace for the City

of Sheffield (1897) after winning the 1st prize in an open competition for its design.

Ramshaw, Wendy (Pls 152, 255)   Born 1939 in Sunderland, England. Studied at Newcastle-upon-Tyne College of Art (1956–60) and at Reading University, A.T.D. (1960–61). Freeman of the Worshipful Company of Goldsmiths; fellow of the Society of Industrial Artists and Designers. Won De Beers 'Diamonds Today' Prize, 1970; Council of Industrial Design Award, 1972; Johnson Matthey Award for platinum, 1974; De Beers Diamond International Award, 1975.
Exhibitions: 16, 98, 103*, 162, 224, 241, 270, 344, 418, 494, 508*, 520*, 521, 530, 553, 572*, 574, 605, 611, 620*, 667*, 718, 767, 831*, 836*, 851, 889, 905* (with David Watkins), 909*, 1048, 1118*, 1120, 1151
Works in public collections: The Worshipful Company of Goldsmiths, London; National Museum of Wales, Cardiff; Philadelphia Museum of Art; Stedelijk Museum, Amsterdam; Schmuckmuseum, Pforzheim; Royal Scottish Museum, Edinburgh; Bristol City Art Gallery; Victoria and Albert Museum, London; Crafts Council, London; The Government and People of Papua, New Guinea; Western Australian Institute of Technology, Perth; State Art Gallery of South Australia, Adelaide; National Gallery of Victoria, Melbourne; The Australian National Gallery, Canberra; The Art Gallery of Western Australia, Perth; The Assembly Rooms, Bath; Maidstone Museum and Art Gallery; Gallery of English Costume, Manchester; Wedgwood Museum, Barlaston; City Museum and Art Gallery, Stoke-on-Trent; The Museum of London.

Reiling, Reinhold (Pls 141, 189)   Born 1922 in Eisingen, FRG (died 1983). Served apprenticeship as engraver (1936–40). Attended Kunstgewerbeschule, Pforzheim (1939–41, 1946–53), and Kunstgewerbeschule (under T. Wende), Dresden. Taught at the Fachhochschule für Gestaltung, Pforzheim (from 1954); professor of jewellery-design (from 1971). Won many prizes in jewellery competitions (since 1955): prize in the 'Dose mit Email' competition, 1955 and Silver Mirror from the Gesellschaft für Goldschmiede; Remington's Sport Prize.
Exhibitions: 161*, 899*
Works in public collections: Schmuckmuseum Pforzheim; Goldsmiths' Hall, London; Evangelische Stadtkirche, Pforzheim.

Riklin-Schelbert, Antoinette (Pl. 291)   Born 1920 in Zurich, Switzerland. Attended Kunstgewerbeschule Zurich (silversmithing under M. Fröhlich) (1939–44). Opened jewellery shop in Zurich and produced one-of-a-kind pieces (1946–59). Since 1972, works using

textile techniques in metal with very fine silver, gold, copper and stainless steel wire.
Exhibitions: 103, 171, 313, 321, 469, 624, 1041, 1127
Works in public collection: Röhsska Konstslöjdmuseet, Göteborg.

Risch, Hildegard (Pls 83, 111) Born 1903 in Halle, GDR. Trained in metalwork under Karl Müller, Burg Giebichenstein and in working non-precious metals (1922–28). Opened her own workshop with Eva Elsässer and first experimented with jewellery-making (1929). Passed journeyman exam in goldsmithing (1931), and master's degree (1936). Moved to West Germany (1963). Received award from the Landesgewerbeamt, Stuttgart, 1969.
Exhibitions: 250*, 476*, 994
Works in public collections: Schmuckmuseum, Pforzheim; Kunstgewerbemuseum, Cologne.

Ross, Ivy (Pl. 240) Born 1955 in the U.S.A. Attended Syracuse University, School of Design (metalsmithing) (1973–75); Fashion Institute of Technology, New York (jewellery design) (1975–77). Won Women in Design International Award for outstanding achievement in the field of design, 1981; 1981 Diamonds Today competition, 1981; Color Core Surface and Ornament Design Competition II, 1984.
Exhibitions: 416, 652, 788, 789, 790, 800, 821, 828, 951, 1067, 1130, 1155
Works in public collections: The Cooper-Hewitt Museum, The Smithsonian Institution's National Museum of Design, New York; The Renwick Gallery of Art, National Museum of American Art, Smithsonian Institution, Washington, D.C.; Schmuckmuseum, Pforzheim; Kunstindustrimuseet, Oslo; Nordenfjeldske Kunstindustrimuseet, Trondheim; The Cleveland Museum of Art.

Rothmann, Gerhard (Pls 171, 243) Born 1941 in FRG. Attended Staatliche Zeichenakademie, Hanau (goldsmithing) (1961–64). Opened his own workshop (1965). Student in the workshop of Hermann Jünger (1966). Collaborated with architects on interior design of churches and public buildings (1968).
Exhibitions: 134, 231, 253, 328, 391, 412, 545, 602, 614*, 809, 814, 819, 956, 1125

Saddington, Tom (Pl. 220) Born 1952 in Birmingham, England. Studied at Guildford School of Art Surrey (1969); Sir John Cass College, London (silversmithing and jewellery) (1969–73).
Exhibitions: 150* (with V. Manning), 411, 556*, 835*
Works in public collections: National Gallery of Victoria, Melbourne; Gemeentelijke van Reekum Museum, Apeldoorn.

Sandoz, Gérard Gustave (Pls 62, 72) Born 1902 in Paris. From a family of watchmakers and jewellers; grandfather and father ran a watch and jewellery shop in Paris (from ca. 1865). Firm participated in the International Exhibition, Milan (1906). After studying art and the humanities, began designing very geometric jewellery for father's firm. Participated in the Exposition Internationale des Art Décoratifs et Industriels Modernes, Paris (1925); was a regular exhibitor at the salons d'Automne and the salons des Artistes Décorateurs (until 1931). Founding member of the Union des Artistes Modernes (1930). Closed the jewellery shop (1931); has worked since mainly as a painter and filmmaker.

Schafran, Hermann (Pl. 224) Born 1949 in Annaberg-Bucholz, FRG. Works in Mannheim (since 1977).
Exhibitions: 35*, 86*, 258*, 267, 441, 442, 443*, 458, 580*, 810*, 891, 949, 1065*
Works in public collections: National Gallery of Victoria, Melbourne; Victoria and Albert Museum, London.

Scherr, Mary Ann (Pls 160, 187) Born in the U.S.A. Attended Cleveland Institute of Art; University of Akron, Ohio; Kent State University, Ohio; Akron Art Institute, Ohio; Academy of Fine Art, New York. Won silver medal at Jablonec, 1971.
Exhibitions: 131, 179, 184, 207, 208, 209, 422, 424, 573, 666, 779*, 786, 907, 974, 977, 1044, 1079, 1148, 1149
Works in public collections: Akron Art Institute, Ohio; Massilon Museum, Massilon, Ohio; Smithsonian Institution, Washington, D.C.; James A. Michener Collection, Kent State University, Ohio; Vatican Museum of Contemporary Art, Vatican City, Italy; Goldsmiths' Hall, London; The American Craft Museum, New York; Yale University Art Gallery, New Haven, Connecticut; The Metropolitan Museum of Art, New York; United States Steel corporation, Pittsburgh, Pennsylvania; Alcoa, Aluminum Company of America, Pittsburgh.

Schlumberger, Jean (Pl. 113) Born 1907 in France. Became top designer for Elsa Schiaparelli's costume jewellery before starting to work with precious metals and stones. Served during World War II in De Gaulle's Free French Forces; afterwards opened a jewellery shop on Fifth Avenue, New York, with Nicolas Bongard as partner. Joined Tiffany & Co. (1956), where he is now a vice-president and has his own salon on their premises. Created a chevalier of the Ordre national du Mérite by the French government (1977).

Schobinger, Bernhard (Pls 226, 228) Born 1946 in Zurich, Switzerland. Attended the Kunstgewerbeschule, Zurich (1962–67). Estab-

lished own workshop (1968). Won Swiss scholarships for Arts and Crafts, 1969, 1970, 1971; German Schmuck und Edelstein Prize, 1977.
Exhibitions: 2*, 97, 100, 247, 297, 298, 474, 602, 689, 920, 921, 1026, 1029, 1035, 1161, 1171

Schuszter, István (Pl. 254) Born 1953 in Budapest, Hungary. Self-taught artist. Participated in several group exhibitions in Hungary and abroad.

Skal, Hubertus von (Pls 120, 221) Born 1942 in Jungferndorf, eastern Bohemia. Trained as a goldsmith in Munich (1957–61), passed journeyman exam (1961). Attended Silberschmiedeschule, Neugablonz (1962); Akademie der bildenden Künste, Munich (1963); graduated (1969). Worked as free-lance goldsmith in Munich (from 1970); cofounder of Galerie Cardillac, Munich (1971). Received grant from the German Academy to study at the Villa Massimo, Rome, 1977.
Exhibitions: 391, 510, 552, 722, 1120
Works in public collections: Staatliches Museum für angewandte Kunst, Munich; Kestner Gesellschaft, Hanover; Kunstgewerbemuseum, Zurich.

Skubic, Peter (Pl. 208) Born 1935 in Gornij-Milanovac, Yugoslavia. Attended the Fachhochschule für Metallkunstgewerbe, Steyr, Austria (1952–54); the Akademie für angewandte Kunst, Vienna (1954–58). Master's degree in gold- and silversmithing (1966). Organized the international symposium 'Schmuck aus Stahl' (Steel Jewellery) in Austria (1974). Professor at the Fachhochschule Kunst & Design, Cologne (since 1979). Won the gold Ehrenmedaille from the Künstlerhaus, Vienna, 1976; stipend from the Cultural Ministry of the city of Vienna, 1976–77; Dr. Theodor Körner Prize, 1977; City of Vienna Prize, 1978. Organized the 'Schmuck International 1900–1980' exhibition, Vienna (1980). Professor at the Sommerakademie für bildende Kunst, Salzburg (1983–84).
Exhibitions: 1*, 97, 194, 195*, 205, 274* (with Gundi Dietz), 297, 331*, 386, 450*, 478*, 481*, 632, 744, 808, 889, 900, 1035, 1041, 1082, 1086, 1087, 1102*, 1104, 1106*, 1110*, 1112*, 1113, 1117*, 1134*
Works in public collections: Museum für angewandte Kunst, Vienna; Museum des 20. Jahrhunderts, Vienna; Schmuckmuseum, Pforzheim; Education and Cultural Ministry, Vienna; Neue Galerie der Stadt Linz, Linz; Neue Galerie der Stadt Aachen: Ludwig Collection, Aachen.

Slutzki, Naum (Pl. 66) Born 1894 in Kiev, Russia (died 1965). At the Bauhaus in Weimar (1919–23); then lived in Hamburg (1927–33). Came to London as a refugee from the Hitler regime (1933); became a tutor in metalwork at

Dartington Hall, Devon (until 1939), where he worked in research on diamond tools used in optics (during World War II). Taught part-time at the Central School of Arts and Crafts, London (1946–50); taught at the Royal College of Art, London (1950–57), where he established and equipped the Product and Design Research studios. Head of the School of Industrial Design, Birmingham College of Arts & Crafts (1957–64). Head of the Industrial Design Dept., Revensbourne College of Art, Bromley (1965).

Smit, Robert (Pls 140, 297)   Born 1941 in Delft, Holland. Studied at the Staatliche Kunst- und Werkschule, Pforzheim (under Klaus Ullrich) (1963–66). Qualified as goldsmith (1966). Winner of Bavarian Staatspreis at the Internationale Handwerksmesse, Munich, 1967.
Exhibitions: 26, 28, 39, 119, 235, 236, 295, 341, 342, 351, 517, 545, 710, 808

Smith, Christina Y. (Pl. 263)   Born in the U.S.A. Attended San Diego State University, San Diego, California, B.A. in art (1974) and M.A. in art/metalsmithing/jewellery (1979). 'California Craftsman 1976' from Monterey Museum of Art, Monterey, California. Attended California State University, Long Beach, M.F.A. in metalsmithing/jewellery (1983). Made jewellery designs for the movie *Flashdance* (1983).
Exhibitions: 137, 249, 462, 691, 776, 783, 787, 800, 932, 945, 946

Sokolsky, Joachim (Pl. 179)   Born 1946 in Warsaw, Poland. Attended the Art Academy, Warsaw. Works as a free-lance goldsmith.
Exhibitions: 106*, 511, 560, 891, 1112, 1140*, 1141*, 1142*, 1144*, 1145*
Works in public collections: Museums of Gliwice, and Kazimiers Dolny.

Steltman, Johannes (Pl. 49)   Born 1891 in Steenwijk, Holland (died 1961). Early training in the jewellery workshop of his uncle in Steenwijk; later studied in Hanau, Germany, where he was also taught enamelling, a technique he perfected with mastery. Opened jewellery shop, The Hague (1917): interior was designed by Hildo Krop. Enlarged his workshop and was joined by Jean Koch, a jewellery designer and master goldsmith (early 1920s). Robert Mack, a silversmith, became member of team shortly afterwards; from that time, they also specialized in hollow-ware. Won Bronze Medal for a silver tea-set, Exposition des Arts Décoratifs, Paris, 1925; now part of the Haags Gemeentemuseum's collection, The Hague.

Stenbak, Birte (Pl. 214)   Born 1938 in Roskilde, Denmark. Served apprenticeship at Poul Bang silversmith (1954–59); worked at a jeweller's workshop, Copenhagen (1959–71). Won Silver Medal at 'Den Massmanske', 1959. Attended Goldsmith's College, Copenhagen (1973–75). Opened own workshop in Copenhagen (1975). Won Paul Frigasi Award, 1976.
Exhibitions: 59, 218, 221, 222, 425, 577, 602, 604, 1028

Tempelman, Jan (Pl. 207)   Born 1943 in Holland. Trained at the Vakschool, Schoonhoven, and the Kunst- und Werkschule, Pforzheim. Awarded the Bavarian Staatspreis in Gold, 1972.
Exhibitions: 30, 33, 98, 122, 163, 165, 256, 347, 348, 352, 353, 734, 889, 891

Templier, Raymond (Pls 57, 72, 79)   Born 1891 in Paris, France (died 1968), into a family of Parisian jewellers. Attended Ecole Nationale Supérieure des Arts Décoratifs (1909–12). Went to work in the family firm. First exhibited at the Salon des Artistes Décorateurs; then in many exhibitions in France and abroad, particularly in Rotterdam and Milan. Member of the High Council for Education in the Decorative Arts; co-founder of the Union des Artistes Modernes, Paris (1930); president of the Decorative Arts section and vice-president of the salons d'Automne. Knight of the French Légion d'Honneur. Did not work directly in the firm of Paul and Raymond Templier during the last years of his life; it was then run by Marcel Percheron, who had worked with Raymond since 1929.

Thomas, David (Pl. 126)   Born 1938 in London, England. Attended Twickenham Art School, London, from age 15 (general art course); won a scholarship to study in Italy and France. Spent a year working in Scandinavia as a jeweller for Bolin and as a silversmith under the designer Sven Arne Gillgren. Entered the Royal College of Art, London (1959), specializing in jewellery and was awarded the title 'Royal Scholar'. Opened his own studio (1961). Work included in the 1st 'International Exhibition of Modern Jewellery', Goldsmiths' Hall, London (1961). Has exhibited all over the world, and has won a number of competitions and prizes. Solo exhibitions held in Australia, America, Japan, Africa, Europe and at the Goldsmiths' Hall, London. His workshop produces large commissioned pieces (Masters' badge for the Grocers Company; the Ladies badge for the Goldsmiths' Company; a Sheriff's badge for the City of London and the trophy for the King George VI and Queen Elisabeth II Stakes) as well as finely made smaller items. Has also designed and produced collections for the National Trust, De Beers Diamonds, and national coinage for the Royal Mint. Liveryman of the Worshipful Company of Goldsmiths, Freeman of the City of London, member of the Goldsmiths' Craft Council and the Goldsmiths'

Design and Technology Committee (with responsibility for purchasing the Company's modern collection).
Works in public collections: The Worshipful Company of Goldsmiths, London; De Beers Diamonds, London; Victoria and Albert Museum, London.

Tiffany & Co. (Pls 4, 19, 110, 113, 121)   First established by Charles Lewis Tiffany (1812–1902) in New York (late 1830s) as a partnership with John B. Young; originally traded in fancy goods and stationery. French jewellery soon added to line; later German and English jewellery as well as Bohemian glass, Dresden porcelain, clocks and cutlery. Tiffany's workshop won acclaim, awards and gold medals at prestigious exhibitions in Paris (1867, 1878, 1889); particularly successful with the mixed-metal techniques of Japan.
   After studying painting in Paris, founder's son, Louis Comfort Tiffany (1848–1933), joined the firm; took over direction on his father's death (1902). Especially interested in the jewellery side of the business; had charge of the workshops during the last years of his father's life. (*See also:* **Schlumberger, Jean**)

Tipple, Barbara (Pl. 289)   Born 1951 in England. Trained at Portmouth Art College (1969); studied at Hornsey College of Art, London (1971–74). Inspired to become a jeweller after seeing Gerda Flöckinger's exhibition at the Victoria and Albert Museum, London (1971). Won two Diamond International awards, 1972, 1984. Currently runs shop with workshop attached in partnership with Gareth Rees (a writer).

Tisdale, David (Pl. 268)   Born 1956 in San Diego, California. Attended University of California, Berkeley, College of Environmental Design (1974–76); University of California, Davis, B.S. in design (1978); San Diego State University, M.A. in jewellery design (1981). Partner in Quadrant Concepts, a design firm in New York (1981–83). Owner of David Tisdale Jewelry Design Firm, New York (1981–84). Member of the faculty at the New School/Parsons School of Design, New York (1981–84) and at the 92nd Street YM&YWHA, New York.
Exhibitions: 174, 650, 651, 780, 800, 939, 948, 953, 1130, 1155
Works in private collections: Malcolm, Sue and Abigale Knapp, New York; Judith and Martin Schwartz, New York; Ronald and Anne Abramson, Rockville, Maryland; Helen Drutt, Philadelphia; Arline Fisch, San Diego; University of California, Davis.

Tortell, Louis (Pl. 283)   Born 1954 in Sliema, Malta. Attended Royal University of Malta, Valletta, B.Sc. (1974); Sheridan College,

Oakville, Ontario (diploma in crafts and design, jewellery major) (1979). Won Silver Medal for Achievement, Sheridan College, 1979; Steele Trophy for best piece, Metal Arts Guild, 1981; Design Award, Metal Arts Guild, 1982; Ontario Craftsmens Grant, 1983.
Exhibitions: 175, 644, 829, 1050, 1055, 1058, 1060, 1062

Toynbee-Wilson, Jenny (Pl. 296) Born 1942 in Edinburgh, Scotland. Attended the Edinburgh College of Art (design) (1961–64). Graduate studies (1965). Lecturer at the Visual Communications Dept., Sydney College of the Arts.
Exhibitions: 10, 455, 1011
Works in public collection: Power House Museum, Sydney.

Treskow, Elisabeth (Pls 63, 130) Born 1898 in Bochum, FRG. Trained at the Kunstgewerbeschule, Essen; the Hagener Silberschmiede, Hagen; the Höhere Fachschule, Schwäbisch-Gmünd, and under Professor Rothmüller, Munich. Master goldsmith (1925). Was working on ecclesiastical restoration in Cologne (early 1920s), when, together with two colleagues, she re-discovered the true technique of granulation as practised by the Etruscans. Taught at the Werkschule, Cologne (1948–64). Has participated in many prestiguous exhibitions all over the world. Won many awards and prizes, including gold medals at the Triennale, Milan, and at the Paris World Fair.

Ullrich, Klaus (Pl. 114) Born 1927 in Sensburg, East Prussia. Served apprenticeship as goldsmith, and passed journeyman exam (1947–50). Passed journeyman exam as silversmith (1950–52). Attended the Werkkunstschule, Düsseldorf (1952–55). Master's degree as gold- and silversmith (1954); began working as a free-lance jewellery designer, Düsseldorf. Taught jewellery design at the Fachhochschule für Gestaltung, Pforzheim (1957). Won Baden-Württemberg Staatspreis, 1961; 1st prize in the international competition 'Der goldene Anhänger', 1963; Bavarian Staatspreis in gold, 1963; gold medal for jewellery at the Triennale, Milan, 1964. Professor at the Fachhochschule für Gestaltung, Pforzheim (1969). Opened jewellery workshop, Pforzheim-Würm. Silver medal for jewellery at Celje, Yugoslavia, 1976.
Works in public collection: Schmuckmuseum Pforzheim.

Van Cleef & Arpels (Pls 75, 85) A famous French jewellery firm; established by three brothers – Julien, Louis and Charles Arpels – and their brother-in-law, Alfred van Cleef (1906), all members of families engaged in jewellery and diamond dealing. Soon branched

out from their headquarters, Place Vendôme, Paris, and opened shops in London, New York and other major cities in many parts of the world. The sons of Julien Arpels (Claude, Jacques and Pierre) are still part of the present management. Van Cleef & Arpels designed and made the crown for the coronation of Farah Diba, wife of the Shah of Iran (1967).

Vasin, Andrei Aleksandrovich (Pl. 237) Born 1952 in Moscow. Secondary education in the arts at the Higher Artistic-Industrial College. Member of the Artists' Union of the U.S.S.R. (since 1979). A free-lance artist; executes individual work for art exhibitions and museums. Continuous participant in exhibitions at home and abroad.

Viehböck, Waltrud (Pl. 212) Born 1937 in Fulda, FRG. Studied art (sculpture and metal-working) in Linz, Austria. Won stipend for decorative art, 1974; Herbert Hoffmann Prize, Munich, 1975; Austrian State Stipend for Decorative Art, 1975; 1st prize (metal sculpture) for the Neue Rathaus, Linz, 1985.
Exhibitions: 376, 380, 381, 382, 467, 480, 482*, 726, 885, 888, 926, 1082, 1092, 1105, 1120, 1132, 1133, 1170

Vigeland, Tone (Pl. 227) Born 1938 in Oslo, Norway. Studied at Kunst & Handverksskolen, Oslo (1955); at Oslo Yrkesskole (1957). Established own workshop (1961). Received Master's degree (1962). Won 'Jacob' Prize, 1965.
Exhibitions: 108, 109*, 319, 601, 655, 656, 657, 697, 805, 824, 825*, 991, 999 1066
Works in public collections: Kunstindustrimuseet, Oslo; Vestlandske Kunstindustrimuseum, Bergen; Nordenfjeldske Kunstindustrimuseum, Trondheim; Landsforbundet Norsk Brukskunst; Det Danske Kunstindustrimuseum, Copenhagen; National Museum, Stockholm; Varmlands Museum; Norsk Kulturrad.

Visintin, Graziano (Pl. 258) Born 1954 in Pernumia, near Padua, Italy. Graduated from the Istituto d'Arte 'Pietro Selvatico', Padua (1973). Won jewellery-art prize 'UNO-A-ERRE', Arezzo, 1973. Teaches jewellery art at Istituto d'Arte 'Pietro Selvatico', Padua (since 1976). Won International Jewellery-Art Prize at the 5th Tokyo Triennale, Tokyo, 1983.
Exhibitions: 66, 101, 102, 199, 385, 395, 720, 721, 723, 727, 740, 822, 842, 898, 903, 1026, 1041, 1123, 1176

Watkins, David (Pls 170, 249) Born 1940 in England. Studied sculpture at Reading University (1959–63). Awarded Crafts Council Bursary, 1977. Artist in Residence at the Western Australia Institute of Technology, Perth (1978). Professor at Royal College of Art,

London (1984). Work included in public collections in Australia, Austria, Britain, Germany and Holland.
Exhibitions: 46, 150*, 153*, 315, 457, 526*, 529*, 545, 578*, 600*, 623, 634, 793, 798, 832, 880, 891, 900, 910, 1118*

Weckström, Björn (Pl. 118) Born 1935 in Helsinki, Finland. Graduated from the Goldsmiths' College, Helsinki (1956). Worked free-lance (1956–63); then as designer for Lapponia Jewelry Oy, Helsinki. Has own gallery in Helsinki; member of the Finnish Sculptors' Union and of ORNAMO, the designers' union. Won 2nd prize in a jewellery-design contest sponsored by the Finnish Goldsmiths, 1962; Grand Prix for jewellery design, Rio de Janeiro, 1965; the Lunning Prize, 1968. Awarded the Pro-Finlandia medal, 1971; won the Illum Prize, 1972.
Exhibitions: 110, 213, 266, 320, 398, 399, 400, 401, 402, 405, 413, 505, 769, 827, 843, 849, 913, 919, 1006, 1033, 1068
Works in public collections: Victoria and Albert Museum, London; Röhsska Konstslöjdsmuseet, Göteborg; Royal Scottish Museum, Edinburgh; Museum für angewandte Kunst, Helsinki; Finnish Glass Museum, Riihimäki.

Wende, Theodor (Pl. 78) Born 1883 in Berlin (died 1968). Served apprenticeship as gold- and silversmith in Berlin (1905); went to Dresden as journeyman. Attended the Zeichenakademie, Hanau, and the Kunstgewerbeschule, Berlin (1908). Was asked to join the Artists' Colony in Darmstadt (1913). Professor at the Kunstgewerbeschule, Pforzheim (1921). Member and honorary Grand Master of the Young Artists' Guild, Pforzheim. Received the Ehrenring from the Gesellschaft für Goldschmiedekunst, 1946. Retired (1951).
Works in public collections: Hessisches Landesmuseum, Darmstadt; Schlossmuseum, Darmstadt; Badisches Landesmuseum, Karlsruhe; Kestner-Museum, Hanover; Schmuckmuseum, Pforzheim.

Wennrich, Wolf (Pl. 166) Born 1922 in Germany. Studied at the Kunstakademie (jewellery/goldsmithing), Hamburg (1947–52). Went to Melbourne, Australia (1953). Lectured in jewellery/design in the Dept. of Gold- and Silversmithing, Royal Melbourne Institute of Technology (1963–80).
Exhibitions: 80, 294, 430, 664, 665, 976
Works in public collections: National Gallery of Victoria, Melbourne; Australia Council (Crafts Board Collection); Melbourne State College Collection.

West, Margaret (Pl. 230) Born [**Margaret Dodds**; known as **Margaret Jasulaitis** (1960–82).] 1936 in Melbourne, Australia. Attended Royal Melbourne Institute of Technology, Certificate

of Art (1955); Diploma of Art (1975); Graduate Diploma of Art (1976); Diploma of Education (1977). Lecturer in Jewellery Dept., Sydney College of the Arts (since 1979).
Exhibitions: 430, 463, 667, 668, 674, 675, 679, 891, 1009, 1158
Works in public collections: The Australian National Gallery, Canberra; National Gallery of Victoria, Melbourne; West Australian Art Gallery, Perth; Queensland Art Gallery, Brisbane; Victorian Ministry for the Arts, Melbourne; Meat Market Craft Centre, Melbourne; Australia Council (Crafts Board Collection); Melbourne State College Collection; Royal Melbourne Institute of Technology; Queen Victoria Museum and Art Gallery, Launceston, Tasmania.

Wilson, Henry (Pl. 29)   Born 1864 in England (died 1934). Attended the School of Art at Kidderminster; then apprenticed to an architect in Maidenhead. On completion of apprenticeship, worked as chief assistant to J.D. Sedding, whom he succeeded when Sedding died (1891). Shortly before that, had become interested in metalwork; set up a workshop that gradually became more important to him than his architect's practice. Began teaching metalwork at the Central School of Art and Design, London, and later at the Royal College of Art, London. (John Paul Cooper [see Pls 24, 25] worked with him before setting up own workshop.) Author of *Silverwork and Jewellery* (1903); the second edition of which (1912) has additional chapter on Japanese metalwork techniques: *mokume gane, shakudo,* etc. Both Wilson and Cooper very interested in working with mixed-metal finishes; gained much of their knowledge from two visiting Japanese professors, who lectured and demonstrated the techniques at the Royal College of Art around that time.

Winston, Harry (Pls 92, 178)   Born 1896 in New York (died 1978). Earned the title 'King of Diamonds' by becoming the world's foremost connoisseur of diamonds, as well as the largest individual dealer in them. Firm still has headquarters in New York; also maintains branches in other countries such as France and has workshops producing gem-set jewellery. Now managed by Harry's son, Ronald Winston (b. 1941).

Wittek, Walter (Pl. 223)   Born 1943 in Schoppinitz, (now Szopienice, Poland). Served apprenticeship as a steel engraver (1958–62). Attended the Akademie der bildenden Künste, Nürnberg (1962–68). Worked free-lance in Düsseldorf (1969–72). Taught at the Fachhochschule für Gestaltung, Hildesheim (1975–78).
Exhibitions: 140, 158, 202*, 204*, 205, 268*, 374, 389, 390, 392, 409, 604, 739, 744, 746, 807

Zehetbauer, Ulrike (Pl. 148)   Born 1934 in Vienna, Austria. Attended the Akademie der bildenden Künste (Professor Rickert), Munich (1951–56). Worked for Juwelier Heldwein, Vienna, for 2 years. Opened her own workshop in Vienna (1958).
Exhibitions: 171, 185, 280, 368, 369, 379, 389, 766, 813, 887, 897, 1047, 1085*, 1088, 1095*, 1096, 1100*, 1101, 1120, 1136*, 1163*, 1170

Zeitner, Herbert (Pl. 108)   Born 1900 in Coburg, FRG. Attended the Zeichenakademie, Hanau (1914–21). Passed journeyman exam (1921) and worked free-lance (1921–24). Master's degree as goldsmith (1924). Taught at the Vereinigte Staatsschulen für freie und angewandte Kunst, Berlin (1924-39); professor there (1935). Member of the Prussian Akademie der Künste, Berlin (1939–45); head of masters' workshop, and member of its senate. Received Ehrenring from the Gesellschaft für Goldschmiedekunst, 1943; the Olympia Medal, Helsinki, 1952; silver medal at the Milan Triennale, 1954; and the Lower Saxony Staatspreis for Crafts, 1967. Worked free-lance in Lüneburg (from 1946). Had solo exhibitions all over West Germany. Participated in many international exhibitions abroad.
Works in public collections: Schmuckmuseum Pforzheim; Neue Sammlung, Munich; Märkisches Museum, Berlin; Museum für Kunst und Gewerbe, Hamburg; The Museum of Modern Art, New York; Städtisches Museum, Lüneburg.

Zotov, Vladimir Alekseevich (Pl. 234)   Born 1934 near Moscow. Graduated from the Surikov Art Institute, Moscow; member of the Artists' Union of the U.S.S.R. (since 1973). Currently a free-lance artist, executing individual works for art exhibitions and museums. Has participated continuously in exhibitions in the U.S.S.R. and abroad. Won silver medal, Jablonec, 1977. Works in the U.S.S.R's major museums.

Zschaler, Othmar (Pl. 262)   Born 1930 in Chur, Switzerland. Served apprenticeship as a goldsmith (1946–50). Opened own workshop in Berne (1960). Won the Bavarian Staatspreis, 1967; participated in the 'Jewellery' symposium, Czechoslovakia (1968).
Exhibitions: 105*, 120*, 229, 230, 232*, 297, 433, 457, 465, 711*, 712, 748, 798, 799, 808, 882, 883, 884*, 889, 891, 900, 928, 986, 1023, 1026, 1030, 1035, 1174*

Zwollo Sr., Frans (Pl. 21)   Born 1872 in Holland (died 1945). Attended art school in Amsterdam; served apprenticeship as a jeweller, Paris and Brussels. Founder and teacher of metalwork classes at art schools in Haarlem (1897), Hagen (1907) and The Hague (1914). Exerted great influence on Dutch metalwork (inter-war period). Won gold medal at the Exposition des Arts Décoratifs et Industriels Modernes, Paris, 1925. A convinced theosophist (a follower of Rudolf Steiner and others), whose beliefs deeply influenced the design and forms of his work.

List of Exhibitions

The exhibitions listed are arranged alphabetically by the cities, countries or continents in which they were held and chronologically under the place names. An asterisk indicates a solo exhibition; (tour) indicates a travelling exhibition. Each entry is numbered; these numbers also reappear under *Exhibitions* in the Artists' Biographies, pp. 201-218, to show the exhibitions in which they participated. The artist/jewellers themselves supplied the information below.

1 Aachen 1978*: Neue Gallerie der Stadt, Ludwig Collection
2 Aarau, Switzerland 1981*: Kunsthaus
3 Aberdeen 1973: Aberdeen Art Gallery and Museum, 'Aspects of Jewellery'
4 -- 1974: Aberdeen Art Gallery and Museum, 'An Invitational Exhibition of Work by 8 American Metalsmiths and Jewelers' (tour: Edinburgh, Sheffield)
5 -- 1975: Aberdeen Art Gallery and Museum
6 Adelaide 1963*: White Studio
7 -- 1975: Jam Factory Gallery
8 -- 1978*: Bonython Art Gallery
9 -- 1982: Royal Adelaide Show
10 -- 1984: 'Worn Issues' (tour)
11 Alaska 1980: 1st Metal Art Exhibition
12 Alice Springs, Australia 1983: Crafts Council of the Northern Territory, 'National Craft Award Exhibition'
13 Amboise, France 1970*: Orangerie du Musée de la Poste, 'Bois des Noll'
14 Amersfoort 1969–73: Galerie Het Kapelhuis
15 -- 1972: International Jewellery Exhibition
16 -- 1972: Zonnehof Museum, 'Sieraad 1900–1972'
17 -- 1975–83: Galerie Het Kapelhuis
18 Amsterdam 1956*: Stedelijk Museum
19 -- 1960: Stedelijk Museum
20 -- 1966*: Galerie Swart
21 -- 1966–71: Galerie Swart
22 -- 1967*: Stedelijk Museum
23 -- 1969*: Galerie Ina Broerse
24 -- 1970*: Art and Project
25 -- 1971*: Galerie Swart
26 -- 1971: Museum Fodor
27 -- 1972*: Galerie Swart
28 -- 1973: Galerie Swart, 'Different Information'
29 -- 1975*: Galerie Swart
30 -- 1976: Galerie Ra
31 -- 1977: Galerie Ra
32 -- 1977: Stedelijk Museum
33 -- 1978: Galerie Ra
34 -- 1979*: Galerie Neon
35 -- 1979*: Galerie Ra
36 -- 1979: Stedelijk Museum
37 -- 1980: Galerie Ra
38 -- 1980*: Galerie Ra
39 -- 1980: Museum Fodor, 'The Critic Sees'
40 -- 1981: Galerie Ra
41 -- 1981*: Galerie Ra
42 -- 1981*:
43 -- 1982: Galerie Ra
44 -- 1982*: Galerie Ra
45 -- 1982: de nieuwe Kerk, 'Kunstmanifestatie'
46 -- 1982: Stedelijk Museum, 'Visies op Sieraden, 1965–1982'
47 -- 1983: de nieuwe Kerk, 'Kunstmanifestatie-83'
48 -- 1983: Galerie Ra
49 -- 1984: de nieuwe Kerk, 'Galerie 84-een jaar hedendaagse Kunst'
50 -- 1984: Galerie Ra
51 -- 1984*: Galerie Ra
52 -- 1984*: Stedelijk Museum
53 Anchorage, Alaska 1979: Visual Arts Center of Alaska, 'Metal Invitational'
54 Annecy, France 1976: Musée du château, 'Textiles appliqués'
55 Antibes 1958–60*: Musée Picasso
56 Antwerp 1959: 'Sculpture Biennale'
57 -- 1980: Diamond Centre, Provinciaal Diamantmuseum
58 -- 1983: Provinciaal Diamantmuseum, '10 Orafi Padovani'
59 -- 1984: Diamond Centre, Provinciaal Diamantmuseum
60 Apeldoorn 1977: Gemeentelijke Van Reekum Museum
61 -- 1978: Gemeentelijke Van Reekum Museum
62 -- 1980: Gemeentelijke Van Reekum Museum
63 -- 1982*: Gemeentelijke Van Reekum Museum, 'Marion Herbst, een overzicht 1969–1982' (tour)
64 -- 1982*: Gemeentelijke Van Reekum Museum (tour)
65 -- 1983*: Gemeentelijke Van Reekum Museum, 'Wendy Ramshaw'
66 Arezzo, Italy 1973: 'Uno-A-Erre'
67 -- 1975: 'Japan/Italy Exchange Exhibition'
68 -- 1981: 'International Jewellery Exhibition'
69 Arnhem 1981: Gemeente Museum
70 Asheville, North Carolina 1970*: Asheville Museum of Art
71 -- 1971*: Asheville Museum of Art
72 Asia 1978–80: 'Finnish Craft Exhibition' (tour)
73 Atlanta, Georgia 1974: Georgia State University, 'Contemporary Jewelry and Metalsmithing' (invitational)
74 Augsburg 1975: Galerie Rehklau
75 -- 1976: Galerie Rehklau
76 -- 1978: Galerie Rehklau
77 -- 1979: Galerie Rehklau
78 -- 1980: Galerie Rehklau, '10 Goldschmiede'
79 -- 1982*: Galerie Rehklau
80 Australia 1974: Crafts Board, 'Australian Jewellery Travelling Exhibition' (tour)
81 -- 1975: 'Australian Jewellery Travelling Exhibition' (tour)
82 -- 1976–78: *see* Germany
83 -- 1977*: Georg Jensen (tour)
84 -- 1981: 'Travelling Exhibition of Enamel Jewellery' (tour from Galerie am Graben, Vienna)
85 Avignon 1980: Les Angles, 'Présence des Formes'
86 Baden-Baden 1981*: Galerie Suzanne Fischer

87 Baltimore: Walters Art Gallery: Johnson Collection of American Crafts, 'Objects USA'

88 Barcelona 1980: Capella Santa Agata, 'Public Presentation of Group Orfebres F.A.D.'

89 — 1980: Reials Drassanes, 'I Mostra d'Artesania d'Avantguarda'

90 — 1980: '80 Anys d'Orfebreria Catalana'

91 — 1980: Palacio de Congresos, Montjuich

92 — 1982: Palacio de Congresos, Montjuich, 'Expocultura 82'

93 — 1982: 'Histories d'amor i d'inquietud', Grup Nou'

94 Basle 1964: Kunsthalle, 'La peau de l'ours'

95 — 1970: Mustermesse

96 — 1974: International Jewellery Exhibition

97 — 1974: Mustermesse (MUBA), 'Kreativer Schmuck'

98 — (Reinach) 1978: Atrium Gallery, 'Schmuckobjekte'

99 — 1979: Swiss Industries Fair

100 — 1979: Internationale Kunstmesse

101 — 1981*: Galerie Atrium

102 — 1981: Internationale Kunstmesse

103 — 1982*: Galerie Atrium

104 — 1983: Art Fair, 'Hephaïstos'

105 — 1983*: Galerie Atrium

106 Belgrade 1974*: Kunstgewerbemuseum + Design Center

107 — 1975: 'Nemacki Nakit 15–20 Veka' (German Jewellery)

108 Bergen 1974: 'Tendenser i Norsk Kunst & Handv'

109 — 1977*: Galeri Ingeerleiv

110 — 1982: Veltlanske Kunstindustrimuseum (Western Norway Museum of Applied Art)

111 — 1985: Vestlanske Kunstindustrimuseum

112 Berlin 1983: Galerie VFK, 'Schmuck Konzentriert'

113 — 1983*: Werkstatt Galerie

114 East Berlin / Karl-Marx-Stadt 1976: 'Junge Künstler der DDR' (tour)

115 — — 1981:

116 — 1981*: Galerie Skarabäus

117 — 1983*: Galerie Skarabäus

118 West Berlin 1963*: Kunstkabinett

119 — 1967: Galerie Lalique

120 — 1969*: Galerie Lalique

121 — 1971*: Galerie Lalique

122 — 1975: Galerie Ofhir

123 — 1975*: Modus

124 — 1978*: Modus

125 Berne 1972*: Incontro

126 Bielefeld 1965*: Werkkunstschule

127 Birmingham, Michigan 1977*: Yaw Gallery

128 — 1978*: Yaw Gallery

129 Birmingham, England 1978: City Museum and Art Gallery, 'Contemporary German and British Crafts'

130 — 1979*: City Museum and Art Gallery

131 Bloomfield, Michigan 1974: Cranbrook Museum of Art, 'Portable World'

132 Bloomington, Indiana 1983*: Fine Arts Gallery, Indiana University, 'Randy Long Works in Metal'

133 Bochum 1963*: Galerie Falazik

134 Bolzano 1980: Galerie Albrecht, '8 Goldschmiede, 8 Orafi'

135 Boston 1980: Harcus Kracow Gallery

136 — 1983: Westminster Gallery, '401 ½ Craftsmen'

137 Bozeman, Montana 1979: Montana State University, 'New Metals – Eleven Contemporary Metalsmiths'

138 Brampton, Ontario 1975*: Public Library Art Gallery

139 Bratislava 1966: 'Užité Uměni z NSR'

140 Bremen 1979: Rathaussaal

141 Brighton, England 1981: Polytechnic, '8 Artist Craftsmen'

142 Bristol, England 1967–73: Arnolfini Gallery

143 — 1967: Arnolfini Gallery

144 — 1968: Arnolfini Gallery

145 — 1969: Arnolfini Gallery

146 — 1971*: City Art Gallery

147 — 1975: Arnolfini Gallery

148 — 1975*: Arnolfini Gallery

149 — 1976: Arnolfini Gallery

150 — 1977*: Arnolfini Gallery

151 — 1978: Arnolfini Gallery, 'Jubilee Celebration Jewellery'

152 — 1978*: Arnolfini Gallery

153 — 1981*: Arnolfini Gallery

154 Britain / Holland 1977–79: 'Fourways' (tour)

155 Brockport, New York 1981: Tower Fine Arts Gallery, State University of New York, 'Metal '81'

156 Bromsgrove (Worcestershire) 1978: International Art Festival

157 Brooklyn 1953: Brooklyn Museum, 'Designer Craftsman USA 1953'

158 Brühl, FRG 1980: Orangerie Schloss

159 Brussels 1958: Swiss Pavilion, Weltausstellung

160 — 1958*: German Pavilion, Weltausstellung

161 — 1968*

162 — 1973: Europalia 73, 'GB Hand and Machine'

163 — 1976: Galerie Neon

164 — 1977: 'British Jewellery'

165 — 1980: Art Prospect Gallery

166 Budapest 1970*: Eötvös Club

167 — 1975*: Mini Gallery

168 — 1977*: Hungarian National Gallery (Magyar Nemzeti Galéria)

169 — 1977*: Helikon Gallery

170 Buffalo, New York 1974: Albright Knox Museum, 'Masterworks of the 70's'

171 Burgdorf, Switzerland 1982: Art Exhibition, 'Internationales Kunsthandwerk'

172 Cadaques, Spain 1978: Galeria Cadaques

173 Calgary, Canada 1978: The Quest Gallery

174 Camden, New York 1980: 'Wire in Art: Artists in Wire'

175 Canada 1985: juried travelling show of Canadian crafts, 'Frontiers'

176 Carmel, California 1979: Concepts Gallery, 'Contemporary English Jewelers'

177 Carrara, Italy 1970: Marina di Carrara, 'Biennale Internazionale de Gioello d'Arte'

178 Chicago 1957*: Art Institute

179 — 1976: Museum of Contemporary Art, 'American Crafts 1976'

180 Cleveland 1949-mid-70's: Cleveland Museum of Art, 'Cleveland May Show'

181 — 1966: Cleveland Museum of Art, 'May Show'

182 — 1967: Cleveland Museum of Art, 'May Show'

183 — 1971–73: Cleveland Museum of Art, 'May Show'

184 — 1977: Cleveland Museum of Art, 'May Show'

185 Coburg 1981: Kunstverein, 'Email International'

186 Cologne*: Galerie MAP

187 — 1961: 'Italienische Kunst'

188 — 1967*: Kunsthaus am Museum

189 — 1970*: Galerie MAP

190 — 1971*: Kunsthaus am Museum

191 — 1975*: Galerie MAP

192 — 1978*: Galerie Der Spiegel

193 — 1979*: Galerie MAP

194 — 1979: Kunstgewerbemuseum, 'Angewandte Kunst in Österreich – Heute'

195 -- 1981*: Galerie Mattar
196 -- 1981: Kunstgewerbemuseum 'Französisches Kunsthandwerk Heute'
197 -- 1981: Atelier Mattar, 'Ready Made'
198 -- 1981*: Galerie MAP
199 -- 1981: Galerie Teufel
200 -- 1981: Kölnisches Stadtmuseum, 'Email-Kunst-Handwerk-Industrie'
201 -- 1981: Kunstgewerbemuseum, 'Arts français'
202 -- 1982*: Galerie MAP
203 -- 1982: Atelier Mattar, 'Sieben Japaner'
204 -- 1983*: Galerie Videre
205 -- 1983: Atelier Mattar, 'Ringe' (tour)
206 Columbus, Ohio 1968: Gallery of Fine Arts, 'Beaux-Arts-Designer-Craftsmen Exhibition'
207 -- 1973: Gallery of Fine Arts, 'Beaux-Arts-Designer-Craftsmen Exhibition'
208 -- 1973: Gallery of Fine Arts, 'Designer/Craftsmen 73'
209 -- 1975: Gallery of Fine Arts, 'Beaux-Arts-Designer-Craftsmen Exhibition'
210 -- 1979: Columbus Museum of Art, 'Beaux-Arts-Designer-Craftsman '79'
211 Copenhagen 1951: Norsk Brakskunst i Kunstindustrimuseum
212 -- 1961: Royal Academy of Arts, 'Lunning Prize'
213 -- 1963: Galerie Gatto
214 -- 1965: American Art Gallery
215 -- 1967*: Det Danske Kunstindustrimuseum
216 -- 1968: Georg Jensen
217 -- 1968: Erling Haghfelt Gallery
218 -- 1970: Gammer Strand Gallery
219 -- 1971: Erling Haghfelt Gallery
220 -- 1973: Erling Haghfelt Gallery
221 -- 1975: Gallery Asbaek
222 -- 1977: Det Danske Kunstindustrimuseum
223 -- 1977: Snedkerhuset Ltd
224 -- 1979: 'British Design Exhibition'
225 -- 1979: Georg Jensen, '75 Year Jubilee Exhibition'
226 -- 1981: Det Danske Kunstindustrimuseum
227 Coral Gables, Florida 1975: Lowe Art Gallery, '200 Years of American Gold and Silver Smithing'
228 Curaçao, Netherlands Antilles 1969*: Galerie R.G.
229 Darmstadt 1964–5: Hessisches Landesmuseum, 'Schmuck-Jewellery-Bijoux'
230 -- 1967: Hessisches Landesmuseum, 'Schmuck von Malern und Bildhauern'
231 -- 1978: Hessisches Landesmuseum '3 Konzepte – 3 Goldschmiede – Bury / Jünger / Rothmann'
232 -- 1983*: Galerie Henning
233 Dartington, England 1977*
234 Darwin, Australia 1983: Museums and Art Galleries of the North Territory, 'National Craft Acquisition Award Exhibition 1983'
235 Delft 1970: Stedelijk Museum 'Het Prinsenhof', 'Bijdrage tot het constructivisme van nu'
236 -- 1973: Stedelijk Museum 'Het Prinsenhof', 'De Volle Maan'
237 Den Bosch (near Eindhoven), Holland 1980: De Moriaan
238 -- 1982: Het Kruithuis
239 -- 1984: Het Kruithuis, 'Objekt en Image' (tour)
240 Denmark 1972: Kolding Art Association
241 Denver 1975: Colorado State University, 'Contemporary Crafts of the Americas 1975' (+ Washington, D.C.: Pan American Building)
242 Des Moines, Iowa 1980*: Art Gallery, Drake University, 'Exhibition of Work in Metal and Porcelain'

243 Detmold 1979: Lippische Gesellschaft für Kunst
244 Dresden 1977: '8th Kunstausstellung der DDR'
245 -- 1982: '9th Kunstausstellung der DDR'
246 Donawitz 1974: International Symposium, 'Schmuck und Objekt aus Stahl'
247 Dubendorf, Switzerland 1974: Galerie Arte Arena
248 Duisburg 1976: Wilhelm-Lehmbruck-Museum, 'Ars Viva'
249 Duluth, Minnesota 1977: Tweed Museum of Art, 'Lake Superior 1977'
250 Düsseldorf 1928–29*: Professor Breuhaus's
251 -- 1970: Galerie Orfèvre
252 -- 1971: Galerie Orfèvre
253 -- 1974: Galerie Elke und Werner Zimmer
254 -- 1975: Georg Jensen
255 -- 1975: Galerie Elke und Werner Zimmer, 'Claus Bury / Rüdiger Lorenzen / Gerd Rothmann'
256 -- 1977*: Galerie Orfèvre
257 -- 1977*
258 -- 1978*: Galerie Orfèvre
259 -- 1979: Palais Wittgenstein, 'Schmuck + Gerat: Schüler und Lehrer der FHS Düsseldorf'
260 -- 1979: Galerie Orfèvre, 'Zwei als Eins'
261 -- 1979*: Galerie Orfèvre
262 -- 1980: 'Light, Form, Shape'
263 -- 1980*: Galerie Orfèvre
264 -- 1981: Galerie Orfèvre
265 -- 1982*: Galerie Orfèvre
266 -- 1982: Stadtmuseum
267 -- 1983: Galerie Orfèvre
268 -- 1983*: Galerie Orfèvre
269 -- 1984: Kunstverein für die Rheinlande und Westfalen
270 Edinburgh 1973: Royal Scottish Museum, 'Aspects of Modern British Crafts'
271 -- 1974: Richard De Marco Gallery: see Aberdeen 1974
272 -- 1975: Scottish Arts Council
273 -- 1975: 'Jewellery in Europe: An Exhibition of Progressive Work' (tour: Aberdeen, Belfast, Cardiff, Glasgow, London, Newport [Isle of Wight])
274 Eichgraben, Austria 1982*: Verein für Kunst und Kultur
275 Eindhoven / Washington, D.C. 1969: Van Abbemuseum/The Smithsonian Institution, 'Objects to Wear'
276 Eisenach 1978*: Kleine Galerie
277 El Cajon, California 1980: Grossmont College, 'Metal/Fibre'
278 El Paso, Texas 1979: El Paso Museum of Art, '11th Biennial Crafts Exhibition'
279 Enschede 1975: Rijksmuseum Twenthe
280 Erbach 1972: Deutsches Elfenbeinmuseum
281 Erfurt 1978*: Galerie erph
282 -- 1979: Galerie erph
283 -- 1979: 'Kunsthandwerk in der DDR'
284 -- 1981: 2nd Quadriennale des Kunsthandwerks sozialistischer Länder
285 -- 1982: 3rd Quadriennale des Kunsthandwerks sozialistischer Länder
286 -- 1982: 'Schmuck aus unedlen Materialien'
287 -- 1984: 'Schmuck und Glas'
288 Essen 1983: Glass Gallery of Essen
289 Europe 1974: 'Schmuck aus Stahl'
290 -- 1978: World Crafts Council, 'The Bowl' (tour)
291 -- 1979: 'SNAG – Selected Works of 41 Artists' (tour)
292 -- 1983: 'International Jewellery Art Exhibition'
293 -- 1982–4: 'Australian Jewellery' (tour)
294 -- 1982–3: 'Australian Contemporary Jewellers Exhibition to Europe' (tour)

510 -- 1971: Electrum Gallery, 'Erotic Jewellery'
511 -- 1971–84: Electrum Gallery, 'Christmas Exhibitions'
512 -- 1971*: Victoria and Albert Museum
513 -- 1971*: Goldsmiths' Hall
514 -- 1972: Electrum Gallery, 'Concepts of Modern Jewellery'
515 -- 1972*: Electrum Gallery, 'Wendy Ramshaw'
516 -- 1972*: Electrum Gallery, 'Objects to Wear'
517 -- 1972: Electrum Gallery, 'Twenty Modern Jewellers'
518 -- 1972: Electrum Gallery, 'Objects and Acrylic Jewellery' (Gerd Rothmann, Claus Bury and Fritz Maierhofer)
519 -- 1972*: Electrum Gallery, 'Susanna Heron'
520 -- 1972*: Goldsmiths' Hall
521 -- 1972: Goldsmiths' Hall South Africa/Japan 1975: '500 Years of Gold Jewellery'
522 -- 1973: Electrum Gallery, 'Aspects of Modern Jewellery'
523 -- 1973: Electrum Gallery, 'Figurative Jewellery'
524 -- 1973*: Electrum Gallery, 'Things Remembered'
525 -- 1973: Electrum Gallery, 'Jewellery and the Human Form'
526 -- 1973: Electrum Gallery, 'Wendy Ramshaw and David Watkins'
527 -- 1973: Electrum Gallery, 'Christmas Exhibition'
528 -- 1973*: Annely Juda Gallery
529 -- 1973*: Goldsmiths' Hall
530 -- 1973: Victoria and Albert Museum, 'The Craftman's Art'
531 -- 1973–74: Goldsmiths' Hall, 'Welsh Arts Council Exhibition'
532 -- 1973–74: '*The Observer* Jewellery Exhibition'
533 -- 1974: Electrum Gallery, 'Jewellery of the Silverscreen'
534 -- 1974: Electrum Gallery, 'Revolt in Jewellery'
535 -- 1974*: Electrum Gallery, 'Norbert Muerrle'
536 -- 1974: Electrum Gallery, 'Five New Jewellers'
537 -- 1974*: Electrum Gallery, 'Susanna Heron'
538 -- 1974: Goldsmiths' Hall, 'Seven Golden Years'
539 -- 1975*: Electrum Gallery, 'Fritz Maierhofer'
540 -- 1975: Electrum Gallery, 'Brian Glassar and Jeremy Ross'
541 -- 1975*: Electrum Gallery, 'David Poston'
542 -- 1975: Electrum Gallery, 'Hermann Jünger and Rüdiger Lorenzen and Their Students'
543 -- 1975: Electrum Gallery, 'The Complete Erté'
544 -- 1975*: Electrum Gallery, 'Roger Morris'
545 -- 1975, 1976: Victoria and Albert Museum, Scottish Arts Council Exhibition, 'Jewellery in Europe: An Exhibition of Progressive Work' (tour)
546 -- 1976*: Electrum Gallery, 'The Amazing Miniatures of Karel Bartosik'
547 -- 1976*: Electrum Gallery, 'Giampaolo Babetto'
548 -- 1976: Electrum Gallery, '6 Contemporary American Jewellers'
549 -- 1976: Electrum Gallery, 'Titanium Jewellery'
550 -- 1976*: Electrum Gallery, 'Nele'
551 -- 1976: Victoria and Albert Museum, 'Royal College of Art '76'
552 -- 1976: Victoria and Albert Museum (jewellery gallery)
553 -- 1976: Victoria and Albert Museum, 'Jewellery in Europe' (tour)
554 -- 1977*: Electrum Gallery, 'Harry Abend'
555 -- 1977*: Electrum Gallery, 'Emanuel Raft'
556 -- 1977*: Electrum Gallery, 'Tom Saddington'
557 -- 1977: Electrum Gallery, 'Kazuhiro Itoh and Takeo Mitsuyasu'
558 -- 1977*: Electrum Gallery, 'David Hensel'
559 -- 1977*: Electrum Gallery, 'Rod Edwards'
560 -- 1977: Electrum Gallery, 'Diamond Story'
561 -- 1977: Goldsmiths' Hall, 'Explosion'
562 -- 1977: Craftwork Gallery

563 -- 1977: National Theatre, 'British Craft Awards'
564 -- 1977: Victoria and Albert Museum, 'Jubilee Jewellery'
565 -- 1977: Victoria and Albert Museum, 'Presentation Pieces'
566 -- 1977: British Crafts Centre, 'Masterpiece'
567 -- 1978: Electrum Gallery, 'Jewellery Grows On Trees'
568 -- 1978: Electrum Gallery, 'Wally Gilbert and Sue Carney'
569 -- 1978*: Electrum Gallery, 'Victor Selinger'
570 -- 1978*: Electrum Gallery, 'Joby Baker'
571 -- 1978: Electrum Gallery, 'Students Work from Bezalel College, Jerusalem'
572 -- 1978*: Electrum Gallery, 'Wendy Ramshaw'
573 -- 1978: Goldsmiths' Hall, 'Rattlesnakes: 4 American Jewellers'
574 -- 1978: Victoria and Albert Museum, 'Objects, the Victoria and Albert Museum Collections, 1974–78'
575 -- 1978: Crafts Council Gallery
576 -- 1979*: Electrum Gallery, 'Martin Page'
577 -- 1979: Electrum Gallery, 'Five Danish Jewellers'
578 -- 1979*: Electrum Gallery, 'David Watkins'
579 -- 1979*: Electrum Gallery, 'Aya Nakayama'
580 -- 1979*: Electrum Gallery, 'Hermann Schafran'
581 -- 1979*: Electrum Gallery, 'William Harper'
582 -- 1979*: Electrum Gallery, 'Paul Preston'
583 -- 1979: Victoria and Albert Museum (jewellery gallery)
584 -- 1979: British Crafts Centre, 'New Faces'
585 -- 1979: Crafts Council Gallery, 'Press View'
586 -- 1979: Crafts Council Gallery (tour)
587 -- 1979: Studio Gallery
588 -- 1979: Goldsmiths' Hall, 'Loot' (tour to Australia)
589 -- 1979–80: Commonwealth Institute, '401½ Craftsmen'
590 -- 1980*: Electrum Gallery, 'Lisa Kodré-Defner'
591 -- 1980*: Electrum Gallery, 'Arline Fisch'
592 -- 1980*: Electrum Gallery, 'Erté'
593 -- 1980*: Electrum Gallery, 'Frank Bauer'
594 -- 1980*: Electrum Gallery, 'Alistair McCallum'
595 -- 1980*: Crafts Council Gallery (tour)
596 -- 1980: Design Centre/Victoria and Albert Museum, 'A Case for the Spectacular'
597 -- 1980: Victoria and Albert Museum, 'Acquisitions, Drawings and Designs'
598 -- 1980: Victoria and Albert Museum, 'Japan Style'
599 -- 1981: Electrum Gallery, 'Onno Boekhoudt and Jan Tempelman'
600 -- 1981*: Electrum Gallery, 'David Watkins'
601 -- 1981*: Electrum Gallery, 'Tone Vigeland'
602 -- 1981: Electrum Gallery, '10th Anniversary of Electrum Gallery Exhibition'
603 -- 1981: Electrum Gallery, 'Miriam Sharlin and Elizabeth Holder'
604 -- 1981: Electrum Gallery, 'The Ring from Antiquity to the Twentieth Century'
605 -- 1981: Design Centre, Council of Industrial Design, '50 Years of Design'
606 -- 1981*: Goldsmiths' Hall, 'Jewels'
607 -- 1981: Patrick Seale
608 -- 1981: O'Casey's Craft Gallery
609 -- 1981: Royal Danish Embassy
610 -- 1981*: 'ICA Sideshow'
611 -- 1981*: Crafts Council Gallery, 'The Maker's Eye'
612 -- 1981: British Crafts Centre, 'Ten Jewellers'
613 -- 1982: Electrum Gallery, 'Titanium by James Ward and Dust Jewellery'
614 -- 1982*: Electrum Gallery, 'Gerd Rothmann "Body Prints"'
615 -- 1982*: Electrum Gallery, 'Bernd Schobinger'
616 -- 1982: Electrum Gallery, 'New Figurative Jewellery'

617 -- 1982: Electrum Gallery, 'Love Tokens'
618 -- 1982*: Electrum Gallery, Christmas Exhibition, 'Wendy Ramshow's Wedgwood Collection'
619 -- 1982: Patrick Seale
620 -- 1982*: Victoria and Albert Museum, 'Wendy Ramshaw'
621 -- 1982: 'Whitechapel Open'
622 -- 1982: I.C.A., 'Craft Council Sideshow'
623 -- 1982: Victoria and Albert Museum, 'Towards a New Iron Age'
624 -- 1982: British Crafts Centre, 'Jewellery Re-Defined'
625 -- 1982: Crafts Council Galleries, 'The Maker's Eye: Crafts Council 10th Anniversary'
626 -- 1982: British Crafts Centre, 'Works in Wood'
627 -- 1983: Electrum Gallery, 'Paper-Plus'
628 -- 1983: Electrum Gallery, 'Grup Nou'
629 -- 1983*: Electrum Gallery, 'Arline Fisch'
630 -- 1983: Electrum Gallery, 'Hephaïstos'
631 -- 1983: 'Whitechapel Open'
632 -- 1983: Aspects Gallery, 'Rings' (tour)
633 -- 1983: Goldsmiths' Hall, 'The Goldsmith and the Grape'
634 -- 1983: Crafts Council Gallery, 'The Jewellery Project'
635 -- 1984: Electrum Gallery, 'Base + Noble'
636 -- 1984: Electrum Gallery, 'Contemporary Jewellery from Hungary'
637 -- 1984: Electrum Gallery, 'Diamonds International Awards Show'
638 -- 1984: Electrum Gallery, 'Contemporary Japanese Jewellery'
639 -- 1984: 'Whitechapel Open'
640 -- 1984: Victoria and Albert Craftshop, 'New Omega'
641 -- 1984: British Craft Centre
642 -- 1984*: Victoria and Albert Museum
643 -- 1985*: Electrum Gallery, 'Verena Sieber-Fuchs'
644 -- 1985: Electrum Gallery, 'Chan, Evans and Tortell'
645 -- 1985: Electrum Gallery, 'Niessing Collection'
646 -- 1985: Olympia, 'Contemporary Arts Fair'
647 -- 1985: Goldsmiths' Hall, 'Fusing Forces'
648 Long Beach, California 1983*; Art Gallery, California State University at Long Beach, 'Open Vessels'
649 Los Angeles 1976*: Los Angeles Craft and Folk Art Museum
650 -- 1982: Freehand Gallery, 'Californians Design: Jewelry'
651 -- 1982: Los Angeles Craft and Folk Art Museum, 'The Belt Show'
652 -- 1983: Los Angeles Craft and Folk Art Museum
653 Madrid 1980: '80 Anys d'Orfebreria Catalana'
654 -- 1982: Palacio de Cristal, 'Oficio y arte'
655 Maihangen 1975: 'Fra serk til Sirene'
656 -- 1976
657 -- 1977: 'Jacob Prisen 20 ar'
658 Malmö 1981*: Malmö Museum, 'Torun Vivianna Bülow-Hübe, 35 Years Silversmithing'
659 Manchester 1967: Peterloo Gallery
660 Marburg 1979*: Galerie in der Hofstatt
661 McLean, Virginia 1981*
662 Melbourne: Standfield Gallery, 'Workshop 3000 No. 1'
663 -- 1968: National Gallery of Victoria, 'The Field'
664 -- 1974: Georges Gallery, '3 + 1'
665 -- 1975: National Gallery of Victoria, 'Crafts Victoria '75'
666 -- 1976: Australian Government + USIA, 'Metals Invitational'
667 -- 1978*: National Gallery of Victoria
668 -- 1978*: National Gallery of Victoria 'Collection Pieces'
669 -- 1978*: Makers' Mark Gallery
670 -- 1979: Makers' Mark Gallery, 'Presentations'
671 -- 1979*: National Gallery of Victoria
672 -- 1980: 'Diamond Valley Shire Art Awards Exhibition'
673 -- 1980: Meat Market Craft Centre, 'Centenary Celebration'
674 -- 1980: Meat Market Craft Centre, 'Australian Crafts'
675 -- 1981: Meat Market Craft Centre
676 -- 1981: 'Diamond Valley Shire Art Awards Exhibition'
677 -- 1981: Makers' Mark Gallery, 'Arm Jewellery'
678 -- 1981: Makers' Mark Gallery
679 -- 1983: 'Diamond Valley Shire Art Awards Exhibition'
680 -- 1984: see Adelaide 1984
681 -- 1984: Meat Market Craft Centre, 'Australian Crafts 1984'
682 Mexico City / Tasco 1974: 'World Silver Fair'
683 Miami Beach, Florida 1981: Bass Museum of Art, 'Good as Gold: Alternative Materials in American Jewelry' (tour 1981–83)
684 Milan 1951: Swedish Pavilon, 9th 'Triennale di Milano'
685 -- 1954: Triennale
686 -- 1957: Triennale
687 -- 1960: Triennale
688 -- 1964: Triennale
689 -- 1970: Galleria Pianella Cantu
690 -- 1973: 15th Triennale
691 Monterey, California 1976: Monterey Peninsula Museum of Art, 'The Californian Craftsman'
692 -- 1978: Monterey Peninsula Museum of Art, 'The Californian Craftsman'
693 Montreal 1967: 'World Exposition 67'
694 -- 1974: 'In Praise of Hands'
695 -- 1982: Centre des Arts Visuels, 'Objets de Métaux Précieux'
696 Moscow/Riga/Tallinn 1973: 'Czechoslovak Jewels in the U.S.S.R.' (tour)
697 Moss, Norway 1971–73: Galleri 15, 'Tendenser'
698 Mount Vernon, Illinois 1984: Mitchell Museum, 'Society of North American Goldsmiths, Distinguished Members Exhibition'
699 Mulhouse, France 1979: 'Grands Artisans d'Aujourd'hui'
700 Munich*: Internationale Handwerksmesse
701 -- 1960*: Galerie van de Loo
702 -- 1962*: Galerie van de Loo
703 -- 1963: Galerie Franke
704 -- 1964–66: Internationale Handwerksmesse, 'Form und Qualität'
705 -- 1966: Galerie Thomas, 'Bildhauerschmuck von Nele, Penalba, Pomodoro, Jünger'
706 -- 1966–82: Internationale Goldschmiede Ausstellung
707 -- 1967*: Galerie Thomas
708 -- 1967*: Galerie van de Loo
709 -- 1967: Internationale Goldschmiede Ausstellung, 'Form und Qualität'
710 -- 1967: Internationale Handwerksmesse
711 -- 1968*: Galerie der Handwerkskammer
712 -- 1969: Internationale Handwerksmesse
713 -- 1971: 'Sonderschau'
714 -- 1971: Internationale Handwerksmesse
715 -- 1971: 'Internationale Schmuckschau'
716 -- 1972*: Galerie für internationale angewandte Kunst
717 -- 1972*: Galerie Cardillac
718 -- 1973: 'The Two Elizabeths'
719 -- 1974*: Galerie Rutzmoser
720 -- 1974: Internationale Schmuckschau, 'Form und Qualität'
721 -- 1975: Internationale Schmuckschau, 'Form und Qualität'
722 -- 1975: Staatliches Museum für angewandte Kunst, Neue Sammlung
723 -- 1976: Internationale Schmuckschau, 'Form und Qualität'
724 -- 1976: Galerie Rutzmoser
725 -- 1976: Galerie Thomas

726 -- 1977: Exempla 77, 'Handwerk und Kirche'
727 -- 1978: Internationale Schmuckschau
728 -- 1978: Galerie Thomas, 'Schmuckkunst'
729 -- 1979: Städtische Galerie im Lenbachhaus, 'Körper-Zeichen'
730 -- 1979: Städtische Galerie im Lenbachhaus
731 -- 1979: Schmuckschau at the Internationale Handwerksmesse
732 -- 1979*: Galerie Apollon die Insel
733 -- 1979: Exampla 79
734 -- 1979: Galerie Thomas
735 -- 1980: 'Austellung Neue Dimension'
736 -- 1980: Exempla 80
737 -- 1980: Galerie Thomas
738 -- 1982*: Schaufenster Nr. 34
739 -- 1982: Internationale Schmuckschau
740 -- 1982: Internationale Handwerksmesse, 'Schmuck und Gerät'
741 -- 1983: Galerie Hermanns, 'Schmuck'
742 -- 1983: Lothringerstr. 13, 'Das Schweizer Gold, die Deutsche Mark'
743 -- 1983: Galerie Cada, 'Eröffnungsausstellung'
744 -- 1983: Spektrum Galerie, 'Ringe' (tour)
745 -- 1983: 'Material, Schmuck und Gerät'
746 -- 1984: 'Schmuck und Gerät 1959–1984'
747 -- 1984*: Galerie Cada
748 -- 1984: 'The 1984 International Light and Handicrafts'
749 Neuchâtel 1961: Musée d'Ethnographie, 'Parures et Bijoux dans le monde'
750 New York: American Craft Museum, 'Jewelry U.S.A.'
751 -- : Museum of Contemporary Crafts, 'Enamels'
752 -- 1958: Museum of Contemporary Crafts, 'Young Americans'
753 -- 1963*: Georg Jensen
754 -- 1964*: Georg Jensen
755 -- 1964*: Georg Jensen, 'The Eloquent Jewels of Sigurd Persson'
756 -- 1964: 'The American Craftsman'
757 -- 1964*: Museum of Contemporary Crafts
758 -- 1965*: Museum of Contemporary Crafts
759 -- 1968*: Museum of Contemporary Crafts
760 -- 1969*: Lee Nordness Galleries
761 -- 1969*: Bloomingdale's, Gallery One
762 -- 1969: Museum of Contemporary Crafts, 'Young Americans '69' (tour)
763 -- 1971*: Lee Nordness Galleries
764 -- 1972: Leslie Rankow Gallery, 'Goldsmiths' Hall'
765 -- 1973: The Metropolitan Museum of Art, 'Gold'
766 -- 1973: Austrian Institute
767 -- 1974: Museum of Contemporary Crafts, 'Collectors' Collections'
768 -- 1974: Museum of Contemporary Crafts, 'Baroque 74'
769 -- 1974: Rosenthal Studio-House
770 -- 1974*: Leslie Rankow Gallery
771 -- 1975: Austrian Institute, 'Creative Crafts of Austria' (tour)
772 -- 1975: Museum of Contemporary Crafts/Bloomfield Hills, Michigan: Cranbrook Art Gallery, 'Forms in Metal: 275 Years of Metalsmithing in America' (competition)
773 -- 1975*: Florence Duhl Gallery
774 -- 1977: Sterling Silversmiths' Guild of America: Lever House, 'Sterling Silver Design Competition'
775 -- 1977: Museum of Contemporary Crafts, 'Young Americans'
776 -- 1978: The Bronx Museum, 'Works in Fiber, Clay and Metal by Women' (National Invitational Exhibition)
777 -- 1978*: The Bronx Museum, 'Art in Craft'
778 -- 1978*: K. Mikimoto & Company
779 -- 1979*: Florence Duhl Gallery

780 -- 1979: Sterling Silversmiths' Guild of America: Lever House, 'Sterling Silver Design Competition'
781 -- 1979: Artwear Gallery
782 -- 1980: Artwear Gallery
783 -- 1980–81: American Craft Museum, 'Young Americans in Metal' (tour)
784 -- 1980: Art Latitude Gallery
785 -- 1980: Galerie La Tortue, 'Art New York'
786 -- 1980: American Craft Museum, 'Art in Use'
787 -- 1981: Elements Gallery, 'The Pin'
788 -- 1981: American Craft Museum, 'Celebration 25'
789 -- 1981: Artwear Gallery
790 -- 1982: American Craft Museum, 'Approches to Collecting'
791 -- 1982: American Craft Museum, 'Patterns'
792 -- 1983: Edward H. Merrin Gallery
793 -- 1983: American Craft Museum, 'New Departures'
794 -- 1984 /Santa Fe: Byzantium Gallery
795 -- 1984*: Byzantium Gallery
796 -- 1984: Cooper-Hewitt Museum, The Smithsonian Institution's National Museum of Design, 'Design in the Service of Tea'
797 -- 1984: American Craft Museum, 'American Jewelry 1984'
798 -- 1984: American Craft Museum, 'Contemporary Trends'
799 -- 1984: American Craft Museum, Jewellery International'
800 -- 1984: American Craft Museum, 'Jewelers U.S.A.'
801 -- 1984: Fashion Institute of Technology, 'S.N.A.G. Distinguished Members Exhibition'
802 Nîmes, France 1977: Galerie de Nîmes
803 -- 1982: 'Salon de la Pièce Unique'
804 Normal, Illinois 1984: Visual Arts Gallery, Illinois State University, '10th Biennial National Invitational Craft Exhibition'
805 Norway 1959: 'Landsforbundet Norsk Brakskunst' (tour: Sweden, England, U.S.A., Israel, Australia)
806 Nottingham 1977: Castlegate Museum, 'Metal Jewellery'
807 Nürnberg 1966: Kunsthalle
808 -- 1971: Norrishalle, 'Gold + Silber, Schmuck + Gerät, von Albrecht Dürer bis zur Gegenwart'
809 -- 1978: see Darmstadt 1978
810 -- 1979*: Galerie Decus
811 -- 1982–83*: Kunsthalle
812 Oberplanitzing: see Bolzano
813 Oldenburg 1972: Landesmuseum für Kunst- und Kulturgeschichte
814 -- 1976*: Landesmuseum für Kunst- und Kulturgeschichte
815 -- 1977*: Landesmuseum für Kunst- und Kulturgeschichte
816 -- 1978*: Landesmuseum für Kunst- und Kulturgeschichte
817 -- 1981: Galerie d'Or, 'Six Artists from England'
818 -- 1982*: Galerie d'Or
819 -- 1983: Landesmuseum für Kunst- und Kulturgeschichte, 'Körperkultur'
820 Osaka 1970: see Tokyo 1970
821 -- 1983: see Tokyo 1983
822 -- 1983: Nabio Gallery
823 Oslo 1952: Kunstindustrimuseet, 'Norsk Emaljekunst i Lyset'
824 -- 1964*: Kunstvernes Hus
825 -- 1978*: Kunstforbandet (+ Electrum Gallery, London)
826 -- 1978*: Kunstindustrimuseet, 'Retrospective G. Prytz-Kittelsen'
827 -- 1982: Kunstindustrimuseet
828 -- 1985: Kunstindustrimuseet
829 Ottawa 1984: National Museum of Man, 'Works of Craft'
830 Oxford 1968: Bear Lane Gallery
831 -- 1971*: Oxford Gallery
832 -- 1975: Oxford Gallery

833 -- 1978: Ashmolean Museum
834 -- 1979: Oxford Gallery, 'Earrings'
835 -- 1979*: Oxford Gallery
836 -- 1980*: Oxford Gallery, 'Porcelain Jewellery'
837 -- 1981: Oxford Gallery, 'Black Jewellery'
838 Padua 1959: Biennale
839 -- 1961: Biennale
840 -- 1963: Biennale
841 -- 1979: International Small Sculpture Biennale
842 -- 1982: Studio GR 20
843 Palm Beach, Florida 1978: Galeria of Sculpture
844 Palm Springs, California 1978: 'British Silver'
845 Paris 1954–68: [for other exhibitions in the century: see the Index] Galerie du Siècle (permanent collection)
846 -- 1960: Italian pavilion at I.C.E. (+ Helsinki)
847 -- 1963*: Grand-Palais, 'Salon des artistes décorateurs'
848 -- 1964: Swedish House, 'Four Lunning Prize Winners'
849 -- 1968: Galerie Clerc
850 -- 1971: Musée des arts décoratifs, 'L'Idée et la forme'
851 -- 1971: Musée du Louvre, 'British Design'
852 -- 1973*: Georg Jensen, La Boutique Danoise, 'Torun, 25 Years of Silversmithing'
853 -- 1974: Maison de Danemark
854 -- 1975: Salon de Bijhorca
855 -- 1975*: Galerie Sven (arranged by Hubert de Givenchy)
856 -- 1976: International d'art contemporain 76
857 -- 1977: Musée des arts décoratifs, 'Artist/Artisan?'
858 -- 1977–78: Galerie Beaubourg, 'Les Bijoux d'Artistes'
859 -- 1978: Galerie Bernheim-Jeune, 'Artisans créateurs d'aujourd'hui'
860 -- 1979: Grand-Palais, 'Salon des Artistes décorateurs'
861 -- 1979: Cercle Foch, 'Libres Bijoux'
862 -- 1980: UNESCO and Generalitat de Catalunya, 'Catalunya avui'
863 -- 1980: Louvre des Antiquaires, Galerie Curia, 'Bijoux 81'
864 -- 1980–81: Musée des arts décoratifs, 'Les Métiers de l'Art'
865 -- 1981*: Galerie Monade
866 -- 1981*: Galerie Faris
867 -- 1981*: Galerie Mercedes Arnuls
868 -- 1982*: Galerie Mercedes Arnuls
869 -- 1982*: Galerie Temporaire, 'Les Noll'
870 -- 1982: Grand-Palais, 'Bijoux 82'
871 -- 1982: Grand-Palais, 'Biennale des Antiquaires et de la Haute Joaillerie française'
872 -- 1982: Jansen, 'D'or et d'Argent'
873 -- 1983: 'D'or et Diamant'
874 -- 1983: Hôtel Drouot, 'Les Années 80'
875 -- 1984: Grand-Palais, Galerie J.M. Capillard, 'FIAC'
876 -- 1984: Musée des arts décoratifs, 'Sur Invitation'
877 Pasadena, California 1965: Pasadena Museum of Art, 'Design Nine'
878 -- 1968: Pasadena Museum of Art, 'California Design Ten'
879 Pennsylvania 1965: Everhart Museum, 'American Jewelry Today'
880 Perth 1978: 'W.A.I.T.'
881 -- 1980: 'Loot' (tour: Adelaide, Sydney)
882 Pforzheim 1967: Schmuckmuseum, 'Tendenzen'
883 -- 1970: Schmuckmuseum, 'Tendenzen'
884 -- 1972*: Schmuckmuseum
885 -- 1972: Schmuckmuseum, 'Halsschmuck in Silber' (+ Hanau)
886 -- 1972: Galerie 'K'
887 -- 1973: Schmuckmuseum
888 -- 1973: Schmuckmuseum, 'Metallkunst aus Österreich'
889 -- 1973: Schmuckmuseum, 'Tendenzen '73'
890 -- 1974*: Schmuckmuseum

891 -- 1977: Schmuckmuseum, 'Tendenzen, Schmuck 77'
892 -- 1978: Schmuckmuseum, 'Schmuck-Tischgerät aus Österreich 1904–1908, 1973–77'
893 -- 1979*: Schmuckmuseum
894 -- 1979: Schmuckmuseum, 'SNAG, The Goldsmith' (+ tour: Hanau: Deutsches Goldschmiedehaus; Gmund: Städtisches Museum; Antwerp: Provinciaal Diamantmuseum; Amersfoort: Zonnehof; Oslo: Kunstindustrimuseet; Helsinki; London [1979–80]: Goldsmiths' Hall)
895 -- 1979*: Schmuckmuseum, 'Therese Hilbert'
896 -- 1979: Schmuckmuseum 'Tendenzen'
897 -- 1980: Schmuckmuseum, 'Email, Schmuck und Gerät in Geschichte und Gegenwart' (+ Vienna: Galerie am Graben
898 -- 1980: Schmuckmuseum, 'Armschmuck' (Jewellery for the Arm)
899 -- 1982*: Schmuckmuseum
900 -- 1982: Schmuckmuseum, 'Schmuck 82 – 'Tendenzen'
901 -- 1983: 'Japanese Modern Jewellery Exhibition' (+ tour: Hanau, Munich, Lausanne, Vienna)
902 -- 1983: Schmuckmuseum, 'Schmucktendenzen – 1983'
903 -- 1983: Schmuckmuseum, '10 Orafi Padovani'
904 -- 1984*: Schmuckmuseum
905 Philadelphia 1973*: American Institute of Architects Gallery
906 -- 1974: Philadelphia Museum of Art
907 -- 1977: Philadelphia Museum of Art, 'The Philadelphia Craft Show'
908 -- 1978*: Helen Drutt Gallery
909 -- 1981*: Helen Drutt Gallery
910 -- 1982*: Helen Drutt Gallery
911 -- 1984*: The Works Gallery
912 Phoenix, Arizona 1977: The Phoenix Museum of Art, 'The Metalsmith' (invitational) (+ Seattle: The Henry Gallery, University of Washington)
913 Pisa 1982: San Zeno Cathedral
914 Pittsburgh 1961: Carnegie Institute
915 -- 1984*: University of Pittsburgh Art Gallery
916 Prague 1968: Galerii na Betlemsken
917 -- 1973*: D Gallery
918 Pullmann, Washington 1981: Museum of Art, Washington State University, 'Contemporary Metals: Focus on Ideas'
919 Quebec 1977: Galerie d'Art
920 Rapperswil, Switzerland 1975: Galerie Seestrasse
921 -- 1976: Galerie Seestrasse
922 Regensburg 1978: Galerie Artmann
923 Reinach, Switzerland 1972*: Galerie Atrium
924 Riihimäki, Finland 1982: International Sculpture Biennale
925 Rome 1974: Galleria La Trinità
926 -- 1977: Centro Artistico Culturale, 'Correnti Attuali'
927 Rotterdam 1964: 'Deutsche Sammler'
928 -- 1965: Museum Boymans-van Beuningen, 'Sieraden'
929 -- 1970: Museum Boymans-van Beuningen
930 -- 1972: Museum Boymans-van Beuningen
931 -- 1979: Van Wilegen
932 Sacramento, California 1983: Crocker Art Museum, 'California Crafts XIII'
933 St Ives (Cornwall) 1964: Fore Street Gallery
934 -- 1964–76: Penwith Gallery
935 -- 1969–72: Marjory Parr
936 -- 1972: Wills Lane Gallery
937 St Louis, Missouri 1967*: Craft Alliance Gallery
938 -- 1978: Steinberg Gallery, Washington University, 'American Goldsmiths – Now' (invitational)
939 -- 1983: Craft Alliance Gallery, 'Iron Age to Space Age'
940 St Paul, Minnesota 1953: 'Fiber, Clay and Metal'

941 -- 1974: Minnesota Museum of Art, 'Society of North American Goldsmiths'
942 Salzburg 1969*: Galerie Welz
943 -- 1970: Multimedia
944 San Diego, California 1973: University Art Gallery, San Diego State University
945 -- 1981: University Art Gallery, San Diego State University, 'Two Decades of Metal'
946 -- 1983: San Diego State University, 'Update: Recent Work from Selected Alumni'
947 San Francisco 1968*: Museum West
948 -- 1978: Bank of America, 'Bank of America California Crafts Exhibition'
949 -- 1983: Contemporary Artisans Gallery
950 -- 1983: Contemporary Artisans Gallery, 'Hephaïstos'
951 -- 1984: The Elaine Dotter Gallery
952 San Marino, California 1955: The Huntington Library, 'American Jewelry'
953 Saratoga Springs, New York 1984: Skidmore College, 'Multiplicity in Clay, Fiber, Metal'
954 Scandinavia 1982: 'Craft Design Exhibition' (+ Japan)
955 Schwäbisch-Gmünd 1953: 'Internationale Silberschmied-Ausstellung'
956 -- 1976*: Museum
957 Scottsdale, Arizona 1979: Hand and Spirit Gallery, 'Collectors Pieces'
958 -- 1981: Hand and Spirit Gallery
959 Scranten, Pennsylvania 1965: Everhart Museum, 'Jewelry Today'
960 Seattle, Washington 1962: Swedish Pavilion, World's Fair
961 -- 1966: The Henry Gallery, University of Washington
962 -- 1981: The Henry Gallery, University of Washington, 'Embellishment Beyond Function'
963 -- 1982: 'Enamels'
964 -- 1982*: Foster White Gallery
965 -- 1982: Museum of History and Industry '1982 Northwestern Crafts Exhibition'
966 Sheboygan, Wisconsin 1975: John Michael Kohler Arts Center, 'Master Craftsmen'
967 -- 1983: John Michael Kohler Arts Center, 'Craft as an Art Form'
968 Sheffield, England 1974: Sheffield Polytechnic School of Art and Design: see Aberdeen 1974
969 s'Hertogenbosch, Holland 1981*: Gemeentelijk Museum
970 Society of North American Goldsmiths (S.N.A.G.) 1970: Goldsmith Exhibition
971 -- 1974: Goldsmith Exhibition
972 -- 1976: Goldsmith Exhibition
973 -- 1978: Goldsmith Exhibition
974 -- 1979–81: European Exhibition (tour: Germany, Holland, Norway, Finland, England, Switzerland)
975 -- 1984: Goldsmith Exhibition
976 South-East Asia 1977: 'Ten Australian Jewellers' (tour)
977 Spokane, Washington 1974: World's Fair, 'Expo 74'
978 Stockholm 1948: Galerie Aesthetica
979 -- 1950*
980 -- 1959: Nationalmuseum
981 -- 1960*: NK, '77 Ringe'
982 -- 1963*: NK, '7 × 7 Armband'
983 -- 1963*: Hantverket, 'Silberne Leuchter'
984 -- 1964*: NK, 'Der Ohrschmuck'
985 -- 1965*: NK, 'Der Halsschmuck'
986 -- 1967: 'British Jewellers Exhibition'
987 -- 1968*: Hantverket, 'Skal'
988 -- 1969: Gallery Bengtsson
989 -- 1970: 'Nutida tysk guldsmedskonst'
990 -- 1970*: '25 Silberkannen unter 33 Jahren'
991 -- 1976: Hasselby Slott
992 -- 1979: Georg Jensen: see Copenhagen
993 Stuttgart 1966: Landesgewerbeamt, 'Internationales Kunsthandwerk'
994 -- 1969: Landesgewerbeamt, 'Internationales Kunsthandwerk'
995 -- 1974: Avantgarde 74
996 -- 1980: 'Design from the Netherlands' (tour)
997 Suhl 1983*: Galerie im Steinweg
998 Sweden 1966–68: 'Sigurd Persson Design' (tour)
999 -- 1974: Varmland and Smaland Museum
1000 -- 1974: Engelholm Art Association
1001 -- 1982: Engelholm Art Association
1002 Sydney 1963: Blaxland Gallery, 'Survey 3'
1003 -- 1963*: Marion Best Design Studio
1004 -- 1973: David Jones Art Gallery
1005 -- 1973: Bonython Art Gallery
1006 -- 1974: David Jones Gallery
1007 -- 1978*: Robin Gibson Gallery
1008 -- 1979: Art of Man Gallery
1009 -- 1982: Crafts Council Gallery, 'The Australian Experience – Elements of Change'
1010 -- 1983: Crafts Council Gallery, 'Workshop 3000 No. 2'
1011 -- 1984: Power House Museum, 'Cross Currents: Jewellery from Australia, Great Britain, Holland, Germany' (tour)
1012 -- 1984: see Adelaide 1984
1013 Székesfehérvár, Hungary 1981*: Chemistry Museum, 'Black Eagle'
1014 Szombathely, Hungary 1984: 5th 'International Bienniale for Miniature Textile Art'
1015 Tel Aviv 1966*: Massada Gallery
1016 Terra Haute, Indiana 1977: Indiana State University, 'Women's Art Symposium, National' (invitational)
1017 Tokyo: 'Metalsmith International Jewelry Arts Exhibition, Triennial'
1018 -- 1967: 'Japan Jewellery Design Show'
1019 -- 1969: 'Japan Jewellery Design Show'
1020 -- 1969*: 'International Exhibition of Goldsmith's Art'
1021 -- 1970: Japan Jewellery Design Show
1022 -- 1970/Osaka: 'Three Centuries of Rings'
1023 -- 1970: International Jewellery Art Exhibition
1024 -- 1971: 'Diamonds International Award' (tour: New York, Sydney, Italy)
1025 -- 1972: Japan Jewellery Design Show
1026 -- 1973: International Jewellery Art Exhibition,
1027 -- 1973: Imperial Hotel, 'Jewellery Show'
1028 -- 1976: Odankya Grand Gallery
1029 -- 1976: Seibu Art Museum
1030 -- 1976: International Jewellery Art Exhibition, 'Jewellery in Europe'
1031 -- 1977*: Seibu Art Museum
1032 -- 1978: Wako Department Store, Ginza, 'Modern Japanese Jewellery Exhibition by 50 Members of Japanese Jewelry Designers' Association' (invitational)
1033 -- 1978: Mikomoto Hall Gallery
1034 -- 1978: K. Mikimoto & Co.: Mikimoto Hall Gallery, Ginza, 'Modern American Jewellery Exhibition'
1035 -- Mikomoto Hall Gallery, Ginza, 4th 'Tokyo Triennale: International Jewellery Art Exhibition'
1036 -- 1979*: Atrium Ginza La Pola
1037 -- 1980: Mikimoto Hall Gallery
1038 -- 1982: 'International Jewellery Art Exhibition'
1039 -- 1983*: 'International Jewellery Art Exhibition'

1040 -- 1983*: 'Jewellery New'
1041 -- 1983: Isetan Museum, 5th Tokyo Triennale, International Jewellery Art Exhibition (+ Osaka: Nabio Galerie)
1042 -- 1984: National Museum of Modern Art: *see* Kyoto 1984
1043 Toronto*: 'International Craft Exhibition'
1044 -- 1971: 'International Exhibition of Contemporary Jewellery'
1045 -- 1971: Art Gallery of Toronto, 'Jewelry '71'
1046 -- 1973: Art Gallery of Ontario, 'Textile into 3-D'
1047 -- 1973: 'Contemporary Crafts of the World'
1048 -- 1974: 1st 'Worlds Craft Exhibition'
1049 -- 1978: Ontario College of Art, 'Aspects of Sculpture'
1050 -- 1978: annual juried exhibition of the Metal Arts Guild, 'The Medium is Metal'
1051 -- 1981: Ontario Craft Council Gallery, 'Ontario Craft 81'
1052 -- 1981: Prime Canadian Crafts, 'The Jewellery Collection'
1053 -- 1982: Ontario Craft Council Gallery, 'Ontario Craft 82'
1054 -- 1983: Ontario Craft Council Gallery, 'Ontario Craft 83'
1055 -- 1983: Merton Gallery, 'The Medium is Metal'
1056 -- 1983: Prime Canadian Crafts, 'Jewellery in Transition'
1057 -- 1983: Ontario Crafts Council Gallery, 'About Space'
1058 -- 1984: Annual juried exhibition of the Metal Arts Guild, 'The Medium is Metal'
1059 -- 1984: Prime Canadian Crafts, 'Constructions in Slate and Steel'
1060 -- 1984: Art Gallery at Harbourfront, 'Celebration '84'
1061 -- 1984*: Prime Canadian Crafts
1062 -- 1985: Ontario Crafts Council, Craft Gallery, 'Jewellery as Art'
1063 Toulouse 1972: Galerie 'At Home'
1064 -- 1982: Galerie 'At Home'
1065 Troisdorf 1979*: Galerie Donath
1066 Tromsø, Norway 1974: Galleri 71
1067 Trondheim, Norway 1985: Nordenfjeldske Kunstindustrimuseet
1068 Turku, Finland 1978: Wäinö Aaltonen Museum
1069 Ulm 1975*: Galerie für Goldschmiedekunst
1070 -- 1981: Studio f
1071 U.S.A. 1952–56: 'Design in Scandinavia' (tour)
1072 -- 1954–57: 'Design in Scandinavia' (tour)
1073 -- 1971–75: American Craft Council Northwest Region Traveling Metal Exhibition' (tour)
1074 -- 1981–84: 'Finnish Design' (tour)
1075 U.S.A./Australia 1982: '1 + 8' (tour)
1076 U.S.A. 1984: Contemporary Artisans Gallery
1077 -- 1983*: 'French Connection'
1078 U.S.S.R. 1979–80*: 'Czech Jewellery' (tour: Moscow, Riga, Vilnius)
1079 Vatican City 1978: Vatican Museum with the Smithsonian Institution, 'Craft, Art and Religion: American Crafts at the Vatican Museum'
1080 Venice 1964: Biennale internazionale d'arte
1081 -- 1966: Biennale internazionale d'arte
1082 -- 1984: Biennale: Ateneo San Basso, 'Schmuck, zeitgenössische Kunst aus Österreich'
1083 Vienna 1964*: Österreichisches Museum für angewandte Kunst
1084 -- 1967: '600 Jahre Wiener Goldschmiedekunst'
1085 -- 1969*: Galerie Nagl
1086 -- 1969: Palais Liechtenstein, 'Maskulin – Feminin'
1087 -- 1970*: Galerie L & K Wittmann, 'Schmuck-Skulptur – Skulptur-Schmuck'
1088 -- 1970: Schloss Schönbrunn
1089 -- 1971*: Zentralsparkasse
1090 -- 1971*: Im Studio Galerie in der Blutgasse
1091 -- 1971*: Galerie L & K Wittmann
1092 -- 1972: Galerie am Graben, 'Eröffnungsausstellung'

1093 -- 1972: Galerie am Graben, 'Angewandte Kunst der Gegenwart'
1094 -- 1972: Österreichisches Museum für angewandte Kunst, 'Schmuck 72'
1095 -- 1973*: Galerie am Graben
1096 -- 1973: Rathaus
1097 -- 1974*: Galerie am Graben
1098 -- 1974: 'Schmuck aus Stahl' (tour: Nürnberg, Berlin, Pforzheim)
1099 -- 1975: Galerie am Graben, 'Angewandte Kunst der Gegenwart'
1100 -- 1975*: Galerie Veronique
1101 -- 1975: Künstlerhaus 'Schöpferisches Kunsthandwerk in Österreich'
1102 -- 1975*: Modern Art Gallery
1103 -- 1976*: Galerie am Rabensteig
1104 -- 1976: Galerie am Graben, 'Multiples'
1105 -- 1976: Galerie am Graben, 'Viehbock, Larsen, Lewers, Chung'
1106 -- 1977*: Galerie am Graben
1107 -- 1977: Galerie am Graben, 'Dosen'
1108 -- 1977: Künstlerhaus, 'Struktur-Textur' (+ Zürich, Undine)
1109 -- 1977*/78*: Galerie am Graben
1110 -- 1977*: Museum des 20. Jahrunderts
1111 -- 1977: Galerie am Graben, 'Dosen'
1112 -- 1978*: Galerie am Graben
1113 -- 1978: 'Schmuck- und Tischgerät aus Österreich (+ tour: Lausanne, Pforzheim, Hanau, Linz)
1114 -- 1978: Galerie am Graben, 'Schmuck und Glas von Anton Cepka und Václav Cígler'
1115 -- 1979*: Galerie am Graben
1116 -- 1970*: Neue Galerie
1117 -- 1980*: Galerie am Graben, 'Ein System'
1118 -- 1980*: Galerie am Graben
1119 -- 1980: Galerie am Graben, 'Email, Schmuck + Gerät' (+ tour Pforzheim, Australia)
1120 -- 1980: Künstlerhaus 'Schmuck International 1910–1980' (invitational)
1121 -- 1981*: Galerie am Graben
1122 -- 1981: Galerie am Graben, 'Arbeiten in Textil und Metall'
1123 -- 1981*: Galerie am Graben
1124 -- 1982*: Galerie am Graben
1125 -- 1982: Galerie am Graben, 'Körperkultur'
1126 -- 1982*: Galerie am Graben
1127 -- 1982: Museum für angewandte Kunst, 'Internationales Kunsthandwerk'
1128 -- 1982*: Museum für angewandte Kunst
1129 -- 1982–83*: Palais Pállfy: Österreichisches Kulturzentrum
1130 -- 1983: V & V Galerie, 'Four American Jewellers'
1131 -- 1983: V & V Galerie
1132 -- 1983: Rathaus, 'Ars Sacra'
1133 -- 1983: Künstlerhaus 'Topografie'
1134 -- 1984*: V & V Galerie
1135 -- 1984*: Galerie am Graben
1136 -- 1984*: Künstlerhaus
1137 Vigo, Spain 1976: International Congress of Young Artists
1138 Wakefield 1984: West Bretton Sculpture Park
1139 Warsaw 1971*: Österreichisches Kulturinstitut
1140 -- 1974*: Galerie 'Passage'
1141 -- 1975*: Galerie DESA, 'Zapiecek'
1142 -- 1977*: Galerie DESA
1143 -- 1977: 'Salon Sztuki'
1144 -- 1978*: Galerie DESA
1145 -- 1979*: Galerie Piotr Nowicki

Bibliography

Amaya, Mario. *Art Nouveau*. London: Studio Vista. 1966.

Arwas, Victor. *Art Deco*. New York: Abrams, 1980, and London: Academy, 1980.

Becker, Vivienne. *Antique and Twentieth-Century Jewellery: A Guide for Collectors*. New York: Van Nostrand-Reinhold, 1982, London: NAG Press, 1980.

——. *Art Nouveau Jewellery*. London: Thames & Hudson, 1985 [forthcoming].

Bott, Gerhard. *Schmuck als künstlerische Aussage unserer Zeit*. Edited by Reinhold Reiling. Königsbach-Pforzheim: Verlag Hans Schöner, 1971.

Dormer, Peter and Turner, Ralph. *The New Jewelry*. London: Thames & Hudson, 1985.

Edwards, Rod. *Techniques in Jewellery*. London: Batsford, 1978. [Published in the U.S.A as *The Technique of Jewelry*. New York: Scribner's, 1977.]

Fisch, Arline. *Textile Techniques in Metal*. New York: Van Nostrand-Reinhold, 1975.

Gautier, Gilberte. *Rue de la Paix*. Paris: Julliard, 1980.

Gere, Charlotte. *European and American Jewellery, 1830–1914*. London: Heinemann, 1975.

Habsburg-Lothringen, Geza von and Solodkoff, Alexander von. *Fabergé: Court Jeweller to the Tsars*. Preface by A. Kenneth Snowman. Trans. by J.A. Underwood. New York: Rizzoli International, 1979, and London: Studio Vista/Christie's and Fribourg: Office du Livre, 1979.

Hinks, Peter. *Twentieth Century British Jewellery, 1900–1980*. London: Faber & Faber, 1983.

Hughes, Graham. *The Art of Jewellery*. London: Studio Vista, 1972.

——. *Modern Jewellery*. London: Studio Books, 1973.

——. *Gems and Jewellery*. Oxford: Phaidon, 1978.

Japan Jewellery Designers' Association. *Modern Jewellery in Japan*. Tokyo: 1978–1979.

Leidelmeijer, Frans and Cingel, Daan van der. *Art Nouveau and Art Deco in the Netherlands*. n. p., Meulenhoff/Landshoff, 1983.

McFadden, David Revers. *Scandinavian Modern Design, 1880–1980*. New York: Abrams, 1982.

Maierhofer, Fritz. *Fritz Maierhofer*. Vienna: Galerie Am Graben, 1982.

Munn, Geoffrey C. *Castellani and Giuliano: Revivalist Jewellers of the Nineteenth Century*. Foreword by A. Kenneth Snowman. New York: Rizzoli International, 1984, and London: Trefoil and Fribourg: Office du Livre, 1984.

Nakayama, Aya. *Kumihimo Jewellery*. Tokyo, 1976.

Oman, C.C. *British Rings, 800–1914*. London: Batsford, 1974.

Penland School of Crafts. *Jewelry Making*. Indianapolis and New York, 1975.

Raulet, Sylvia. *Bijoux Art Déco*. Paris: Editions du Regard, 1984.

Reiling, Reinhold. *Goldschmiedekunst*. Königsbach-Pforzheim: Verlag Hans Schöner, 1978.

Schollmayer, Karl. *Neuer Schmuck*. Tübingen: Ernst Wasmuth, 1974.

Schweiger, Werner J. *Wiener Werkstätte: Design in Vienna, 1903–1932*. New York: Abeville Press, 1984, and London: Thames & Hudson, 1984.

Snowman, A. Kenneth. *The Art of Carl Fabergé*. 2nd rev. ed. London: Debrett's Peerage, 1980.

Turner, Ralph. *Contemporary Jewelry: A Critical Assessment*. London: Studio Vista, 1976.

Untracht. Oppi. *Jewelry Concepts and Technology*. New York: Doubleday, 1982.

Vever, Henri. *La bijouterie française au XIXe siècle*. 3 vols. Paris, 1906; 1908.

Ward, Anne; Cherry, John; Gere, Charlotte and Cartlidge, Barbara . *The Ring: From Antiquity to the Twentieth Century*. Fribourg: Office du Livre and London: Thames & Hudson, 1981. [Published in the U.S.A. as *Rings Through the Ages*. New York, Rizzoli International, 1981].

Weckström, Björn, *Björn Weckström*. Helsinki: Lapponia Jewelry Co. 1980.

Wilcox, David. *Body Jewelry*. Chicago: Henry Regnery, 1973.

Photo Credits

The author and the publisher are extremely grateful to everyone who helped them assemble the photographs. All those photographs not credited below to specific photographers or institutions are by courtesy of the artist/jewellers themselves. The numbers refer to plate numbers.

Abel, Oslo   227
Katrin Aitken   245
American Craft Museum, New York   103, 107
Augenstein   154
AURUM magazine, International Gold Corporation, Geneva   260
Australian Crafts Council Collection, Sydney   239, 242
Michael Bruce   7, 14, 25, 32, 36, 52, 67, 70, 85, 91, 94, 131
Cartier, Paris   26, 34, 46, 47, 48, 54, 73, 74, 99, 101
Barbara Cartlidge, London   2, 3, 10, 18, 24, 37, 41, 42, 53, 55, 58, 66, 76, 82, 84, 86, 90, 96, 106, 110, 132, 136, 144, 147, 156, 161, 167, 171, 177, 179, 180, 182, 186, 190, 209, 210, 211, 214, 215, 220, 226, 228, 232, 243, 246, 257, 265, 281, 286
Christie's Geneva   35
Christie's, New York   19, 69, 75, 121
Bob Crump   152, 170
De Tio, Stockholm   97
M. Lee Fatherree   95, 104
Jan Faul   17
Thomas Michael Franke   271
Gimpel Fils Gallery. London   116
Andrew Grima Ltd   145
Bob Hanson   109
Eric Hesmerg   21, 27, 31, 49
Tomas Heuer, Paris   57, 59, 62, 64, 65, 68, 72, 79
Andrew Holmes   150
Georg Jensen, Copenhagen   112, 119, 135
Seth Joel, New York   98
Graham Kirk   174, 202
Kunstgewerbemuseum, Cologne   63, 83, 130

Kunstgewerbemuseum, Staatliche Museen Preussischer Kulturbesitz, Berlin   266
Lapponia Jewelry Oy, Helsinki   118
Eric Lechtzin   200, 293
Mikimoto Company, Tokyo   20, 39
Musée des Arts décoratifs, Paris   33, 50; (photos L. Sully-Jaulmes: 51, 77, 260)
National Gallery of Victoria, Melbourne   166
Louis Osman   137, 138
Österreichisches Museum für angewandte Kunst, Vienna   16, 28, 38, 40, 43 (photos Narbutt-Lieven, Viennna)
Pietinen, Helsinki   139
Paul Podolsky, London   115
Enzo Ragazzini   153
Salmi   194
Schmuckmuseum, Pfozheim   1, 8, 9, 15, 23, 44, 78, 108, 111, 114, 129, 141, 143, 181, 189, 219 (photos Günter Meyer, Pforzheim)
Philipa Schönborn   120
Sotheby's, New York   98
Soviet Artists' Union, Moscow   234
Sune Sundahl   159
Joseph Szasztai   90
TAG Oeuvres d'Art S.A., Paris   93, 100
Teigens Fotoatelier A/S, Oslo   124
Thomas GmbH, Karlsruhe   224
Eveline Tietze, Vienna   208
Tiffany, New York   113
Victoria and Albert Museum, London   12, 22, 30, 45, 80, 81, 89, 102
David Ward   238
David Wardle   294, 295, 296
Wartski, London   4, 5, 11, 13, 56
Harry Winston, New York   92, 178
Worshipful Company of Goldsmiths, London   29
Ulla Zernicke   269, 270, 272
Jan Zweerts, The Hague   60, 61

Acknowledgments

I would like to express to my family and to my many friends all over the world, my sincere appreciation and gratitude for their encouragement and help, so freely given to me while engaged on the task of writing this book. My special thanks to:
Dr. Fritz Falk, Schmuckmuseum Pforzheim; Dr. Rüdiger Joppien, Kunstgewerbemuseum, Cologne; Shirley Bury, Victoria and Albert Museum, London; Jane Stancliffe, Victoria and Albert Museum, London; Marie-Noël de Gary, Musée des Arts Décoratifs, Paris; I. Meij, Nederlands Kostuummuseum, The Hague; Annelies Krekel-Aalberse; Ida Boelen van Gelder; Susan Hare, Goldsmiths' Hall, London; Toni Wolf; Barlach and Laurence Heuer; Gilberte Gautier, Cartier, Paris; Geoffrey Munn, Wartski, London; Oppi Untracht; and to the many artist/jewellers whose wonderful work has made the writing of this book so enjoyable and worthwhile. Last not least, my thanks to my editor, Barbara Perroud, for her patience and understanding; I am glad to say we are still friends after all this time.

Barbara Cartlidge
London, May, 1985

Index

This book was printed in July, 1985 by Imprimeries Réunies Lausanne S.A., Renens, Switzerland. Setting: Typobauer Filmsatz GmbH, Ostfildern, West Germany; Photographs: Planning Group, Verona, Italy; Binding: Schumacher A.G., Schmitten, Switzerland.
Design and Production: Emma Staffelbach.
Editorial coordination: Barbara Perroud-Benson.

Printed and bound in Switzerland.